"Ministers of Christ and Stewards of the Mysteries of God."
1 Corinthians 4 vs. 1

TABLE OF CONTENTS

PREFACE

"But the Comforter, which is the Holy Ghost, whom the Father will send in my name, shall teach you all things, and bring all things to your remembrance, whatsoever I have said unto you." *St. John*, XIV, 26.

Truth is eternal and everlasting. That which was, is, and forever shall be; manifest variously as it may. One of the mightiest of truths is the mystical meaning of that which is inculcated in the universal teachings as to the Divine Mother.

In every Age, in many languages and religions, under many names and symbols, does the loving Mother speak to Her children. In ancient Egypt as Isis—the feminine aspect of the Godhead, the Productive Principle, the Bringer Forth, both in Nature and in man—She bade Her children gather together and prepare for the manifestation of Her child as Horus. In that Age the Divine Mother was depicted as gathering together and restoring to oneness, but burying (making esoteric) the severed members of the body of Osiris—the Egyptian term for the great Creative Aspect of the Godhead which manifests to the Cosmos as the Cosmic Cause, to our universe as the Sun and to humanity as God, the Father of all—or that united body of Universal Truth given to all mankind, the Grand Plan of Manifestation and Redemption. This body has indeed been broken in many pieces by mankind throughout the ages, and only the understanding Love of the Divine Mother can gather the pieces together and reveal them as one, the eternal living Body of Truth.

In Jerusalem the Son of the Divine Mother for the Piscean Age, in bidding farewell to all His faithful followers, tells them that the Divine Mother shall remain with them "even unto the end" (of the dispensation) as the Holy Ghost, the Comforter, to teach them all things and bring all things to their remembrance; for the esoteric Truth has always remained with the Faithful, altho hidden under exoteric creeds and dogmas. But the Age has now dawned when that which was hidden shall be revealed and this buried Body must be uncovered and restored to life and manifest exoterically in the hearts and lives of mankind. This is but another call for the ingathering of all who love the Father-Mother-God, that there be but one universal sheepfold and one Shepherd.

As the new Aquarian Age, so long foretold, dawns for humanity, the outbreathing of the Holy Ghost, the Comforter, again speaks, and in no uncertain tones, to all children who recognize Her, and proclaims to them: "Behold, it is I. Be not afraid!" At the ushering in of this Aquarian Age She comes under the name of Aquaria. And, true to the promise of Jesus, She brings to our remembrance all that He has told us concerning the New Dispensation when there "Shall appear the sign of the Son of Man (the sign Aquarius) in heaven."

Lest any there be of Her children who fail to recognize Her as the Divine Mother or who fail to see the signs and wonders brought forth by the outpouring of Her Divine Love, as the gates of the New Age swing open, these lessons—which have been given through those who know whence they come—are sent forth to all Her children for their comfort and instruction and to announce the re-appearance and prepare for the recognition and welcome of Her Son.

May the followers of Universal Truth in every land and clime gather together at Her knee, feel the warmth of Her Mother-love and the protection of Her arms around them and listen receptively and understanding to Her momentous words, knowing that they be no new words, nor only cunningly contrived conceptions of the mind of man, but age-old Universal Truths reiterated again and again in every Age, in language suited to the time and the people to whom they are given, and now again brought to the remembrance of all who through Love can recognize their truth and who are ready to respond to Her call.

Thus does *The Message of Aquaria* naturally follow *The Voice of Isis*.

—THE AUTHORS.

San Francisco, California
September 15th, 1921

MESSAGE OF AQUARIA

CHAPTER I

THE MYSTIC LIFE[1]

"Your life is hid with Christ in God . . . where there is neither Greek nor Jew, circumcision nor uncircumcision, Barbarian, Scythian, bond nor free: but Christ is all, and in all." *Colossians*, III, 3, 11.

O, Thou Divine Reality! Thou who fillest all heavens and all earths! Thou only art God. Thou only art One in all blessedness, glory and honor, forevermore." *Teachings of the Order*.

After the days of horror through which the peoples of the Earth have been and still are passing there is already arising from out the stricken nations, and also from those others who have sickened at the sight, an insistent cry for new ideals of life. The old conceptions have been weighed in the balance and found lamentably wanting, hence the eyes of millions are looking for something new, perhaps for signs and wonders, that will give them some vital ideal, some new conception of life to guide them during the new dispensation now dawning. The mere repetition of the old orthodox conceptions can no longer satisfy. A hell after death can no longer appall after their mortal eyes have seen a hell on Earth. No mere promise of a negative heaven of supine and insipid bliss can inspire or comfort after the deeds of heroism and self-sacrifice they have beheld in the days of carnage. The cry already goes up for "a new heaven and a new earth" in which righteousness shall dwell, omitting all reference to hell.

One aspect of the Divine Law is that there can be no longing for the ideal born in the human heart that is not a re-flection of a Divine Reality which the Soul dimly senses

---

[1] Abstract of an address made by Dr. and Mrs. F. Homer Curtiss at the Annual Convention of The Order of Christian Mystics, July 9, 1917.

as a truth. Hence there cannot be a Soul-cry or a sincere demand for righteousness, peace and harmony that will not bring its own fulfillment in due season. Perhaps this universal demand which the horrors of recent years have created is the next step in the spiritual unfoldment of the Race. Therefore, those who know where to seek for the answer must be up and doing, ready to spread the glad message of cheer and comfort that is found in a realization of the Mystic Life.

But to convince others we must first prove by experience and expression in our own lives that living the Mystic Life is a practical possibility. For the majority think that mysticism and practicability are like the opposite ends of a magnet, while in reality they form the central point where both blend.

We must prove to the world that the Mystic Life does bring to the heart and into the life of every devoted follower a new heaven in which dwelleth righteousness, the righteousness of inspiring ideals, noble deeds, great sacrifices and love for Earth's children, giving him the ability to share this righteousness with others, thus creating new Earth conditions for all who enter into this new realization. In past ages mankind sought retirement from the world in an effort to create the new heaven within himself, but the modern mystic realizes that to be practical he must seek his heaven in the very midst of the turmoil of life wherever the Great Law has placed him and bring it forth, not only within himself, but within his environment so others may benefit by it. This is the ideal manifestation of the Mystic Life.

All manifestation comes from the unseen. Everywhere we see the inner molding the outer. The plan in the mind of the architect determines the size and form of the building. Our ideas, as they seek expression, determine our words and acts. The ambitions of a selfish monarch plunge the world into war, while the ideals of freedom, right and justice inspire millions unselfishly to sacrifice their lives to counteract the results of that selfish ambition. So must the ideals of the Mystic Life be spread until they inspire millions to manifest peace, love, brotherhood, co-operation and harmony within themselves ere those qualities can manifest among nations; for as our enlightenment increases so does our responsibility for local and world conditions.

The causes (realities) are always mystic and unseen. The objective form is but the manifested aspect of the cause. That which is manifested in the outer world is but the outer husk, the vehicle through which some inner form of the One Life is seeking expression in this world of matter. One of the most fundamental and obvious characteristics of the manifested universe is its sentience. Everywhere, from the amoeba to the solar system, we see both the evidence and the results of a directing consciousness which organizes, controls and directs the activities of the various manifestations toward specific ends. In fact, the physical form limits the expression; for every form of life is far greater than it is able to manifest through its physical vehicle. The cause back of the acorn is far greater than the acorn or even the tree into which the life-force, in its desire for expression, forces the acorn to expand. The seed contains the potential tree, but its source is hid in mystery. In fact, all life is a manifestation of the Divine Life or Cosmic Christ-force seeking expression that it may complete the cycle of its outgoing and return to its Source. It is this inner pressure for an ever greater and more perfect expression that is the cause back of evolution.

As we see the Mystic Life expressing itself in Nature, according to the Law of Growth, so is it with man. The Mystic Life is the life of causes; the Inner or Real Life, the life of the Soul; that life whose will to express results in the best outer manifestation the Soul has learned, through experience in matter, to produce, each incarnation being a step toward the goal of perfect expression. Our Mystic Life is the life of our Higher Self, the Real Man, the life we live in the higher realms, our life in our Father's home.

Hence the discouragement, loneliness, even disgust for the outer life we are living which sweeps over us at times; for we realize how far short we fall from living our real life and manifesting our Real Self. It is the source of all our life, even the physical life; for if we do not renew our life by returning to bathe in its Source every few hours through deep sleep, our physical body becomes exhausted and dies, no matter how much food, water, Sun and air it may receive. If we need to leave the outer world behind and cease to react to its stimuli and seek the Inner Life for the sake of bodily health, how much more should we seek it, through meditation and devotion, for our moral and spiritual health!

We have an outer shell of a life in the world as our casual acquaintances know us and as history might record of us. Then we have a more inner life, such as our family and close friends know, and finally we have the real Inner or Mystic Life of the Soul, known only to the Father, but which it is our duty to recognize and correlate with or truly live on Earth, even as it is done in heaven.

This is the life of the Soul which is striving to guide and train us to follow its direction until all our outer activities are but an undistorted expression of that Real Self. With the majority this Inner, Mystic Life has not yet been recognized, nor has it found a direct channel for expression. Hence their Soul-life is but an over-shadowing influence which tries as best it can to inspire and guide the outer personality toward harmonious and constructive ends.

At this stage of spiritual unfoldment the majority dwell in the outer senses, in the vibrations of and reactions to the outer world. The urge for satisfaction—which can ultimately be quenched only through union with the Higher Self—the majority endeavor to satisfy through sensation, excitement and the struggle for the attainment of outer things. They make the acquisition of money their standard and aim in life; money and ever more money, even when they have sufficient for the normal needs of life. They desire more comforts, even luxuries, when they already have ample for a simple, happy life. They spend their spare time in a rush for pleasure, seeking through sensation to drown the persistent craving for peace, love and harmony. Peace, however, is not the result of certain outer circumstances, but is an inner state of consciousness. The tranquility they seek can be found only within; by quieting the outer vibrations of the body and mind and responding to "the peace that passeth understanding," which is theirs for the seeking.

All this struggle and striving, however, is but the result of the inner Mystic Life pushing outward for fuller expression, so that in the earlier stages of the unfolding inner consciousness the rushing from one outer condition to another or from one teacher to another is but the natural result when the personality fails to listen to the inner guidance. And it is this blind responding to the stimuli of outer conditions which is the cause of most suffering; for without a recognition of the Inner Guidance man cannot know or follow the Law of Harmony, except as he learns it laboriously and painfully through experience. Therefore, those who will not listen must be left to learn through experience.

Since the inner urge of the Mystic Life keeps us striving for its expression in one way or another, this chapter is an effort to explain to those who are ready to listen just what they are more or less blindly striving for and how they can attain it; for both the end and the means to its attainment should be known if we are to work effectively and efficiently.

The majority are like a butterfly that fell into a pond. It struggled tremendously to get out of the abnormal conditions in which it found itself, and it made excellent progress, but being ignorant of the direction of its goal, it was swimming away from the shore! Just so the majority of mankind are ignorant both of their Source and the goal they are destined to attain, hence all their misdirected striving but exhausts them and takes them farther from the desired attainment or discourages them until they often say, "I cannot believe in anyone or anything." Ignorance of the Higher Self and of our final destiny is, therefore, one of the greatest obstacles to spiritual unfoldment. But this should not be true of those who have been attracted to the teachings of this Order by more than passing curiosity; those who sincerely desire to attain peace, harmony and true satisfaction. For, as we have said elsewhere: "The only true satisfaction is the response we feel to the force poured out through some form of union with the Divine. The only real satisfaction is experienced in the thrill of oneness that comes when a Ray from the Divine within us finds expression in manifestation on any plane, physical, mental or spiritual, from the thrill that results from an unselfish deed, a kind word or a generous forgiveness, to the ecstasy of conscious union with the Higher Self in the highest Initiation."[2]

Some scientists attempt to define life merely as a series of reactions to various stimuli (causes). This is true to a limited extent, and to that same extent it is as true mentally, morally and spiritually as it is physically. But the great point to remember is that it lies with us to determine which stimuli we will react to, the outer or the inner. If the finger touches a glowing coal it is quickly snatched away. If something threatens the eye the lids are instantly closed. These reactions to stimuli from without are carried out by the subconscious mind long before we have time to think about what has taken place. The reaction is not mental, but instinctive. We feel hunger and cold and we naturally seek food and shelter. Here a mental reaction is involved in seeking to satisfy these stimuli for the welfare of the body. We hear a statement with which we do not agree and our uncontrolled mind reacts with an argument, a dispute or perhaps a blow. A criticism that slights our pride, dignity or self-esteem may cause our uncontrolled emotions

---

[2] *The Key to the Universe*, Curtiss, 108.

to react in anger. Yet we may listen to so-called spiritual teachings at variance both with common sense and also with those teachings which we have accepted and made our own, and altho the Inner Self sends out strong impressions that such teachings are not true, we may fail to listen or respond to the Inner Self and unthinkingly say, "Are they not beautiful?" especially if they be given by some impressive personality.

In such cases we are reacting almost as blindly as does the body from the hot coal or the danger to the eye. But we have an Inner or Higher Self to whose stimuli we should learn to react just as readily as we now react to the outer. And the Aspirant who desires to unfold his Real or spiritual nature more rapidly than those who drift through incarnation after incarnation with the slow tide of an evolution gained only through suffering, must rise above the animal plan of instinct by the power of the currents of the Mystic Life. For there are currents of power which the mystic can call to his aid—Nature's finer forces—which are just as real and just as vital as are the invisible currents of air, the currents of magnetism, electricity, etc, in the outer life. He must begin consciously to control his mental and spiritual reactions, so that the Real Self shall enable him to respond with calmness, patience, love and wisdom instead of allowing the response to be determined by the little vanities and prejudices of the personality. If the society leader and business man restrain and control their reactions and expressions—at least outwardly, even when not conquered within—from a motive of social or business expediency, how much more should the Aspirant for spiritual advance control not only his outer, but his inner reactions!

As the effort is seriously made to let the Mystic Life manifest and control our reactions we find that it requires more than an 'intellectual recognition of its desirability. We cannot accomplish it through the strength of the personality alone. We must seek and rely upon the power of the

Christ within. Many, many weary Souls see the illusions of the outer life, the vanities, the temptations, the shams, the camouflage—all the long list of instinctive reactions— and crave the real, satisfying Inner Life of tranquility, content and peace in activity, but they have not the strength to resist and overcome the habits of reaction formed before their awakening to the Mystic Life.

Many desire initiation into the mysteries, but no Soul ever passes the Great Initiation in his outer consciousness until he has first found the Mysteries within himself; until he has learned to withdraw his consciousness from reacting to the outer happenings of life and learned to live in close and intimate contact with the Mystic Life in that inner chamber of the Soul where the Christ stands with outstretched arms before the altar of the Most High—from which flow the hidden streams of all life—crying, "Come unto me and rest in peace." Here in this inner shrine must we seek for the power of the Christ that shall enable us to manifest the Mystic Life. "When thou prayest, enter into thy closet, and when thou hast shut thy door (*i.e.*, shut out all vibrations of the outer life) pray to thy Father which is in secret (the Higher Self); and thy Father which seeth in secret (our inner motives) shall reward thee openly." That is to say, He will enable us to manifest our inner ideals openly in our outer life. And this is the only reward the true mystic should expect and the greatest boon that could be given him.

Manifesting the Mystic Life in our outer conditions means a spiritual growth, and all growth and expression involves change. The physical body changes with the growth of the cells within. Just so the outer life must change as new spiritual ideals (cells) are built into our spiritual life. But if the tender sprout clings to the old husk which it has outgrown, or endeavors to carry the husk along with it, the sprout suffers and its growth is hampered or perhaps distorted. Just so do we suffer when we cling to or continue to depend upon old ideas, outer conditions, physical things or personalities when the great tide of the Mystic Life is sweeping us on into new conditions, into new fields of expression where new lessons and opportunities for usefulness await us.

The more we resist the inner current of the Mystic Life the more we suffer, until the Great Law is forced to tear from our bleeding hands the things which retard our unfoldment and which we should have gladly let go long before. Therefore, if we would live the Mystic Life we must not cling to tradition, to precedent, to old forms and dogmas, to old habits of life or thought, not even to old family or friendly ties *if they hinder* the unfoldment of our Inner life. For while we must ever do our duty and strive to live in peace and harmony with those Souls with whom we find ourselves associated, yet often there comes a time when our association brings to them inharmony and, moreover, calls down abuse and misunderstanding on us and our chosen religion or ideals. Hence, it is but helping to push them farther away and delay their following of the still small voice which is continually calling to us all, "Come unto me," if we remain on intimate terms with such persons and refuse to follow our urge to make a change. For the Mystic Life is ever an advance in understanding and expression, and it must have room to grow unhampered by things and conditions which our Soul has outgrown.

One mistake, however, which many make who start out to live the Mystic Life is in thinking that they must carry nothing of their old life with them. They feel that the whole past life must be disowned and cast into the fires of sacrifice. This is a wrong conception, for often what seems at first sight to be but faults and failings only need readjusting to become strong factors in the new life. If we try to leave behind all joy, laughter and companionableness or all association with friends, we are leaving out of life one of its greatest blessings and giving to the new life only the dregs of the old without the wine. If we have led a gay, thoughtless life, we must not kill out the joy, but prove our sincerity and the reality of the new step by finding a greater and more satisfying joy and pleasure in helping to make glad this saddened world. And so with many other qualities which now hold us back because misapplied or misdirected. Also in establishing our new life we must realize that we have outgrown many things, just as in moving into a new house we find many things in the old household that are not worth moving, yet which have served a useful purpose in the old life. We wisely decide to leave them behind, yet we do not condemn them, crude and imperfect as they may have been. Let this be the attitude of mind with which we prepare to step over the threshold of our old life in the world and enter the new manifestation of the Mystic Life. Leave behind that which is outgrown, but give thanks for the service it gave, for the lessons it taught.

When we are through with the sorrows of war, the cataclysmic changes of the Earth's surface and the disasters which may be expected to descend upon humanity, we will begin to realize that there is another and deeper world of consciousness whose changes, altho marked and definite, are nevertheless of quite a different character. And it is this inner world into which our consciousness has been born which is destined to manifest in the New Era of the world as it never did before, throwing all the happenings of the outer world into their proper perspective. Hence, we may expect that ere long, as men mark time, there will sweep over the consciousness of all who are awakened, waiting, eager and ready to receive it, an outpouring of the graciousness of the love of God toward man. This may not be noticeable at once in the outer world, for there will still be many inharmonious conditions to face, but it will occur, not only in the inner lives of individuals, but also in the inner mystical lives of the nations.

Therefore, all of us who have begun to feel the new life surging through us and desire earnestly to break through the hampering bonds of misconception that separate us from our brother-man, must awaken and pray without ceasing that we all may light within our hearts the Lamp of Truth and Wisdom and be ready to go forth and shed our Light within our own environment. This Order, with its all-inclusive cosmic philosophy, its devotional exercises and its personal help for each student, is especially prepared to gather in from the highways and byways all who will listen to the call and feed their hungry hearts with the Bread of Life and quench their thirst with the Waters of Life of which those who eat and drink shall hunger and thirst no more.

The secret of the Mystic Life is a realization that the Christ fills us whether His power is recognized and utilized or not; that sleeping or waking, in meditation or when engaged in the daily tasks, His Divine Presence is always with us, close to our heart's consciousness, like a loving companion to whom we can turn at any time and whose love is always the greatest reality in life. This is what is meant by being "hid with Christ in God," *i.e.*, the Christ has become flesh in us, even as it did in Jesus. This does not mean that we will never again make a mistake, think a wrong thought or lose our temper, but it does mean that when these things occur our reaction will be at once to fly to our loving Christ for strength to overcome and transmute such feelings and by His love and counsel grow stronger for the experience, just as we love more deeply one whom we have wronged or hurt yet who has forgiven us.

How important it is then to learn the path to the little door of the inner shrine within which the Christ dwelleth; to understand its power and learn whence it cometh and whither it is bearing us. For in this sacred shrine of the Mystic Life we find the great Hierophant who gives us the "Lost Word," who shall touch our foreheads that the

Eye of the spirit may open. His touch it is upon our hearts that makes us feel the great waves of love and compassion which encompass the world, yet which have their ebb and flow within our own hearts. It is here that we drink of the chalice of the Holy Grail, and here it is that the Christ turns the Water of Life into the Wine of the Spirit.

Let us strive then each one of us to live close to the realities. Learn how to open the little Door of the Heart. Watch for the Light that streams from it, even tho opened but a crack. Let our thoughts recur constantly to the Mystic Life until they wear deep channels through which it can flow to us, as we kneel in meditation before the Heart of Divine Love. Rest assured that we will never find that little door barred or locked, but ever waiting to open to our knock. And when we have entered, there we will find the Christ, the lover and comforter of our Souls, ready to wipe away all tears and fill our hearts, be they ever so sad, with comfort, love and joy; for His love is not of this world, neither can the world take it from us nor bar our way to its shrine.

Determine, therefore, that each day our Souls shall enter that sacred crypt and kneel before the altar and be bathed in the stream of the Mystic Life, as our body is during sleep. Then some day, when we least expect it, we will see the shrine illumined by the Divine Presence and He will place His mark upon our foreheads and give us the true Initiation into the Mysteries which the manifestation of the Mystic Life has prepared us to enter.

CHAPTER II

THE SIGN AQUARIUS

"And then shall appear the sign of the son of man in heaven: and then shall all the tribes of the earth mourn. . . . And he shall send his angels with a great sound of a trumpet, and they shall gather together his elect from the four winds, from one end of heaven to the other." *St. Matthew*, XXIV, 30, 31.

As we enter into the great Aquarian Cycle[1], in spite of the confusion and unrest which the adjusting and closing of the old cycle (Piscean) and its overlapping on the next brings to all nations, we cannot help feeling the mighty stirring of a new and greater day which all classes of mankind are sensing more or less clearly and seeking to understand and define. We say in a general way that this is the Aquarian Age, but having said it, few besides special students are much further enlightened. We therefore wish to point out in this *Message of Aquaria* the significance of some of the more important phases of the sign Aquarius and the age.

As we have said elsewhere: "As the earth, in its yearly journey around the Sun, passes through a sign of the zodiac each month, so does our solar system, during its great journey around the Central Sun of this universe (Alcyone), pass through each sign of the zodiac; but in this greater cycle, instead of a month, our solar system requires approximately 2160 years to traverse each sign."[2] "This period is called a Day or an Age. Thus we have had the Taurian Age when the vernal equinox of the Sun appeared in the sign Taurus, at the close of which occurred

---

[1] See *The Voice of Isis*, Curtiss, Chapter II
[2] *Ibid, 39*.

the exodus of the Hebrews from Egypt and during which the Bull or Calf was the object of worship and was represented with the golden disk of the Sun between its horns; the Arian Age, during which the Ram was worshiped as the symbol of the Sun-god; the Piscean Age, whose symbol of the Fish was the symbol of its Great Teacher, Jesus, the disciples of whom were all represented as fishermen and called 'fishers of men.' And our solar system has recently entered the sign Aquarius or 'the Sign of the Son of Man in heaven,' referred to in the *New Testament* as the time of the New Dispensation or Age."[3]

In the *Bible* the sign of Aquarius is called the Sign of the Son of Man, and in astrology the Water Bearer, and is represented by a man emptying a water pot. The sign Aquarius is the eleventh sign of the zodiac, and kabalistically its numerical value is also eleven. As is explained fully under that number,[4] eleven symbolizes the first step in a new cycle; a new condition or undertaking. And as the Aquarian Age dawns our Earth and its humanity is preparing to take a new step, to enter into new cosmic fields, gain new experiences and outline the great discoveries to be brought forth in the generations yet to come.

Aquarius is an airy (emotional) sign and marks the middle of the winter season (Jan 20 to Feb 19). As the winter season is the middle of the darkest period of the year, yet is also the prelude to the springtime, so will this first step into the New Age mark the middle of the darkest period for humanity and the prelude to the joy and beauty of the new cycle which it ushers in. In itself the cycle of the Aquarian Age will be marked by its four seasons, just as is the cycle of the year.

Aquarius is now one of the fixed signs and occupies the upper right hand or dominating point of the fixed cross,

---

[3] *The Key of Destiny* Curtiss, 36

[4] *Ibid*, Chapter I.

signs, which will give us a firm foundation on which to erect the temple of our spiritual life.

The sign Aquarius is "the sign of the son of Man in heaven," hence we find the Man dominating the cross. This is not the lower, personal man, but the Man who can dominate, indraw, and transmute all the lower potencies; the Man who must master the dual sign Scorpio, which in its lower aspect is the scorpion, "an adder in the path, that biteth the horse's heels, so that his rider shall fall backward," *i.e.*, the lower aspects of the scorpion (sex) blunt man's understanding and make him fall backward or make man, instead of being a rider who controls and directs his horse (thought), fall backward into the mire and wallow under the horse's feet.

The Aquarian Man, however, must lift up this force until it becomes the Eagle which brings forth its young upon the mountain top and soars into the very eye of the Sun. He must also conquer his heart (the Lion) and tame it, turning it from a raging beast that devours all into a docile and obedient servant. In other words, he must have the strength of a Samson to open its jaws, render it harmless and find in its carcass the honey of wisdom.[10] He must conquer the Bull or ox (Taurus), that great and powerful force of the animal nature which, if permitted to follow its own instincts, bellows, tears up the earth in a cloud of dust and with its eyes closed blindly charges, even to its own destruction, anything it fears or cannot understand. Yet, when this animal force is mastered and harnessed by man, it becomes powerful and patient to labor and bring forth; in fact, its tremendous force must be turned into channels through which it can be directed to express as the untiring labor and painstaking toil, without which the Neophyte cannot overcome and attain. Thus, through victory over the lower aspects of these animal signs man must attain to the pinnacle of his development. Because this highest at-

---

[10] *Judges*, XIV, 8.

tainment is necessary to become the Man, Aquarius is often represented by an Angel instead of a man, the Angel Gabriel, who is associated with the Disciple John; for the four Gospels, in their mystic symbology, are but another representation of the fixed cross and the zodiacal signs which mark its four corners.[11]

Astrologers tell us that Aquarius is an intellectual sign, the Captain of the Host. They say that it is ruled by Saturn, and are apt to enumerate all its negative qualities, just as in the Dark Ages man was described by his negative qualities as inherently evil, a worm of the dust, etc., instead of as a son of God, made in His image.

Like all the signs, Aquarius is divided into three decans of ten degrees each, the first one being ruled by Saturn, the second by Mercury and the third by Venus. But thus far humanity has never been able to manifest more than the lower aspects of the first decan. In other words, this sign has largely been but a prophecy of that which it would bring into manifestation when the New or Aquarian Age dawned. In previous cycles humanity was not sufficiently developed to respond to and express its forces. And even now few persons born under this sign are able to manifest its higher aspects, for the solar system in this cycle has only just entered the Aquarian Age, hence its vibrations are not registered in full, either upon the substance of the globe or in its humanity. In rare instances where a native of this sign approximates a balanced manifestation of the sign, he has brought the advancement over from incarnations in other great cycles or from other planets which have passed through this important era and manifested its forces. From the above it is easy to understand why this has been such a mysterious sign and why humanity has never comprehended more than the outer significance of its first decan.

Uranus is conceded to be the esoteric ruler of Aquarius, but in truth it is a Ruler of Rulers and, according to *The*

---

[11] *The Key to the Universe*, Curtiss, 146-7.

Secret Doctrine, belongs to another system. From an occult standpoint it is the mysterious forces consciously sent forth from Uranus which determine the changes in the cycles of ruling of the planets of our system. For instance, in the individual life one may be ruled for a long period by the denser and more material aspects of the planets, but after a certain spiritual growth is attained (Initiation) and because of it, it is decreed that he shall pass into a more ethereal zone, where the higher mental, psychic and spiritual aspects of the planets will then be the strongest influences felt. This is one reason why it is so difficult correctly to interpret the horoscope of an advanced student. Both with the planet and with the individual, it is Uranus who decides when these changes or advanced steps shall be taken, but until this stage of spiritual growth is attained Uranus has very little effect, because the individual cannot respond to the high rate of vibration of its forces. Uranus is said to bring about sudden changes because it is not strongly aspected until the student is about ready for such steps.

Since we are now standing on the threshold of this New Age and its doors are swinging outward, it is time that we understood something of its positive qualities and what the Earth and mankind may expect to meet and gain from it during the next two thousand years. During this period the human race must penetrate deeply into the mysteries of Aquarius, which are the mysteries of Man. For man has now grown up, become a Man. Hence, to study Aquarius we must study man. We must now take up in earnest that which our lips have so glibly repeated: "Man, know thyself." And step by step we must prove and demonstrate to the world the knowledge thus gained.

Just as Saturn, during all the ages, has been garnering the golden grain out of individual hearts, and teaching them through experience the unwisdom of disobeying the divine Law of Harmony, so in the first decan of Aquarius does Saturn take his place upon the throne of this world and, as the Water of life is poured forth by the Son of Man, gather in his harvest from both the planet and from mankind. He it is who sees that the tares are burned in the fire unquenchable—unquenchable because necessary and inevitable, hence must not be quenched as long as tares infest the wheat. But he also sees to it that the wheat is carefully gathered into the granary of the King. Jesus has said of these conditions: "Woe unto the world because of offenses! for it must needs be that offenses come; but woe to that man by whom the offense cometh!" or by whom the seed was planted which bore the crop of tares. The first woe which we are told is past,[12] was the planting of the tares among the wheat. Their growth and the suffering incident to the experiences which their growth among the wheat brought about during the past centuries was the second woe, while the third woe is the karmic reaping the world has been undergoing at the close of the old cycle.[13]

Ever since the childhood of the race man has been disobedient to his Divine Guidance; has been ambitious, selfish and self-indulgent, cruel and bloodthirsty, yet, in spite of this, civilization has steadily advanced in a cyclic and spiral fashion. This has been accomplished through the Great Law constantly working with man in its sevenfold manner,[14] always trying to inspire him with higher ideals, always utilizing for his learning, through the Law as Karma, the suffering he brings upon himself. This Law is enunciated in the *Bible* in the words: "Whatsoever a man sow, that shall he also reap. One jot or one tittle shall in no wise pass from the law, till all be fulfilled...... Inasmuch as ye have done it unto one of the least of these my brethren, ye have done it unto me." Through this law, which is Divine Justice, man is taught through actual experience that he cannot love God and hate his brother; that he cannot truly worship God while he oppresses even the

---

[12] *Revelation*, IX, 12. Also chapters XIX and XX herein.
[13] See *The Philosophy of War*, Curtiss.
[14] See *The Voice of Isis*, Curtiss, 192.

least of the ignorant little ones who are his brethren in Christ, without in some life, either now or in the future, himself suffering from injustice, hatred and oppression, until Saturn has gathered all the crop of unbrotherliness his heart has brought forth.

The *Bible* tells us that when we see this Sign of the Son of Man in the heavens we may expect the end—not of the world, but of the old dispensation, the reign of the sign Pisces—and as this sign is now beginning to dominate or reign in the heavens we naturally expect a new outpouring of the vital Water of Life to rain down upon humanity, which will be just as real as was the rain of meteors from their "radient" in the constellation Aquarius. Just as the farmer waters his crops and the water exercises its life-giving power to bring forth whatsoever seeds are in the ground, so Aquarius, the cosmic Water Bearer, pours forth the divine Water of Life upon the world, not for the purpose of bringing forth judgment and sorrow, woe and disaster, but like the rain which falls alike upon the just and the unjust, to fructify whatever seeds have been planted. And as it has been man who has planted the tares among the wheat, during the first decan of this sign, Saturn, the great Reaper and Adjuster, must gather in the harvest and separate the tares from the wheat. Then, during the second decan, under the rulership of Mercury, the Messenger of mankind must be fructified, while during the third decan, under the rulership of Venus, the spark of divinity in each heart will be quickened through direct contact with Divine Love and man will then bring forth the true brotherhood and rule his kingdom with the golden scepter of Love.

The Planetary Deities (The Elohim) who rule the signs and their decans are not separate Gods, as would seem at first sight from St. Paul's words: "As there be gods many, and lords many,"[15] but are the seven aspects of the One God, just as man to be a real Man (Aquarian) must manifest all his seven attributes; for this is the Image of God into which he is growing. "To us there is but one God, the Father, of whom are all things, and we in him."[15] For instance, the same man might have to deal with a business issue where the cold scrutiny and stern Justice of Saturn would be required, the power to know and separate good from evil. In another instance he might have to manifest the wisdom and power to rule of Jupiter; in another the great intellectual acumen of Mercury; in another the persiflage and light laughter of the Moon; in another the enlightening power of the Sun; in another the comforting mother-love of Venus, and in another the stern warrior spirit of Mars, who fearlessly fights all evils and protects the weak, yet through all these manifestations it would be the one man expressing his various attributes.

Since the affinity between man and the planet has always been recognized, as this stage of the Earth's evolution is reached we may expect many Souls to incarnate under these new and specially prepared conditions, who will come as real Aquarians, ready to respond to and express, not vaguely but definitely, the higher mental, psychic and spiritual forces of the planets which rule the three decans of this sign. As time goes on we will therefore find slowly taking the place of the humanity of today, a humanity which will be ruled by the forces from the higher and more ethereal globes of each planetary chain.[16]

In the Aquarian Age man should reach a point where he no longer acts like a mere child, swept hither and thither by the currents and eddies of the Great Law; for, in this Age the majority of mankind will reach a point of intellectual and spiritual development which today is reached only by a few; where they recognize their responsibility for the conditions from which mankind is suffering and for the

---

[15] *I Corinthians*, VIII, 5-6.

[16] See *The Voice of Isis*, Curtiss, Chapter XV.

condition of the planet, and the lower kingdoms as well. They will grow into the realization that each man is his brother's keeper and that all, from the least to the greatest, are brothers; that no real happiness can come to any living Soul if it has to be attained at the expense, misery and despair of his brothers. This lesson is now being learned as the result of the world's experience, but will be fully grasped only as the Aquarian Age enters into the second decan, in which man responds to the finer forces of Mercury, instead of to its denser forces as at present. Mercury is called a vacillating planet, and those who have it strongly ruling in their horoscopes are apt to be loquacious, to exaggerate, and may even be called liars, for they can soar into the higher realms of thought and relate experiences or conceptions which, to the average plodder, seem but lies.

Being essentially the planet of reasoning and thought, Mercury is called the Messenger of the Gods, as it is through thought that the will of God is made known to man. It is vacillating only as thought is vacillating until we have learned to control and direct it. Hence, as man enters the second decan of Aquarius and comes under the finer forces of Mercury, he will have a wonderful intellectual awakening, amounting almost to illumination. In fact, he will begin to open his Third Eye and blend intuition with understanding. And to this will be added, during the third decan, the Divine Love and Spiritual Will of Venus. For just as each zodiacal sign has its three decans, so the great Aquarian Age will have its three lesser cycles during its great cycle of approximately 2160 years.

Today we see the Spirit again moving upon the face of the troubled waters of humanity. The brooding of this Spirit brings forth the Son of Man or something that has been born from man, a child or offspring; a new consciousness which is awakened and brought forth amid the birth-pangs of anguish which humanity has suffered during the past cycle and is still suffering so cruelly today as the New

Age is being born. When this new consciousness or Son is so completely brought forth and manifested that it emanates from man and is lifted up to the heavens; that is, when humanity has accomplished this new birth and the cry of it reaches the heavens, "Then shall appear the sign of the Son of Man in heaven." This Son is the essence of the sign Aquarius, no longer merely overshadowing, but now brought forth in humanity; the manifestation of the Water of Life which shall make all things new.

Do not confuse the Son of Man with the Son of God, for the Son of Man is the higher spiritual realization which is born of man's inner experience; a new-found understanding, joy and at-one-ment. The Christ is born in Capricorn, but as He grows and His influence in humanity spreads, the Son of Man is brought forth in His image in Aquarius and reigns, first as an essence in heaven, then in its embodiment in man on Earth. But His reign on Earth will be only when men and women in sufficient numbers and with sufficient love, devotion, realization and spiritual power, have united to form a nucleus of those whose spiritual consciousness can sway the thought of humanity, and through gradual accretion in numbers, leaven the rest of the Race.

And after the reaping, when the golden grains have been gathered by the Four Winds from all the fields of Earth— those who have come "out of great tribulation," and whose garments have been made white "in the blood of the Lamb"— then the mighty down pouring of the Water of Life will just as surely bring to fruition the seeds of man's divine nature as it already has the lower: those spiritual seeds of which St. Paul spoke: "Sown in corruption; it is raised in incorruption: it is sown in dishonor; it is raised in glory: it is sown in weakness; it is raised in power: it is sown in a natural body; it is raised in a spiritual body." For the world this new spiritual body will be the Aquarian Age, and for each individual first a new conception of love, light, power and life; the actual unfolding of the Christ-consciousness and a manifestation of its power in the life.

But first there must come the realization that because Saturn must reap the tares we have sown, he is not to be thought of as evil, but as one of the Sons of God who, in divine love and compassion, clears the ground that we may bring forth the Christ-seed and reap our spiritual harvest. And just as Saturn is an aspect of God, so also is Mercury, he who takes our every aspiration godward, our every effort toward victory and our every realization, to the very throne of God, until through the intercession of this winged Messenger, Venus or Divine Love enters and builds her nest in our heart and brings forth her young. As we thus become real Aquarians, we will at last realize that because we have loved much, much has been forgiven.

Note: *The Birth of Aquarian Age*—"On Feb 12th, 1912, Uranus returned to its ruling sign Aquarius for first time in 84 years, and the Sun by precession also entered it. The Moon also entered the sign with the Sun." *Astrological Bulletina*, 1912.

CHAPTER III

ARE THESE THE LAST DAYS?

"And ye shall hear of wars and rumours of wars: see that ye be not troubled: for all these things must come to pass, but the end is not yet. For nation shall rise against nation and kingdom against kingdom: and there shall be famines, and pestilences, and earthquakes, in divers places. All these are the beginning of sorrows." *St. Matthew*, XXIV, 6-8.

"We must not accept a general principle from logic only, but must prove its application to each fact; for it is in facts that we must seek general principles, and these must always accord with facts." *History of Animals*, Aristotle, I, 6.

"Coming events cast their shadows before" is an age-old saying which, like all such sayings or "wise saws" that have survived the ages, has an occult basis in fact. In this case the saying is based upon the fact that all events take place first in the higher realms and later descend into physical manifestation, as the great naturalist, Agassiz, recognized when he stated that "All things had their origin in spirit—evolution having originally begun from above and proceeding downward, instead of the reverse."[1]

In the Realms of the Eternal there is neither past nor future, all is one everlasting now. Hence, at the moment of creation a composite picture of the event and its working out through its positive and constructive, also its negative and destructive, aspects is instantaneously photographed upon what is called the Akashic Records or more commonly the Screen of Time. While the necessity for the manifestation of the event on Earth is a destiny that must necessarily be fulfilled, it is not fate; for by its power of free-will choice humanity determines in which way the destiny shall be fulfilled, either positively and constructively, in peace and harmony through correlating with the Law, or negatively in

[1] *Principles of Zoology*, 154.

composed of the four signs, Aquarius, Leo, Taurus and Scorpio, which in earlier ages formed the cardinal cross.[5] From an occult and mystical standpoint this fixed cross is of the greatest importance, and is called the Foundation of the Universe, the Four Corners of Earth, the Four Winds and the Four Breaths. In fact, not only are the signs at the ends of this cross looked upon by astrologers, occultists and mystics as of great importance, but we find many allusions to them in the *Bible*. For instance, the "wheels" of Ezekiel are none other than these signs in motion. He describes them as coming out of a cloud as follows: "Also out of the midst thereof came the likeness of four living creatures. And this was their appearance; they had the likeness of a man. (♒) .... As for the likeness of their faces, they four had the face of a man, and the face of a lion (♌) .... the face of an ox (♉) .... the face of an eagle (♏)."[6] Yet they were all blended into and expressed through the likeness of a man, hence Aquarius, the Man, must synthesize these forces. The same figures are also described by St. John in *Revelation*.[7]

Again, when Ezekiel describes his vision of the valley of dry bones which he was to endow with life, he exclaims: "Come from the four winds, O breath, and breathe upon these slain, that they may live."[8] The four winds[9] or Divine Breath are the four aspects of the Divine Life Spirit manifesting through these four signs, and when they are focused upon humanity, even tho humanity spiritually be but a valley of dry bones, the dry bones shall arise and become a mighty army for the Lord. There are many other similar allusions in the *Bible*, but all go to show that there is some important significance attached to the figures on this fixed cross and some mystical potency to be attained through understanding and correlating with these four

---

[5] See *The Key to the Universe*, Curtiss, 143, footnote.
[6] *Esekiel*, I, 5-10.
[7] Chapter IV, 7.
[8] Ezekiel XXXVII, 9.
[9] See Chapter X, herein.

sorrow and suffering through opposition to the Law because of
the refusal to follow the principles of its spiritual teachings.

The Seers who reach up in consciousness to the plane of eternal
verities (in the fourth dimension) usually see first only the negative
phase of the event that is to be, for that is the densest and closest
to the Earth, and thus fail to penetrate to the positive expression
which is in a higher state of vibration. They thus see the event as
a moving picture of which both the past events leading up to it
and also the ultimate working out or fulfillment are cognized by
the inner spiritual consciousness. But since the majority of Seers
see only one side of the picture, according to their affinitization
to any one phase, they report the ultimate fulfillment of either
the positive or negative aspect of the event, which would seem
to them absolutely predestined. In the case of one affinitized only
to the lower negative aspect or one with a pessimistic attitude of
mind, he would probably enlarge upon the many failures, sorrows
and evils which must be overcome ere the complete fulfillment
was possible. Another, affinitized to the higher positive aspect
would report only the glory of the ends to be attained and entirely
overlook the necessary conditions which humanity must prepare
if the positive aspect is to receive expression. Thus each would
give but half truths.

Therefore, in considering prophecies we must always make
allowance for this natural human tendency in their transmitters.
For instance, the destiny of the present sub-race is that the Earth
and its humanity must be purified and take an advanced step, both
in consciousness and in physical affairs, to prepare conditions
necessary for the coming of the more spiritual sixth sub-race.
Naturally, its past creations of selfishness, greed, impurity,
injustice and unbrotherliness must be faced and redeemed ere
it can enter into the new cycle. This redemption could have
been accomplished by the majority of the sub-race sending out

great streams of love, harmony, tolerance and brotherhood to manifest in the actions of individuals and nations in such power that they would neutralize and transmute the accumulated evil. Then there would have been no world war. But since this was not done, in spite of the many teachers sent to arouse the people to the necessity of higher ideals, the adjustment had to be precipitated physically in the negative and destructive aspect of physical warfare.

Most comments on the prophecies of the *Bible* are based upon a literal interpretation of the symbols given. Altho there is generally an actual historical incident, place or personage upon which the symbol is based, and while the prophecy will also have some form of physical fulfillment, the vital point to understand is the spiritual meaning of the symbol rather than the physical, *i.e.*, the spiritual event which is to manifest either positively and constructively or negatively and destructively. For only as we learn the lesson intended by the symbol can we profit by the experience. Merely to hear that certain events are to transpire either fills us with fear or elates us with joy, and we quite forget that all depends upon our reaction to the lesson intended.

Modern interpretations are usually calculated from some such period as the Babylonian captivity. From the known astronomical observations of seven great eclipses left by the Egyptian astronomer Ptolemy, the date of Nebuchadnezzar's accession has been accurately calculated as having taken place in 604-3 B.C. This is commonly believed to mark the times when "Jerusalem shall be trodden down of the Gentiles, until the times of the Gentiles be fulfilled."[2] Computing the "seven times," which Daniel says must elapse, as seven cycles of 360 years each we have a total of 7x360=2520 years, and this added to 603 B.C (2520 minus 603 equals 1917) gives us 1917 as the year when the rule

---

[2] *St. Luke*, XXI, 24. It should be borne in mind that the term, "Gentiles" refers, not merely to the non-Hebrew peoples but to all who do not follow the Divine Law, symbolized by Moses, while the "chosen people" are all who do follow that law, no matter what their race or form of religion.

of the Gentiles shall end and a new dispensation begin. And 1917 saw Jerusalem freed from the rule of the Gentiles (Turks) and under the rule of the Christian King of England.

Dr. Grattan Guinness, who is looked upon by many as an orthodox authority on biblical calculations, makes his reckoning from the beginning of "the abomination that maketh desolate," which he considers began with the Turkish occupation of Jerusalem, and which he is quoted as placing at 622 A.D., altho the *Encyclopedia Britannica* gives the date of the entry into Jerusalem by the Caliph Omar as 637 A.D. By a similarly obscure method of his own he calculates the "thousand three hundred and five and thirty days"[3]—or lunar years, according to the lunar measurements used in the Hebrew—of Daniel as equaling 1295 solar years, and from this concludes that the "time of abomination" ended in 1917 (1295 plus 622 equals 1917). But no matter how historically inaccurate the dates assumed above may be, the occult addition of the number given by Daniel gives 12 (1+3+3+5=12) or the number of a complete solar cycle, showing that the end of a cycle is clearly indicated, even tho the orthodox method of calculating the exact date is unreliable.

"According to Mr. Norris, the period of 1917-1918 is the termination of three great prophetic periods. It is the termination of the 1260-1260-75 lunar years from 602-1 B.C., when Judah became tributary to Babylon; secondly, it is the termination of the 2520 solar years from 604-3 B.C, when Nebuchadnezzar saw the vision of the great image, and thirdly, the termination of the 1335 lunar years from 622 A.D., the commencement of Mohammedanism. . . . Again, adding the 70 years Captivity period to the year 1847-48, the date of the second downfall of the temporal power of the Papacy, we read the downfall of all evil (altho we still have evil with us). Further, if we add the 40 years of probation

---

[3] *Daniel*, XII, 11

experienced by the children of Israel, to 1877 A.D., the year of the defeat and dismemberment of Turkey through the Russo-Turkish War, we reach 1917, the final destruction of all desolation of abomination.... If we take the end of a cycle of fifty years, we come to what Pastor Russell speaks of as a Jubilee of Jubilees, Earth's Great Jubilee, or Times of Restitution (Acts, III, 21). . . . Reckoning from the beginning of the 70 years desolation under Babylon (*Jer.* XXV, 11), the Great Cycle ends with the year 1875. Six cycles of seven years each from 1875 brings the date up to 1917, the commencement of the seventh cycle. . . . Pastor Russell and his many followers are daily expecting the great world change. This the prophecies of the *Bible* show (so he claims) is coming in 1917. They think that at any moment Christ may appear, and then the thousand years' millennium will start."[4]

An anonymous author writing in 1895 and using the Grand Gallery of the Great Pyramid to symbolize the Christian dispensation says: "The termination of the Grand Gallery, 1910 inches, gives the third of December, 1910, as the end of the present era. . . . The total length, including the height of the great step at the end, is 1917.7 inches, which would bring us to the 12th of November, 1917. The top of the great step is much worn. Probably it originally indicated Tuesday, the 4th of December, 1917, as the theoretical date of the end."[5] Thus do many modern prophets, having been duly impressed with the idea of the near ending of certain cycles, laboriously seek to pin the events down to certain specific dates, even tho they are forced to distort history to make their theories figure out as they think they should. But as a rule the methods by which such calculations are made will not bear mathematical and astronomical investigation, even tho the cycle may end at approximately the date given.

---

[4] *Noted Prophecies*, Zalinsky, 151-2-3-4-5-6.
[5] *Ibid*, 156.

But how are we, who require some scientific basis for our belief, to regard these various calculations, even tho we prefer to consider the symbolic rather than the historical interpretation of the symbols? Since all creation as manifested in Nature and in the history of nations follows a parallel course, these prophecies point unmistakably to the close of some great period; not the "end of the world," as many think, but the end of a dispensation, the end of a great cycle, in this case the end of a sub-race. One peculiarity of racial manifestation is that every sub-race foreshadows in a manner that which will be more fully and completely expressed and manifested by the succeeding Great Race of the same number."[6]

For instance, the coming sixth sub-race into whose beginnings humanity is now entering will not usher in the millennium referred to in the biblical prophecies, but will foreshadow and prepare for it, sow the seed, as it were. That is, there will be such a tremendous uplift and advance over previous conditions as they existed before the World War—spiritually, mentally and physically—that to many it will seem to be the dawn of the millennium. It will in truth be but the dawn of the seed-time of that which can be fully manifested only at the close of the Sixth Great Race; for the true millennium can come only during the period of the Seventh Great Race, or the great Sabbath Day of rest of this World Period, altho there will be a minor millennium in the seventh sub-race.

As to when we may expect the millennium to be ushered in, since we demand facts rather than theories, let us refer to the well-known astronomical calculations of the Eastern Sages. It is known that the Assyrians preserved astronomical records covering a period of 270,000 years which have been confirmed by our modern astronomers as far back as 48,000 years before the Greek era. The far more ancient

---

[6] See *The Voice of Isis*, Curtiss, 238.

Hindu calculations are based upon the following table of cycles
or yugas, 1,000 Maha Yugas (4,320,000 years) making one Kalpa
or Day of Brahm. Each of these Maha Yugas is composed of four
cycles as follows:[7]

The *Krita Yuga*, or Golden Age	1,728,000 years
The *Treta Yuga*, or Silver Age	1,296,000 years
The *Dvapara Yuga*, or Bronze Age	864,000 years
The *Kali Yuga*, or Iron Age	432,000 years

We are now living in the early part of the Kali or Iron Age
of this Maha Kalpa[8], concerning which the *Vishnu Purana*
prophesies: "Property alone will confer rank; wealth will be the
only source of devotion; passion will be the only bond of union
between sexes; falsehood will be the only means of success in
litigation . . . dishonesty will be the universal means of subsistence,
weakness the cause of dependence; menace and presumption will
be substituted for learning; liberality will be devotion; a man if
rich will be reputed pure; mutual assent will be marriage; fine
clothes will be dignity. . . . He who is the strongest will reign."

The figures given above are not the calculations of biblical
students, who have had no training in the philosophy of world
cycles, who have only theories, mere estimates which they think
plausible. Neither are they the result of revelation or psychic
information. *They are the mathematical results of astronomical
calculations capable of verification in any age, and therefore
irrefutable.* They have been proven correct to within 1 degree
in 4,883 years! According to these calculations, the *Kali Yuga*
or Iron Age—in which there are, of course, innumerable lesser
cycles and subcycles—began with the reputed death of Krishna.
Astronomically this was when Mars, Mercury, Saturn and
Jupiter were in conjunction in the **6**th degree of Aquarius. This
conjunction occurred between February 17 and 18, 3102 B.C.,
at a time when the four great stars which form the points of the

---

[7] *The Secret Doctrine*, Blavatsky, II, 73.
[8] Vol. I, 404.

Heavenly Cross were in balance, *Aldebaran*, the Eye of the
Bull, and *Antares*, the Heart of the Scorpion, being exactly at
the equinoctial points, while *Regulus*, the Heart of the Lion, and
Formalhaut, the Southern Fish, were near the solstitial points. We
are therefore only in the beginning of this Iron Age of 432,000
years, the first 5,000 years of which ended in January, 1898
(5000—3102 equals 1898). We therefore have 427,000 years
left before the close of this Iron Age! Hence no one need worry
about "the end of the world" coming at all soon! For the sixth and
seventh sub-races of our present Fifth or Aryan Race, and then the
entire Sixth and Seventh Great Races, with their seven sub-races,
each with its many family races, each composed of many nations,
must all have their evolution before the close of this Kalpa.

To gain some conception of such vast periods let us consider
the cycle of our present Fifth Great Race, the Aryan. This began about 1,000,000 years ago, before the complete sinking of
the ancient continent of Atlantis, at the beginning of the Glacial
or Ice Age. *The Secret Doctrine*[9] tells us that the first sub-race
saw the doom of the Giants of those days, also the flood, while
the fourth saw the disappearance, 11,000 years ago, of the last
islands left by the sinking of Atlantis. Each sub-race endures
for approximately 210,000 years, its seven family divisions extending over some 30,000 years each, and the many national
divisions from 3,000 to 4,000 years. We are now just entering upon the beginning of the 210,000-year period of the sixth
sub-race, altho the period will be considerably shortened owing to the shortening of all periods as a great cycle draws to a
close. Then will follow the even shorter cycle of the seventh
sub-race. Then the Sixth Great Race will have to have its evolution of nearly 1,000,000 years before the Seventh Great Race,
when the great Kalki Avatar or the Christ will descend to reign

---

[9] Vol. II, 452.

upon Earth "forever and ever," that is, until the end of this great Day Period or Round.

Nevertheless we are at the end of a sub-race cycle when its old accounts must be balanced, a minor Iron Age preparatory to the minor Golden Age of this sub-race cycle, for each race, sub-race and family race has its Iron and other ages. The "end of the world" will therefore not come suddenly, nor as long as there are forces and materials in the Earth which are undeveloped and unutilized for the benefit of all. Only when the very earth itself and the forces now existing within it have been raised up to a higher expression can we have a new heaven and a new Earth in which these advanced materials and forces will be incorporated as fundamental essences, just as our advances in one life are built into our bodies in the next incarnation, and as our faculties are expanded as we enter the astral world.

Man must become the "Lord of Creation," the ruler of the Earth and all its forces. But this will not be attained through a miracle. We must first conceive the idea of what is intended, then gradually bring it into manifestation. For instance, we must learn true efficiency, not that all things may work together for success merely in war or business, but for the best good of all humanity. All waste must be eliminated and all resources utilized for the good of all.

Great strides are now being made in guarding the health and conserving the man-power of the nations, also in reducing infant mortality. But greater strides must be made in protecting humanity from the burden of the defective and unfit. They are the less evolved Souls who will strive to incarnate for a time in the advanced conditions now being ushered in, altho they are not far enough advanced to correlate with those conditions and take their places as co-workers, and hence would have to be taken care of by the more advanced, as they are today. In the New Age those who are sufficiently advanced to correlate with the new conditions must be permitted to advance in this new cycle without the handicap of carrying the less evolved, or the rapid advance necessitated by the new era and the wisdom needed for their proper care could never be attained, the Race being already nearly 5,000 years behind the development it should have reached.

The less evolved will have their opportunity later on in the minor cycles of a succeeding sub-race, at which time humanity will have advanced to a point where it can wisely and understandingly care for and help on their evolution far more efficiently and quickly than now, while still struggling for advance itself. The compensation the undeveloped will receive for waiting certain cycles, as the animals are now waiting for entrance into the human kingdom—no animals having been admitted into the human kingdom after the beginning of the fifth sub-race of the Third Race[10]—will be the tremendously increased and far easier advance to be made then than now. Therefore the great importance of arousing all who will listen to a recognition of the necessity of taking advantage of the great opportunities now offered for rapid progress and setting out in earnest on the Path or striving to live the Mystic Life. For this is truly "the end of the world" (cycle) for those who utterly refuse to respond to the higher ideals that are now being set forth for humanity's standard and attainment. All such will live out the natural life of this incarnation and will have every opportunity given them to contact, if they will, the truths of the higher life, *i.e.*, to hear lectures, read books and meet with those whose lives are manifesting the higher ideals. But if they refuse to listen or pay attention, after the close of this present life-period they will remain out of incarnation until the end of this racial cycle. They will then incarnate only when the great mass of humanity which has continued to

[10] *The Voice of Isis,* Curtiss, 54-5.

advance has progressed to the point where it can carry such laggards; where their ignorance, indifference, ridicule and even active opposition can no longer retard the progress of those who are striving to live up to their highest ideals. In short, when such backward ones next incarnate they will find themselves in a hopeless minority and will have to be classed among the laggards and unfit.

Therefore it is most important that each earnest student sow the seed wherever the soil seems propitious—not forcing it upon others—and leave the harvest to the Great Law. Let no one say he lacks opportunity. The seed can be sown in whatever environment we find ourselves if we carefully prepare the soil.

Just as disease is rapidly being abolished by the intelligent application of our resources, vibratory, physical, mental, psychic and spiritual, so must poverty be gradually abolished, not by the confiscation of the wealth of others, but by abolishing the power and prestige now given to the possession of wealth, increasing the intelligence and efficiency of the masses, and utilizing the resources of Nature more fully and under a just and efficient governmental control for the benefit of the people as a whole.

The fetus of the New Humanity is already stirring in the Womb of Time, and, like the human mother, humanity must learn to eliminate its waste materials and poisons and give the fetus proper nourishment or the life of both the child and mother will be endangered, as in cases of eclampsia. This is the work of the present transitory conditions, and it is a waste of time and energy, hence will delay the fulfillment, to speculate on the details of that which is to come only after many hundreds of thousands of years in the future. The entire thought and aim of today should be to meet present day conditions as they confront us, but meet them with an intelligent conception of the advanced conditions in humanity and its organization toward which the present day events are tending and which may be attained the more quickly by taking wise advantage of the opportunities now offered.

CHAPTER IV

COMETS AND ECLIPSES

"Comets, importing change of times and states,
Brandish your crystal tresses in the sky;
And with them scourge the bad revolting stars."
   King Henry, VI, *Shakespeare*, Act I, Scene 1.
"When beggars die, there are no comets seen;
The heavens themselves blaze forth the death of princes."
   Julius Caesar, *Shakespeare*, Act II, Scene 2.
"The heavens declare die glory of God: and the firmament
sheweth his handiwork." *Psalms*, XIX, 1.

Cosmic and sidereal changes directly affect the Earth and therefore its inhabitants. For instance, it is well known that the so-called "sun spots" markedly alter the magnetic conditions and hence affect the magnetic and atmospheric currents of the Earth with such regularity that important changes in the weather can be predicted a month or more in advance within a few days after the sun spot appears. This is because the Sun, altho but the physical reflection of the Spiritual Sun, is nevertheless the heart of our system. And like the heart of man it has its rhythmic beat, its systole and diastole. But instead of its pulsations requiring less than half a minute to complete the round of circulation, as in the case of the blood of man, the Sun requires a period of eleven years to complete the circulation of its life-blood to the planets and return.[1] And as the sun spots are one of the phenomena attending the dilation (diastole) of this great cosmic heart, when the life-forces are being indrawn, astronomers are quite correct in stating that this phenomenon will recur with special intensity every eleven years.

Throughout the ages comets have been universally recog-

[1] For details see *The Key of Destiny*, Curtiss, 8.

nized by occultists as celestial messengers ("His angels"), which bring great forces to the systems and planets whose orbits they intercept. The major ones which contact the Earth's atmosphere are followed by great mental, moral, social and political changes. The major comets are remarkable for approaching nearer the Sun at perihelion than does the orbit of any other known body, passing through the Sun's corona with a velocity of more than one hundred miles per second without suffering any retardation. During this passage they gather the message of the Regent of the Sun, together with its radiant energy and actual physical materials composing it. The visit of a comet to the Sun is followed shortly thereafter by a shower of meteors (so-called "shooting stars") from a focal point in some particular region or constellation which is called its "radient" or the radiant center and source of the meteors. As the meteors enter the atmosphere of the Earth they bring not only new magnetic, ethereal and spiritual *forces*, but actual *physical materials* from their distant sources in the heavens.

The advent of former notable comets was followed by showers of meteors from Andromeda, Perseus, Leo and Lyra. But it is of the greatest importance to an understanding of this new Aquarian Age to remember that the advent of the great Halley's comet in 1910— which really ushered in the Aquarian Age (1910=11, the number of Aquarius) and which left in the Earth's atmosphere the *physical materials of its entire tail*, some millions of miles in length— was followed by a great shower of meteors coming for the first time *from Aquarius* as their radient or source! Therefore physical science corroborates the occult teachings that at the beginning of this New Age the Earth has received not only new forces, but has received actual *material substances* from the constellation Aquarius. It is any wonder then that, with the advent of the forces and materials from Aquarius, its ruler Saturn, the Reaper, should begin to reap the crop of tares sown by man during the cycle

(Piscean) now closing and clear the field for that which is to be brought forth in the New Age?

Among celestial phenomena the appearance of comets has always been heralded as a harbinger of strife, war, pestilence and troublous times. The first great comet commonly mentioned in history was seen in western Asia in 604 B.C., when Nebuchadnezzar was on his way to the conquest of Palestine. The Jews of that day regarded it as a portent of the speedy downfall of their kingdom. In the year 66 A.D., according to Josephus, "a star shaped like a sword" hung over Jerusalem for a whole year before the beginning of the great war which ended in the destruction of the city by Titus and the great annihilation of the Jewish state in A.D.70. Sixty-eight years later another comet appeared, at the time of the rebellion led by Bar Chochebas which resulted in the slaughter of half a million Jews by the Roman armies and the complete dispersion of Israel among the nations. Since that time rulers and military leaders have always given attention to the appearance of comets. "Th' illustrious stranger passing, terror sheds on gazing nations." For instance, the comet of 1811 confirmed Napoleon in his plan for the invasion of Russia, altho his misinterpretation of its significance proved most disastrous to him.

In reality comets are messengers which literally bring powers, forces, intelligences and *physical materials* from the far distant regions they have traversed. Most of them have regular orbits and appear regularly at longer or shorter intervals, the one discovered by the astronomer, Wolf, at Heidelberg, having an orbit whose cycle is said to require the enormous period of 60,000 years for its completion. Halley's great comet, which has a period of approximately 76 years and which recently visited us in 1910, brought not only new mental, psychic and spiritual forces to this planet, but the *actual physical materials* of its enormous tail, all of which were bound to modify not only the minds of men—as has been so markedly evident in the upset mental conditions of the nations—but also their astral and physical bodies, as well as the Earth itself, just as the clouds of volcanic dust which were sent high into the upper atmosphere from a recent volcanic eruption in Alaska encircled the Earth and affected its climate for many months. Many of the former visits of this comet were followed by war and marked changes among the nations, its visit in 1066 being followed by the invasion of England by the Normans; that of 1456 by the Turkish invasion of Europe, its huge scimitar-shaped tail exciting the greatest consternation throughout Europe.

Great changes in humanity inevitably follow the appearance of such visitors not because the comets bring war as such, but because they bring new physical and spiritual forces, ideas, materials and intelligences destined to usher in a New Era, either minor or major. The required advance usually necessitates the destruction of many old conditions, ideas, forms of government, social conditions and religions, just as every new cycle of spring necessitates the destruction of the old forms of the last season's vegetation. Hence the appearance of comets should be regarded as the dawn of a new springtime for humanity, a new cycle and in some cases a New Era in the evolution of mankind and the planet. They therefore bring good tidings, in spite of the changes necessary for the new manifestation.

Altho there are two eclipse seasons of the Sun and one of the Moon of about a month's duration in each year, eclipses are nevertheless important in marking the duration of cycles, some major and many minor. The cycle of eclipses occurring every 18 years is called a *Saros*[2] and is especially important because in each Saros the eclipses are repeated in nearly the same consecutive order, and are of a similar character, *i.e.*, either total, annular or partial.

---

[2] Later (especially the last four centuries B.C) angular measurements were made (by the Babylonians) in 'cubit-degrees and inches' (Kugler). These observations resulted in the discovery of the eighteen-year period, which the Creeks called 'Saros'." *Origins of Civilization*, Prof. James H. Breasted.

We are taught that as the Moon is eclipsed by the shadow of
the Earth when the Earth passes between it and the Sun, the Earth
while thus hiding its lesser luminary is gathering up and absorbing more occult, mystical and wonderful potencies and preparing
for a new expression. And so must it be with each individual and
with this Order. Since *The Order of Christian Mystics* is a true
cosmic Order, ever since its conception it has noticeably followed
the trend and laws of cosmic events. It has passed through many
periods of partial eclipse when darkness seemed to settle over it,
yet like the planet, during those periods of semi-darkness it was
gathering greater powers and more wonderful potencies that it
might manifest more powerfully in the new day, just as the individual learns his greatest Soul-lessons and has his most vital
experiences while passing through periods of darkness or eclipse.

And as in the cosmic system, each atom (personality) that is
drawn into the onward sweep of this Order has its place and
its special end to attain. Again like the Cosmos, the Order is
governed by a mighty and immutable law which predestines
each Soul who correlates with its force to reach the perfection
of Sons, yet gives to each the widest latitude of free-will, as
to the manner and the length of time required, to work out his
destiny; for all are destined ultimately to reach such perfection.
Because of his free-will he can refuse to work in the little
personal ways that mark the beginning of all great endeavors
and wander like an embryonic Sun which, through countless
eons, is apparently lost in space, or again like others, he can
be drawn into the influence of some system whose day of
manifestation is progressing, and there apparently be swallowed
up as an independent entity, obeying the law of that system
and adding his force to it. Yet altho he senses the untrammeled
scope of the work in which he is destined to participate, and
the importance of the fulfillment of the end, he often forgets

his own individual responsibility and is inclined to leave such matters to the leaders of the organization, society or church with which he is concerned, and thus greatly delays the time of his perfection.

The vision of the glory to be attained is ultimately sensed by every advancing Soul. Even tho it looms but dimly before the mental vision it thrills every fiber of his being, much as an autumnal landscape, veiled by a faint violet haze through which the Sun shines with a softened glow idealizing land and sea, fills the heart of the beholder with an ecstasy of longing. Yet the same objects viewed in the full glare of the mid-summer Sun stand out as naked physical objects to be met and conquered through effort; grain to be garnered; fruit to be sprayed that it may be saved from the ravages of insects; everywhere the need of honest toil to reap the harvest; or seen in early spring will suggest only hope and possibility; a spur to the needed toil and effort. Hence none should waste time in dreaming of the end, but should do each task as it is presented with the realization that thus the end will be attained as surely as the harvest follows spring and summer.

The eclipse of the Moon on July 14th, 1916, marked the close of a secret major cycle of long duration, and from an occult standpoint was one of the most important for many centuries; for it marked an absolute change from one era to another. In other words, the Earth's position in relation not only to the Sun, but to its great journey through space along with its companion planets was uniquely different from any similar position which it had ever occupied before. That eclipse marked an entire climatic, mental, psychic and spiritual change for the Earth and its inhabitants; the beginning of the fulfillment approaches. The baptism of blood in the World War had reached its first stage of completion and had entered upon that which was indicated by the excess of green color that was visible as the eclipse progressed. When the eclipse was watched closely the red in its darker, angrier and more disastrous form was seen to be followed by the green, which symbolizes the lower mind, the dominance of the intellectual or *lower manas* by means of which physical supply is obtained. But after the war that, too, will pass away, just as it was seen to pass over the Moon; for the reign of intellect over the world, as used by so-called "big business" selfishly to control the supply of the necessities of God's children, is about to be eclipsed. This did not come immediately after the war nor will it come even quickly, but it is destined to pass away; to be swept from the planet by devastations of war and anarchy, as well as the physical devastations that will prevail over all the globe. As we have said, the first step, or as the *Bible* puts it, "the first woe," is accomplished and the second seal has been opened.

At 6:30 P.M., on March 2nd, 1918, another most occultly momentous astronomical event occurred, one which marked the close of the long cycle of the cosmic reign of Saturn in the Greater Zodiac and the beginning of the reign of Jupiter,* which is to last throughout the entire sixth and seventh sub-races or until the Sixth Great Race is ushered in. For altho this present Aquarian Age is said to be ruled by Uranus, since Uranus is a Ruler of Rulers, it will rule largely through its influence on Jupiter, giving to the influence of that planet greater power and potency, just as the powers of Saturn were made more potent during the past Piscean Age. At the above mentioned hour there was a great rejoicing and jubilee in all the realms of the worlds of this system, from the glad dancing of the fairies and elementals up to the sacred joy of even the Arch Angels; for at that hour the Mystery Planet so long hidden behind the Moon showed, for the first time since the forces of its laya centers were transferred to this planetary chain [3] a glimpse of its bright rim beyond that of the Moon and shed

---

* The beginning of the cycle of the sixth sub-race.
[3] See *The Voice of Isis*, Curtiss, 204.

its glorious light directly upon all the kingdoms, as our entire system entered the new configuration in space.

When we speak of a Greater and a lesser zodiac it must be understood that we are using the terms Greater and lesser in the same sense that the physical human body is a lesser expression of the greater Divine Self, the Immortal I. And being the microcosm of the macrocosm man manifests through cycles of zodiacal influences corresponding to those through which the planets pass. We speak of the Path of Evolution through which the personality passes and the greater Path of Manifestation through which the immortal Soul is evolving, yet each includes the building in of the forces and lessons from the zodiac.

The Earth passes through the twelve signs of the zodiac in one year, while "Our whole planetary system moves in retrograde direction through the twelve signs of the Zodiac, which like a gigantic ring encircles our Cosmos with numerous other solar-systems. All these solar-systems revolve around one *Central Sun*, which is supposed to be in the constellation Pleiades (Alcyone)."[4] To make a mental picture of this is somewhat difficult unless we compare it with man, comparing the lesser zodiac, whose constellations we can see and study with the telescope, with man's physical body and the Greater Zodiac which we cannot see with the physical eyes to the Soul or the true I, the movement being retrograde because the Soul is going back to God as it revolves around the central Spiritual Sun.

The eclipse of 71 per cent of the light of the Sun on the evening of June 8th, 1918, which threw a line of shadow fifty miles wide diagonally across this country from Aberdeen, Washington, to Ormond, Florida, was also of great significance to this country, as those will recognize who have eyes to see and hearts to understand.

The total eclipse of the Moon on the night of April 21st, 1921, marked another important step in the manifestation

---

[4] *Astrology, Its Technics and Ethics*, C. Aq. Libra, 17.

of the Mystery Planet and an important stage in the life expression of *The Order of Christian Mystics*. The sum of the numbers forming that date (4-21-1921) equals 20, which number is called "The Dispenser of Wisdom."[5] And it was during that eclipse that "the Lord of Life and Love and Wisdom," the Real or Divine Self of the Order or the great Spiritual Being for whose special manifestation the Order was put forth, actually descended to take up His abode in the aura of the Order and become "the Dispenser of Wisdom" for it, while those who form the true atoms of the body of the Order must become the points of radiation of His force and consciousness and responsible for the Order's influence in the world.

We are therefore standing before the Mighty Portals, waiting for the curtain of time to rise upon the New Age. Its rise will be gradual, first illuminating our feet (understanding), then our hands (power to accomplish), our hearts (power to bring forth) and finally will bring illumination to our heads (power to rule). Let us, therefore, prepare ourselves for that which is approaching so swiftly.

But opposed to every seemingly evil omen, portents of good also appear. The new star called *Nova Aquillae*, which was recently discovered on the verge of the Milky Way between *Altair* and *Eta Serpens*, thus falling in the sign of Capricorn, is one of the most important phenomena that has appeared for many centuries. As referred to by one authority: "The famous star which appeared in Andromeda about the time of the Nativity, and which later was seen by Albumazar, the Arabian astronomer in 945 A.D., again in 1264, and towards the end of the sixteenth century by Kepler, is one of those stars which have an orbit of great eccentricity with the major axis towards the solar system, so that they appear 'end on' when entering the field of vision, make a brief incursion, during which they appear to grow in luminosity, and then recede again and are lost

---

[5] See *The Key of Destiny*, Curtiss, 278.

to view for a period of many years. . . . It thus falls in the Sign
Capricorn, and this sign is affected during the years 1921-2 by a
malefic conjunction of Mars and Mercury in the world horoscope.
. . . Falling as it does in the Sign Capricorn, astrologically
associated with political and governmental affairs more than any
other sign of the zodiac on account of its correspondence with the
tenth division of the heavens, this 'star' holds for us portents of
singular interest. . . . Perhaps new stars have another significance
than that which belongs to comets. It may herald the appearance or
birth of a new and great political leader or the rise of a new world
power in the domain of politics. That it falls in the solar decan of
the sign Capricorn is at least significant of such a probability."[6]

Since Capricorn is the most mysterious and esoteric sign of all
the zodiac[7] its chief significance to us as Mystics is that Capricorn
is presided over by the great Spiritual Beings called the Kumaras,
whose special function it is to bring forth for the race the Avatars
or those "Superior Gods" who manifest themselves to men. The
Kumaras are also concerned in the destruction of lower forms of
life and manifestation that higher forms may take their places,
also the lower passions and appetites of men, thus helping man
to evolve to his higher destiny through the exercise of the power
of *Kriyashakti*, the power of Spiritual Creative Thought which
enables one to produce external, tangible phenomena by its own
inherent energy. This means that while man is still dwelling here
on Earth in separated sexes his higher creations will ultimately
be brought forth not through sex, but through this mysterious
creative power of Spiritual Thought. And Capricorn is the sign
where these mighty Beings, of whom St. Michael was one,
preside. It is for this reason that all Avatars or Saviors of mankind
are born or rather appear in Capricorn, or as it is commonly

---

[6] Sepharial in the "British Journal of Astrology," July, 1918.
[7] See *The Key to the Universe*, Curtiss, 178-9.

expressed, are "laid in a manger," Capricorn being the sign of the manger. It is also the sign of the goat, an animal that is very strongly sexed, thus plainly showing that the power of creating through thought and will must proceed from the same spiritual source as the lower sexual creations, but pure and undefiled and manifesting through other centers. That is to say, the sexual conditions will be supplemented, not superseded, by *Kriyashakti*. An Avatar, as we know, is not born sexually of mortal woman, yet is truly "born of a virgin"—the sign Virgo being on the horizon as Capricorn rises—and "laid in a manger" where the animals come for their food.[8]

What is the significance of these great cosmic events for us as Christian Mystics and students of occult philosophy? The cosmic life-blood permeates not only the planet, but the very substance of our bodies, the physical as well as the finer. For the last few years the very air we breathe has been so charged with new forces and substances that it has been more difficult than formerly for advanced and supersensitive persons to breathe, especially during periods of low barometer which would naturally intensify the physical effect. It is the influx of these new currents of life-force and finer substances which is eliminating the accumulated effluvia from the mind and aura and body of humanity like a purging draught, that it may be cleansed and ready to enter into the New Era and correlate with the new forces now being poured out upon mankind and the planet. Naturally the more sensitive persons who have some diseased or even weak spot in their bodies, or who have something in their minds and auras which requires elimination, find this period of purgation a trying and confusing time. Yet they should remember that the power of the Christ within them is greater than all that can oppose their advance if they will but correlate with and utilize it.

Also, altho the nervous ether of the planet is impregnated

---

[8] For explanation see *The Voice of Isis*, Curtiss, 137.

with man's vileness and is bringing back to him for redemption that which he has created and sent forth, nevertheless it is also filled with a new influx of the vibrant life-force of the Cosmos, the very Christ-power. Therefore we should recognize the meaning of the transitory conditions under which we are living and refuse to respond to or correlate with anything but the constructive life-forces in them. If our bodies are strong and healthy and do not suffer we may find other effects of these new forces springing up; new expressions of temper to subdue, irritation to conquer, selfishness to rise above and temptations of the flesh to overcome. In short, everything in the Earth's atmosphere and aura is intensified, both the good and the evil. Hence we must make a still greater effort than we have made in the past to "stand on the Lord's (Law) side."

In these days of confusion, when the last of the old cycle is overlapping the new—like the period of convalescence after a disease has run its course ere the new cells can be built in and perfect health restored—the great end which these changes in conditions and affairs are striving to bring about is one of purification and balance and a harmonizing with the higher spiritual note that has been sounded in the cosmic scale. Unless we strive to correlate with this aim and bring about these changes voluntarily within ourselves and our environment we are placing ourselves as impediments in the circulation of the blood of the Cosmos. Hence, like all impediments in a swiftly flowing current, we must either be stranded and left behind or be swept along to be buffeted and suffer until we are purified and have become one with the stream or one with the Law. And since man has free-will he can make himself either something that must be purged from the life-stream of humanity or he can become a white warrior corpuscle or leucocyte, which aids in the destruction and elimination of impurities and in the building up of the new tissues in the body of mankind.

This is a vital subject for us as practical Mystics to

understand and take advantage of, a practical result toward which we should strive; for it shows us why conditions in the world are so unbalanced and also toward what ends they are tending. It further shows why our personal conditions are more or less unbalanced and inharmonious. And just as when our blood is polluted we should not wait for the purifying process to force out the impurities through painful boils, etc., but should purge ourselves within and without and wash out the impurities with great draughts of sparkling water, so during this period in evolution we should drink in copious draughts of the divine Waters of Life, the force of the Great Mother-love, which shall purify our minds and hearts from selfishness, jealousy, resentment and antagonism, and also purge from our mental and astral bodies all impure desires which attract to us similar conditions and forces from the mental and astral worlds.

Having experienced the first stage—the Awakening—ere we consciously started out on the Path, through following the above suggestions we can pass the second of the stages of the Mystic Life—the Purgation—and prepare ourselves for the three final stages—Illumination, Crucifixion, Union—in which we shall become conscious channels and agents of the cosmic life-forces in their work for the regeneration of humanity and the planet itself, thus making the "last days" of the old dispensation a vital preparation for the new.

CHAPTER V

THE LAW OF GROWTH

"Seek out the way. . . . Seek it by study of the laws of being, the laws of nature, the laws of the supernatural; and seek it by making the profound obeisance of the soul to the dim star that burns within." *Light on the Path*, Collins.

To understand the causes underlying the many questions which are pressing upon all thinkers for solution today, we must recognize the motive power back of the evolution of both our individual lives and the Race, as well as the planet upon which we dwell. All manifested creation is produced as a result of vibratory differentiation of Eternal Motion and its resultant Force. Spirit and matter are but convenient terms used to express degrees of retardation of Absolute Motion, which in turn is the expression of Divine Will. Without Motion and its resulting Force the universe would be a dead, cold, solid and immovable cinder upon which no life could exist. The power of the Sun and wind, the waves of the sea, the waterfall, of steam and electricity are but various expressions of Divine Will going forth into manifestation. As long as there is motion, which is vibration or life, we cannot get away from God, for it is in this God that "we live and move and have our being."

One reason why Saturn is spoken of as the Regent of the Earth is that the force sent out by that cosmic center of force is stability and inertia. It is, therefore, ruler in so far as, without stability, Motion would have nothing on which to act. Saturn is also called the Adversary, because his force of inertia is forever opposed to Motion. And it is that impassive shore against which the sea of humanity is forever beating in restless activity until an equilibrium between the two is attained. Perfect balance or equilibrium is the "rest that remaineth for the people of God." Stillness and apathy as well as strife and inharmony result in death, but equilibrated Motion is eternal life.

As the child grows in body, mind and Soul in response to this Law, which expresses in every atom of its being as growth, expansion and unfoldment, so it is with the planet upon which we dwell. Today mankind is awakening to a realization that we are living in a new and transitional age in which changes are taking place so rapidly that we must become more thoroughly acquainted with new aspects of many of the forces of the universe with which we once thought ourselves familiar, but which daily surprise us with new expressions. Yet this is only the same surprise we feel when we meet one whom we had known as a child only a few years ago, but who now must be treated as a man. The explanation is that the Race and the planet have grown up to their young manhood and have entered in earnest upon their real life expression.

Just as the variation or special form of the Eternal Motion which produces our individual lives also determines our vibratory place, decides the possibilities of our attainments and marks out the path of our evolutionary destiny, so with the Earth. It, too, is traveling its appointed Path, unfolding and manifesting the various stages of its evolutionary cycle and taking its true place in the universe in obedience to the same law. It is the same Force whether pushing a planet or solar system onward to the fulfillment of its destiny or acting within the heart of a tiny seed causing it to expand and burst asunder its confining husk or shell and gradually unfold into the type of plant its destiny has ordained.

The reason we are not astonished and awed by the wonderful transformation of the acorn into the oak is that we have grown familiar with the miracle. But because we know that the invisible pattern of the oak lies embedded within the acorn awaiting only for its unfoldment and embodiment in matter to manifest the tree, it is none the less a miracle. So familiar are we with this phenomenon that we forget that according to the same law the ideal or potentiality within the seed of a world or a humanity or an individual Soul must likewise pass through all its various phases of unfoldment and ultimately manifest the ideal which the Divine Will has implanted within it. The process followed is the same as that of the planet, *i.e.*, assimilating the elements needed by each individual from the environment in which it finds itself, and building those elements into the pattern provided by its destiny.

Once we awaken to the method by which the ideal manifests through the Law of Growth we will realize that we have not discovered a new force in Nature or harnessed a new energy as we advance, but that whenever a force is contacted it indicates that the seed is taking a new step in its growth, for the completion of which it must utilize a higher aspect or expression of the One Life. The man who thinks he has discovered a new force has merely unfolded within himself a new phase of consciousness by which he recognizes and vibrates to a similar force within Nature and himself. And like the seed, at every unfoldment of the God-consciousness within him he enters a new field of force in Nature to which his physical body and his consciousness have responded ere it was possible for him to take the step.

For instance, until recently aeroplanes, the wireless apparatus, radium and so on were impossible, not because the laws of aviation and radiant energy did not exist, but because man's consciousness had not reached a point where it could contact, recognize and understand those laws. He had not unfolded into that realm of consciousness. Similarly at present he is not able to understand how to utilize the dynaspheric force and thus draw power for his aeroplanes and other engines directly from the air without the use of fuel, or how to use it to heal his disease and satisfy all his needs, by correlating it with the powers which he will some day awaken within himself, just as Nature manifests all her marvels by utilizing the forces already within her. But this, too, will be grasped and understood in a comparatively short time.

The coming New Age into which science is now entering has been called by some the Magnetic Age, and already, by charging them with magnetism, Dr. Ross has been able to preserve without ice for over three years fruits, vegetables and meats which remained as full of life-force and as fresh as the day they were prepared. The Magnetic Age will as far surpass the achievements of the present Electrical Age as the latter has surpassed the Age of Steam. But the Magnetic Age, in its turn, will be superseded by the still more wonderful Dynaspheric Age. Man and Nature must unfold together in manifesting the Divine Will.

If the Earth were merely an inert mass thrown off from the Sun or other planet and projected only by its initial velocity it would have slowed down and ceased the manifestation of its forces long ere this. But the fact that it is constantly unfolding new expressions of force and manifesting new powers—the effect of more rapid vibrations—shows that it is not an inert mass blindly following so-called mechanical laws, but is a living entity gradually unfolding its inner ideal according to the Law of Growth, just as the inner ideal present within the acorn unfolds into the oak, for the most powerful microscope can find no trace of a pattern in the acorn. The difference is similar to that between a projectile fired from a cannon, which continually and rapidly decreases in velocity, and an express train that picks up speed as the result of the increased application of power at the will of the engineer, that it may conform to the schedule or destiny set for it. The present age is truly called a "speed" age, because the Earth is picking up speed and events are rushing toward us and flying past like the scenery viewed from a speeding train.

Once understand that the Source of Power is within and is gradually unfolding our possibilities according to the Law of Growth and we can begin to work consciously with the Law. We will not strive to conquer Nature's forces only from without, but will realize that really to know and master a force we must unfold the consciousness of it within ourselves; for we cannot conceive of a thing of which the consciousness has not been unfolded within us, any more than an undeveloped mind can understand a complicated scientific instrument or process, even tho it is presented to it and carefully explained.

To grow we must drink in the Divine as the seed drinks in its nourishment from the elements, realizing that the Divine Consciousness contains all the forces, all the ideas, inventions, etc., necessary for the advancement of the Race in all ages, and that these will be unfolded as fast as man is ready to correlate with them. Those most attuned to each phase or idea will grasp and respond to it first. One who is accustomed to vibrate to the mechanical expression of a force or idea would be the first to bring it forth as an advanced mechanism, while a scientist, musician or painter would express the same idea or force, each in his own field. Only thus can we work in unison with the Great Law to bring about the manifestation of the ideal or Real Self within us and the real Sabbath for the Race.

While we remain unenlightened we are the victims of great currents of force, swept this way and that by the swirling currents of adverse and inharmonious forces which man's opposition to Divine Will and his perversion of Divine Love have brought forth. In fact, unenlightened man today is quite as helpless in the desire and mental worlds as was primitive man in the physical world during the early ages of the Race when the conflicts of the elements were of such a devastating and awe-inspiring character. For today man is meeting in the astral and mental worlds the same problems which he faced in the physical world in the early days.

There is a kind of faith which man must attain—a living faith in the certainty of the working of the Great Law—which will carry him through every experience and make him the ruler of his destiny. This faith is the result of an inward correlation with the mystic forces of the universe, an inward realization that he is one with those forces; that his whole life is but a manifestation of them. Hence, nothing in the universe is apart from him, nor is he apart from them.

Manifested God (Good) is the Divine Outpouring from the Absolute, eternally going forth into creative activity and returning to its Source, according to cyclic law. Hence the result of the mandate, "Let there be light!" was not the creation of a new world so much as it was the result of the activity of Divine Love reaching out into and through all chaotic conditions that the living Light might penetrate into and transmute and evolve the materials thrown off unperfected and unredeemed from a previous world system, yet containing the seed of a future world,[1] materials which were waiting in the darkness for the Light of their new day to dawn. In the same way the seed lies in the darkness of the earth, where it is subjected to the disintegrating forces necessary for its transmutation, and there awaits the quickening ray which shall start its evolution. God did not say, "Let us make a new earth for man to dwell in and rule," but the cyclic motion of the ever outgoing Divine Will and Love sent forth a quickening Ray into the world-seed dropped by a previous world system, which seed contained all the various substances and forces which the previous humanity, in all its various phases, was unable perfectly to correlate with, for the faculties and powers necessary to master such conditions were not yet evolved in man as a whole.

---

[1] See *The Voice of Isis*, Curtiss, 325.

This is the secret of the forces back of present day conditions. We look around us and note man's marvelous advance in science and invention, how he conquers the air, harnesses the oceans and subdues the mountains and we are inclined to say, "Behold how wise and powerful is man." But all this advance is merely the natural result of the cyclic push given to all evolution by the outgoing Cycle of Manifestation through the great Law of Growth, the cyclic urge to a higher and more perfect manifestation of Divine Will. In other words, man cannot make practical his new discoveries until the evolution of the planet has produced the necessary conditions and the discoverer has evolved the analogous forces within himself. Hence the motive power back of all growth and evolution is the One Life, which proceeds from Divine Will to bring forth through Divine Love, ever unfolding within us and in all creations higher and higher stages toward ultimate perfection.

When man awakens to this truth and understands that he has not evolved unaided all the advance which today is so rapidly unfolding, he will begin to have faith that the power of the One Life, as a Ray of the Divine, is working within him to unfold and bring to perfection the seeds of his Divinity. Only his refusal to open his heart to the stream of quickening life-force and his refusal to work with it can keep him back from the mastery of his powers; for it is only through his Will to correlate with the One Life that he can keep pace with the possibilities in himself and the planet and become a conscious co-worker with God.

At present man too often seeks to use the powers of God for his own selfish ends without regard to the ideals toward which all evolution is advancing. One phase of teaching says, "Kill out desire," and another holds up desire as the motive power by which alone man can advance, claiming that whatever man desires he should have. Others limit desire to one set of emotions and functions which they elect to call evil, and much family discord, sorrow, suffering and even sin result. Thus the average student is confused and knows not which way to turn. The truth is that human desire is but a negative manifestation of Divine Will and has its seat or focus in the astral world. Since we should never cultivate the negative aspect of anything, instead of allowing ourselves negatively to be ruled by desire, we should carefully discriminate between the objects of our desire and then positively will that which we have chosen as best for us.

The astral world contains all the unfulfilled desires of humanity, as well as those Souls who have passed away from the physical life, but who are still seeking to gratify their desires on Earth. All these forces of desire float out aimlessly over humanity like clouds of exhaust steam, ever seeking expression through man and sweeping him first this way and then that, expending their energy with no constructive object in view. An erroneous idea of certain modern teachings is that man, undeveloped as he is today, is omnipotent and that by the mere exercise of his Will, the control of his breath and life-forces, he can attain oneness with the Divine Will or enter Cosmic Consciousness. But the esoteric teaching is that only by correlating with the currents of the One Life through meditation and heart devotion can the life-forces of man's body become attuned to their parent Source and allow the One Life to flow through him in perfect harmony. In other words, it is not by merely willing to breathe in a certain way that the higher consciousness is induced, but through proper meditation and correlation, the breath will automatically follow the rhythm of the One Life and thus unite us to the ideal upon which we are meditating. But woe to him who thinks to master any force, even those manifesting in his own body, for himself alone or without working in harmony with Divine Will and Love!

The Race is now passing through a transitional state in which one sub-race (fifth) is overlapping the next (sixth);

a night between two day periods. For just as we find no hard and
fast lines of demarcation between the forces of Nature, so with
Races. Day and night and the seasons of the year overlap and
blend the one into the other; the colors of the rainbow merge into
each other and the last note of the musical octave becomes the
first note of a new octave. So in the greater cycles of Races and
sub-races there is a long period in which the forces especially
operative in the fifth sub-race must either find their perfection,
fulfill their highest good and be garnered into the storehouse of
the Race or be swept away and disintegrated into their original
elements, to come forth again when the new humanity is far
enough evolved and unfolded to grasp and deal with that which
it failed to perfect in the past.

Nothing is lost, either in the personal life or in the life of the Race
or the planet. In each incarnation we either master the conditions
we meet and learn their lessons — in which case the experience
gained is stored up as vibratory power in the Higher Self — or the
present forms of those problems which have proved too hard for
us are disintegrated (another manifestation of force) and await
the Soul at its next incarnation, when the same tendencies and
problems must be faced and the victory gained.

The same law operates with every Race and sub-race and with
the planet itself, for every planet is a reincarnation of a previous
planet, every Race of a previous Race and every sub-race a
reincarnation of a sub-race of a previous Great Race. The storms
and cataclysms which occur at the end of each sub-race and Race
are the result of the forces of disintegration, and correspond to the
changes of disintegration which take place in man's physical body
at the end of its life-cycle and later on in astral and mental bodies.

Both the planet and the Race have been passing through
a minor night-period or *pralaya*. All that has been given
to man to understand, use and rule, that he may become a
conscious co-worker with God for the good of all — but which

his selfishness, unbrotherliness and inhumanity and his refusal to work with the Divine Will has perverted and abused—must now be gathered up in a mighty harvest, the tares and the wheat together. In fact, this period of overlapping may be likened to the Mill of the Gods in which the harvest is tested and all but the golden grain is driven out. As *The Voice of the Silence* says: "The worthless husks it drives from out the golden grain, the refuse from the flour." But the husks and refuse will, after their disintegration, form the materials and forces which fertilize the crop of new conditions in which the humanity of the new day-period must now sow its seed.

Every Soul who has awakened to a realization of the law of the One life has within him the key which will not only unlock all doors, but which will solve all mysteries and show him how safely to ride the storms of this period of transition is God's ambassador on Earth; for he understands that the conditions he fearlessly faces, the Great Law will give him the strength to conquer.

How then can we "help nature and work on with her," correlate with the mighty stream of Divine Will and Love that is rejuvenating the planet and the Race and preparing them for a new and greater period of manifestation? Divine Will is the active, centrifugal, masculine aspect, as Divine Love is the passive, centripetal or feminine aspect of the manifesting Godhead expressing according to the Law of Growth, while desire, which holds sway in the lower realms, may be likened to the exhaust steam of an engine. But just as the efficient engineer utilizes the exhaust steam in a secondary cylinder to add to the power of the whole, so when desire is conquered, controlled and directed by the purified Will it becomes an auxiliary cylinder to the engine which is bearing us toward the goal of our destiny.

Out of a negative desire to be kind and loving we must evolve a Will to be so; out of a desire to know and understand we must Will to; out of a desire to work in harmony with the Law of Growth we must Will to work with it. As Éliphas Lévi truly says: "To will well, to will long, to will always, but never to lust after anything, such is the secret of power. . . . The Magus thinks and wills; he loves nothing with desire; he rejects nothing in rage."[2] *The Secret Doctrine* tells us: "The Higher Mind directs the Will; the lower turns it into selfish Desire."[3]

Divine Will and Divine Love, united in expression through the Law of Growth, bring into action the force of the Divine One Life, the Christ-force, the motive power of the universe, the power back of all evolution. Once we correlate with it by willing to let the Christ-force manifest in us as a definite determination to conquer and we will have entered that great stream of Divine Creative Force; will have attached our individual car to the express train that is carrying humanity and the planet on to their destination. If we go through life with desire instead of Will for motive power, spiritually we are drifting aimlessly with the tide. And there is no more hopeless person than one who merely desires to be good, desires to be liberal, to be happy, to be thought well of, etc., yet who makes no definite effort of Will to attain his ideal. Since the dynaspheric force is the servant of the purified and trained Will, no one can hope to utilize it, either in himself or in the world, who is still controlled by desire.

Many come into touch with these Teachings because of a desire to gain all that is possible without serious effort on their part; because they desire to advance without the effort to correlate with the positive force of Will, perhaps thinking that the desired development will soak into them like a shower of rain on a thirsty field and with no special effort on their part to understand and utilize the higher forces. Their Wills are dormant and the motive power of their lives is but the exhaust steam of desire. They are like the dogs which by the very onward rush of an automobile are

<hr/>

[2] *Transcendental Magic*, pp. 237, 238.
[3] *The Secret Doctrine*, Blavatsky, III, 559.

impelled to run along beside it for a time, imagining that they can keep pace with it. Naturally such persons run here and there with no fixed purpose and no Will to attain. And they are often astonished to see others who have Will behind them push past them and press on toward their goal.

These Teachings are the result of positive Willing to enlighten and inspire humanity, not merely on the part of those agents who started out to accomplish this task through a special avenue of force, but on the part of those Great Teachers who through Will have taken their places at the head of the great stream of evolution which ordains that humanity shall have avenues through which the Law of Growth may be taught it, with as little personal bias as possible, and with Will and Love co-equal. Therefore, the great whirlwind of Divine Will which sweeps over mankind at the close of certain cycles has gathered together an atom (personality) here and an atom there, as many as were willing to be lifted up out of their old conceptions and be swept out into the great stream of unselfish service for humanity, with nothing to hold them together but Divine Love. With these there may be gathered some who are but like chaff, who have no momentum, no Will. But those soon drop out, for they are blown hither and thither by every passing breeze in the lower levels of desire. But when the time of hill-climbing comes they will fall away long before the attainment of that which the Will of the Teacher has ordained, and will drop back contentedly into their old habits of thought and life, to be picked up and swirled around by the next current of force that passes by.

To correlate with the One Life and become conscious workers with the Divine we must transmute desire into Will and be dominated by the Will to Grow. Awaken then to the necessity of Willing and taking definite steps to correlate with the Christ-consciousness of the One Life, knowing that all life is an expression of Eternal Motion.

Better is he who with an open mind Wills to do and makes a mistake, than he who stands still or drifts along on the exhaust steam of desire. For if he is earnestly pressing forward, the imperfect or mistaken attainment of today will be left behind without a sigh tomorrow, for the advance he has made will give him a fuller understanding and a greater appreciation of what is best for his spiritual unfoldment and he will see his goal draw closer and closer as he draws closer and closer to the perfect manifestation of Divine Will and Love.

Make life forceful, with Will standing back of everything we do or think. But at the same time draw close and let the Mother-love pervade and bring forth the Christ in us, so that all who meet us will recognize that while we are positive and forceful we are also loving.

CHAPTER VI

THE BIRTH OF THE NEW AGE

"And then shall they see the Son of man coming in the clouds, with great power and glory. And then shall he send his angels, and shall gather together his elect from the four winds, from the uttermost part of the earth, to the uttermost part of heaven."*St. Mark*, XIII, 26-27.

In the early ages, ere the masculine and feminine principles were separated into independent men and women, ere the dawn of the days, symbolically recorded in the first chapters of *Genesis*, and while the two principles were expressing in the one organism, there was a period in human evolution corresponding to the transitional period through which humanity is passing today. But conditions were so different then that we of separate and corporeal organism can scarcely realize or even imagine how beings of an incorporeal and ethereal substance—half astral and half physical—could think, act and function. For it must be remembered that the humanity of that time had not yet reached the lowest arc of its cycle of descent into matter.

As we have explained in *The Voice of Isis*,[1] "These misty forms became more and more dense by the gradual absorption of a new element, earth, until 'The Second Race . . . . . . being also sexless, evolved out of itself, at its beginning, the Third, Androgyne Race by an analogous, but already more complicated process' . . . . . . Only toward the middle of the Third Race (Lemurian) did solid bones develop, the sexes separate, the body become 'clothed with coats of skin' and take on human form as we know it today."

---

[1] Page 231.

The dense materialization began about the middle of the Third Race and was completed by the middle of the Fourth (Atlantean) Race, by which time, owing to the density of the physical conditions in which they must ultimately manifest, the separation of the sexes was completed. The separation was inevitable, for it was necessary that both expressions—active and passive, positive and negative—manifest fully and completely and learn independently, yet together, the lessons of this lowest and densest phase of the Cycle of Manifestation. This could not be accomplished all at once, for physical conditions were then so crude, dense and hard that only by the complete dominance of the positive and masculine element could the organism survive, and this permitted little free expression of the feminine element

It must be borne in mind, however, that when speaking of the masculine and feminine elements expressing through one organism we must not picture man and woman as known today. Neither must we construct an anatomical anomaly in which the two sets of physical organs are equally developed, for we are contemplating that which, while it had been projected into the physical plane, had not as yet taken on physical expression. It was expressing in ethereal and astral matter and was tending toward the density of the physical embodiment, but the masculine and feminine functions had not then focalized themselves into bodily organs. They only existed in potentiality or at most in rudimentary form.

It was then that the masculine and feminine Principles thus projected into Earth conditions began to manifest. The masculine functions are the result of the outpouring and embodiment of the masculine Principle of Will, intellect, courage and the power to fructify and express in form. The feminine functions are the result of the outpouring and embodiment of the feminine Principle of Love, compassion, intuition and the desire to bring forth in form. The masculine Principle, being an expression of the divine Father-aspect of the Godhead, manifests as a great, overwhelming and self-sacrificing desire to project and fructify, even at the expense of itself, while the feminine Principle, being an expression of the divine Mother-aspect of the Godhead, manifests as an overwhelming desire, yearning and eagerness to bring forth, cherish and preserve, even at the expense of its own substance. The chief manifestation of the masculine Principle is creativeness. The chief manifestation of the feminine Principle is motherhood, both expressed in perfect purity.

If this short summary of the creative Principles in manifestation is understood and borne in mind many of the difficulties arising from the contradictory teachings of others as to sex will be avoided or solved.

Altho the feminine Principle is focused in and expressed largely through the female sex, it does not do so exclusively, for there are many men who express more of the motherhood, the yearning, loving desire to bring forth and cherish something more ethereal and spiritual than has as yet manifested in their physical expression of life, than do some women. For there are many women who are not true to their birthright, who are not seeking to bring forth and cherish their higher spiritual realizations in their lives. Conversely, many women express more of the masculine qualities than do some men.

Both men and women today are waking up to a realization of the possibility of manifesting greater and more perfect expressions of themselves; the possibility of bringing forth their higher ideals to manifest in their outer lives. And just as the unquenchable desire of the feminine Principle of Love and compassion to bring forth in freedom and perfection resulted in the separation of the sexes in those early days, so today the same unquenchable longing must result in a more definite separation, independence and freedom for woman. But now, instead of being directed downward into matter, this great urge of the mother-force is projected upward to bring forth higher ideals for the Race.

The separation of the sexes is recorded in the *Bible* in the allegory of Eve being created from a rib taken from Adam's side during his sleep. This marks a real "fall of man," or the "descent into matter," but it was not a fall or descent due to sin. It was brought about by the same great Principle of Divine Love and Wisdom, the Voice of the Deity sent forth, the Word that was spoken and sent through all the spheres. The projection is always creative, but only through the loving mother-force can the creation be brought forth. This "fall" was not a "sin," nor due to the use of the sex functions, for man was distinctly told to "Be fruitful and multiply, and replenish the earth." The sin was that man, after being given the power to create at will, in learning to use his new-found function, used it largely to gratify the desires of the animal body in which he was manifesting upon Earth instead of using it only under the guidance of the Divine. And, alas, in sin and sorrow were the fruits of the Tree of Life plucked and eaten, hence the resulting curses from which mankind has suffered since are of his own creating.

It is said that it was woman who tempted man, but this does not mean that woman was seducing man, selfishly desirous that he should participate in sinful pleasures. It means that woman tempted man in the sense that the Great Mother-force, the love and yearning to bring forth, was then for the first time focused in separate forms. Before that period all the love and desire to bring forth was hidden within the androgynous being, hence was indefinite, like the spiritual longings we feel but scarce understand. They seem vague and far away, yet we all recognize them as efforts of the One Reality, the Higher Self, to express and bring forth in us. And it will be just as great a test or temptation to us, when in the fullness of time we find our spiritual body a definite reality to our waking consciousness, and our power to "make dreams come true" also a reality to our senses, to decide whether we will use our spiritualized creative power to bring forth "in His image" or whether we will again go astray and again debase our god-like power to minister to the selfish desires of the personality.

A rib is an important part of the dense physical framework of man's body, and this very expression tells us in one graphic word that woman is not a separate being newly created and subordinate to man, but is a natural differentiation of the one Spiritual Being which expresses through the two co-equal sexes, an integral part of the very framework of his being; for without the ribs, man's form would be impossible. It is much as tho the moisture of the air, as it is condensed into a cloud, might separate into two parts, yet each part be an expression of the one center of force.

The deep sleep which fell upon Adam, or the advanced humanity of that early ethereal Race, was the sleep of a Race night-period or *pralaya* during which all activity ceases or rests in a deep sleep, to come forth at the dawning of the new day-period in a more perfect manifestation. It is, of course, understood that the Adam of the allegory was not one man or Eve one woman. The literal meaning of Adam is "red earth," hence Adam stands for the first earthly Race of the Red Ray, red coming first because it is the lowest, most material vibration of the solar spectrum, the previous Races being too super-physical to be classed as earthly. But with the first glimpse of the mysterious Orange Planet back of the Moon[2] the Orange Ray has begun to mingle with the Red Ray and have its influence as the forces of the New Age overlap those of the former.

On the descending arc which enters dense physical conditions, as the feminine attributes were separated from the

---

[2] See Page 53 herein.

masculine, it might be said that woman was born from "man." But today humanity, as a whole, has passed the lowest and densest point and is on the upward arc into more ethereal and spiritual conditions, has, indeed, already reached the point on a level with and corresponding to the point on the descending arc at which the sexes separated. Hence, according to the laws of cycles and correspondence, there must be conditions which correspond to those of the former cycle, but in a higher form. Therefore we may now expect a more spiritual separation or birth of the sexes preparatory to a subsequent unification when the conditions of Earth are so changed that mankind, as a whole, manifests in ethereal conditions instead of physical. Thus, once more will woman be born from man, but now upon the mental plane.

Adam, or the Real or Divine Self, will once more give up a "rib" or a part of the framework of his mental body and out of it will be fashioned once more a help-meet for him. In other words, during the past ages of the world it has been man who has built up the mental conceptions and ideals which have influenced, moved and controlled the business and social fabric of society, while woman has had her place in the intellectual and spiritual background, hidden within the body of man, so to speak, altho always an important upholder of the structure of the man-made society. But in this coming Woman's Age, which is now dawning, she will take her place as a co-equal part of the framework of human society, no longer merely a rib in a man's world, but having ribs and a complete independent structure of her own, which shall henceforth work as a co-equal with man in bringing forth the new conditions of humanity.

It is not good for man to be alone, for he has proved his inability, while working alone and dominating, to use the feminine Principle, either within himself or in the Race, for the best good of all mankind. Today there is once more sent out from the Lodge of Masters the thought received by them from the Elohim—the assembled gods of all worlds and systems—"It is not good for man to be alone." Once more there is a fresh and greater outpouring upon humanity of the Mother-force from the jar of the Water Bearer (Aquarius), who falls on his knees to pour out the Water which shall enlarge and deepen the channel of its manifestation in mankind as does a freshet in the springtime.

The feminine aspect of creation is sweeping the Earth. Even in the most materialistic quarters we find women waking up to the thought that they have something more to do in the affairs of the world than heretofore. This in reality is the result of a current of force deliberately sent forth into the world from on high, and only as it is able really to manifest and not only the women of the land wake up to their great possibilities, but also the womanhood of the Race or the feminine qualities in both men and women—the love, intuition, sympathy and compassion that can bring forth, even in man—can humanity as a whole receive its New Birth.

There is hovering over the Race a desire to bring forth something greater; new conditions of physical and spiritual life; new conceptions of brotherhood; new realizations of the oneness of all flesh. No longer do men ask, "Am I my brother's keeper?" They are beginning to find out that all mankind are brothers and are each other's keepers; for that which hurts one hurts all; that which benefits one benefits all, as was clearly shown in the recent World War. The old false conception was but the separating of the mother-love from the masculine-intellect; from the conception that each man must be a law unto himself and create for himself material wealth and comforts and strive selfishly to enjoy them alone.

All this is being conceived and born of the new great outpouring of the Divine Mother-force. Even those women who are seeking political changes and political recognition, altho sometimes in misguided ways, are nevertheless obeying the feminine life-wave of the period. But to those who can hear and understand there comes a higher message, the message of the Great Mother, namely, that there must soon be born the coming manifestation of the Christ, the Avatar. Like all Christs, He must be born, not of one woman through the gate of physical birth—for humanity has passed beyond the point where this is necessary—but He must be born from the outpourings of feminine force from both man and woman, thus setting the example and becoming the pattern for the type of birth which will ultimately be reached by humanity as a whole. That is, it can only be through the deep abiding love, sympathy, understanding and intuition, together with the will, faith and eagerness to prepare a place in the heart and give of the life and of the devotion of the heart and mind, that such a divine outpouring can be focused and made to manifest in an embodiment on Earth.

This preparation must not be to save ourselves or from any selfish desire that we may be recognized and placed in high position where we can exult over or dominate our fellowmen, but must be made because of an overwhelming and unselfish desire that new Light, comfort and spiritual help may be given humanity; that new conditions may manifest; that a force of Divine Love great enough to uplift poor, suffering humanity may manifest on Earth. This is the expression of the real mother-love of the Woman's Age, and while woman must be its focus and bear the greater part in the preparation, yet man must also share in this great work and lend his positive qualities to help establish it upon Earth; for only of such combined qualities can a mighty matrix or Divine Womb of pure spiritual love-force be created into which the Divine One can descend and materialize upon Earth, even as He has already descended and manifested in the higher realms and in the hearts of His faithful followers.

This means far more than the mere bringing into the

Earth's atmosphere of a Great Teacher, for many a Great Teacher has come before and given his message, only to be stoned or crucified and his message either misinterpreted or ignored. All the outpourings of Divine Love and Wisdom which the Great Teachers of previous ages have sent to this dark star have been greatly limited and modified by the dense material conditions which then obtained. But it cannot be too strongly emphasized that the Earth and her inhabitants are passing out of her most dense conditions of limitation; are dying to the old and being swept and garnished; in fact, are today passing through the terrible throes of the birth of a new cycle of manifestation. Hence, every earnest heart who longs for better conditions of any and every kind has a great work to do, namely, to see to it that the united forces of man's and woman's virgin love-nature be so expressed and given forth that the coming Divine One shall be indeed born of woman, the Divine Motherhood of the Race, which also includes the love-nature of man.

In the text which heads this chapter this Great Teacher or Avatar is called the Son of Man who is born of a virgin (meaning pure), or of the feminine aspect of humanity, and hence will be able to manifest the Christ-power in the proportion that man has been able to conceive of and prepare for it, and will therefore become the flower and fruit of humanity. Each Avatar comes as a new outpouring of the universal, Cosmic Christ-force and in Him is expressed all of the highest conceptions of the race thought, together with a foreshadowing of that to which it can attain. And, like Mary of old, the women of today are crying, "How can I bring forth this New Age, 'seeing I know not a man?'" that is, without man's co-operation. But the answer is the same today as of old: "The Holy Ghost shall come upon thee, and the power of the Highest shall overshadow thee; therefore also that holy thing which shall be born of thee shall be called the Son of God."

Hence, an Avatar is always the Son, or more correctly the Sun, of man. He comes not in physical clouds, but in the mists of glory which can be penetrated only by the eye of spiritual discernment, *i.e.*, His teachings will be so far above the full comprehension of the masses of the immediate time that the humanity of all the following cycle will find new truths hidden in the letter of His words, while even the surface and obvious meaning will be comforting, helpful and inspiring to the masses.

This Great Teacher will not come to any one school of philosophy, sect, society, order or church, but to mankind; for He must be born of the combined Mother-love and Will of humanity. Hence, only those who give of their love, will, devotion and intuition will know Him when He comes; for they will be affinitized to the divine force which He manifests and will know Him as a mother knows her child.

It is not a matter of the Race, society or church to which we belong, for if we have manifested this mother-force and are pouring it forth we are one of His own. But there will be, indeed there is now taking place, a selection, a gathering together from the Four Winds, not according to the organization to which we belong, but according to how much of the true mother-force, *i.e.*, how much real love and devotion, we are giving to make this divine birth possible.

He shall shine from the East even into the West, like the rising Sun. By the East is meant not a geographical point, but a point in the racial heart of humanity, the point of conception or the birthplace of the Buddhic or Christ-consciousness. By the West is meant the place of reaping, the complete understanding of all that the cycle was to bring forth, "Every eye shall behold Him," but only the eye of Spirit shall recognize Him. We are especially warned against those who proclaim themselves to be the coming Teacher or who permit others so to proclaim them. "Take heed that no man deceive you. For many shall come in my name, saying, I am Christ; and shall deceive many. . . . . .

For there shall arise false Christs, and false prophets, and shall shew great signs and wonders. . . . believe it not." Remember *an Avatar is not a mortal* born of physical woman, but a phenomenal manifestation of a Divine Being.

To those who are ready, even if but a few; to those whose hearts are open, who can conceive even vaguely of this great truth, comes this message: According to your heart's desire, so shall it be. We speak to you as to the mothers of the Race. Be ye men or women, it is to the mother-force that we appeal. Awaken, ye mothers of Israel! Let it not be said as of old that the voice of Rachel is heard in the land mourning for her children and cannot be comforted, for they are not. Determine that the children of your love and eager desire shall be brought forth and they will be. The birth pangs both you and the Earth are now suffering. But if you understand and know that the time is at hand for the birth of the New Age and its Great Teacher, you will hold fast and patiently bear your sorrows and tribulations, knowing you are bearing them for the world. This is not a time to weep, not even to mourn. It is a time to focus all your attention on the great truth that humanity shall bring forth a Child and shall call His name Emanuel, "God with us." And He shall dwell with us forever more. Amen.

Chapter VII

JACOB AND ESAU

"And the Lord said unto her, Two nations are in thy womb, and two manner of people shall be separated from thy bowels; . . . behold, there were twins in her womb. And the first came out red, all over like an hairy garment; and they called his name Esau. And after that came his brother out, and his hand took hold on Esau's heel; and his name was called Jacob." *Genesis*, XXV, 23-26.

As we enter into this Aquarian Age we hear, as with a trumpet blast, the angelic hosts proclaim: "The days of judgment are upon you, O Earth; the days when the mills of the gods which for ages have ground out the meal of life so slowly yet surely, begin to revolve with greater speed, and the chaff and dust fly in more stifling clouds. The grain is ripe. The grinding has begun. Already the angels who are the reapers are gathering the meal into the storehouse of the ages."

It is being proclaimed on every hand that the New Age is upon us; that the New Race is being born, the New Humanity; that the New Day has dawned, the New Dispensation. Much of this is the echo of a divine truth proclaimed from on high, written in the stars. But much of it, like echoes ringing from an overhanging rock, but repeats the last word uttered and gives us no connected sentences and conveys no consecutive thought.

All the great events in the life of the planet, the Race and the individual are brought about by the turning of the mighty Wheel of Time, each revolution marking a new day or New Age, which is as definite as the day of twelve hours brought about by the turning of the Earth upon its axis, or as definite as the summer that follows the winter. Hence, if we would know more than an echoed word of what this new turn of the Great Wheel may bring us, we must consider the ushering in of past ages. The baker who would know how to bake his loaf today must consider the loaf of yesterday and put into the new loaf the same measure of meal and of shortening and of leaven. But today he may have new and more advanced ways of baking it. Instead of a rude oven of clay he may have a fully equipped electric oven; instead of kneading it with his hands, he may have an efficiently designed machine which kneads the dough and fashions the loaves.

So is it with the New Age. It is well to heed the past, yet not to live in it and say that that which has been is all that ever can be, but intelligently reason from underlying principles which are the same yesterday, today and forever, altho they find ever greater facilities for more perfect expression as evolution advances. The Tree of Life grows from age to age and puts forth fresh branches and leaves and fruit perhaps undreamed of when it was but a sapling; nevertheless, it grows always from the everlasting Root, and but expresses that which was present altho unmanifested within the seed. And ever is it the same fundamental process of Nature which puts forth its new expressions.

Among the wonderful symbolic allegories of the *Bible*—that presentation of the Wisdom Religion most familiar to the Western World—we find in the story of Jacob an accurate description of the beginning of a New Age. Jacob—the meaning of whose name is "the supplanter"—passes through the various steps of Initiation which lead him from his early mistakes up to final Mastery.

Jacob was one of twins. Esau, his elder brother, is represented as a mighty hunter, and is described as red and hairy. He symbolizes the personal or animal self, while Jacob, born afterward and holding to his brother's heel, is the Real Self which is to be embodied in the flesh, but which does not come into full contact with the lower animal man until the personality reaches a certain stage of unfoldment, hence, may be said to hold to his heel—the point of contact with the Earth—while in the cosmic cycle Jacob represents the Aquarian Age. Despite Esau being the first-born, it is Jacob who obtains his birthright, as the Higher Self must ever do, altho it is obtained by what at first might be called trickery; for the Higher Self is destined to take the leading place, inherit the birthright and dominate the lower self. And altho Jacob again supplanted his brother in obtaining the blessing intended for Esau, which concluded with the words everlastingly true when applied to the Higher Self: "Cursed be everyone that curseth thee; and blessed be he that blesseth thee," nevertheless Esau received an appropriate blessing, namely, "Thy dwelling shall be the fatness of the earth," *i.e.*, the lower self is blessed with physical health and the ability to supply his animal needs in abundance, and is happy and contented only as he serves his brother, the Higher Self. Hence, only as the Higher Self takes precedence, can the lower self obtain the blessing, yet because of this the animal self often rebels and resists and seeks to pull down and slay the Higher Self.

We next find Jacob taking stones from the wayside to make a pillow on which to rest his head for the night while on the Great Journey. Here he had the wonderful dream of the ladder set up on Earth yet reaching into heaven, with angels ascending and descending. "And, behold, the Lord stood above it." Thus is the Real Self awakened and its mission foreshadowed. And especially will the comforting assurance, "I am with thee, and will keep thee in all places whither thou goest," awaken an answering thrill in the heart of each one who really seeks to let the Real Self manifest. For this promise is given to Jacob not as one man, but to the one whom he symbolizes, *the Man Who Conquers* and becomes one with his Father-in-heaven, *i.e.*, the Aquarian

Man. But like all visions, Jacob's vision simply pointed out that which could be accomplished.

After this we find Jacob recognizing in Rachel his divine counterpart or complement and feminine aspect—love and intuition. But after serving for her seven years—a cycle of perfection—he finds that he has gained only Leah, not the real inner, Soul-love or the Voice of Intuition speaking to him independently from within or Soul illumination, but a substitute or the voice of authority, the dictum of others instead of the divine knowing of one who has made the correlation within. This often happens. How ardently many sincere students serve through a long cycle of perfection only to find that they are wedded to Leah, and even bring forth children by her, that is, many advanced students have gained a certain intellectual understanding of the Wisdom Religion, yet dogmatically insist upon the interpretation of all Truth exactly as former students have expressed it. Such students accept nothing that has not already been said in some occult book which they consider authoritative. And because they refuse to listen to the Voice of Intuition, which would give them a more direct meaning or personal application, the voice of Rachel cannot speak and so they find they must still serve another perfect cycle ere the real inner Voice can speak.

We also find Jacob giving of his flocks and herds to Esau. These herds, as we have explained elsewhere,[1] represent our thoughts, desires and feelings which we must watch over and guard. Yet, when Jacob, the Higher Self, sends them to Esau the personality, they represent great wealth, the gifts of the Higher Self. Moreover, they are sent to Esau across the river Jordan, that invisible river of force[2] which separates the outer physical life from the inner and invisible life. Jacob also says, "With my staff I crossed over Jordan," *i.e.*, the staff is the power of the One Life which

---

[1] See *The Voice of Isis*, Curtiss, 315.
[2] See *Realms of the Living Dead*, Curtiss, 27.

enables the Higher Self to pass over Jordan and not only incarnate in the flesh, but ever to pass back and forth to guide, train and enrich the lower personality until Mastery is reached and the two become one as Israel. Thus must the Higher Self ever help and bless the lower, for only as this mission is fulfilled is Jacob met by the Angel, with whom he wrestles until he obtains the blessing. All alone in the darkness of the night he wrestled until break of day and refused to let the Angel go until he blessed him, even tho his hip was put out of joint. This symbolizes the final Initiation; for the Angel told him: "Thy name shall no more be called Jacob (supplanter), but Israel (power of God), for as a prince hast thou power with God, and with men, and hast prevailed."

As Israel—meaning soldier, champion or Power of God—Jacob summons to his deathbed his twelve sons who are to succeed him. He blesses them and prophetically assigns to each his place and work in the age then dawning. Symbolically the twelve sons of Jacob, the twelve disciples of Jesus and the twelve months in the cycle of the year refer to the twelve signs of the zodiac, which rule the several months, sons and disciples.[3] At the beginning of each Age these twelve sons become the sons of "the man who has prevailed" and are blessed by him and sent forth. Jesus also called his twelve together and blessed them and gave to each his work. When we attain this point in our individual ongoing, we are no longer ruled by the signs, but are able to bless them and direct and guide their forces toward the fulfillment of the Divine Law.

Thus the true Aquarian becomes a worker with the Law. Hence, the perfected man who, like Jacob, has "prevailed with God," is one who has attained to the great understanding of what the forces of the universe are evolving; who can see all life as a mighty ladder up which the Angel in man is ascending rung by rung, step by step, back to his

---

[3] See *The Key of Destiny*, Curtiss, Chapters V and VI.

divine estate, and down which the divine helpers descend to man with their blessings and their power. In the course of its spiritual unfoldment every Soul—while sincerely trusting to or resting upon the stones of traditional truth taught in his religion, yet realizing their hardness and incompleteness—will surely receive the vision of the Ladder of God or the positive realization of the actuality of the angels and their power to ascend and descend. He can thus see that all things must ultimately help bring to birth the Divine Seed hidden within, no matter how dark or vile the intervening stages of unfoldment may seem to be or how great the suffering the birth pangs cause.

The twelve tribes of Israel are, therefore, the twelve aspects of the "Power of God" which are sent forth to accomplish their ultimate work in evolution in each Age; the Power which draws upward all things that are down and assists all things that are in the heavens to descend into manifestations on Earth in glory. The physical manifestation and embodiment of this Power is the physical Sun, but its human embodiment is the awakened Soul who can grasp the end from the beginning and consciously work on with that end in view.[3]

At the beginning of this new Aquarian Age this great Power is once more calling together its twelve sons that they may be blessed and be assigned their work. As it is written, "And then shall appear the sign of the Son of Man in heaven. . . . And he shall send his angels (messengers) with a great sound of a trumpet, and they shall gather together his elect from the four winds, from one end of heaven to the other."[4] This gathering is now taking place and, as we have explained elsewhere[5] the four winds are the creative cosmic currents of force focused in and emanating from the four signs at the corners of the fixed cross of the zodiac.

---

[4] *St. Matthew*, XXIV, 30-1.
[5] Chapter X herein; also *The Key to the Universe*, Curtiss, 143-6

The first of the four is Aquarius the Man, the source from which comes the outpouring of the Water of Life or the great Mother-force contained in the ewer carried by the Water-bearer, symbolizing the Womb of Time, of Nature and of man. For into this ewer-man throughout the ages has been pouring the true Mother-force developed in him as a result of his experience, suffering and efforts toward overcoming; that force which alone can make of man Superman and make the Earth truly bring forth her increase as foreordained in the Grand Plan.

From the opposite end of the cross the force generated by Leo the Lion is both great strength and abiding love, while from the point crowned by Scorpio the Eagle, comes the force of sex regenerated and lifted up. While the power of the scorpion is that which "biteth the horse's heels, so that his rider shall fall backward," yet when the fullness of the Aquarian Age shall dawn it shall be lifted up to become the poise and the power of the Eagle to soar undaunted into the higher realms, into the very eye of the Sun. At the other end of the cross stands Taurus the Ox with the mighty strength to labor and endure, unfaltering patience and endless perseverance.

These four fixed signs therefore represent what the Sign of the Son of Man in heaven must accomplish during its Age or cycle of over two thousand years. It is quite likely that ere this Age has progressed far we will find the influence of these signs expressing their higher aspects instead of their more material, and finding expression through various leaders or "men who have prevailed with God." For the New Age could not be ushered in or manifest in all its phases if all twelve sons or tribes were not represented, for it is through them, together with the influence of their corresponding zodiacal signs on the children born under those signs, that those forces must find expression in humanity.

Today, each of the twelve tribes has heard the command of the Great Law: Go forth and gather out of thy tribe the Children of the Lord (those who have fulfilled the Law), who have not bowed the knee to Baal and who have not received the mark of the Beast in their foreheads nor in their hands! Not only are all the nations of the world standing today before the judgment seat of the ages, but each nation, nay each individual, must consciously or unconsciously respond to the force that is today drawing them to the center of all Being. And in that drawing each is passing through a mighty testing. The seal placed by the angel on the foreheads of the chosen ones is the Light of Understanding which shines from the eyes of everyone who has found his or her true place and tribe.

We are told there were twelve thousand sealed out of every tribe. This, of course, being but symbolic, means those who have gathered sufficient experiences from all twelve signs of the zodiac to enable them to recognize their tribe and the banner of its leader.[6] This also shows unmistakably that no one tribe has an advantage over another. Yet this fact must not be taken for a right to remain unattached to any tribe and to say: "Since there is good in all, I can go from one to another without giving allegiance to any particular one." For only those who uphold the banner of their tribe and march forward into the New Age with their leader, are sealed and counted among the chosen ones, *i.e.*, those who, having recognized their tribe and given their allegiance to its banner are sealed or chosen as conscious and intelligent instruments to leaven the great mass of humanity. Some day the banner of our tribe will be presented to each of us, and we will recognize it with a thrill of joy as we would our country's flag. We do not have to go into distant lands. We do not have to go into strange conditions. We have only to prepare our hearts and minds and be ready to respond when the banner is seen.

Remember, that while there are many other banners, and they all stand round about the Sun, the banner which this Order holds up before you is the banner of the Lion of the Tribe of Judah, which calls to all whose hearts and minds

---

[6] *The Key of Destiny*, Curtiss, 46.

and lives respond to the call of the Heart Doctrine as presented by its Leader, the Teacher of the Order. If you recognize the call, give it your heart's allegiance and your support. Make it a vital factor in your life, that you may be sealed by the Great Ones as one of the Workers for humanity in this great New Age under the banner of Judah.

The countries of Europe, each under its own banner, have been passing through their baptism of blood and their purification by fire,[7] and will so continue until their lessons are learned; for only thus can their sins be washed away and their chaff and evil weeds consumed. Each country or nation on Earth is the vehicle for the expression of the forces of a certain Star which is its Genius, and from that Star emanate the vibrations which give the country or nation its peculiar characteristics. And as certain Stars disappear from our system their nations also disappear. And when new Stars appear or their forces reach us, new nations arise which express their forces. Even the banner or flag of a country is chosen because those who fashion it are impressed to use the colors and symbols which in some measure express the vibrations from its Star of Destiny. America must also lift high her banner and take her place in the purifying fire, ere her mystical twelve thousand can be chosen and sealed, since only those who go forth at the call and endure to the end receive the blessing. For out of this terrible baptism there shall arise a purified humanity.

As we have said elsewhere: "A banner or national flag not only symbolically embodies the highest ideals of the people over whom it flies, but it also symbolizes the highest attainment and ultimate perfection of that people. The flag of the United States of America symbolizes and foreshadows the greatest possibilities of any flag ever designed. Altho there are many flags having the same colors, yet in none are they combined in a like manner. The colors of a flag are like the letters spelling a word or the notes of music forming

---

[7] Written in March, 1917.

a melody. Therefore the flag of each nation proclaims that nation's word and sounds its key-note, hence rallies to it the elemental powers and forces belonging to its colors and symbols.

"In our flag the red symbolizes the life-force, the martial force, its clear bright shade representing all the higher possibilities of the courage, energy and power of Mars, the masculine forces of the solar system and in humanity, as well as the intensity of love that will fight for a principle. "Also the red of Mars is alternated at equal intervals with the white of purity, sanity, righteousness, justice and brotherhood. This proclaims to the world that we will fight if we have to, not because we seek to spill our brother's blood, or for aggrandizement, but for righteousness, justice, freedom and liberty, for these must be maintained by the force of Mars if necessary, else our flag is unbalanced and the principles for which it stands are betrayed. But we should continually strive to let the white so blend with the red that they shall ultimately manifest as the pure rose-pink of love. It also indicates that war is not the governing spirit, but is blended and balanced in equal proportion with the desire for peace honorably won and maintained by the higher aspects of Mars.

"Blue is the color of the Great Mother-force, the power which brings forth and which cherishes all that is beautiful and lovable, as well as those things which the force of Mars energizes. In other words, it represents the force of Venus or Divine Mother-love.

"No other flag has the arrangement of these two colors as found in our flag. Others have the blue, but not in one great mass like a sea of color on which the five-pointed stars are arranged side by side in harmonious color.

"And because the white and the red are co-equal, our victories must be won as much by the powers of the white as those of the red. If there were a large field of white it would tend to symbolize peace at any price, but since it is equally balanced by the red, it symbolizes peace, but peace attained and maintained if necessary by a righteous warfare.

"Since the five-pointed star symbolizes man,[8] the white stars, *i.e.,* the purified men and women, set in their field of blue, symbolize the gathering together of all humanity into the lap of the Great Mother. They stand for the united brotherhood which holds out its arms to all mankind to come and become one of US. And if they come in love and harmony and are willing to rest in the lap of their adopted mother, each in his proper place and ready to obey her decrees, laws and requirements, they are welcome. But if they cannot take their places thus on the field of blue, the flag has no other place for them.

"In its emblem this country thus proclaims to the world that it has conceived and set before its children the high ideal and glorious opportunity of becoming the leader in liberty and freedom in that it offers freely a home for all God's children, a country in which to found the New Humanity. The responsibility is great. Will we as a nation live up to it?

"Each one of us should be glad that we have a flag with such a wonderful meaning, and each should study its higher, esoteric symbology; for it enables each one to say, I belong to a new country and a new people. I will do all I can to make this country and this people all that our flag symbolizes. I will do my duty in all ways to keep the flag waving over this country, and also over the whole world in the sense of upholding the highest ideals of freedom, justice, righteousness and brotherhood.[9]

There are many other nations which are bearing high their banners and passing through their testings. Therefore, we should not give too great heed when we hear it stated that America has been chosen to be the seat of the new sub-race, or that any special location in the United States has been chosen for its center. All nations and countries are in the

---

[8] See *The Key to the Universe*, Curtiss, 181.
[9] From *The Philosophy of War*, Curtiss, 59-62.

melting pot, and the one whose people come forth most fitted will be the one chosen, altho America has a natural advantage as the new continent and the youngest people and is being peopled by many reincarnated Atlanteans who took part in a similar period at the beginning of their sixth sub-race.

Neither should we be supercilious if some person or society should say to us that the Great Teacher is coming to their particular society, and make it the head of the new civilization. Instead say: "Welcome, brother. All shall find their Leader and their exact place in the New Civilization, be it head or heart, hands or feet, according as they show their fitness during these years of testing. We recognize that each division of the great Army of the Lord must march, as did the Children of Israel, under its own banner, and that it requires all the twelve banners to lead the hosts through the fiery trials, battles and victories of the wilderness on into the Promised Land. Hence each must march in the company or tribe at whose head his banner flies, and greet as comrades those who march under all the other banners." The New Age will have twelve leaders and twelve seats, all in their true place around the Sun. Only when each of the twelve has lifted up its banner and has reflected the rays of Divine Truth so brightly that all who belong under that banner will gather together and learn from the Leader of their tribe the golden precepts of understanding of the great Ladder of Life (evolution); only when each has taken the very stones in his path, *i.e.*, the hard hearts, the misunderstandings and cruelties of life, and out of them has built a cairn of sacred memory, consecrated to the God of Gods, so that the twelve cairns shall complete the circle; only as each learns that co-operation and brotherhood mean each Soul worshiping with his whole heart and giving of his life and substance in his own place and under his own banner, all singing together a paean of praise and adoration to the one Central Sun, can the Great Teacher descend outwardly among men.

This is an allegorical picture of the conditions which must prevail ere the Great One comes to make His dwelling openly among men, altho He will appear to and give forth His teachings through His chosen disciples (the twelve Leaders) long before mankind as a whole is ready to receive Him. Then will He gather His own out of all the tribes, not to make of them a new sect, but to help each one the more perfectly to be true to the inner, divine truth as it has been revealed to him under the banner of his tribe. And out of all will be gathered those who can stand around His throne, even as the twelve signs of the zodiac stand around the Sun, each receiving the one pure Light and Teaching direct from the One Source, yet each pouring it out for the world in terms and phraseology which will appeal to and be understood by the minds attuned to that tribe or Ray of Truth: for if all men were intended to think alike there would be no need of the twelve tribes or of the twelve signs of the zodiac into which the Sun pours his rays that they may be broken up and express his Light and Life and Love (warmth) in diverse manners. "As above, so below." As we find it expressed in the physical universe, so will we find it in the spiritual fulfillment; for one Law rules the world, and the entire universe is an expression of that one Law.

CHAPTER VIII

MASTERY AND THE MASTERS OF WISDOM[1]

"The Masters of Wisdom are Great Souls, who, through repeated experiences and determined efforts through many Earth lives, have obtained Mastery, firstly, over the passions, appetites and desires of the personal self; and, secondly, over the forces of their bodies and over the life-currents of the Cosmos. Hence they have become one with the Fount of all Wisdom. . . . . Jesus was such a Master, in fact, was and *is* a Master of Masters." *Letters from the Teacher*, Curtiss, 63.

The words Mastery and "the Master" hold for each Soul who is ardently striving to make definite progress upon the Path of Attainment such a mighty potency and power that it is important that a fuller understanding of just what is meant and implied should be given, that through ignorance none shall stumble and fall or take steps which they must later retrace in sorrow and suffering. Mastery is not a sudden attainment, nor a gift bestowed upon certain especially favored ones. Neither are the Masters of Wisdom afar off, hopelessly separated from the mass of humanity and only to be contacted after long and wearisome search, bitter struggle and failure, alone and without guidance or help. Nor are they Beings who calmly watch our trials and temptations from afar, unmoved by our struggles and untouched by our tears or cries for help and our efforts to find a solution to the perplexing and trying problems of every-day life. They are our big, grown-up or Elder Brothers and Sisters; for there are many feminine Souls who have reached Mastery. But because of the dense and inharmonious conditions on Earth during the past ages

---

[1] Abstract of an address made by Dr. and Mrs. F. Homer Curtiss, at the Annual Convention of The Order of Christian Mystics, July 9, 1917.

the Great White Lodge of Masters decreed that until the Aquarian Age was well established, only masculine Masters would be sent to work in Earth conditions; for the masculine Souls are positive or active on Earth where the feminine are negative or passive. The feminine Souls are positive in the higher worlds, hence accomplish their work best from the higher realms.

Mastery is attained in accordance with the Law of Growth which we see manifesting in all the kingdoms below us. It is attained as a result of overcoming every obstacle as it is presented, neither denying nor shirking a condition, but resolutely facing it, learning its lesson and conquering it, thus leading to the unfolding and manifesting of the perfected being, the ideal pattern of which has been sent down by the Higher Self to be manifested in this world of matter that the will of the Father—the attainment of perfection in manifestation—may be done on Earth in a dense physical body, even as it is already done in heaven or the Soul-realm from which we have descended to complete this lowest arc of our cycle of expression ere we can return to our Father's home in a spiritual body.

Many have asked, who are the Masters, and where are they? Why do they not appear to us and speak to us and teach us here in America? Others have said, We do not wish to meet a Master in the flesh, for the racial appearance and habits of his personality might be a great disappointment, and if he had not mastered all the traits and conditions which we considered necessary we might be completely disillusioned. We prefer to contemplate our ideal and commune only with the Higher Self or at least with the disembodied consciousness of the physical Masters.

There is indeed a Lodge of Masters, organized as we have described elsewhere,[2] with many members of its lower orders still mortals, living in their physical bodies and still subject to the laws of the physical plane, also to many of its limita-

---

[2] *The Voice of Isis*, Curtiss, 187.

tions. These physical Masters are of various degrees of attainment. They are of many groups and have many schools in various parts of the world, often in mountain retreats difficult of access. They have mastered many wonderful secrets of Nature and the universe; have developed great psychological and magical powers; have attained great learning and wisdom. They could teach us many wonderful things, help us to unfold mental and psychic powers, but they could not confer upon us any power which had not already begun its development within us, nor could they develop it before we had reached a suitable stage of unfoldment

They might know of us psychicly and might help and encourage us if we were sufficiently developed to commune with them, but to know them in the flesh we would have to find out just where their monastery or retreat was located, have some kind of an introduction to them, etc. And being still mortals and having attained their degree of mastery through certain schools of thought, religion and philosophy, they still retain a certain imprint of those schools and naturally think that the methods by which they reached their attainment are the best for those to pursue who seek their aid.

"Every class of Adepts has its own bond of spiritual communion which knits them together. . . . The only possible and effectual way of entering into such brotherhood. . . is by bringing one's self within the influence of the Spiritual Light which radiates from one's own Logos. I may further point out here. . . that such communion is only possible between persons whose souls derive their life and sustenance from the same divine Ray, and that, as seven distinct Rays radiate from the 'Central Spiritual Sun,' all Adepts and Dhyan Chohans are divisible into seven classes, each of which is guided, controlled, and overshadowed by one of the seven forms or manifestations of the Divine Wisdom."[3]

---

[3] *The Secret Doctrine*, Blavatsky, I, 628.

There are, therefore, far higher orders of Masters than those mortals now on Earth who have entered the lower degrees, wonderful as their attainments may be. There are Masters so high, so pure, so spiritual and divine that they no longer dwell on Earth. And it is the Masters of this invisible Lodge, not in the astral but in the higher spiritual realms, who have put forth *The Order of Christian Mystics*, and from whom its Teachings come. This Order is put forward from an entirely new standpoint. Its students are not asked to go to some far distant land or to seek entrance to some ancient monastery where they may be told that to do without all comforts, conveniences and sanitary arrangements and to live on coarse and frugal fare, will free their minds from attachment to physical things. For the Western type of mind to try to adapt itself to such a radical change of habits and environment, instead of bringing quiet, ease and freedom of mind, it would require years of training of body and mind to accustom itself and become indifferent to the discomforts and rigid discipline of such a life.

If the mind of the average American aspirant is to be trained for spiritual things, to become quiet, free from disturbances and able to develop its higher faculties and commune with the highest, this can be more quickly and successfully accomplished if he is given a quiet, comfortable and orderly home life in which the comforts to which he has been accustomed are neither luxuries nor temptations; they are taken as a matter of course and are not given a second thought, whereas their absence would cause great diversion of mind. In such a home life he would be subject not to the dictates of Abbot, Priest or Master; nor to the rigid discipline of a monastery, but to the discipline of "living the life" of aspiration and devotion in the midst of the world's affairs, being "in the world, but not of it" and subject only to the dictates of his own divine Higher Self.

The two systems of development differ because of a difference in racial thought and habits of life. In the East from childhood students have been accustomed to give obedience to some one in authority over them, but in America the whole attitude of mind is one of freedom and independence. Therefore the Masters back of this Order set before its students not rigid outer observances, discipline and physical requirements, but give them an understanding of the basic principles and laws of manifested life and let each student discipline himself as may be necessary to live in accord with those principles and laws, under the guidance of his Higher Self, each one progressing according to the effort he makes toward self mastery.

The principle of Mastery or overcoming is as inevitable in its working and results as the Law of Growth. Following the Law of Growth, which is the assimilation of the food (or experience) in the conditions surrounding it, the seed overcomes and masters every obstacle in its path until it at last unfolds into the perfect flower whose ideal pattern was implanted in the seed. Man's physical body, under the guidance of his animal soul, also demonstrates to a wonderful degree this same Law of Mastery, for in spite of the many handicaps of environment, social and climatic conditions, etc., which modify the growth and expression, his body will approximate the fullness of its ideal physical pattern. It will keep on growing until it reaches a certain size, height and weight, that is, until it has filled out its astral pattern; for no man by taking thought can add one cubit to his stature.

Because man is endowed with free-will, in his mental, moral and spiritual growth he can refuse to make the effort necessary to overcome obstacles in his environment, hence can retard for a long time the ultimate attainment of Mastery. But some day, be the time ages long, and after many, many incarnations or here and now, each of us must definitely determine to become the master of his destiny, even tho that determination is the result of the suffering brought about by our refusal to recognize the goal in any other way.

All the years and perhaps incarnations that we have been

playing with life and neglecting our opportunities those Great Souls whom we call the Masters of Wisdom and Compassion have been watching over us and have been aware of our truancy. And even when in our ignorance or perversity we have turned from them, scorned all inner help and even denied their existence, they have exerted an influence on our lives. But they cannot compel us to follow their guidance, neither can they interfere with our reaping the results of the causes we set up, for they too must work with the Law.

The ancient axiom "when the pupil is ready the Teacher appears" does not mean that the moment we feel a desire to advance, partly to satisfy curiosity or self-satisfaction and partly for genuine growth and desire for service, a mysterious vision or manifestation of one of the Great Ones will be vouchsafed to us or that some astral guide will appear and tell us to do this or that thing and henceforth lead us like puppets along a smooth path up the Mount of Attainment. Nevertheless the axiom is absolutely true; for the Master who can best help us, because we belong to his Ray and naturally respond to his currents of thought and spiritual force, will send us some form of help.

Here it may be noted that many students, especially those who have recently come out of orthodox conceptions, resent the idea that there can be any Master save Jesus. As we have explained elsewhere[4] Jesus is a Master of Masters, the "first fruits of them that slept" or those who are not yet awakened to the mystic Inner Life of the Christ within and begun to strive for its attainment. The Christ-life which animates and is the life of all creation fills and finds complete manifestation through Him. But there are Masters of lesser degree on every step of the Path, just as there is no break in evolution between the lower kingdoms.

Man, who is created to be the Lord of Creation, embodies all the lower kingdoms within his body, so that we might

---

[4] *Letters from the Teacher*, Curtiss, 63 and *Gems of Mysticism*, Curtiss, Chapter 5.

well say that the mineral, the vegetable and the animal essence has become one with man, and because they are incorporated in him he has the power to master them. And as each kingdom has its Ruler or Master, when man has attained mastery over himself he may be called a Master of Masters of the lower kingdoms. For each portion of any of the lower kingdoms that a man masters within himself gives him, thenceforth, power over all that portion of the kingdom and it will obey him. For instance, if one has a wolfish trait within him, when he masters it he will find that he has gained a power over all wolves. No matter how much of the Christ-power we are able to express, if there is any animal trait still unconquered within us this condition will be sensed by animals of the kingdom to which it belongs and they will not obey us. Thus it is that the physically embodied Masters can dwell in forest or jungle and be on friendly terms with the fiercest wild animals, even poisonous serpents, for such Masters have conquered the forces of those kingdoms and are recognized as Lords of those kingdoms.

Just so Jesus, having become one with the Divine Father and been incorporated into Him, stands at the apex of the Christ manifestations, hence can rule or master the expressions of the Christ in all forms below Him. And just as there are grades in man's mastery over the lower kingdoms some who have mastered the earth and can make it produce abundantly; some who have mastered the air and can use and navigate it; some who have mastered the water and turned it to man's use, and some who have mastered fire in its subtler expressions, such as electricity, etc., so there must be many degrees of expressions of the Christ, each Master who attains to the mastery of any one manifestation turning it to the use and upliftment of all, and especially to those who need that particular phase of help.

The help which a Master gives, however, may seem to be quite a natural and commonplace happening, far from the phenomenal or miraculous. For instance, perhaps we will meet some person whose words will be used as the channel to give us just the mental and spiritual idea which at that time is needed to take us the next step onward. Or we may hear a lecture in which the word spoken touches and awakens within us the mystic chord whose vibrations open to us that inner chamber of the heart where we find that which we were seeking. Or perhaps we may find our help in a book which has been called to our attention and there find our answer, or we may be drawn into some society, order or other expression of thought which is helpful and enlightening for that stage of our growth. But whatever way it comes, if we but follow the leading and recognize in it the workings of the Law of Growth, we will have taken at least one step toward the final attainment of Mastery.

Mastery means firstly mastering the little things in our daily lives, our wrong ways of thinking, our wrong ways of speaking, acting and living. We are thus led to master our little inharmonies, our temper, jealousy, pretense and foolish chatter. And everything we master carries us one step onward until finally we find ourselves standing close to the Masters, because we are attaining to their stature and doing their work. The master of a trade or craft, while he may be cognizant of and supervise the first awkward efforts of an apprentice, does not work beside him. But when the apprentice has mastered the main features of his trade and is ready for the intricacies which only the master of the craft can teach him he will then come under the master's personal supervision. So is it with our spiritual apprenticeship. For the Law of Mastery is the same above as it is below.

The Great Souls whom we call the Masters of Wisdom have reached their high estate of spiritual development by taking one step at a time, mastering one thing after the other. But remember that we have the same power of Mastery latent within us awaiting development and use, namely, the power of the Christ, and we have the same forces to work with and also to contend against. But it is easier for us in these days to tread the Path to Mastery than it was for them, firstly, because they have gone on ahead. Everyone traveling this Path has helped to make it just that much easier for those who come after, just as every auto which passes over a rough road wears it down and helps to make it smoother and easier. Those who have attained Mastery have left a trail of glory behind which those who follow can see as plainly as the children of Israel could see the pillar of cloud by day and the pillar of fire by night.

Secondly, in these days there are many more phases of spiritual teaching given out by those whom the Masters inspire to become their servants and helpers and the guides and leaders of their fellowmen. And the ratio of such help is increasing continually. For example, every student who grasps these Teachings and incorporates them in his life becomes a helper to others ignorant of or less familiar with them than himself. Every such a one is thus utilized by the Masters to spread their Teachings. While the many differing phases of teaching may seem confusing to the beginner, yet the diversity helps greatly to develop his intuition; teaches him to think, to weigh, ponder and discriminate and to follow his guidance from within. Moreover it must be remembered that each one who is sincerely giving out teachings to help mankind is expressing them according to his type of mind and stage of spiritual unfoldment. And since all men belong to the seven basic types symbolized by "the seven churches which are in Asia," each expression of truth will help the many who belong to the same type or who are approaching a similar stage of unfoldment.

Since the Masters have reached the heights of their attainment by facing and conquering the little things of life as they came, we must not imagine that to reach perfection we are to discard or neglect our daily duties, disturb our family life, upset our home and make others uncomfortable, thus creating a gulf between us and our friends and family, often embittering them and turning them against all higher and advanced teachings. Neither are we to make ourselves peculiar or become recluses and refuse to play our part in our environment. Such ideas are the remnants of the misconceptions and wrong teachings of the Dark Ages both in Europe and the Far East.

The thing to be remembered is that Mastery is to be attained right in the environment where the Great Law has placed us. For until we can master those conditions or the Great Law takes us elsewhere or removes them from us, we are not ready for others. We may turn away, seek some other life and endeavor to escape them, but only to find the same problems confronting us in another form. But we should also remember that each thing we master we are through with and hence are free to go on to other lessons. And if the old problems do appear under different aspects to test us, we have gained the power to recognize and master them.

Altho we must face and conquer conditions for ourselves, since no one can do this for us, still we are never left to struggle on alone, are never without help and helpers; for the force of those who have mastered similar conditions forms a reservoir of power upon which we can draw to conquer these particular conditions, if we will but correlate with it, even tho many of the modern problems are peculiar to this age. But to correlate with and utilize this force we must keep our consciousness open to it continually. This is one reason for the injunction to "pray without ceasing," praying not for material things, but for self-knowledge, for love, courage, persistence and determination to conquer. Every such a prayer will be answered, for the Masters can pour into our hearts the Divine Love which alone can fill us with the ardor of achievement and the ability to bring it forth in our lives as the fruits of love. The Masters cannot and will not give us money or power or glory, but if through love we follow close in their footsteps we will gain the power to create and attain all things *as they are needed* to accomplish the manifestation of the ideals we are following.

But we never can do or attain the big things until we have grown big enough to know how to use them for the best. And whether we will use them thus is the great test they bring to us. While we are children we must learn to master the lessons of children, for they are fundamental and must be learned ere we are ready or able to take the more advanced steps. Some of these earlier steps are so simple and commonplace that they are often overlooked or are not recognized as having an important place in the life of the occultist; for the real Path of Attainment is so different from that which our enthusiasm often pictures it. In the round of plain daily living the great ideals which aroused our enthusiasm often seem to evaporate and we find only the tasks of daily life and all seems stale, commonplace and profitless.

One of the first of the early steps to be gained is the simple quality of courage, not only the dumb courage to suffer, endure and plod on, but the courage of the Christ-man as illustrated in the life of Jesus. Not only the physical courage required to ride in triumph into the city where He knew His enemies awaited Him; the courage to cleanse the temple of the money changers; not merely the courage to enter the Garden and face His accusers, His trial and the cross, but the courage required for a great Spiritual Being to leave the higher realms and manifest in the dense limitations of a human body of flesh and live in a commonplace environment and among people from whom He could not expect comprehension, to say nothing of sympathy, appreciation and understanding; where He would have to endure their indifference and their rebukes for talking with the elders in the temple, eating with publicans and sinners, etc.; the courage to be thought simple because He was not making great claims for Himself.

This is the courage of living and working and radiating the

joy and peace and love of the Inner Life even tho misunderstood and unappreciated; the courage to be about His Father's business in spite of all the doubts which His nearest and dearest heaped upon Him. In the daily life this often becomes the courage not to Do but to Keep Silent; to refuse to answer back or quarrel, to trust to the Divine Law to straighten out all misunderstandings, smooth out all inharmonies and solve all problems, provided we listen and follow the Inner Urge of the divine ideal that is seeking to manifest through us.

Picture the Christ-man during His earlier unfoldment as being unable as yet to manifest the divine ideal. Then say to yourself, that is my position. The Christ in me is hampered in its expression by a body that is still imperfect; through a personality that has faults and failings, habits of thought and expression that need to be corrected, uplifted and transmuted. But the Christ within gives me the power to pick up all these burdens and push steadily and calmly on and let the Christ-light shine out through me in spite of all. It gives me the courage to endure in spite of the spiritual growing pains; to say I'll trust and manifest and overcome; to stand alone with my Christ and watch the Law work out my problems.

Another seemingly simple quality which the occult student should develop is attention; the attention which reports to his consciousness not merely each outer happening, but reveals its inner significance. Not the cold outer attention of the scientist who seeks to understand a flower or bug by dissecting its outer form, but the attention that gathers the meaning and life-message of the flower or insect; that responds to its consciousness and thus is able to correlate with, understand and interpret Nature. This is the kind of attention that gets behind and beyond the outer and into the heart of things.

We should study our loved ones, friends and all humanity, with this kind of attention and our knowledge of the hearts and motives of mankind will grow; for we see in things and in people those qualities to which we are affinitized, either the beautiful or the sordid. Therefore we should learn to send our consciousness through the outer into the heart of things and find out our points of contact and oneness with all. Then we will be quick to recognize the true from the false, the inner from the outer, and help it into expression.

Ability to see the inner heart of things leads to the development of another important quality which should be cultivated, that of simplicity and truth in all things. The pretense, sham, hypocrisy, the boasting, exaggeration and great claims of those in the world around us are easily seen to be untrue, a false expression of the Real Self, a vanity of the personality. Seeing this we should strive to make our whole lives manifest exactly what we are, without striving to shine except as our innate qualities silently shine forth.

If conditions are not what we desire we will not pretend that they are ideal and that we are perfectly satisfied with them, for if we do so the Great Law will take us at our word and allow us to remain in them; for since we claim they are satisfactory there is no need for better. Let us be true with ourselves and about ourselves, striving ever to higher ideals and better conditions through gaining the best out of those we have and thus outgrowing them.

Among the ancient Egyptians simplicity and truth were the marks of breeding and refinement just as they are in the world today. With them nothing was so despised as pretense, the jackdaw masquerading in peacock's feathers and thinking that it deceived the world! In the great simplicity of their temple service the differences in rank among the priesthood and temple attendants were largely indicated by the texture of their robes. The robes of the more humble servitors were of coarse weave, while the difference in rank among the priesthood sometimes could be told only by counting the number of threads to the inch, each one depending on the quality of his garment to proclaim his position, for no boasting or claims could conceal it. Just so must the Soul wear coarse garments of flesh until it has learned the lessons from them and has been able to manifest the joy and beauty of the Inner Life in spite of them; for it is by manifesting that joy and beauty that the garments (bodies) are purified and made finer of texture.

In their carvings, hieroglyphs and paintings the Egyptians are represented with bare feet. This was not because they never wore any coverings or protection for their feet, but to symbolize that to advance spiritually the understanding (feet) must be uncovered and unhampered by outer and limiting forms. Their feet are represented as flat and placed in a straight line, one exactly in front of the other, in a posture no one would or could readily use in walking. This was to indicate that if we are to tread the Path to Mastery we must be straightforward and true, progressing in a straight line one step after another, each step taken firmly and flatfootedly so that our position cannot be shaken. The straight lines and angular figures used in portraying the human form were used, not because the Egyptians did not appreciate the curves of the body or because their sense of beauty was poorly developed — for their portrait statues show a highly developed sense of art — but the straight lines were used so that no suggestions of sex appeal would detract from the symbology of the drawing.

The above are only a few of the many simple steps that must be taken, but they are enough to show that it is not by great deeds, by the attainment of psychic powers, nor by passing frightful tests in the astral that Mastery is won, but by following the Law of Growth, conquering each event and extracting out of it its spiritual force and building it into spiritual growth just as the plant extracts the particles of food from all the forces of its environment and builds them into sprout, twig, leaf and bud and finally into the full-blown flower.

We will find the Path to Mastery fully outlined in the symbolic story of the life of Jesus. Therefore, those who "take up the cross of the Christ" and follow understandingly in His footsteps are treading the Path to Mastery.

CHAPTER IX

MOTHER EARTH

"Cursed is the ground for thy sake; in sorrow shalt thou eat of it.
. . . .In the sweat of thy face shalt thou eat bread." *Genesis*, III, 17-19.

"The Root of Life was in every Drop of the Ocean of Immortality, and the Ocean was Radiant Light, which was Fire, and Heat, and Motion. . . . . Light is Cold Flame, and Flame is Fire, and Fire produces Heat, which yields Water—the Water of Life in the Great Mother." *The Stanzas of Dzyan*, III, 6-9.

As the great Wheel of Time turns in its ever-recurring cycles, closer and closer do we come to that inner sphere of Nature which might be compared to her laboratory; for there Nature is working out, through the transmutation of the atoms of the globe, the mighty secrets hidden in her bosom since the beginning. Here and there among the children of men there are a few who have sensed the fact that man is indeed the microcosm of the macrocosm or a little universe within himself, and that there is but One Life and One Law manifesting in both man and the universe. Hence they know that man is one with the mighty forces which today are sweeping the world and bringing all flesh to judgment.

Many are sensing their oneness with the mighty struggle of the elements which has recently manifested visibly among men as the great World War. Such also feel that the very Earth itself is preparing within her hidden depths for the baptism of cleansing which is even now taking place in all lands. Even tho they cannot explain the exact workings, they feel the mighty cosmic forces moving upon the waters of life, and they almost hold their breath in expectation of that which is to come, while like little children they still hold fast to their Father's hand, knowing that thus they will be safe whate'er betides.

Just as man's body is composed of many elements and myriads of atoms, electrons, mentoids, etc., so is the Earth made up. Just as man has seven principles and four bodies[1]—physical, astral, mental and spiritual—so our Mother Earth has her seven distinct layers of differing qualities and essences and her four bodies or kingdoms in which the elements and their constituents are manifesting. These kingdoms we will call the body of Fire, which vitalizes all things; the body of Air, which feeds every atom of the planet; the body of Water, which refreshes and quickens, and the body of Earth, which supports. Each of these kingdoms is a distinct body, made up of living infinitesimal sensate lives, centers of radiant energy, yet all are interblended with and interdependent upon each other; all working in perfect harmony.

The seven principles of the Earth are like seven layers, each expressing a quality or essence of its own, which is imparted to all that comes under its influence, and these, like the four kingdoms, are overlapping and interpenetrating, making a harmonious whole. It is the influence of these qualities or essences of the Earth Entity which brings about the various changes in the vegetation, the types of living creatures and the racial differences in man. Each of these seven layers or zones, as we will designate them, is ruled by one of the seven Divine Hierarchies. And each zone is marked upon the crust of the Earth as one might outline a country on a map. Hence the difference between the people of one district— also the flora and fauna of their country—and those of another, not

---

[1] See *The Key to the Universe*, Curtiss, 255.

only in appearance, but in bodily constitution and modes of thought, is not one merely of education or manner of life, but a fundamental elemental difference brought about by imbibing and in-building the elemental forces belonging to the zone of the Earth in which they were born and brought up.

We have given elsewhere[2] the facts as to how each Hierarchy rules in succession, while the others become subservient during such rule. But when the change takes place from the rule of one Hierarchy to that of another, it is felt, especially throughout its own kingdom, in all the atoms and elementals composing it. Hence, there must necessarily be a great rearrangement and readjustment of all the atoms of the Earth, since every atom contains the potencies of each kingdom. Naturally, then, this planetary readjustment reacts upon and is felt throughout the Races of mankind, as well as by the lower forms of life. In his unconscious effort to adjust himself to this change in the essences of his environment, man, with his usual blindness to all things occult, turns to a purely physical explanation for the causes of the changes and upheavals; even goes to war with his brother-man.

At all such cosmic and planetary periods there is a great change in man's ways of thinking. Nations and whole Races are swept with new ideas, ambitions and aims in a comparatively brief time, almost like wild-fire sweeping a dry prairie. Such periods are easily traced in history by their dominant ideas, as for instance the Crusades, the Renaissance, the beginning of physical science, the rapid spread of prohibition and of universal suffrage, etc. The causes of these changes in man, in his outer life, and in his spiritual, mental, astral and physical bodies, can be traced to the changes in the four elemental kingdoms of the Earth of which he is a part and to which he must react, those of today being the result of the out-

---

[2] See *The Voice of Isis*, Curtiss, 186.

pouring of the Water of Life at the beginning of the present Aquarian Age.

As we enter into the Aquarian Age the change from the rule of one Hierarchy to another is most marked, because both humanity and the Earth itself are becoming more sensitive and more responsive to inner conditions. In each sub-cycle, however, the element of that cycle has a predominating influence, subservient only to the Hierarchy of the Great Age of which it is a part. For instance, air, which is the element of Aquarius, has now begun to rule, but it will be subservient and more or less dominated by the water Hierarchy until it has passed beyond the overlapping period of the Piscean Age.

During its cycle — approximately 2160 years, not counting the centuries of overlapping — there will be planted in the planet and in man the seed of that which will be fully perfected when, at the end of the seventh sub-race of the Fifth, the Sixth Great Race begins its reign. Aquarius being an airy sign, the atoms of the Earth's surface must be readjusted so that the air can influence and rule it. This means that there must be a great stirring up and etherealization of all its atoms into a higher and finer state. Each element must enter, in greater quantity and purer quality, into everything that the Hosts of Air shall rule. To this end the zone or layer belonging to this element must come closer to the surface and the little elementals called Sylphs come into closer rapport with man, both to learn from him and also to help him and teach him the mystical lore of their kingdom. This will be increasingly evidenced as we enter more completely into the Aquarian period, for as yet we have entered only into its shadow or overlapping.

The coming changes will affect all man's bodies. His spiritual conceptions will be higher, broader; his mentality will be uplifted, more expanded and more capable of expressing the outgoing Breath of the Spirit or air in its highest mystical aspect, and he will be able to grasp more subtle ideas and express them more fully. His astral powers will have a great and wonderful unfoldment, and his ability to use and live in the air in many now undreamed of ways in addition to aviation, will be derived and brought down from those Realms where the ideals and perfected inventions await his ability to reach up and grasp them. Even his physical body will become less dense and more buoyant, sensitive and beautiful.

During the Aquarian Age man will advance enormously in his conception of brotherhood and true humanitarianism. In fact, it is in this period that the Great Teacher must come to pour out the Water of Life on humanity and to impart to it higher ideals and conceptions of life and to teach how to bring them forth. Also, being a feminine cycle, woman must begin to take her true place. But just as Jesus set for the Piscean Age the ideals which only the comparatively few have been able truly to manifest since, so must we not look for the full glory of the Aquarian Age until we have had many a hard struggle in subsequent incarnations.

Science tells us that the center of the Earth is probably fiery and molten. This is a shrewd deduction, which, to a certain extent, is in harmony with the esoteric or secret teachings. We should note here that these teachings are secret in the same sense that the repeatedly proved problems of higher mathematics and much other scientific knowledge are secret to a schoolboy, namely, not because they are hidden from the child, but because he is incapable either of grasping or wisely using the information they convey. It would not only be useless to explain them, but were he confronted with and compelled to solve such problems ere he could lisp his multiplication table his brain would be stultified. Such teachings are a part of the statistics of the Great White Lodge, which has kept records, not only of the Races of man, but of the cosmic events and planetary changes, since the manifestation of this system and the creation of this planet. These records are kept on a basis similar to that by which the Geological Society keeps a record of the physical changes through which the Earth passes, as shown in its rock strata, erosions, etc. The great difference is that the Lodge of Masters has always had representatives who have personally lived in and studied and recorded all the conditions of past Ages, even as They do today. It is from such records, therefore, that we learn that Fire, the element least understood and least controlled by man, lies deepest in the Earth's crust; also that as each new Race and sub-race is born and a new Hierarchy rules, the element of that Hierarchy comes closer to the surface and manifests more definitely to man.

While the scientists have drawn the reasonable deduction— from the estimated pressure and the steady increase of temperature which has been observed as far as man has penetrated into the Earth's crust—that ere the center of the Earth is reached all solids must be not merely molten, but volatile or gaseous, they are still far from the true solution. To be sure, as far as we have descended toward the center of the globe, the temperature does increase, and the esoteric teachings tell us that the core of the Earth is Fire, but something far more than fire in the sense in which the scientists of today understand the term. They would probably call it force or radiant energy, altho in reality it is Spiritual Fire or Divine Energy. It is that Divine Life which gives to the Earth as a living, breathing entity its life-force; for without this core of radiant Spiritual Fire the Earth would be a dead planet. Man also has within him the same Spiritual Fire manifesting as radiant life energy.

In referring to the Earth as a living entity, do not get the idea that it is a form shut up in this sphere of energy at the center of the Earth, or that the varying forces of the planet are confined to particular zones, any more than it could be said that the Soul of man was shut up in his heart, and that the bones, nerves, muscles, blood, breath, etc., were marked off and confined to separate areas in the body. No part of the body is without these, altho each has its special zone of manifestation. Just so it is with the Earth. For while the zones are marked off distinctly, still the forces and essences of each are constantly changing and interblending. The life-force is penetrating every atom, piercing through dense matter and bringing forth both within and upon the planet.

Each of the four elements which constitute the four kingdoms or bodies of the Earth is a servant of the Divine One Life. Each element is composed of myriads of elemental lives—the elementals—which are the ingredients that are continually being transformed and transmuted as they are built into the ever-changing forms of Nature.

When we speak of the Nature elementals we must not think that each flower or blade of grass or grain has a separate elemental spirit informing or connected with it, but that all flowers, grains, etc., of one variety are each of them under the guidance of a living sentient being, who directs their activities of growth, form, color, perfume, etc., toward perfection that they may accomplish their part in the evolution of the planet and of man. For there is no form of growth that has not its special and necessary part to play, either in the preparation of the soil for more advanced vegetation, to feed man or the animals, to furnish him healing forces or some other definite work to accomplish. Even the humble sagebrush, which covers the most barren and desolate regions of the Western States, is doing a valuable and constructive work in adding humus where no other plants will grow and in preparing the soil to produce more useful crops. And even the sagebrush itself contains many medicinal properties useful to man. Other vegetation in arid regions, such as cactus, yucca, mesquite, etc., has its particular work in helping to redeem the soil and preparing better conditions, also other helps for man.

All this is not accidental, but is a part of the Divine Plan, brought into manifestation through the guidance of the hierarchies of elementals working under the Divine Law, each lower order receiving its guidance from the one just above. These Nature elementals are to plant life what a group soul is to a species of animals and the individual Soul to man—simply higher grades of intelligence all working under the hierarchies of their own Rays to perfect everything in that Ray so that it may blend with the others into the one White Light of Divine Manifestation.

In a similar way the particles of the food we eat, which are made up of infinitesimal living forces, are taken into our stomachs and transformed into bone, muscle, brain, energy, etc. It is the activity of this process of transmutation that produces heat, both in the body of man and in the body of the planet. "Light is Cold Flame, and Flame is Fire, and Fire produces Heat" when it meets resistance, the *Stanzas of Dzyan* tell us. Hence, it is the resistance which the dense matter of the Earth's crust offers to the passage of the central Spiritual Fire that produces the heat discovered by those who have penetrated deeply into the Earth, only as yet man has pierced but the outer layers of the Earth's crust.

As one Race draws to a close and a new Race begins its reincarnated life-cycle, it is necessary that new conditions obtain in the Earth; that new forces be liberated, new energies brought to man's attention, and this is correspondingly true, altho in a lesser degree, as each sub-race is ushered in. For at least the advanced ones of the Race or sub-race, those whose work for humanity consists in preparing for the New Age as teachers, inventors, scientists, poets, artists, reformers, etc., must reincarnate under conditions in which they can not only live, but can utilize the new-found energies and prepare for the great influx of the New Race or sub-race. It is, therefore, the fore-runners, leaders and teachers of the

New Age who incarnate first that they may educate the mothers of the new humanity. Throughout the past cycle of the Piscean Age, the Great Mother-principle (Rachel) has been "weeping for her (spiritual) children, and would not be comforted, for they were not" (incarnated).[3] But the coming leaders and teachers will prepare conditions of peace, harmony, love and purity in which the more spiritual and sensitive Souls can incarnate. For without these great teachers and helpers it would be almost impossible for the masses of mankind to reach the development required to usher in the New Age.

If man fails to face these problems and consciously recognize and utilize the finer energies of the Earth to bring about the necessary adjustments, then in some other way the Great Law will work out the problems without or even in spite of him. For Mother Nature attends to her needs and readjusts her forces and atoms in many ways, often through great wars, storms, floods, upheavals and cataclysms of various kinds. But, however it occurs, the outer surface, which the human race up to the present has tilled, polluted and well-nigh exhausted, must be broken up so that the new energies of the deeper layers may be utilized. The small amount of life-force which the constant interchange of the Spiritual Fire, sweeping through the outer crust leaves behind is largely used up or perverted so that the soil constantly requires artificial fertilization. At a certain depth there is a hard crust which in ordinary cultivation is seldom disturbed or broken up because no plow goes deep enough, and the necessity of artificial fertilization must the sooner be resorted to. Artificial fertilization is but an expedient by which life-force is gathered from another source and added to the exhausted soil, much as a sick man must add to his vitality by taking tonics, etc.

As with man, so with the Earth. As we have said, in speaking of the dynaspheric force, the Earth normally

---

[3] See pp. 62, 70.

develops everything from within herself. Life-force sufficient for all its wants is stored up in its hidden depths. The sick man must break through the crusts of old habits of life and thought and correlate with the deeper currents of the One Life and let them flow through him unimpeded if he would conquer disease, and for the planet the old used-up crust must be broken up, sloughed off or in some way disturbed so that the One Life manifesting in the deeper layers may come to the surface. Below this layer of crust or "hard-pan" as it is called, the roots of grains, vegetables and many fruit-trees cannot penetrate, hence will not flourish without the life-force being supplied in an artificial way.

Today the surface of the Earth is not only depleted, but it is saturated with the blood shed in all the wars of mankind throughout the ages; all the vibrations of inharmony, selfishness and enmity; and all the effluvia and off-scouring of man's impurity. This pollution has gone on until the whole crust of the Earth is impregnated with disease and death, even where modern man has never trod, so that the planet as a whole is nauseated with it. Hence the soil is today unfit to bring forth the higher types of food that will be required by the coming more sensitive Souls who will constitute the new sub-race. The fore-runners of this sub-race must, therefore, begin to teach mankind how to overcome all these adverse conditions; for in eating the vegetables and fruits grown on Earth at present man is imbibing the effluvia he cast off in the past, and also the results of his wrong thinking, which have polluted the Earth. The small amount of life-force the foods now contain and the prevalence of disease both in the plants and in man is, of course, a part of the Karma man must reap, for it is a part of the curse of the ground which he must redeem.

When the foundations of the Earth were laid, preparation was made for the sustenance of all the seven Great Races and their seven sub-races, nations and tribes, including the greater needs of its later and more sensitive Races and sub-races. Underneath the seemingly impenetrable outer layers of the crust are stored up, waiting for the advanced Races, all the demerits of nutrition and life-force which those Races will require to nourish their finer bodies and enable them to live under the new conditions in which they will find themselves; for the Spiritual Fire, in traversing the various zones and layers, leaves behind in each the proper potencies belonging to that proper zone. One of the effects of the World War is the breaking up of the crust, by shot, shell and mine explosion, so that the air elementals of the deeper zones and layers so long imprisoned are being set free, while those of the surface air are able to penetrate more deeply and mingle with the soil and thus help to purify it and prepare for the next step.

St. Paul tells us that "We know that the whole creation groaneth and travaileth in pain together until now." All the entities of all grades of consciousness in Mother Earth are laboring together mightily to complete the purification, evolution and perfection of the globe, and must so work until the spirit of the Cosmic Christ is born in mankind as a whole and man takes his place as the Lord of Creation or the husbandman of the Lord God on Earth.

Already man is learning a new lesson, for the great fertility of the land devastated by the war is attracting the attention of scientists. No longer do they claim that the increased fertility is due merely to the saturation of the soil with blood, altho that is a factor; the effect of the upheaval is also being considered. But another phase of this problem is already causing alarm. From the bloodstained fields of battle myriads of insect pests, plant diseases and blights have recently arisen—such as the mysterious chestnut blight that swept the world some few years ago—entailing great labor to combat and doing much to counteract the increased fertility of the soil. The occult student will quickly recognize that these pests are simply materialized expressions of the perverted life-force and the inharmonious and destructive thought-forces, which have been accumulating in the astral and are now precipitated upon Earth.

Man must learn to draw upon the inexhaustible resources of Mother Earth and to remember that the creative forces poured out upon her in the beginning still vibrate through all the kingdoms of Nature and will go on and on vibrating and creating and re-creating as long as the planet endures. When man awakens to these mighty truths he will no longer believe that it is the blood shed on the battlefields that really enriches the Earth; for this is but the life-force which has passed through the human organism and is filled with the waste products of man's body, and its emanations are impressed with the misuse of his forces. Man himself has continually to renew and purify the life stream in his body if he would retain his health. The land is therefore enriched less by the blood poured out upon it than by the release of the life-forces stored up in the deeper layers or zones of Mother Earth.

As he awakens to these forces, man will also find an explanation and cure for the ever-increasing menace of the insect plagues and plant diseases, which has had such a sudden and enormous increase in all parts of the world since the war. These have ravaged the world's crops until the agricultural authorities have issued warnings that man will have to fight a battle royal with these perverted forms of life if he would enjoy the increase of his labors. There is, therefore, a reasonable basis of truth in the predictions of many astrologers that the World War will be followed by a great famine over all the Earth, even the increased crops that are raised being devastated by both storms and pests.

But as long as man remains ignorant of the resources hidden in the depths of the Earth he must continue to suffer from the curse: "Cursed is the ground for thy sake; in sorrow shalt thou eat of it all the days of thy life." As most of the pests are the manifestation and embodiment of "man's inhumanity to man," together with his wasted and perverted creative powers which have been accumulating in the astral, they will naturally be at enmity with man their creator until he learns how to utilize the forces of the One Life, both in himself and in the planet, to protect himself from and transmute these enemies of mankind.

But if he is to understand wisely how to prepare the Earth to raise improved foods, not only for the millions who have made great sacrifices that peace, justice and righteousness may prevail for all mankind, but also to prepare for the more advanced Souls of the new sub-race who will require purer, more nutritious, more concentrated and more life-giving forms of food, he must learn that it is necessary to break up the soil to a depth never before attempted. He has already made a start in this direction by planting his orchards with the use of dynamite and he finds that they not only make a three years' growth in two, but are better able to resist both insects and disease. This must be done not merely to allow the roots to strike deeper and to draw the water to them by capillary attraction through the loosened soil, but to permit the readjusting of the elemental lives within the crust of the Earth that the new order of vegetation may be ushered in and that he may intelligently hasten the day when "the desert shall bloom as the rose." For only when the quality and life-giving properties of the vegetables, fruits and nuts have been thus increased, purified, refined and perfected can a strictly vegetarian diet satisfy the needs of all classes of mankind. Such perfected foods will not only be disease-resisting, but they will be disease-preventing when eaten by man.

Another lesson that man in southern climates must learn is that the soil requires cycles of rest and recuperation, even tho the climate makes it possible to grow crops almost continuously, through irrigation and other methods of forcing. The enforced rest entailed by winter in northern climates allows the life-forces to collect and concentrate for expression during a short summer season. The life-force manifests in fruits as flavor, aroma and satisfaction of taste and in flowers as perfume, pungency, etc. Flowers growing in mountainous regions, where the altitude is great and the seasons short, are usually far more vivid and brilliant in their coloring than those grown in low altitudes and where the seasons are long. Also it is well known that altho southern fruits may be larger, they are usually coarser in fiber, and altho they are most attractive in appearance they lack the flavor and satisfying qualities to be found in northern fruits, just as the northern flowers make up in perfume for their smaller size, less showy appearance and the shortness of their season.

In the beginning of the Race all these things were taught to infant humanity by the super-human and godlike Beings who came to this planet for the purpose of instilling into the minds of man the essence of wisdom and instructing him in all the arts and sciences. It is this stored-up fund of knowledge and wisdom upon which mankind has been drawing during the succeeding ages, as the evolutionary changes demanded it and the more advanced minds were able to correlate with it. Scientists might say that man, by the development and use of his mighty intellect, had discovered new forces and new ways of using forces previously unknown, but the occultist knows that all those things were provided for man's use during the first six "days of creation" and manifested during the first six sub-races of the Third Great Race (Lemurian). For it was only then that the Earth was materialized into solid form. Then during the seventh sub-race of the Lemurians there was a long Golden Age or period of rest, while the planet was being further cooled off, materialized, solidified and beautified for man's occupancy.

We are told that God created every plant of the field *before it was in the Earth*, and every herb of the field *before it grew*.[4] Thus even before the Earth was materialized, every condition, force and material needed for the evolution of the Earth itself and for the evolution and spiritual unfoldment of all the Races and sub-races of man was prepared for in advance. We are also allegorically told that out of the dust of the Earth God made man, as well as every tree and herb and living creature. This, of course, does not mean that God gathered up a handful of dust and fashioned man out of it, but it does mean that the Divine Ideation, through the creative power of the Cosmic Consciousness and the manifesting power of the One Life, first conceived the idea and then projected it into objective manifestation—through the outbreathing of the Great Breath—first of the Earth and all things pertaining to it, and finally of man himself, all fashioned out of the same fundamental and undifferentiated Cosmic Substance, and then clothed in a body of flesh composed of earthly substances. All these manifestations of the Divine were vivified by the same Divine Life-force which we call the Christ-force, because it is the "only begotten son" or the only outgoing current of Divine Life-force sent down into the manifested Cosmos to be its life and aid in evolving godward. This divine Christ-force must therefore be present in every molecule of the Earth and in everything brought forth from or upon the Earth. We therefore know that the life-force is stored up in the various layers and zones of the Earth waiting to bring forth in each day-period and sub-race the forces and products needed for that day or sub-race.

---

[4] *Genesis*, II, 5.

As we have been passing through the dark night-period which always separates one racial day-period from another—the period during which the scavengers are at work gathering up the debris of the last day and cleansing the Earth for the new—we look forward with faith to the New Day now dawning, instead of bewailing the passing of the old and being appalled by the outlook. We should turn our minds toward finding the "open sesame" that will swing wide the doors of God's storehouses where He has laid up for this particular time all that humanity needs.

Therefore, if man would be the child of the New Age he must begin at once to get acquainted with the mystic potencies of Mother Earth and to correlate with the elemental lives which do her bidding and which she uses to bring about her miracles. Let man ask seriously what she holds for him. Let him step out of the rut of the commonplace and experiment and he will find out the truth of that which is told us in *The Voice of the Silence*: "Help Nature and work on with her; and Nature will regard thee as one of her creators and make obeisance. And she will open wide before thee the portals of her secret chambers." (*i.e.*, zones.)

CHAPTER X

THE FOUR WINDS

"Fohat takes five strides, and builds a winged 'wheel at each corner of the square for the Four Holy Ones. . . . and their Armies." *Stanzas of Dyzan*, V, Sloka 5.

"There is Occult philosophy in the Roman Catholic doctrine which traces the various public calamities, such as epidemics of disease and wars and so on, to the invisible 'Messengers' from the North and West. 'The glory of God comes from the way of the East,' says Ezekiel; while Jeremiah, Isaiah, and the Psalmist assure their readers that all the evil under the Sun comes from the North and West." *The Secret Doctrine*, Blavatsky, I, 147-8.

"Prophesy unto the wind, prophesy son of man, and say to the wind, Thus saith the Lord God. Come from the four winds, O breath, and breathe upon these slain, that they may live." *Ezekiel*, XXXVII, 9.

Four is the number of the Earth-plane. It signifies the completion of Earth conditions, the foundation stone upon which all that manifests on Earth must be created. Its symbol is the square, the base of the pyramid. In the evolution of man four indicates the Fourth Race of the Fourth Day-period, when the four lower aspects of Nature and of man had reached their perfection and were made the material basis upon which the higher aspects must manifest. Applied to man four represents the understanding, the foundation which completes the merely human, and when illumined by the Light of Spirit, makes Divinity attainable.

Four is used in many ways in the *Bible* and in all other sacred scriptures as well as in occult literature. The Holy City must be laid four square, the mystical "white stone" is square, and there are four cardinal points, North, South, East and West, presided over by four great Angels or Regents, symbolized by the four sacred animals of *Ezekiel*, *Daniel* and the *Apocalypse*, namely the Bull, the Lion, the

Eagle and the Man. In the Orient these Regents are called the Four Great Kings or Maharajas and are related to the Four Lords of Karma or the four great Powers which make square, balance or adjust the workings of the Great Law that love, justice, peace and harmony may ultimately prevail. The powers and forces thus symbolized are not mere abstractions, but are the intelligent, entitized forces so often referred to in the writings of the Christian Fathers as the "Messengers," "Angelic Virtues," "Spirits" or "Angels."[1]

In the temples of Egypt a great curtain was drawn over five pillars separating the Holy Place from the congregation. This symbolized the veil which hangs between our five senses and the Divine Mysteries. The curtain was of four colors, blue (spiritual aspiration), purple (understanding of the astral), scarlet (purification of earthly conditions) and gold (truth combined out of all), again representing the four cardinal points, the four elements and the Four Winds. Also the Children of Israel after their sojourn in Egypt were instructed to make a tabernacle which went with them during the Exodus. It was to have a veil made of blue, purple and scarlet, to be hung upon four pillars of shittim wood overlaid with gold, upon four sockets of silver.[2] The whole setting in both cases symbolized that it is through the four Powers ruling the Four Winds that our five senses become cognizant of the hidden mysteries of life. In other words, through the forces which are manifested by these high Rulers of the Four Winds does man grow in the understanding of the mysteries of Nature, and by relating himself to Nature, of the mysteries of his own being.

Primitive man learned that during the season of the East Wind—Spring—he must till the ground and plant the seed; during the season of the South Wind—Summer—the crops spring up and grow; during the West Wind—Autumn—the crops mature and the harvest is gathered, and during the

---

[1] See *The Key to the Universe*, Curtiss, Chapter XXIV.
[2] *Exodus*, XXVI, 31–2

season of the North Wind—Winter—all the life-forces are
indrawn and must lie in the tomb of winter. Also "the way of a
ship in the midst of the sea," spoken of by Solomon as one of the
four great mysteries, had to be learned by a study of the winds.
Even today, be his ships ever so marvelous, man must still reckon
with the winds and tides. We find a recognition of the importance
and the sacredness of the four elements, the four cardinal points,
and the Four Winds in every religion and in all ages, and applying
the occult axiom, "As above, so below," by studying the physical
manifestations of the Four Winds we can understand and correlate
with the Powers of which they are expressions.

As we have said elsewhere: "The four beasts also symbolize
the four corners of the earth and the four winds of heaven. The
wind, like the breath of the physical body, is a manifestation of
the Spirit, which comes we know not whence and goeth we know
not whither. *Jeremiah*, *Isaiah* and the *Psalms* assure us that from
the North and West come all disease, catastrophes, and afflictions,
while from the East and South come all benefits." Symbolically
this means that when we turn from the Spiritual Sun we have long
dark nights of cold, and are breathing in the effluvia of the Earth
whence come disease and death. Equally so when for us we let
the Spiritual Sun set in the West.

While if we mentally face the mystic East and greet the rising
of the Spiritual Sun or bask in its full radiance in the South
continually, we can breathe in all spiritual blessings. While this
is symbolically true, yet by a careful analysis of each Wind we
will find that none are evil, but that all four are presided over by
beneficent Powers and their manifestations are for the ultimate
good of mankind.

Enoch tells us: "I also beheld the four winds which
bear up the earth, and the firmament of heaven . . . . . I then
surveyed the receptacles of all the winds, perceiving that
they contributed to adorn the whole creation, and preserve

the foundation of the earth . . . . . The first wind is called the eastern, because it is the first. The second is called the South, because the Most High there descends, and frequently there descends *he who* is blessed forever. The western wind has the name of diminution, because there all the luminaries of heaven are diminished, and descend. The fourth wind, which is named the North, is divided into three parts."[3]

The East Wind is the wind of the morning, the wind that brings the freshness of the new day. *Ezekiel* says that the glory of God "comes from the way of the East." Just as the East Wind brings renewed life to the Earth, so does the mystic East Wind bring renewed life and power to the Soul. As the first breath of day comes from the East so should the first waking breath correlate with the power of the East Wind by repeating some sacred text, such as the Morning Prayer of this Order.[4] There is a mystic potency in the first thoughts held and the first words uttered, for they strike the keynote for the day. Therefore concentrate upon some uplifting text, prayer or thought and let it abide with you in the undercurrents of your consciousness during the day.

The South Wind is the wind which brings growth, unfoldment and perfection to the Earth and causes the Soul to put forth in a greater fullness in the everyday life the strength and beauty garnered and assimilated during the wintertime. The South Wind brings the summertime of the Soul when all things seem to go well, altho even during this period the husbandman of the Soul-life, like the husbandman of the soil, must watch for and guard against the little insects that prey upon his crops; must protect them from drought and storms and prune off all abnormal growths that they may reach perfection. While the South Wind is balmy and pleasant it does not carry the mariner

---

[3] *The Book of Enoch*, XL, XXVIII, LXXVI.
[4] See Appendix.

on his way as rapidly as the fiercer winds from the North and West, yet its force must be utilized to advance the progress of the ship toward its port.

The West Wind is said to be disastrous, but only as it brings to the individual life its fulfillment and to the Earth its harvest. It brings the rest and refreshment of eventide, both to the life and to the Earth, the period when both enjoy the fruits of their labors. Hence we may expect our compensation and the complete understanding of the lessons of life to be brought to us by the wind from the West. The West Wind brings sadness only if the harvest we have sown be tares instead of wheat. But even so, only as we courageously reap the harvest can we learn to sow more wisely. It is in the West that we may look for the close of the present turbulent conditions and for a peaceful garnering of the fruits which ripen as the result of the lessons which humanity has learned.

We are told that at the second coming of the Christ His light shall shine from the East even unto the West. This is but one of the many prophecies indicating that it is in the West that the great gathering of the elect will take place to make ready for the coming of the great World Teacher so soon to appear. For it is "in the cool of the day" or as the Sun sets in the West that we must meet the Lord in the garden or the place where the fruitage of experience is garnered. Here we may sit at His feet after the strife and turmoil of the day and learn the great lessons which shall prepare us for the new day of the Sixth Great Race, for the sixth and seventh sub-races are the eventide or closing period of the Fifth Great Race.

The North Wind brings the chilling blasts which strip the leaves from the trees, scatter the seeds far and wide and usher in the winter season. The sky is leaden, frowning, ominous. The wind comes in vicious gusts that chill and shrivel all living things, or it howls and shrieks in a terrifying gale which wrecks the ship that is not staunch and true and well captained, and that sweeps before it everything that is not well rooted or established on a firm foundation. It spreads a protecting sheet of ice over the streams and lakes that the life within them may be protected. It brings the whirling, blinding snow which spreads its mantle of white over the Earth and the children of its bosom that they may be protected and find that rest and peace in which the forces of life may be indrawn into Mother Earth and the experiences of the summer digested, that they may be prepared to manifest anew under new conditions. So must it be in our lives, for the North Wind is none other than King Desire whose fierce breath chills and shrivels and brings disaster. He has his seat in the sign Scorpio, the Adversary whose sting poisons the whole man, yet when conquered and lifted up becomes the Eagle, the Bird of Life and Freedom, which can gaze unflinchingly into the eye of the Sun.

Desire as a principle—the negative aspect of Divine Will, an expression of the desire of the Divine for manifestation—in one sense is the fundamental cause of all manifestation. But when this principle becomes personalized in the individual as human desire it reaches both upward and downward, governed and controlled by free will. As long as there is any experience or sensation on Earth which attracts us our desire is turned outward, downward, earthward, and we must experience that desire ere we are satisfied, unless we transmute it by a higher desire or by our will. As long as our desires turn earthward—desires for possession of things, of place, of approval or applause; for the gratification of sensation and self-indulgence, etc.,— their satisfaction always leaves the sting of the Scorpion. Only when we realize that our Father-in-heaven will supply all things needed for our best good on Earth and we no longer waste our thought-power desiring physical things, can our desires fly upward like the Eagle into the higher realms and become one with the will of our Father and so do His will on Earth, even as it is done in heaven. "Thought arises before desire. The thought acts on the brain, the brain on the organ, and then (animal) desire awakens. . . . The student must guard his thoughts."[5] Understanding this we will realize the significance of the promise: "Seek ye first the kingdom of God, and his righteousness; and all these things shall be added unto you . . . . For your heavenly Father knoweth that ye have need of all these things." With this understanding King Desire becomes not our tempter, but a most beneficent helper on the Path of Self-Mastery.

The North Wind blows in many ways in our lives as individuals, for each and every one must meet this great King and conquer the power of his icy breath. For the effect of the North Wind (desire) is cold and shriveling to the Soul, and like a blast of wind forced into a furnace, it transforms the steady, quiet flame of Love into a raging, consuming passion. The North Wind comes to us to test the strength of our roots, to see if we are rooted in truth, to wipe out old conditions and prepare for the new. The North Wind will also play its part in bringing to the Earth the disasters which will mark the beginning of the cataclysmic changes which are to come and which are even now taking place. But as these apparent disasters come, both in our individual lives and to the Earth, realize that they are but the great North Wind sweeping away that which is holding us back from entering upon the new conditions. They do not come by chance, but are guided by the Divine Love of wise and beneficent Powers for the best good of ourselves, humanity and the planet as a whole.

It is the force generated by the mystical North Wind that shall roll away the stone from the sepulcher of our lives. And as we find the stone rolled away many of us may start back appalled to find only empty graveclothes where we thought to find the Christ. How many of us

---

[5] *The Secret Doctrine*, Blavatsky, III, 573.

have had something we valued above all else, that which seemed to be our Lord of Life, taken from us and we have laid it in a tomb and have sealed it with a great stone! Often this stone is fashioned from our hearts grown hard and bitter because our Lord of Life has been taken from us and we know not where they have laid him.

There are many, many such, many who are carrying through life the memory of such a death and burial; many whose hearts close the mouth of a sepulcher in which their hopes and dearest wishes lie buried. This may be the physical loss of a loved one who seemed necessary to lean on but who may have been removed only to teach the Soul to lean upon its own inner touch with divinity. Or it may be some disappointed hope or some affliction of the body which they have sealed up in the tomb of the mind, where they often go to weep and lament or to curse the fate that has willed it so. Then comes the great North Wind and sweeps them off their feet, tears from their lives all those things to which they have clung so long. By its force the stone they thought so firm is torn from its foundations and rolled away and they find in their sepulcher no Lord of Love, no cherished idol, but only the graveclothes of that which has passed away long since. Moreover, if they come to this sepulcher at dawn after the bitter North Wind has blown all the night long, they will find an angel waiting for them saying, "He is not here, for he is risen. Why seek ye the living among the dead?"

What is the meaning of this symbol? It is this, there is no thing that is called out by our true, unselfish love that can rest in the grave. Its essence must rise and become a part of our True Self, for we cannot lose anything that is true and pure. Do not hover over the graves in life, for nothing can remain in the grave but the mere outward covering which we ourselves have woven about the thing we loved. There are no sepulchers which require the hardening of our hearts to seal up, no dark and dismal caverns where our loved ones rest. No thing that has awakened in our heart one living spark of Divine Love and has then apparently been taken from us is dead. Nor can it rest in the grave, for it is risen, risen into the great and mighty oneness of Divine Love, which includes the little things of life as well as the great.

When the bitter North Wind blows and our lives seem to be going to pieces, when petty cares, like the dust and debris cast up by the wind, are flying about us on every hand, perhaps blinding us; when the Sun of Righteousness and the Moon of Intuition are darkened and the Star of Initiation seems to have withdrawn its light, look up, for behold our redemption is nigh. When we have looked up we will realize the lesson and go fearlessly into the tomb and see for ourselves that our Lord of Love has risen, for the stone of misunderstanding and hardness of heart has been rolled away by the King of the North Wind.

True love is divine, immortal, hence can never die. No force of love that we have ever experienced can ever be lost, for as we rise we shall find the full essence of all the love we have poured forth manifesting to us in a higher expression. For as the Eagle in us flies upward it will find all that we thought dead and buried waiting for us in the heart of the Sun. Often they are taken from us that our desires may be drawn upward and become the will for a higher expression.

Thus we find that each of the Four Winds has its times and seasons and each its work to accomplish in the development and perfection of the Soul-life. Let us enjoy the pleasant winds while they blow, but also let us trim our sails to take advantage of the North Wind when its season comes. Let us take comfort in the knowledge that tho the North Wind is fierce and cold it will sweep us most rapidly on our journey, will call out all our powers and seamanship and will take from us only those things which retard our progress.

Thus do the Regents of the Four Winds, with their hosts or armies of living powers, bring to the Earth and to mankind their particular forces without which evolution could not be completed. From this we learn the great lesson of unity in diversity; that each Soul must work out its own salvation in its own way, just as the winds accomplish their own work even tho apparently adverse. As well might the South Wind condemn the North Wind or the East Wind the West as for students to condemn those who accomplish their work in life in different ways.

Meditation upon this chapter should awaken in the student a larger idea of the necessity of making use of every wind that blows. Be it from the North or South, the East or West, let us utilize its power and make it our servant. In other words, *let us learn the lessons from every event and circumstance in our life and environment* that we may make our life one with the Great Law.

CHAPTER XI

THE THREE JOHNS

"And in those days there came John the Baptist. . . . and Herod sent and beheaded John in prison. Now there was leaning on Jesus' bosom one of his disciples, whom Jesus loved. . . . And he sent and signified it by his angel unto his servant John: who bare record of the word of God, ... and of all the things that he saw." *St. Matthew*, III, 1; XIV, 10. *St. John*. XIII, 23. Revelation, I, 1-2.

In previous chapters we have learned that the sign Aquarius in its mystical significance symbolizes Man: not undeveloped or animal man, but the spiritually awakened intellectual man symbolized in the *Bible* under the name John. But we find that there were three Johns—*John the Baptist*, *John the Beloved* and *John the Revelator*. These three Johns have the same symbology as the three decanates of Aquarius, all synthesized in Jesus, the perfect Man. Considering the three Johns together we therefore have a composite picture of man as he unfolds and manifests his three decanates or the three stages of unfoldment into his highest attainment as the real Man.

The three Johns also represent the three offices which the Aquarian Man must hold or manifest in the course of his spiritual unfoldment, *i.e.*, Prophet, Priest and King, or Man claiming the three-fold powers of his Sonship. For it is only the manifestation of the Son in man that can truly make him either Prophet, Priest or King. The mere predicting of coming events, through the use of clairvoyance, prevoyance or other psychic faculties, does not constitute a Prophet; for a Prophet is "one who speaks for God" or interprets the will of the Divine to man, and prediction plays but a small part in his life and work. The mere graduating from a theological school and being ordained cannot make a man a true Priest, unless in addition he has unfolded the Christ within his heart and his intellect has been so illumined that he can stand before the altar and sacrifice his lower nature to the Divine. In many instances the wearing of an earthly crown is but a parody on true kingship; for the crown which marks the real King is the radiance of his purified aura and the emanations of his illumined intellect which enable him to rule with justice. Such a crown each of the three Johns wears, yet the crown of each differs from that of the others according to the kingdom over which he rules.

In the *Bible* there are also three great elevations or Mounts which correspond to that which is meant by the three Johns. The first, which agrees with John the Baptist, is Mt. Sinai in the wilderness; the mountain from which the Law is given amidst lightnings and thunders so that the people are overawed. From this wonderful Mount comes their Law, their instruction and their call to repentance. The second Mount corresponds to John the Beloved. This is the Mount of Divine Love from which Jesus gave the message of blessedness: "Blessed are the peacemakers," etc. The sermon is very mild. If we heard it today we would be inclined to say it was negative. But the other side of this Mount is Calvary, the Mount of Crucifixion; Divine Love gives out its message from a height so great that it is always misunderstood and the giver crucified. The third is the Mount of Transfiguration. Here stands Moses the Law-giver or the first John, and Elias, the blessed John, both coming with the third John who has lost his identity in Jesus; for the Revelator does not speak his own words, but those given him from on high. And as the world passes through the sign Aquarius there must be a blending of these three phases.

The first decanate of Aquarius, which is ruled by Saturn,

is symbolized by John the Baptist; the man clothed in the skins of wild animals and wandering in the wilderness. Yet this is not primitive man, but man crowned with high intellectual attainments. Because his awakened intellect has recognized the superior power of the Christ-consciousness, the one who is "mightier than I, the latchet of whose shoes I am not worthy to stoop and unloose," he becomes a Prophet crying: "Prepare ye the way of the Lord (Law), make his paths straight." The number eleven, the number of the sign Aquarius, signifies the beginning of a new and higher cycle; and the kabalistic value of the name John is nine, the number of Soul Initiation. Hence we see that as the first decanate of this sign begins to manifest, man will have an intellectual awakening which will initiate him into a new and higher world, a consciousness which transcends the outer, the visible and the merely intellectual, and shall usher him into the world of spiritual realization. And as there are three decanates, we may expect intellectual man to pass through three distinct phases, all of them but steps in the unfoldment of the fifth principle (*Manas*) in man, that which gives him supremacy. Manas is commonly divided into *Higher Manas* and *lower manas*; Higher when joined to the Soul (*Buddhi*) principle and called *Buddhi-manas*, and lower when joined to desire (*Kama*) and called *Kama-manas*. But it also has a third and distinct expression wherein it is neither the one nor the other, but vacillates between the two. The two lower must be mastered and transcended ere man can become the true Aquarian.

The first stage in this mastery through which all must pass is the John the Baptist stage. This is the stage when, after man's intellect has awakened to the fact that there is something greater to be attained, he is still wandering in the wilderness of the outer life seeking to prepare the way, through a study of the philosophy and laws of the higher life, for the coming of the greater consciousness, the Christ-consciousness, in his heart. At this point he is exceedingly solicitous that others should awaken to the higher conceptions which have so enthused him, hence he is continually crying, "Repent ye," and striving to have everyone who will listen follow him. He lays great stress upon outer conditions and observances. He is clothed in skins, *i.e.*, the simplest form of attire, and his physical body and its care and subjugation occupy a very prominent place in his life. He lays great stress upon the simplicity of his raiment and upon what he eats, drinks, etc. This is well, for at this stage the mastery of pride of appearance and the control of appetite are important steps.

But he is confronted on every hand by many and diverse paths or teachings, all seemingly pointing to the goal, yet leading in different directions. And since the seeker during this stage is still depending upon his intellect to guide him he feels that he must investigate all movements and teachings in an effort to find the true inner Path which shall lead him to the Christ. At this stage it is right that he should do so, and without being thought vacillating and insincere. Jesus plainly showed what attitude of mind we should hold toward this stage of development when He replied to His disciples as they tried to rouse His condemnation for one who was so unsettled: "What went ye out into the wilderness to see? A reed shaken with the wind?" *i.e.*, a vacillating or weak-minded person. Then He continued: "But what went ye out for to see? A prophet? yea, I say unto you, more than a prophet."

We should take this to heart, and when we see sincere persons running here and there seeking intellectually to make a straight Path through the many devious teachings, we should not think of them as reeds shaken by every wind of doctrine that springs up. For their very activity in proclaiming and seeking the Christ is a prophecy and forerunner of that which they shall attain; that other John, the

beloved of the Christ, into which they will evolve. For some day
they will step into the Jordan, see the Dove descend and hear the
Voice proclaiming that the Christ, the only begotten Son, has
been found. The Law is: "Ask, and it shall be given you; seek,
and *ye shall find*; knock, and *it shall be opened unto you*; for
everyone that asketh receiveth; and he that seeketh findeth, and
to him that knocketh *it shall be opened.*' This seeking attitude of
mind is the turning point, the turning from the old, the outer, to
the new, the inner. For there must be the intellectual conception
before there can be the perception. This stage corresponds with
the first decanate of Aquarius and is ruled by Saturn, who must
test and judge and make stable all things, so that the rulership of
Mercury can begin.

When this step in the unfoldment has been taken and
John the Baptist has recognized and baptized the Christ, his
intellectual supremacy and dominion must wane while the
Christ-consciousness waxes, as it is said: "He must increase, but
I must decrease." Then the seeker enters into the second stage,
symbolized by John the Beloved. In this stage he has not only
found and recognized the Christ, but sits at meat with Him and
rests on His bosom. At this stage he is little concerned with either
raiment or food, for his Master, on whose bosom he rests, came
both eating meat and drinking wine. No longer does he exhort the
multitudes to repent, but rests quietly in the great love of the Christ
and waits patiently for his work for humanity to be given him, yet
he helps the world greatly by his love and example. No longer
does he eagerly run to and fro after the latest popular teacher or
to investigate the latest psychic phenomena; for he has found his
spiritual home, where he finds the Christ and sits at meat with His
disciples. This phrase "sits at meat" may puzzle some, especially
used as it is here in connection with the spiritual home which
each Soul will some day find. But it is correct so to use it, for

the Christ here spoken of is the universal cosmic Sun (life) Principle which is the spiritual life of and must feed each and every Soul. It refers to that mystical food of which Jesus spake when He said: "I have meat to eat that ye know not of." This "spiritual meat,"[1] this feeding in the heart or real assimilation of spiritual truth can only be fully accomplished when the pupil sits down at the table which is spread by the teachings which satisfy most completely his intellect and feed most satisfyingly his heart hunger and thus promote his spiritual growth, even as well assimilated physical food will promote the harmonious growth of both body and mind in proportion to its nourishing power and the pleasure and contentment its eating brings.

As with physical food, so with spiritual. Not only must the food be wholesome in itself, but it must be prepared and presented in a way that will appeal to the taste and satisfy the appetite. Similarly the spiritual food for each must be presented in the various ways that will appeal to each. The old adage, "God sent food, but the devil sent cooks," has its application here. For while all spiritual food comes from on high, yet unenlightened man, in his own limited intellectual conceptions, often distorts or disguises the truth until it is like badly cooked food, acceptable only to an undeveloped, unsensitive or perverted palate. Hence, intellectual development, study and discrimination are necessary before one is fitted to prepare spiritual food. For, as in the miracle of the loaves and fishes, it is always the Christ who blesses and breaks the bread and gives it to His disciples, who in turn transmit it to the multitude.

Therefore each should seek until he finds a table spread whose spiritual food is appetizing to him, nourishing and easily assimilated by him. And once having found it he can rest on the bosom of the Christ and give all his allegiance, love and devotion to the avenue through which he is fed, as

---

[1] *I Corinthians* X, 3.

he gladly pours forth all the worldly help which the Great Law enables him to give. Such an avenue of teaching is his Soul's resting place, a spiritual home in very truth. And its welfare and growth, enabling it to extend its food to the many other hungry hearts, is his dearest wish; something to be held ever in mind, to be prayed for, to be worked for and to be sacrificed for.

Thus is it found with those who at this stage are brought by the Great Law into touch with *The Order of Christian Mystics*, after having searched in the wilderness among all other teachings. Those who truly belong to it, whose enlightened intellect and quickened heart have enabled them really to grasp its Teachings and to correlate with the great currents of force back of them, are contented to rest in it, for in it they have found and recognized a manifestation of the Christ and know it to be their spiritual home, hence feel no inclination to seek elsewhere. But there are many others who come to these Teachings, as they do to many others, seeking for just the expression of spiritual truth and the currents of force to which their stage of unfoldment will enable them to respond. These may stay with us a shorter or longer time and then find their home elsewhere. Many, on the other band, after going forth again into the intellectual wilderness, return and find rest and satisfaction. But all are welcomed as honored guests, and such as do not become "Children of the Household" are cheered on their way when they depart with a blessing and a hearty "Godspeed" and a sincere hope that they may soon find the Christ manifesting in some other spiritual home so that they may rest on His bosom and go no more out.

The second John does not make a great stir in the world. He is not a great teacher or preacher. He does not go out and cry unto the people so that they flock to him in great numbers out of curiosity, either as to his peculiar manner of life and dress or as to his teachings. He simply rests on the bosom of the Christ and solves the problems of life through the mystic power of the Christ which he finds in his heart. He blesses the world silently and hence is often misunderstood and persecuted; for the world cannot understand or accept him. Yet his own heart is always cheered because he is resting in the absolute knowledge that he has found the Christ and has imbibed the force of the heart while resting on His bosom. This is the end, we might say, of the second John; the end of the second decanate of Aquarius, which is ruled by Mercury, the great intellectual planet, yet the one which is so variable and so little understood by the world.

But there comes a day in the life of every true disciple when, after the dominance of the intellect has given way to the illumination of the intuition, through the power of the Christ with whom he has dwelt in so intimate a relationship, he feels impelled to call upon the intellect which has now been illumined by the Divine Light, and use it to reveal to man that which is to be. He has heard the Voice cry from out the Silence: "It is not well; thou hast reaped, now thou must sow." This is the third and last John, the Revelator. The last decanate of Aquarius is ruled by Venus or the power of Divine Love. Through his realization of Divine Love John has gained another crown. He has learned to love the world of humanity and labor for it. Through the persecutions he has passed he has penetrated into the very heart of life and has seen the possibilities and needs of mankind. Having entered into the oneness and drawn down the glory of the Shekina he is crowned with glory unspeakable. The intellectual brilliancy of the first John and the heart warmth of the second are swallowed up in the spiritual radiance of the third John in which all are melted, blended together and sublimed. But this cannot be expressed in words; it must be realized. For to John the Revelator all worlds are one, and as he lives therein he becomes the Revelator of the Divine to man. He has not only entered into the Spirit on the Lord's day, but he has heard the Voice and has turned and glimpsed the glory of the Ancient of Days. He has heard the thunders of the Seven Churches and has held in his right hand the powers of the Christ. The Mount upon which he stands is the Mount of Transfiguration. He is still man, but he has become more than a man, a true Aquarian.

CHAPTER XII

CHILDREN OF THE HOUSEHOLD

"Ask, and it shall be given you; seek, and ye shall find; knock, and it shall be opened unto you." *St. Matthew*, VII, 7.

"Now therefore ye are no more strangers and foreigners, but fellow-citizens with the saints, and of the household of God." *Ephesians*, II, 19.

PRAYER FOR DEMONSTRATION

I am a child of the Living God.

I have within me the all-creating power of the Christ.

It radiates from me and blesses all I contact.

It is my Health, my Strength, my Courage.

My Patience, my Peace, my Poise.

My Power, my Wisdom, my Understanding.

My Joy, my Inspiration, and my Abundant Supply.

Unto this great Power I entrust all my problems,

Knowing they will be solved in Love and Justice.

(Here mention all financial and physical problems pertaining to your outer life, environment and *worldly affairs*[1] with which you desire guidance and help, that they may work out *in the way that shall be best* for you. Meditate a moment on each until visualized, then conclude with the following words):

O Lord Christ! I have laid upon Thine altar all my wants and desires. I know Thy love, Thy wisdom, Thy power and Thy graciousness. In Thee I peacefully rest, knowing that all is well. Not my will but Thine be done.

How familiar to our ears are the numerous texts pertaining to the efficacy of prayer! Yet many, many Souls in these dark days seem to be losing much if not all faith in prayer as an actual and compelling power. Many, as they look around the world today, realize that we are living in the last days of the old dispensation, hence are tempted to ask with Jesus, "Nevertheless when the Son of man cometh, shall he find faith on the earth?"[2]

To some this chapter may seem too simple and obvious,

---

[1] For spiritual unfoldment use the *Prayer for Light*. For healing, harmony, comfort, etc., use the *Healing Prayer*, for protection the *Protecting Invocation*, etc. See Appendix.

[2] *St. Luke* XVIII, 8.

especially to those who have grown tired of the faith that looks for positive answer to prayer and who have turned their backs upon what seems to them but a mere ceremony belonging to the old garment of religious thought they have thrown aside as impractical. Nevertheless, we ask all to have patience, for even those who have turned away because they did not understand the Law, yet who feel within them the cry of the Soul for some definite comfort from on high; whose hands still reach out gropingly in the intellectual confusion and spiritual darkness of this age for some strong, powerful hand to which they may hold fast, need just the understanding and help which this chapter endeavors to bring.

On the other hand, many earnest and devoted students have a faith of a sort, yet do not know how to ask aright. And since this *Prayer for Demonstration* has been given us in answer to the above need, the following analysis and instruction as to its use is now given out to all.

"I am a child of the living God"

This is not a mere assertion without any foundation in sober fact, neither is it a mere affirmation of something we would like to see manifested in reality, yet which we have to question and qualify in our minds as we say it. It is a plain statement of fact. All humanity are children of the living God in the wider sense, but as used in this prayer the thought to be held is that the Children of God who really enjoy the advantages of childship are those who definitely recognize their relationship to the Father. We realize that the Father we address is not the incomprehensible Absolute, so separated from His children and so lacking in sympathy with the frailties of humanity as to be approachable only in fear and trembling. We understand that the Living God has sent forth not only His "only begotten Son," but has also enshrined in each human heart a direct Ray of Himself, which we call our personal Father-in-Heaven, our Higher Self, our Real Self. Similarly, the physical Sun embodies a vital portion of itself in every seed without which the seed could not germinate and unfold, no matter how much earth, air and water were supplied. In this sense every plant that grows is a child of the Sun.

We realize that our Divine Self is a part of the Living God as a drop is a part of the ocean or as a ray of sunshine is a part of the Sun, containing all its potencies. This Divine Being, because truly our Father, knows and understands even our personal and physical needs, and because a Ray from the Living God, can flash our petition to the very Fount of all Outpouring, even as pushing an electric button can bring back from the central power station a force which shall perform our most trivial household tasks. Also, since this Ray of God came to Earth to complete the Cycle of Manifestation of the Divine within, it cannot accomplish its mission until we, its earthly embodiment, have been so purified and developed as to manifest its perfection.

Those who grasp this idea as a vital realization of the immanence of the God within, step out from the mass of mankind and enter the spiritual Household. They recognize that the Lord God or the Law of God is the vital force of that Divine Love which brought forth the manifested universe in consecutive order, from the Absolute to man, without a missing link, and which implanted within us that manifestation of the Divine which pushes us on and on into ever greater stages of unfoldment and expression of the Divine in us.

While exoterically there is a crude manifestation of childship in all, esoterically the true Children of the Household are those who choose to dwell in the Household and submit themselves to its laws, because they have taken the trouble to study them instead of merely following a set form of words (prayers) which have little meaning, but which they must accept and believe or be cast out.

"I have within me the all-creating power of the Christ. It radiates from me and blesses all I contact."

Once we have recognized our relationship to the Divine and our position in the Household, we will understand its intimate and necessary provisions for our personal comfort and spiritual maintenance. Then we gain the ability to manifest that power which is the only begotten of the Father-Mother, the Christ-power. It flows through our veins and manifests as a vital factor in our lives, as the knowledge of his family blood courses through the veins of an aristocrat. Yet only through practice in expressing its characteristics in the daily life can we prove our childship. Altho it is the heritage of every child of God, in the majority it lies dormant because no attempt is made to develop and express it. If we are consciously striving to let it shine through us, *i.e.*, dwelling in its Light and meditating on it in our hearts, it cannot help radiating from us and blessing all we contact.

"It is my health."

By claiming our childship we become obligated to strive for the expression of the ideals of the Household, one of which is health. If, however, we put health first and demand it of our Father before all else, we may receive it to the exclusion of the gifts of the Spirit. On the other hand, if through our spiritual advance our bodies become more sensitive to small imperfections and inharmonies which would not affect one who was less advanced, hence make us react more easily to inharmony of body or mind, we must recognize that the keynote of the Household is harmony and that this is brought about and maintained by the adjustment of all inharmonies, through the all-creating power of the Christ. While the observance of the well-known laws of bodily health is an important factor in maintaining this harmony, the Children of the Household should have some instruction as to the inharmonies that arise even when all the physical laws have been obeyed to the letter. Hence this chapter.

Bodily Health. Bodily health is but the ultimate expression of a harmony manifesting in the inner bodies and expressing on the physical plane, according to the degree of its attainment, even tho the unfoldment of the higher spiritual faculties is but slight.

Since it is an anatomical fact that the cells of our body are continually dividing and multiplying, each new born cell bearing the imprint or characteristic vibration of our state of mind at the time of its birth, perfect health can be greatly facilitated and ultimately attained by our deliberate recognition of this fact and a conscious impressing of a mental picture of the perfection of the Christ upon each new cell as it is born. To accomplish this, each morning on waking, give thanks for the watchful care of the Divine Mother who has been helping us to imprint the image of perfection upon each new cell during the night. Also the last thing before dropping asleep ask that the great stream of Divine Life (the Christ-force) may flow unimpeded and uninterrupted through the body and bring each cell to the perfection of its manifestation.

If atoms and cells which cannot vibrate to the new keynote which we have sounded in our life have to be thrown off through cataclysms of illness, do not try to hold on to the old atoms. Let them go, but hold strongly the idea of *building into their place finer and more perfect atoms and cells*, which will respond to our new keynote. Hold the thought, however, that this change and rebuilding shall be gradual so that great masses of atoms and cells will not be eliminated at one time, but gradually, thus making cataclysms of illness unnecessary. But if illness does come, always regard it as a cleansing and rebuilding process, and take every means and form of treatment that will help Nature make the readjustment quickly and thoroughly.

Mental Health. This is the result of right thinking. Therefore we must learn so to order our thoughts that they shall be constructive and helpful. We must also study the laws of mind[3] so that we may work in harmony with them and not waste our mental forces in vain imaginings or fritter them away in worry, etc. We aid the manifestation of our mental health (harmony) by learning to think sanely on

---

[3] See Chapter XIV.

all spiritual as well as physical questions; not to be fascinated or carried away by half-truths or by teachings whose logical basis is indefinite or not clear, but to turn each question over and look at it from all sides. We must train our mind to work in harmony with our ideals and principles of life, and it will then radiate harmony and health.

It is often ignorantly said that all ills of the body are caused by the mind. This, of course, is obviously untrue, for all physical injuries, external poisonings, psychic disorders and disorders resulting from improper diet are not caused by the mind; they come from without. But all the *sensations of illness* are experienced through the reaction of the mind to the inharmonious cause of the sensations.

Psychic Health. In some schools of thought it is taught that to develop the higher spiritual and psychic powers one must be separated from all contact with humanity. The reason they give is that the higher development can be attained only when the body has become so depleted, anemic and negative that it is almost defenseless against the magnetism, psychic influences and miasmic thought-forces of the common herd. To such an extreme do some carry this idea that we find them wearing gloves when obliged to associate with their fellows, lest by touching one of their lesser developed brothers or sisters they might be contaminated by a lower animal magnetism! Since this is not the teaching of *The Order of Christian Mystics* we wish to go into the matter somewhat fully, that we may make clear our fundamental teachings on this subject.

The physical body, when dense and heavy, and ere the development of the higher faculties is begun, is indeed a protection against those astral influences which envelop the Earth as with a mantle of fog and which contain many kinds of semi-material forms of life which perpetually seek to contact mortals, since their great desire is to manifest in the material world.

As we advance spiritually we naturally etherealize and

sensitize our bodies; for altho to mortal eyes no difference can be observed, yet as we allow the inner spiritual body to unfold within us it must penetrate to the outermost atom of the physical body. Hence the physical body gradually becomes no longer a thick, dense shell, which of itself is an automatic protection from both physical diseases and astral influences. But instead of teaching that at this stage we must withdraw from all human contact and immure ourselves in forest, jungle, convent or monastery, this Order teaches that as the body grows more and more sensitive and less and less a natural barrier to finer forces *of all kinds*, the sensitive must dwell apart not in body, *but in mind and in his response and reaction to* undesirable influences. He must build up within him a vital thought-form and ideal of the spiritual Household in which he dwells, and of the mighty protective power of the indwelling and radiating Christ principle. The *Bible* tells us truly that this Christforce is a consuming fire, but the disciple can dwell in this fiery furnace, as did the three prophets, Meshach, Shadrach and Abednego, when the Christ walks with him.

Primitive man gathered clay and from it made a crude form of pottery. It was coarse, thick and heavy, and if it was to contain water or resist the forces of the elements, he made it still thicker. More developed man also gathered clay and made pottery, but he found out how to make it thin and transparent and beautiful. To strengthen and protect it he covered it with a glaze and subjected it to an intense heat, which made it more enduring and more impervious to water and the elements than the much thicker, crude pottery. It is a somewhat similar protecting glaze which the buddhic fire of the Christ-force, burning steadily within, forms around the bodies of the Children of the Household, the Ring Pass Not, which enables their bodies to become as delicate and transparent as a piece of the finest Sevres porcelain, yet more enduring, protective and impervious than the more dense bodies of the undeveloped. Only to such does the promise apply: "There shall no evil befall thee, neither shall any plague come nigh thy dwelling (body) .... Thou shalt tread upon the lion and adder: the young lion and the dragon shalt thou trample under feet. Because he hath set his love upon me therefore will I deliver him.[4]

The realization of our spiritual oneness, the attainment of mental balance and the manifestation of the Christ-force will give us power in the astral body or body of sensation which stands as the middle point upon which our health is focalized; for above it is the spiritual perception and mental realization, while below it is the physical body and the activities of the outer life. The astral body expresses health or ill health according as it responds to the combined influences from above and below. Most diseases focalize in our sensations. We may suffer a serious bodily mishap, but if there were no sensation we would make little of it. We may receive a great mental shock, but if it brings little suffering (sensation), we soon recover. We may be spiritually blind, but if it brings us no suffering we are scarcely aware of it.

If the sensitive Children of the Household would have perfect health, they must begin to radiate the buddhic Fire of Divine Love; to let the Christ-force dominate the body of sensation; must begin to sense this Divine Fire as a great current of Life thrilling them with a great vibration of Love, coming in through the heart and radiating to the centers of the astral body and flowing up into the mind and Spirit and down into the physical body.

But in striving to cultivate this Love, care must be taken that the sensations of mere physical attraction or magnetism shall not be cultivated under the false name of love. The Love we refer to is a realization of impersonal and all embracing Divine Love, the purest, most godlike and holy vibration to which the Soul of man can respond. It compares with pure, human love only in its great longing for one-

---

[4] *Psalms*, XCI, 10-14.

ness with its Source. To give rein to physical attraction under the mistaken idea that it may awaken the higher Love is a most dangerous and pernicious teaching, much more likely to give rise to lust, a fire of the nether world which attracts to the astral body terrible diseases from the astral world.[5]

Whenever contact with astral conditions brings an astral chill[5] or a feeling as tho a cold wind were blowing over one, if it is allowed to continue its manifestation, some form of illness is apt to follow. This often takes the form of disturbances around the heart or solar plexus, such as palpitation, suffocation, nausea, or abdominal pain, or excessive eructations of gas, due to a poisoning of the astral body. On such occasions we should not try to personalize the force and think that some enemy or inharmonious person is sending us an evil force which upsets us, for usually this is not the case. We have simply allowed ourselves to respond to a low astral force of some kind. To dispel it we should use *The Protecting Invocation*[6] and concentrate on the thought of the Fire of Divine Love blazing steadily within us, warming, vitalizing and protecting us. In using *The Protecting Invocation*, the pupil must be fully aware that he is touching a tremendous dynamic force. Hence only as we recognize that the Ring of Fire is the very heart of creative substance which can create, preserve or destroy with equal force, is it safe to use it. Remembering this, we must maintain the reverent attitude of mind that is willing to take the consequences, *i.e.*, that we hold a Love so holy that it will create in us a closer, more intimate and sensitive oneness with Divine Fire; that it will preserve in us this sensitiveness and destroy or take from us all that in us may impede our growth in godliness. Therefore, we must repeat this prayer reverently, knowing that carelessness may be disastrous. Never repeat it unthinkingly or carelessly.

The astral body is the sensitive plate which records our ex-

---

[5] See *Realms of the Living Dead*, Curtiss, 89-229.
[6] See Appendix

periences, and if it has responded to many sensations it has become so sensitized that it can easily respond to new impressions, not only from the outer world, but also from the astral and mental worlds as well. Those who are not striving to master sensation and gain poise and balance, often live more in the world of sensation than in the physical world. To such, sensation is life, and so they give way to it. But only when they have gained the victory over sensation and taught the mind to control it *by controlling its reactions* to sensation, only then can they expect to manifest perfect health.

Life and evolution depend upon sensation for their expression, and sensation results in experience. Hence age is marked by acquisition of experience, not by the mere lapse of time. The Soul that has responded to the most sensations has experienced most. But we truly experience only the things we really feel. Thousands of things around us pass us by and make no impression, hence they bring up no experience. The plate upon which their vibrations fell was not sensitive or responsive to them. That which makes a Soul young in spiritual unfoldment is that the personality is not sensitized enough for higher events and finer forces to make much impression upon it, hence altho not lacking experiences it is lacking in experience.

This matter of response and reaction to sensation is a vital problem to advanced students who desire to become Children of the Household. Many suffer in this life because in past ages they gained terrible experiences through suffering, often not because they suffered repeatedly, but because they hugged suffering to them and thus had terrible experiences along that one line. They also grew old in self-condemnation, for they deliberately reacted to condemnation and minute and agonizing self-analysis. They made their sensitive plate so thin that even today the least hint of condemnation awakens a memory picture of the long days and weeks and years of vigil and prayer and self-condemnation.

Such Souls are old only in one direction, hence have a great field of other experiences awaiting them, and should not waste time living over and responding anew to the suffering of the past. Others are old along another line, because they have experienced so many disagreeable things, known so many disappointments and disillusions. While they were born with a new brain and a new astral and physical body in this life, ready for new experiences, yet they have built into it the astral permanent atom which bears the impress of the past sensations, the response to which makes them lacking in enthusiasm over anything. It is hard for them to respond to that which is most beautiful and admirable, either in Nature or in their fellowmen. This is not because they do not see and recognize the beauty, but because their one-sided development of sensation has made them feel so old in the ways of the world that they are world-weary, hence find it difficult to respond to new beauties or new ideas. For them this life is but another day's weary journey, for their vague, haunting memory of the intermediate states of glory in the higher worlds frequently renewed in deep sleep, contrasts so hopelessly with their experiences in Earth life. Thus it is difficult for those with a strong development along one line to grasp what others are experiencing. Yet it is through the experiencing of sensations that we develop spiritually, just as a definite organ of sight (the eye) was developed as a result of the sensations suffered because of its absence.

But health results from the mastery of sensation, whether from the outer or the inner worlds, whether in this life or in the past. Giving way to emotions or sensations in the astral, even during sleep, tends to tear the physical body to pieces, gives the face a drawn, depleted look and leaves a mental depression. Hence the necessity for the mastery of our emotions. While all diseases and disasters of physical life which result from self-condemnation and misery, as well as psychic ills, have their scat in the astral body, we must also remember that the realization of all the beauties, the joys and enthusiasms of life, as well as the memories of the glorious experiences in the higher worlds, also impinge upon the body of sensation. Hence these should be dwelt upon instead of the mistakes, disappointments and sufferings. This realization does not admit discouragement, nor allow the Soul to sink into the despondency that results from response to the other class of sensations.

True health requires the ability to abide in outer conditions and still maintain our equilibrium, neither sinking into despondency nor going into ecstasies of joy, but maintaining our poise so that we understand the why and the how and react accordingly. Since we have at hand all our beautiful memories of glory, joy and beauty, the more we respond to their sensations the greater our ability to sense other joys and beauties in life, instead of using our memories and sensations to inflict greater suffering upon ourselves.

If conditions are inharmonious and irritating and we use the power of mind and will to repress response, we are merely putting pressure on a sore spot. We should do all in our power to adjust and make conditions harmonious and then turn our minds to the contemplation of the beauties and ideals of life and allow ourselves to react to them. We must use our sensitiveness to respond to the sensations desired, and then express them. Refuse to vibrate to lower forces, but focus on the higher. Live among the angels who do not worry about anything on Earth, yet gather its forces, experiences and lessons.

If we are sensitive to pain, inharmony, misunderstanding, irritation and unhappiness, we are just as sensitive to joy, harmony, peace and happiness. Which shall we choose to respond to and express?

Spiritual Health. Realizing our oneness with the power of the Christ, the moment we let its buddhic Light manifest and radiate from us our spiritual health is assured; for that is determined by the degree of our at-one-ment with our Source of Being.

CHAPTER XIII

CHILDREN OF THE HOUSEHOLD

(CONCLUDED)

"If the 'Doctrine of the Heart' is too high-winged for thee, if thou needest help thyself and fearest to offer help to others—then, thou of timid heart, be warned in time; remain content with the 'Eye Doctrine' of the Law. Hope still. For if the 'Secret Path' is unattainable this 'day' (life), it is within thy reach 'tomorrow'." *The Voice of the Silence,* Blavatsky, 34.

"Now unto him that is able to do exceeding abundantly above all that we ask or think, according to the power that worketh in us." *Ephesians*, III, 20.

Continuing our analysis of the *Prayer for Demonstration*, we come to the statement

It is my strength.

All earnest students seek to work most effectively for the Master; to accomplish; to attain; and it is a law of life that strength is gained through exercise, for "function makes structure." A growing child must have its increasing strength directed into safe channels, else that strength will be exerted in mischievous or even destructive activities. Hence one of the vital problems of child-training is to see that safe and helpful channels are provided for the constructive use of the increasing powers, so that all shall work toward the joy of a well rounded life, instead of becoming sources of trouble. Most of us are still in the state of spiritual childhood. But we are growing daily and are finding that the promise of old is being fulfilled in us, "As thy days, so shall thy strength be." Hence we, like the child, must look to some guiding and directing power to teach us the proper use of our growing strength, as the child looks to its parents.

Let us look for this guidance, not to any outer source, but

realize that the Christ which is our strength is also the wise directing Consciousness which can teach us how to use it. So many who feel this growing strength, and sense the mighty dynamo of force that is supplying it, think they must use it to accomplish great things all at once. Yet they seem held down by daily tasks that are more or less distasteful. What does this mean? Must we use all our new found strength merely to accomplish physical or mental tasks?

This is the phase of the growing child during which it is gaining moral strength to perform its tasks cheerfully and well, even when it wants to go out and play. We must accomplish our tasks, but when we realize that the Christ is the source of our strength, enough will be supplied, not only for the tasks, but to enable us to learn our lessons out of them. And, like the development of the child's strength through directed activities, each task accomplished advances us just that much onward toward the end in view. We must realize, however, that it is not only strength to accomplish that comes from the Christ, but strength of character, which only a faithful accomplishment of little things can build. And if the Christ is our strength he is our strength to grow, as well as to accomplish. He can also furnish us the strength to accomplish the task now and learn the lesson at once, leaving us free to go on. When a severe storm sweeps over a field of growing grain and the stalks are prostrated by its force, after it has passed some will quickly rise to their former upright position because they have the strength not only to grow but to resist and react resiliently. Others lacking this resiliency remain prostrate on the ground, altho ere the storm struck them they appeared as strong and vigorous as any. Just so it is with us, we all may be laid low by storms at times, but only those who have the resilient strength of trust and faith can properly readjust themselves to conditions and bear fruit, a little more perfect perhaps because of the experience.

The Christ within is ever saying, "Onward! Upward!"

yet how often, even when we have prayed for greater usefulness and have faithfully performed all the preliminary tasks, we cry "I cannot!" We hear the cry of the Great Captain of our Souls saying, "Go on," yet, because we cannot see just how to proceed and are not given a map of the country we are told to traverse, nor see the means by which we are to reach our destination, we still desire to cling to the hand of some earthly helper. The result is sure. We will never be given another similar task until we have proved our trust and faith and confidence in the strength of the Christ; for if He is our strength that strength will never fail us.

It is my Courage.

We can scarcely separate strength from courage. Yet, even courage has its seemingly negative, as well as that positive expression which enables us to step out into the waters of the Red Sea all alone in the darkness of the night, depending only upon that which we have attested and proved as Truth, namely, that the Christ is both our strength and our courage.

The daily routine is often quite different from the Path our first enthusiasm pictured. When it comes down to plain everyday living, the big things, the great ideals, seem to be lost to sight as our eyes are fixed upon the details of the daily round. All seems stale and profitless and we are apt to say that life needs neither inspiration nor courage, only dogged, plodding endurance. Yet the courage of the Christ, as exemplified in the life of Jesus, was not only the courage that led to the cross; that enabled Him to bear alone the bitter agony of the garden; to stand alone when all His followers and disciples forsook Him, and to forgive His dastardly betrayal, but also the courage which enabled a Divine Being to leave His heavenly home and put on the limitations of the flesh and live among conditions of sordid materialism, even to be rebuked by His mother for the presuming to enter the temple and be about His father's business. This is the kind of courage His life points out; the courage of working and living His own life even when misunderstood and unappreciated, except for His ability to accomplish with His hands.

The courage of the Christ is also the courage to stand in the presence of the Masters. Picture the Christ-man here, not as being great and glorious and filled with Divine Power, but with His feet in the mire of Earth, hidden from the sight of men, unable to demonstrate His mission, without opportunity to prove His courage. Then say to yourself, "At that stage He was like me. The Christ in me is tied to Earth, to this unmastered physical body; this mass of habits and desires; these faults and failings; this impatience; these faulty ways of thinking, yet I know the power of the Christ is there developing and ready to manifest as opportunity offers. I know how great within me this Divine Light shines; how it makes me pick up the little burdens of the day and go on and on in spite of all that seems trying to hold me back. Therefore I will rely on that strength and courage and Keep Silent and wait patiently on it, knowing that it will bring me into the fulfillment I have visioned and lived for." This is the courage that goes with the strength to grow; the courage to endure while the growing-pains are severe and hard to bear; that rebounds resiliently after every storm; the courage to say: "I will manifest and overcome. I will not look back nor count up my failures. I will not lean on anyone. In the strength of the Christ I will stand alone and be myself, I and the Christ within."

It is my Patience.

This is the patience that endures and is not easily upset. It is not impatience if we use energy and speed in getting things accomplished. But it is impatience if we are ill at ease and fretful at our own lack of accomplishment and rapid advance. Remember that spiritual advance is a growth which requires time. Patience must begin with our being at ease with ourselves. "Rest in the Lord (Law), and wait patiently for him: fret not thyself because of him who prospereth in his way."[1] Know well that the thing that is best will be brought to pass. If we fret, worry or are impatient we consume the forces within which should be directed toward bringing it to pass. We thus shrivel and contract the centers in our bodies which should be vibrating to the radiant energy of the Christ-light. Hence, while the dynamo is there and in perfect working order, yet the switchboard is out of order and we cannot receive the power.

Often, however, we feel a sort of impatience, hard to overcome, because of the effort of the Higher Self to make us realize that we have left something pertaining to our daily tasks undone. Therefore, when we feel impatient with no apparent cause, we should stop and ask ourselves, what have we left undone? What duty have we neglected? What have we forgotten that should have received attention and which our Higher Self is urging us to do? If it is not apparent, ask in the Silence and soon the forgotten task will be remembered. Then at once we should stop what we are doing and attend to the neglected task. If we have spoken an unkind word we must have the courage to go at once and apologize. If it was an unjust act, we must have the courage to right it at once. For every such thing left unfinished puts its pressure upon us and acts as an irritant on our finer bodies and causes corresponding irritation.

Patience means that we are resting in harmony and at ease with the Higher Self. We are so at ease that we can listen to its promptings. We do not fight either the conditions or the forces which seem to be sent against us, yet we are ever alert to better the conditions in every way possible. And since we remain at ease we can see how the conditions can be improved and mastered. Employed thus

---

[1] Psalms, XXXVII, 7.

we forget to complain to the Father about the little trials of the daily life. In short, true patience is not inertia nor a stolid putting up with things because it is too much trouble to find ways of bettering them, but is the expression of our degree of at-one-ment with the Higher Self.

It is my Peace.

Peace includes so much. We cannot have true peace while there is anything within or without that urges us on to fight. But even here we need not lose our poise. We must have peace within ourselves. True peace is a part or piece of what? It is a piece of the Divine Poise, the "peace which passeth all understanding." If we have it we must rest in it, and we cannot grow weary if we are resting in a part of God.

The great lesson to learn is to rest in this consciousness. If difficult conditions arise we should say to ourselves that now is the time to be quiet and trust that the Christ is sending through us streams of living power and peace, even tho we cannot manifest them all at once, and especially while the world is in travail and giving birth to a new social and spiritual consciousness and a new sub-race.

The "peace which passeth all understanding" is not affected by outer conditions. God rests in perfect peace while all creation groans and travails in birth; while man strives with man in bitter war. This is not because of any lack of sympathy or loving kindness toward either Nature or man, but because of the Divine Wisdom that knows all things must be worked out according to the Law of Manifestation, working in its seven-fold[2] manner, if the wonderful peace which is perfect harmony with God's Grand Plan is to overcome and transmute all the elements of inharmony and unrest.

We cannot have peace within until we have vanquished

[2] See *The Voice of Isis*, Curtiss, 192.

every thought that is out of harmony with the Christ which is our peace. We cannot have peace on Earth until we have vanquished every force among nations which stands in the way of the manifestation of God's harmonious Plan for all His children, as announced by the angelic hosts so long ago but never yet realized.

We will have peace on Earth only when we have Good Will among men of all nations. Good Will means much more than a truce because we are tired of fighting. It means a definite recognition of the all-including power of the Christ in the world and in each heart. It also includes an awakened and strongly developed Will that all shall do His bidding, and a never-ceasing effort to make straight the paths for the manifestation of the Christ. In short, we cannot have true peace until we have a Good Will directed toward all men. Just as the individual must have a strong Will that Good shall manifest, so must the nations Will strongly that the Good or the peace of God shall manifest on Earth. Then, no matter what we have to endure, we can hold the ideal and rest in the consciousness of peace, even while we strive for it. We will not weep nor lament over the necessary adjustment of old conditions in our lives or in the world, even tho they may seem terrible. Neither will we hold back and refuse to play our part in them. We will do our best to settle our problems bravely and justly, then rest in the consciousness of peace, knowing well that in due season the birth of new conditions will be accomplished in our lives and in the life of humanity.

It is my Poise.

As we have already mentioned poise as an element of peace, let us here consider it in the sense of good temper, for one who has poise will have good temper. We use the words tempo, temporary and temporal with the meaning of but a passing phase. Also let us look at temper, not as an evil force in itself, but something that should be used to temper and prepare the Soul for higher states. We temper steel for a bridge or for a fine cutting tool, and the Lord tempers the wind to the shorn lamb. But the steel does not find the process a pleasant one nor does the lamb find only warm sunshine in the spring weather. At first it has to snuggle up to its mother, but later it finds itself tempered and made strong. The wind does not stop blowing because the lamb has been shorn, but the life-force in the lamb adjusts or tempers itself to the new conditions and finds itself strengthened.

To have a good temper does not mean that we are to allow ourselves to be imposed upon or that we will have no temptations or aggravations, but that the North Wind[3] in conditions of life will continue to buffet us until our fiber is improved and strengthened, just as the lamb suffers until it learns that it can keep warm by varying its activities, or as steel has its flaws pounded out by the hammering it receives. The Great Law brings us analogous poundings to make us sensitive and strong and to show us how to use our newfound qualities of strength, courage, patience, peace and poise, to conquer.

Without being tempered we could not meet and endure the strain of the rapidly advancing vibrations and conditions of life, any more than cast iron could stand the strain of increased traffic if built upon a bridge. Through poise we must gain the ability to stand the tempering processes of Earth conditions, understand the why and so make the correlation more quickly with the desired end. If we find the little irritations which we ordinarily call temper are running away with us we are like a workman who, instead of letting the trip-hammer drop on the iron he is tempering, lets it fall on and injure his foot (power of understanding) or his hand (power to accomplish).

---

[3] See Page 132.

It is my Power.

Our power is the power of the Christ-life which is the power back of all evolution; the power that makes the seed to sprout, the mind of the child to unfold, the awakened Soul to delve into ever deeper and truer conceptions of life. In short, it is the power that will and must bring all things into manifestation in exact accord with the pattern sent out by the Divine Mind. Hence nothing can stop the working of this power, altho its ultimate achievement of perfect manifestation may be temporarily diverted and delayed.

Since "God saw *everything* that he had made, and, behold, it was *very good*," the divine constructive power of the Christ-life must bring all those seeds of good sown by the Father into fullness of perfect manifestation. For the Father has sown only good seeds in His field of manifestation. But man, whom the Father made His husbandman, has slept. And while he slept his enemy—his own lower nature, which tends to act selfishly and destructively when the higher nature sleeps—came and sowed tares in the field of his life. So when the good seed sprang up, behold, tares were present also. Nevertheless, while the uprooting and burning of these tares will delay the harvest, ultimately the power of the Christ-life will garner in the perfect grain. In the meantime we must remember that it was the same power of the Christ-life, diverted into wrong channels, that made the tares grow with the wheat and that through the experience of mastering them man should gain greater mental, moral and spiritual power. Also remember that it is the power of this same Christ-life that enables us to endure all the results of the tares and gives us the wisdom and courage to recognize and the strength to gather and burn them and thus utilize the residue of their activity (ashes) to fertilize the ground and bring forth better crops in the next cycle.

It is my Wisdom.

Wisdom is the essence of experience, love and understanding. We will never attain wisdom until we begin to love deeply, experience intensely and understand both. We love deeply only after experience. We understand fully only after we love and experience. But the instant we understand, how our burdens fall away and our problems work out! For we are always confused, blinded and irritated until we do understand.

Wisdom is a god-like quality and he who attains it advances toward godhood. Therefore seek wisdom. How? Not merely by accumulating information from books, but also by cultivating the god-like qualities within, recognizing that the Christ within is the central point from which all our forces emanate. Every nerve in our bodies receives power, not merely from the food we eat, but from centers in the astral body, the body of sensation, the bridge between the spiritual and the physical. Without it we would be without sensation and hence without experience. The higher spiritual body is the Christ-child, which must be born within us and must have its correlation with the physical. It sends down a ray of itself into us, and over this bridge of Light it is capable of revealing to us out of our experience, love and understanding, that which we call wisdom.

Make a picture of the Father-in-heaven endowed with the power and glory of all the worlds and possessed of the infinite wisdom of the ages. Then think of Him as planting the seeds of that wisdom within us, and by the power of the Christ-light which comes direct to us in a pathway of glory from the Father, bringing those seeds to fruition in our lives. And as we strive to return to the Father up this Path of Glory we will be bathed in the power to attain wisdom, which is more than experience, love and understanding. This wisdom then must be gathered out of every little thing through understanding. In this sense the Christ-light within becomes our wisdom in proportion as we understand that which the Light reveals.

It is my Understanding.

Understanding means that we must store up every experience, be it psychic or of the outer life, and like Mary ponder these things in our hearts until we comprehend that which the experience was meant to teach. We should not run to this, that and the other one and ask for explanations, nor even to those who are qualified to teach us, until we have prayerfully sought for the light of understanding within ourselves, else we may get many contradictory solutions. In every experience the Soul passes through there is some deep personal question involved, something which we alone can know, either some deep hidden fault to correct or some deep Soul-mystery to unravel. This we must learn to understand, for only through understanding can we learn the lessons which the experiences held for us.

It is my Joy.

Out of understanding springs joy, the deep abiding joy which knows that every cloud has a silver lining and every dark night is glad morning. The mark which the angel places in the foreheads of the 144,000,[4] who are the Saints to be gathered out of all the tribes, is the look of one who has gained true Understanding of the Divine, Divine Wisdom, hence has a full Understanding of life. The eyes hold in their depths the profound happiness of one who has rested on the bosom of the Christ and can never more be afraid. This is the mark placed by the angel in the forehead of those who are sealed. This is the Joy which the world can neither give nor take away.

It is my Inspiration.

Jesus left with those who are His sincere followers "the Spirit of Truth" which shall abide with us always and which

---

[4] See *The Key of Destiny*, Curtiss, 228, 245.

shall bring all things to our remembrance whatsoever we had been told. Inspiration is a recognition of this Spirit of Truth and the inspiring or breathing in of all that it holds for us. One who has thus attained Wisdom, Understanding and Joy can live in the Breath of the Spirit and at any time draw in or be inspired by the Truth.

It is my Abundant Supply.

Realize just what we mean by supply. If we limit it to food and clothing and ability to pay our debts, and admit that those things are all we need to enable us to unfold and express our Real Self, then they are all we can expect to attain by our utmost efforts. To gain mere selfish desires is to grow in selfishness, hence we will not get answers to such prayers except as the Father sees that we need to learn the bitter lessons which their attainment will teach. Yet, abiding firmly in the faith that our Father will give us that which we have asked *if and when it is best*, we do not harass Him, like a petulant child, by asking again and again. We have planted the seed-thought of that which we desire, and if it be good seed, we must allow it time for growth and fruition. Therefore, we must simply water it with love and firm faith in the Wisdom and kindness of the Father to give it if it be best, and let the sunlight of our spiritual realization shine upon it, and not keep pulling up the seed each day to see if it is growing.

The abundant supply is not merely of physical things and conditions, but of the things we need so much more,—love, peace, poise, unselfishness, understanding, wisdom, etc. When we have an abundance of the Light of the Christ within we have no need to ask for the rest, for all those things shall be added unto us as needed. We must make in our hearts a Temple for the Living God, with an anteroom into which all the forces of the universe can come and bring their gifts, for all are ministers to us for the Christ. If we let the angels, the elementals and the Winds of Heaven lay their gifts at our feet as we minister to the Christ in our Temple, then we will have no wants unsupplied, for all is made subservient to the Divine. And we must be careful not to put a limit upon the power of the Christ by saying that such and such a thing is impossible; for *whatever is needful* for the manifestation of a beautiful, happy and normal life is ours, when we have entered into our heritage as "heirs of God, and joint-heirs with Christ."

CHAPTER XIV

MAN, KNOW THYSELF

"Saith the Great Law: In order to become the knower of ALL SELF, thou hast first of SELF to be the knower.' To reach the knowledge of that SELF, thou hast to give up Self to Non-Self, Being to non-being." *The Voice of the Silence*, Blavatsky, I.

"Ignorance is the cause of imperfection. Men do not know themselves and, therefore, they do not understand the things of their inner world. Each man has the essence of God, and all the wisdom and power of the world (germinally) in himself." *Paracelsus*, Hartman.

Every student of mysticism is familiar with the axiom that man is a microcosm of the macrocosm, and has grown familiar with the idea, at least in a superficial way, that in some mysterious manner man is an epitome of the universe. Let us try to comprehend this idea and make of it a greater reality, a more vital help toward the unfoldment of our inner life; for a *fundamental object of mysticism is to find back of everything the reality which gives it life*. This is as true of a trite axiom or an idea as of anything in the manifested universe.

We look upon the physical universe and admire the beauty and diversity of its manifestations. We enthuse over its outer wonders; its trees and flowers; its rocks and streams; its wondrous store of wealth hidden beneath the surface; its rivers, mountains and its oceans. Truly a marvelous world! Then we look deeper and find in the sea a vast universe inhabited by an infinite variety of lives. The microscope reveals a still more minute, but no less wonderful world of life in every drop of water. The telescope overawes the intellect and thrills the Soul with the mighty revelation of shining stars, flaming comets, glowing suns

millions of times larger than our own,[1] and vast cosmic systems
too great for comprehension, while chemistry and physics tell us
that the electrons within an atom of substance are relatively as far
from each other as the planets in our solar system, yet all, both
great and small, are moving in majestic harmony.

And behind and within all these outer manifestations we find
an infinite number of tribes of living, conscious forces having the
earth, the air, the water and the fire for their habitat, as well as
the great hierarchies of Angelic Beings in the still more ethereal
worlds. Each and all of these forms of life and consciousness
follow their own appointed way, have their own evolution and
fulfill their destined role. No wonder the unenlightened exclaim,
"Do you mean to tell us that man is such a universe? that he is a
microcosm in exact similitude to this macrocosm?"

As we enter the first gate upon the Path of Attainment we
must stop and consider the mandate which is carved over its
portal, "Man, know thyself." What a vast knowing this must be!
First, to know man in the aggregate and then to know thyself
in particular. In the study of man we are wont to consider
him under at least three divisions and say that he is a Spirit
manifesting through a mind and a body. Or we may consider
him under seven divisions, four lower pertaining to his bodies
and three higher pertaining to his Soul,[2] an overshadowing
triangle whose apex reaches up and puts him in touch with the
vastness of the great universal One Life. But even such a division
is little more than as if we were to divide the universe into its
four constituent elements of earth, air, fire and water, and its
three higher ethers, and ignore the component parts and the

---

[1] One star (*Betelgeuse*) of the many thousands in but one constellation (*Orion*),
according to Prof. A. A. Michelson is 27,000,000 times larger than our sun, indeed,
far larger than the *orbit* of our Earth and nearly equaling the orbit of Mars!
[2] See *The Key to the Universe*, Curtiss, Chapter XXVIII.

forces and intelligences which manifest through them; for within each division there are innumerable minor ones. But altho the subject is endlessly complex we can begin with the physical body, as it is the lowest and most easily understood division.

How shall we go about knowing it? A study of its anatomical parts reveals to us a most complicated mechanism, yet of wondrous delicacy and marvelous adaptability to the requirements of life. It is a mechanism, therefore, which must have all the careful and intelligent treatment that we would give to the most sensitive and valuable scientific instrument. A study of its functional activities will acquaint us with the fundamental laws and principles of physiology, which must be observed in a common-sense way if we are to keep it in a clean and healthful condition as a fit temple for the indwelling of its divine occupant, the Real Self. Not only must we observe the well-known laws of hygiene, diet and sanitation, but we must realize that all its activities are the result of the countless currents of the One Life sweeping through it, the Life which builds up the bodies through which we are manifesting in each of the worlds.

Realize that life here in the physical world is not something separate from Life in the higher realms, but is simply a continuation of that Life downward into a denser medium of expression. We also find that the body is not a mere mechanism, but a living and highly intelligent animal with the functions, desires, appetites and habits of any animal. Hence it needs training and control, just as does any other high-bred animal, if it is to become a willing, obedient and efficient servant of its lord and master. Hence, through the directing power of thought we should strive to make the body express our highest ideals; become an embodiment of the Real Self. Yet, if after complying with all the laws of physical health the body still seems to lack, we should

strive to hold vitally to the thought that we are standing in the
glowing stream of the One Life, reaching out and gathering up
and assimilating the forces of the River of Life, as a rose gathers
from the soil and Sun the nourishment that goes to make up its
life abundant, and feel this Divine Life gently permeating and
vitalizing us and fulfilling all our needs.

After considering the needs of the body we must recognize
those of the mental expression of the indwelling Real Self. We
must learn to discriminate and recognize those thoughts and
desires which well up into our minds from the subconscious mind
or the mind of the animal self whose seat is in the solar plexus,
and realize that they are not our thoughts and desires, but those
of the animal body asking us to recognize and gratify them.

Many students, not understanding its nature and functions,
concentrate on the solar plexus in an effort to attain spiritual
enlightenment. This being the center of the animal consciousness,
concentration upon it quickens the forces of the animal nature,
and if at the same time the student is trying to master that nature
the conflict is apt to bring about an unbalanced condition. It is
much like speaking kindly to a dog to get him to perform his best
tricks and then beating him for performing. It is the forces from
the physical Sun, together with astral currents, which center in
the solar plexus, and not the forces from the Spiritual Sun. And
since the function of the physical Sun is to bring forth the physical
life in Nature, concentration upon its center in the body naturally
stimulates our *physical forces, not our spiritual.*

The focus of the Spiritual Sun is in the heart. Hence, if we
desire to stimulate our *spiritual* growth we should not concentrate
upon the solar plexus, but upon the heart; not, however, upon the
physical heart, but upon the development and expression of the
heart qualities.

We must recognize the currents of thought which come

from the rational mind—the intellect of the personality, which operates through the cortex of the brain as the subconscious does through the ganglia of the solar plexus, both containing similar tri-polar nerve cells—as it seeks for the comfort and aggrandizement of the personal self. This aspect of the mind also needs training and control, for it often fails to understand, hence doubts, worries and becomes discouraged. Hence, just as the subconscious mind must be taught to submit its desires to our decision, so must the rational mind be taught to submit to and rely confidently upon the guidance of the higher, *superconscious* or spiritual mind of the Soul, which guidance is always given in answer to aspirations and sincere prayer for guidance.

If the mind grows discouraged at the seeming lack of conditions for peace, harmony and spiritual advance, point out to it the analogy in Nature. Where does the rose get its nourishment and the materials for its growth and development? All the materials needed to put forth leaf and bud, blossom and perfume? Out of the commonplace materials of its environment; yet not out of the materials themselves, but out of the Divine Life-force that is back of all. How does it perform this miracle of transmutation? By keeping confident and poised and allowing the One Life to flow through it in perfect harmony to manifest its destiny. Therefore, in times of doubt and depression we should say to ourselves: "I will keep so calm and poised, so cheerful and confident and in such close touch with the stream of the divine Christ-force within me that I shall draw all things to me that are needed for my growth and development, for strengthening my roots and perfecting my blossoming. But to do so I must open my heart to the Sun of Righteousness and allow the Christ-force to manifest through me in thought, word and deed that I may express my inner or Real Self and thus fulfill my destiny."

Remember that one of the fundamental laws of mind is that, *Every thought tends to express itself in action unless counteracted or neutralized by an opposite thought of greater power.* Therefore we must refuse to think the kind of thoughts we do not wish expressed through us. But *never fight them*; for to do so we are concentrating upon them and giving them greater power. Instead of resisting or fighting them, even to pray over them, we must simply *turn our minds away* from them by concentrating on and *filling our minds with the opposite* kind of a thought, one which we do wish to have expressed through us. Another fundamental law is that, *Every thought we admit into our minds and contemplate, we give a power over us.* We do not have to admit into our minds, contemplate and go over and over every thought that may arise in or be presented to our consciousness. We can turn away from and refuse to dwell upon those thoughts which do not measure up to the ideals of our lives. Therefore, remember that *we do not have to admit or contemplate evil thoughts unless we choose to do so.* Learn these rules by heart.

The currents, thoughts and forces from the astral world must also be recognized. If we find that we are becoming more sensitive to the thoughts of others and are responding to psychic conditions, here also we must learn to discriminate and respond only to those forces which are harmonious and constructive. We must protect ourselves from undesirable forces by realizing that the power of the indwelling Christ-force is the great Protector and the great Adjuster of conditions, both in the inner life and in the outer. With the consciousness of this protection, as our higher faculties begin to unfold, we can use them to expand our consciousness, deepen our understanding and advance our spiritual unfoldment; for we will realize that whether the finer forces of which we are now conscious come from the thoughts of others, or from our disembodied friends; from the planets under which we were born or from the kingdoms of the elementals, *they must all be ruled* and made to contribute toward our ongoing, instead of being allowed to find uncontrolled expression through and rule us. We must also learn to recognize and discriminate between the sources from which we are receiving these influences.

The rational mind should always look up to and receive its inspiration, not from our disembodied friends or from the thoughts of others, but from the superconscious or spiritual mind of the Real Self. Then, by means of the higher illumination thus received, it should guide the activities of the personality and also reach down and train and control the subconscious mind. The spiritual mind is always the court of last appeal, for stored up in it is the experience or lessons learned from all past incarnations, and this experience it seeks to impress upon the rational mind of the personality, if we will only listen, respond and give it expression.

Conscience is the steady pressure of the consciousness of the spiritual mind which all feel to a greater or lesser degree. It is the consciousness of the Real Self reflected upon the rational mind for the purpose of illuminating and guiding the personality. In the earlier stages of spiritual unfoldment it manifests simply as a strong impression of right or wrong, to do or not to do, without giving explanations, reasons or arguments. But as the Aspirant becomes conscious of his Real Self and seeks to become one with and express it, gradually that Divine Self is able to speak to him direct and guide, admonish, encourage or rebuke in a definite way.

All these phases of the Self and the forces which beat upon it should be read about and studied, but they cannot be *mastered* by the intellect alone or by the unaided powers of the personality. Only as the Knower, the Thinker, the Real Self is recognized and given supreme direction of our lives can they be *really known* in the mystical sense, *i.e.*, as a personal realization and comprehension. This Knower, this Thinker, this Self, this I Am, stands in the center of our individual universe, just as the Sun is in the center of the physical universe, and is the ruler over it; the source of its life, light and power. In fact, it is the Maker of our heaven and our earth, the Evolver of our personal self, and is also its Redeemer.

And because this Real Self is the Ambassador of the Christ and is of the same essence as the Cosmic Christ which vitalizes all divisions of the vast universe, through acquaintance, realization and correlation with this Self we can enter into an understanding of those cosmic centers of life, force and consciousness which have their miniature centers and points of contact within our bodies. The man who has thus found himself, through realization and correlation with this inner Self, has found the Christ enthroned in the midst of his universe, and by identifying his consciousness with that indwelling Christ-consciousness he can enter into the consciousness of all things in the vaster universe, hence can learn to know himself as those forces manifest in his personal universe or microcosm.

In Nature we find the mighty Christ Principle expressing harmoniously according to the great Law of Manifestation, vitalizing and bringing into manifestation the ideals in the Divine Mind. And as we learn to identify ourselves with the Christ in us we aid it in bringing forth in us the divine ideals until we reach the point where we are able to realize and know that we are Sons of God. "For as many as are led by the Spirit of God, they are the Sons of God."[3]

After the Christ has been born in the heart of man, has been laid among the animals in the manger of his physical existence; wrapped in swaddling bands of mind-stuff, subconsciously manifesting in the astral, and awakened and manifesting in his spiritual nature, then may the Jesus man, the Divine Physician, the Healer, be said to have come to Earth in our lives. For only as the personal man is taught to follow the Jesus-life can the Christ manifest consciously in him.

Like the story of Jesus, we must pass through all phases of that life. We must be the carpenter's son, constructively

---

[3] Romans, VIII, 14.

doing his duty in the lowly station of life in which he finds himself, striving to build his temple by compass and square; yet through the power of the Christ, whose swaddling bands of consciousness he is day by day unwrapping, he must learn that all events that come to him are but the carpenter's tools with which he must carve out his temple and accomplish the works of his Father. He must remain in the obscurity of Egypt for a season while the Herod (King Desire) who rules the personality seeks to slay Him who is ultimately to become the ruler of the life. He must heal the sick, cleanse the lepers and feed the multitude within his own body with spiritual food. He must strive; he must suffer; he must be misunderstood and condemned, yet never must he forget his real mission. He must hang upon the cross of material conditions until, in the very depths of his being, in the agony of the higher consciousness that has been born within him—that consciousness which strives to uncover and reveal the Christ Child to a world that cannot understand— he cries out "I thirst."

In one aspect this is the thirst of the despairing personality for the old life in the world and its seeming satisfaction, its happiness and security. But in another and higher sense it is the cry of the awakened man for more wisdom; how best to do the works of his Father; how best to lift up the Christ-light that all men shall be drawn into the radiance of that Light. He realizes the mighty power of the Christhood within him and thirsts for the ability to manifest it without crucifying it. But he finds the task too great and lays down the burden crying: "It is finished . . . . Father, into thy hands I commend my spirit." Only when the awakened personality realizes that it cannot achieve, through its own intellectual powers, the destiny that has been glimpsed, and places all the ardor and enthusiasm of his desire to accomplish into the hands—symbol of power to accomplish—of the Father, the Real Self, and ceases to struggle, is the crucifixion over.

This is the most important step in the Soul's unfoldment. We may think that when we reach great heights of mastery, when we can rule the elementals, use our psychic faculties, levitate the body, etc., we have taken wonderful steps. But the most important step that can be taken by man is that symbolized by the crucifixion, namely, when the personal man has learned, through great suffering, that no matter how unselfish or devoted; no matter how great the work he is doing, he cannot make the final attainment in his own strength. He must be willing to be crucified, not rejoicing in the crucifixion as a sign of his superiority over others, but recognizing that it is only a crucifixion of the lower man that the glory of the Christ within might shine forth the better. In fact, the Christ could accomplish His work more perfectly without the distraction which the suffering of the personality brings upon Him, *if the personality could learn and respond* without the crucifixion.

O this crucifixion through which humanity insists on passing! How the Great Physician, the Healer of Souls, struggles with the personality and hangs upon the cross of agony! What is it all for? It is to awaken in intellectual man an abiding sense of the indwelling Divinity and its power to overcome all things, once the opposition of the personality has ceased. He must realize that he is something more than man; that there is something his cultured mind cannot grasp, which must come as a revelation *from the heart*; that he must call upon the Christ within; must yield up the sense of his sufficiency and superiority; for his god, the intellect, has forsaken him, cry he never so loud.

As we found at the beginning of this chapter, man being a universe in himself, every part and division of his nature has its own inhabitants. In his intellectual world[4] he is not tempted from without, but from within. He is not sent down in the lower worlds to be set upon by powers of evil, demons, elementals, creatures of which he has no consciousness and

---

[4] For temptations from the astral world see *Realms of the Living Dead*, Curtiss, 70.

consequently no power to conquer. Everything that comes thus to tempt him is an inhabitant of his own mental world; for through the creative power of his thought-force he has peopled his world with all kinds of creations which seek expression through him, and he has thus opened the door to all the corresponding forces in the surrounding worlds. His tempters are creatures of his own fashioning, living upon the tender leaves his Tree of Life has put forth, just as the infinitesimal lives that the microscope reveals feed upon the leaves of a tree and, if allowed to go on unchecked, destroy it. He has permitted his lower self to lead in procession all the forces and inhabitants of his world because it has put forth a great intellectual branch which reaches up into the mental world, while the Real Self, the Divine Being within, remains imprisoned within that world, realizing its own god-hood, yet unable to induce the personality to manifest it.

But just as our physical bodies and our astral and mental worlds have their inhabitants, so does the spiritual world of each individual have its inhabitants. The Real Self in the spiritual world has many angelic beings and forces attached to him because they inhabit his world, altho most of us are quite unaware of it. Yet, if we will open the door to them as we do to the inhabitants of our lower worlds they will just as surely minister to us and manifest through us, not destructively, bringing about inharmony and suffering, but constructively, bringing about harmony and joy.

Therefore, as we learn to know ourselves and our creations in all our worlds we will end the crucifixion by saying of our personal reliance on outer conditions and forces, "It is finished . . . into the hands of my Divine Self I commit my Spirit." Then we will begin to open our consciousness to the angelic forces from the spiritual world and will know ourselves as Sons of God in the process of unfoldment and manifestation and learn to manifest the Real Self as wholeheartedly and completely as we have hitherto manifested the lower self or personality.

CHAPTER XV

ORDERLY SEQUENCE

"For God is not the author of confusion, but of peace. . . . Let all things be done decently and in order." *I Corinthians*, XIV, 33-40.

"There is one glory of the sun, and another glory of the moon, and another glory of the stars; for one star differeth from another star in glory." *I Corinthians*, XV, 41.

Law and order rule the universe.

This globe, and all that is upon and within it, as well as the Cosmos of which it is a part, has been manifested as the result of definite law. The planets move around the Sun in orderly procession, each in its own orbit, each drawing its life-force from the central Sun, yet utilizing that force to unfold its own particular possibilities according to the law of its being. On Earth every plant, tree, animal, or other form of life, draws its life-force from the Sun, yet manifests it according to the law of its individual expression, each being a necessary part of the whole.

There is but the One Life, manifesting according to the One Law, yet there are infinite varieties of expression. If individual man would unfold his life as successfully and harmoniously as he sees life unfolded in the Cosmos and in Nature around him, he, too, must follow the same Law and walk the same Path; he, too, must draw to himself the One Life and build it into his individual life expression according to definite law and order. But this must be of his own volition, for to man alone of all creation was given free-will.

Certain references have been made in these Teachings to a Great Work to be accomplished for humanity and to the opportunity each one has of taking part in that Great Work.

But ere this opportunity can be grasped and its promise fulfilled, each one who desires to participate must have a certain understanding of the Law ere he is prepared to take his place in the activities which are now at hand. Each one who is in earnest in his endeavors, unselfish in his desires and is a faithful follower of the Teachings—and we trust that this includes all—each is striving to accomplish the Great Work in his own body, in his life, and in his environment. If this Great Work is to be accomplished intelligently, either individually or collectively, it is necessary to call attention to one very important and definite law, *i.e.*, the Law as Orderly Sequence.[1]

Order is said to be heaven's first law. And it is equally important in the unfoldment of those who seek to make heaven manifest here on Earth, in their consciousness, in their lives and in their environment. Even the modern business world recognizes this law and bases all the new methods of efficiency upon it. The man or woman who builds his or her life upon law and order lays the foundation for success, not alone in the material life, but in the higher life as well.

There is a distinction, however, between plan, order and routine. Plan has to do with the whole scheme of life and includes a more or less clear outline of the end to be attained and the methods by which it is to be achieved. Those who "have no plan in life, no objective to be attained, no goal toward which all their activities are working, are merely drifting, subject to every breeze that blows and driven hither and thither by every current of force that may impinge upon them. How can such persons expect to attain any definite accomplishment? To be efficient in life's day at school a philosophy should be sought which is so all-inclusive that it explains where we came from, why we are here, what the destiny is to which we are expected to reach, and what our

---

[1] See *The Voice of Isis*, Curtiss, 193-4.

individual place is in the whole mighty scheme of the universe, and how we are to attain it.

Order has to do with the harmonious relations between things, ideas, actions, etc. The old adage, "A place for everything and everything in its place," has an occult basis; for such an arrangement between physical things not only tends toward orderly arrangement of ideas in the mental world, but it also arranges orderly and *non-interfering lines of force* in the astral and psychic realms. The orderly arrangement of a desk, a room, or a home, for example, is constructive and helps to create a calm, peaceful and poised atmosphere or aura, while a disorderly room, household or office is destructive, for it tends to create confusion and crossed lines of force, hence tends toward irritation, inharmony and disintegration. This idea, however, should not be carried to such extremes as to exclude all else. For instance, in the olden days the parlor or best room in the house was kept closed and the family excluded from its every day use, lest its orderly arrangement should be in the least disturbed. In fact, many persons are even today so restricted in their own homes by the housekeeper's exaggeration of order that the home is made unattractive by it. A reasonable insistence upon order, however, is a more important factor in the mystical and spiritual life than is generally known or appreciated.

Routine has to do with the orderly carrying out of a sequence of events necessary to the working out of a plan. The plan should include a certain time set aside for study, for recreation and for meditation and spiritual realization, as well as for the activities of the material life. And this routine, once carefully laid out, should be followed religiously, but with such reasonable latitude that the routine does not become the master instead of the servant; that the follower does not become pedantic, intolerant or fanatical, instead of becoming a well-balanced, poised and adaptable Soul. But he who seeks to attain the highest by following one impulse today and another tomorrow, unbalanced by discretion and wisdom; who does one thing today because it appeals to his mood and neglects all other parts of the plan and all other duties, cannot expect to advance in a well-balanced manner.

He, who, because he is sensitive and psychic, becomes erratic, who dips first into one teaching and then into another in a superficial way, may have a speaking acquaintance with many words of many syllables, yet he lacks that plan, that order, that routine persistence, which is essential to mastery, whether in the things of the world or the things of the Spirit. He who begins the day with a realization that many things should have prompt attention, and then allows himself to be diverted from the orderly sequence of his duties by becoming so engrossed in the task of the moment that he forgets all others or pushes them back to some more convenient tomorrow, cannot succeed. For tomorrow never comes. When it comes it is today, with its own demands, its own activities, and there is no time in which to go back and pick up wasted moments or perform forgotten tasks.

Picture for a moment a Cosmos built in such a way. Suppose God had said, "Let there be light," and then had forgotten what He had decreed! Suppose that as the Light penetrated into the darkness of Chaos He overlooked the details of the plans He had started into manifestation! Suppose He had said, "Today we will make a great light and a lesser light and tomorrow we will create man in our image," and then had forgotten man! Or suppose man had been fashioned before the Earth was ready to receive him! Think you the work of creation would have been accomplished in six days? Yet those who are striving to attain the higher life are apt to despise the exactitude of business methods and look down upon those who methodically perform each allotted task as it is presented in the routine of the plan and according to definite rules.

The self-discipline of a definite plan, developed in a certain order and according to a general routine, makes for well-balanced and harmonious progress in the spiritual life as in the physical. Yet man must be the master and dictator of his own life, never a slave to his self-appointed and needful rules; for over all these rules is a higher law whose mandates must be observed, *i.e.*, the guidance of his Real Self. His daily life should be arranged in such an orderly fashion that he can easily set it aside temporarily at the call of the Real Self, without upsetting it. This he could not do if his life was in confusion. To listen to the Voice of Intuition and to be ever responsive to inspiration is essential to spiritual progress, even if it temporarily interrupts the routine. But there is much to be accomplished between the periods of inspiration, if the new ideas thus received are to be worked out and made to manifest effectively in the life. Inspiration will be more dependable if there be a regular time set apart for its recognition and reception. By following this method the inspiration becomes so frequent as ultimately to be a continuous conscious guidance in all things, both great and small.

Many think they have nothing to do while waiting for their inspiration; that they can work only when they are given a special outpouring of power. And because of this attitude of mind many a Soul who has been chosen as an important instrument in a Great Work has ended his days in inaction, failure and disappointment. Instead of beginning humbly and proceeding methodically, according to some plan of accomplishment, he has waited year after year for some great manifestation of divine glory and power that would miraculously accomplish the work his inspiration had revealed to him; that would fill him and make the world recognize him in his greatness. Yet all the time he neglected to take the routine steps necessary ere the plan could be materialized in Earth conditions. Such are not the practical mystics these Teachings hope to develop. They are merely dreamers and visionaries, those who help to bring mysticism and the ideals of the higher life into disrepute as impractical and inefficient, simply because they fail to take the practical steps necessary to correlate the ideal with its realization.

Many hear the divine call within, "Come ye out and be ye separate. . . . Take my yoke upon you. . . . Feed my Lambs." And they answer, "Yea, Lord, here am I." And in that day they go forth so full of ardor and enthusiasm that they feel impelled to proclaim to everyone their wonderful experience and the fact that they have been chosen as an instrument in the hands of the Great Law. But they find the hungry lambs indifferent to food that is merely promised; they find the world not ready to bow down before them and acknowledge them to be the great leader or teacher they were told they *might* become. Thus they spend their day of enthusiasm and use up the power given them for accomplishment, not in methodically making a practical beginning, but in dissipating and wasting it in telling the world what they are *going* to do or be at some future time. Then when their evening comes they are in despair and loudly lament the ignorance and stupidity of mankind or bemoan the unbrotherliness of other teachers who fail to recognize them as a chosen disciple who has been sent forth with a badge of honor upon his breast, or perhaps they weep bitterly over the cruelty of a world which demands deeds rather than words, results instead of promises. They desire to sow and immediately reap without the trouble and routine work of preparing the soil, cultivating, weeding and tending the growing crop.

A similar temptation is experienced by every Neophyte, whether chosen for a great work or not; for the first great work for every Soul is to learn to work in harmony with the Law. Until this is learned, no greater work can be entrusted to it. Similar failure can be avoided only by having plan, order and routine for the inspiration to illumine, expand and accomplish through. "There is no royal road to knowledge," nor to spiritual attainment. It requires the same painstaking preparation and training of body and mind as any other important work in life.

The *Bible* tells us that the six days of creation were each divided into two periods, morning and evening. And only on the fourth day were the Sun and Moon created, the greater to rule the day and the lesser to rule the night. What does this allegory signify in the life of the Neophyte? It means that he will pass through three periods of morning-evening, corresponding to the first three days of creation and to the three days in the tomb, before his Sun and Moon are created, during which he must methodically gather fresh the promised manna on which to feed; periods during which he will experience the glory of the mornings, when all is bright and smiling, when he hears the Voice saying: "See the blessings in store for humanity! Come, take, eat, and give unto the hungry," and he is all enthusiasm. Then will come the evenings, when he finds the world indifferent, tired or asleep: when his enthusiasm has evaporated, his powers seem exhausted and his comrades turn their backs upon and slight him. During these three days he works almost blindly, for his Sun and Moon are not yet created, and he cannot see what definite work he is to do.

But if through these three periods of vagueness and semi-light he has followed his guidance faithfully and has gathered his manna fresh from heaven each morning and evening no matter how dark and cold or how weary he might be, and has performed each little task methodically as it was presented, without wasting time in dreaming about the great attainment pictured in his vision, he will have built for himself a firm foundation, which, like all foundations, must be laid stone on stone deep down in the darkness of Earth conditions, below the surface, where it does not receive the recognition or applause of men.

But on the fourth day two Lights will be created, the Spiritual Sun to rule his days and the same Sun reflected in him through intuition to rule his nights. This means that when his mornings of enthusiasm come he will find that the Great Light—the Sun of his Soul—has arisen to illumine his consciousness and enable him to see clearly the plan of his work. It will also reveal to the world the foundation he has already laid. From these periods of illumination there will be reflected through his intuition the comfort, assurance and strength necessary to carry him safely through the night, until he is ready to rest in the midst of his works on the seventh day and pronounce them good. It will also reveal the fact that the night is the time to rest, gather the forces of the Earth and assimilate the experiences of the day, that he may be prepared for the activities of the new day, resting meanwhile in trust and confidence in the workings of the Great Law, until finally he re-enters his Eden and there meets the Lord God (Law of his Good) walking in the cool of the day, the entire Law making its home in his spiritualized body (the Garden of Eden).

During its early days this Order has quietly laid its foundation in the darkness and obscurity of Earth conditions. Then its two Lights were created and set in its heaven, the greater to rule its days, *i.e.*, the positive knowledge that the life-stream of the Christ (the Sun of Righteousness) fills all its world with Light, life and power, which shall germinate all the seeds sown in the twilight of the earlier periods; the lesser to rule its nights—the periods of human discouragement—with the intuitive knowledge that the Sun of Righteousness still shines, even tho only its reflected Light can be seen. Therefore, during the night-periods the Order is able to rest in the assurance that the words of the old familiar hymn,

"Sun of my Soul, my Savior dear,
It is not night if Thou be near,"

are mystically true. For the Sun of God is also the Sun of the Order, just as it is the Sun of each individual Soul. Hence it must rise again in the glory, power and fullness of a new day of greater opportunity after every night period.

As each new day dawns for the Order it must "be fruitful and bring forth abundantly." Each new day will be almost like a new incarnation. And as in the reincarnation of a Soul, there must be the karmic fulfillment—to each student individually, as well as to the Order as a whole—of exactly that which each has sown in the past, both for himself and for the Order. Therefore, all who put the welfare and work of the Order first, who make sacrifices for it and give it their faith, love, devotion and service, will participate in its new developments, and will find comfort, joy and inspiration in the activities of each new day. The Law as Karma and the Law as Growth is working in this day of the Order just as it does in the new Earth life of an individual. In the earlier days there was only the plan, later the astral pattern, and then the beginnings of a materialization comparable to a fetus. But today, as a result of the throes and travail of birth through which it has passed, its physical body has been born. It is not perfect or powerful as yet, for it is but the body of a babe, but it is rapidly growing in stature and in favor with God and man, and is capable of being developed into the giant which it ultimately must become.

But as the body of the Order is composed of many cells (individuals), to make it perfectly fitted to accomplish its real mission each individual must begin with himself, outline his plan of life and his relation to the Order, and then begin to work toward its fulfillment with order and system. In overcoming the tendencies toward disorder, inharmony and lack of perseverance, each has free-will either to yield to the destructive forces and be overcome by them or to overcome them by utilizing the very power which makes them effective. There is no great Being who says that we shall or shall not. But if we wish to conquer, if we wish to draw close, if we wish to let the divine principle of Law and Order work through and manifest perfection in us, then we must begin to correlate with the Law. Begin with

an outline of the end to be attained. Then take up the things of
the outer life, even those which seem to have no connection
with spiritual attainments, and establish order and system in our
lives, remembering that to allow time for spiritual studies and
for meditation is as important a duty as to allow time for meals,
work or recreation.

The same system should also be applied to finances. As definite
a portion should be assigned and consecrated to the support and
spread of the spiritual Teachings as for any other expense. When
Moses enjoined upon the Children of Israel that they should
dedicate a tenth of all they possessed to the support of their priests,
he was but inculcating a deep occult principle which would react
to their own prosperity, materially as well as spiritually, and
become an important factor in making them a great nation. Let
each Soul who reads this book sincerely ask in the sanctuary of
his own heart and in the presence of his Real Divine Self, if the
enlightenment of the world and the betterment of humanity cannot
be more efficiently brought about through the co-operation of all
who accept the principles these Teachings set forth, rather than
by many scattered units trying to work independently. And if the
answer be in the affirmative let him act accordingly. We must
begin just as the Light was manifested. When we say we will do
a thing we must do it. When we make a carefully considered plan,
we must carry it out. When we make a promise, even to ourselves,
we must keep it. When we begin a thing, we must finish it and be
done with it, just as business efficiency demands that the office
desk be cleared before leaving it.

Let each day be a day of creation. But remember that we
cannot create and bring things into manifestation unless we
attend minutely to every duty as it is presented and fulfill
it. The habit of putting off and forgetting is so disorderly,
confusing and inharmonious that instead of drawing to us
the divine constructive forces of the Law, we set up within

ourselves and in our environment forces which produce storms
of opposition, which make us feel impatient, irritable and as tho
we would fly to pieces. Why? Because the Great Law we have
invoked and promised to obey is trying to work in its orderly
fashion and force us to attend to the necessary details in their
regular order and rhythm.

Humanity is a Cosmos in the process of formation. Like the
planets in the heavens each individual has his own orbit, and
this is commensurate with the work he is to accomplish and the
forces he is to utilize. The forces within this orbit manifest as
his natural tendencies, abilities, disposition, etc. As each Soul
evolves along his own path around the Spiritual Sun he finds
that his orbit touches, parallels or perhaps intersects the orbits of
many others. In following the law of his being he must consider
the various aspects he makes with those he contacts. He must
recognize that it is not intended that he force himself to sustain
the same relations toward all, except those of law and order.
With some he finds himself in the so-called malign aspects of
opposition, square, semi-square or sesquiquadrate, while with
others he is in the benign aspects of trine, sextile, conjunction
or parallel. But the Law of Cosmic Order decrees that while all
draw their forces from the central Sun and must work together
in harmony, each must keep to his own orbit and follow his own
plan, without allowing himself to be deviated from it, and without
striving to deflect others from their orbits or force upon them his
personal plan of life.

Each must sound his own keynote and send out his highest and
best forces and make use of whatever influences he receives from
each one he contacts, be they benign or malign, recognizing that
all are parts of the Divine Plan, even if not manifesting perfectly
or harmoniously, just as the lower influence of Mars brings war
and bloodshed and that of Saturn testing, and disaster to all that
cannot pass the test, yet both are Sacred Planets and have their
divine work to do.

Remember that Law and Order are the foundation of the

universe; that this Law must work out in little things as in great; that only he who is faithful in the little things is made ruler over the great. And if we are to be faithful and true and loving we must begin to manifest these qualities in our hearts, in our lives and in the performance of our duties, accomplishing each one, be it ever so distasteful, in the name of the Christ and for the sake of the Christ. Then no duty will be too irksome, no task too sordid, no routine too exacting to be performed cheerfully "for His sake."

CHAPTER XVI

THE SPIRAL OF LIFE

"Fohat traces spiral lines to unite the Sixth to the Seventh—the Crown. An Army of the Sons of Light stands at each angle; the Lipika in the Middle Wheel." *Stanzas of Dzyan*, V, 4.

"Unless one is well acquainted with the philosophical metaphysics of a beginningless and endless series of Cosmic Rebirths, and becomes well impressed with the immutable law of Nature with its Eternal Motion, cyclic and spiral—therefore progressive even in its seeming retrogression—it is difficult to comprehend." *The Secret Doctrine*, Blavatsky, II, 84.

The course of human events, like the entire solar system, is ever sweeping onward and upward in a great spiral of evolution, never standing still and never repeating itself. While we are apt to think that life is ever the same and that the same events happen over and over again, and while this seems true in a certain sense, yet if we study the life of an individual or group of individuals we will find that all are moving onward in a great curving spiral.

Life means eternal progress. We never return to the same position or to the same conditions; some elements are changed. While we often seem to return, we have simply rounded another curve of our Spiral of Life and have come to a point directly over our former position and should be able to look back over our career and learn its lessons. An understanding of this law of life will prevent many heartaches and much sadness, for with this understanding we see that even the process of growing old, which is so often feared, is also progress, and the meetings and partings which seem so important are but transient and seeming. Friends meet and part and seem separated, yet if they are centered at heart they are anchored in the very center of gravity or the point around which the spiral of both their lives is eternally sweeping, hence are never really separated except in outer form. And even in the outer life they will meet again and again most unexpectedly each time the life-cycle sweeps around the spiral.

In each mighty sweep of the Spiral of life we should leave behind us all the sorrows and sufferings which we brought upon ourselves because we would not learn the needed lessons without them, and carry with us only the resulting experience, all that is true and vital out of the past experiences. Often we part from a friend in sorrow or anger yet later meet again in joy and love; for the anger, being but a gust of the passions of Earth, has long since died out and the thread of love, being the life-thread which holds us all together, reunites us. The sorrows and sufferings were but the results of the burning karmic fires, hence as the pure gold of Truth is freed from all impurities and dross, that which is left as a result of the burning is but ashes. And if we were to remain eternally in one spot and continue to do the same thing over and over the ashes would accumulate mountain high in that spot and extinguish all the joy and fire of life. This does not mean that we are not to remain in one home or city or employment year after year, but that *we are not to remain at a standstill mentally and spiritually*; that we are not to remain in one spot in consciousness, but must ever strive upward and onward.

Each nation, as well as each individual life, has its own spiral of evolution. Hence, when we gather a number of persons together in an Order such as this, where they are all inspired by the same ideals and objects to be attained, we must take into consideration, not only the sweep of the individual lives and the special course of the Order, but also the sweep of the life-cycle of the nation and of humanity as a whole; for each of these spirals is turning on its own axis and at the same time traveling onward through space.

We might picture this great sweep of life as a broad ribbon made up of the seven colors of the rainbow, each color with its own vibration and its own individual expression of life, yet all wound round and round the fiery core of a mighty spiral. If we looked closely at this broad ribbon with its various colors moving majestically onward and upward as a whole, we could see that it was made up of many whirling evolving units, and units within units, even as the hour is within the day, the minute in the hour and the second in the minute, yet all having their individual part in the same onward flight of time. In the same way the various units of evolving individual lives are sweeping along in their personal orbits and at the same time are a part of the great spiral of the Order which in turn has its place in the evolution of humanity. And as we find in this Order many students who belong to different nationalities, their life-spiral must in a measure parallel the spiral of the nation of their birth. But if this Order be the heart center of their individual life-spiral they will always swing around this as their real spiritual center. Thus will this spiritual center do much to unite many nationalities into one Spiral of Love. The individual lives are like the stars in the heavens, each turning upon its own axis, yet all being swept around and onward with the great sweep of the evolving Cosmos.

This is true of all manifestations of life, and especially is it noticeable in the life of this Order and the individuals who compose it; for the Order has reached a point where its Teachings are taking a more decided place in the world's affairs; where it is taking a new turn on the upward arc of its spiral. It is now at what might be called a cross-roads. Not a cross-roads in the sense that it turns from its course and goes at cross purposes or deviates from its former teachings or ideals, but a cross-roads in the sense that its onward and upward sweep crosses over the lower levels of its former path and hence must gather up the karmic seeds left behind at the previous turn and carry them with it.

It is much like a cyclone that sweeps up into its heart at each turn all that is not utterly destroyed, with the great difference that in the case of the force of the Order the seeds of experience, truth, beauty and strength are gathered up not to be destroyed, but to be saved and carried forward into the new day and age.

At every turn of the great cyclic Wheel of Life the Great Ones send out their messengers; mortals selected from those who have taken certain steps in unfoldment, who have received special training and gained certain qualities from the fiery experiences of the last sweep of their spiral. "The 'Army' at each angle is the Host of Angelic Beings (Dhyan Chohans), appointed to guide and watch over each respective region, from the beginning to the end of a Manvantara."[1] These Great Ones say to their messengers: "Go forth into all the world carrying with you neither purse nor scrip. Teach, comfort, help and gather in all who answer your call, even those at a great distance." The words "purse and scrip," have generally been misinterpreted and associated with the thought of a beggar who has no money and who depends entirely upon the Lord to supply his wants. This is a very materialistic and limited interpretation, for in its symbolic meaning to travel without purse means to go forth with nothing to tie one or hold one in bondage to money, while "no scrip" means that there are no contracts, papers or binding conditions of business which demand our attention and hamper our activities.

When in *St. Luke* we are told to "carry neither purse, nor scrip, nor shoes: and salute no man by the way,"[2] by wearing "no shoes," the meaning is that the disciple is to have his understanding uncovered and unhampered by preconceived opinions; by saluting no man it means to be so settled in his own mind as to what his ideals are and so determined to fulfill them that no controversy can turn him

---

[1] *The Secret Doctrine*, Blavatsky, I, 144.
[2] *St. Luke* X, 4.

aside; for as long as he is not firmly grounded in his faith, and as long as he has any duty or business that binds him he is not free to go forth as a messenger of the Lord. In other words, going back to our first simile, such messengers are glowing coals heated by the flaming core of the spiral which, while free and independent, have not lost their fiery hearts or been burned to the dead ash which must fall back to Earth and wait until the experiences of a new life-wave have again started their hearts to glowing.

These messengers must go forth because many of the units composing its true Inner Flame have reached a point in their cyclic sweep where they must touch the inner Heart of the Order. By those composing its true Inner Flame we do not mean merely those who are gathered at the earthly Center, for many have been drawn close and have made the personal touch and felt the warmth and power of the Heart Center and then the cyclic sweep of their lives has carried them out and far away. And so must it ever be. But those whose consciousness has correlated with the Heart of the Flame around which the spiral of the Order is revolving, and have found it to be the same center around which their aspirations and spiritual life is centered, will find themselves evolving ever close to the Heart of the Order, no matter how far away they may live in the flesh, and some day will find themselves united, even as a living cell, in the very Heart of the Flame. And it is necessary that many other lives in many different parts of the world shall also be given an opportunity to draw closer and feel the magnetic forces and the spiritual attraction of the Flame of Love which is the true center and core of the Order.

All members of the Order are sweeping onward in their personal orbits while at the same time they are a part of the evolution of the Order. Some, in their individual evolution, follow closely the changing conditions of the Order, while others are apparently going off in other directions. Yet this is only apparently so, for they are still a part of the great sweeping spiral of the Order. For example, a fly confined in a car of a swiftly moving express train might be crawling or flying in the car in the direction opposite to that in which the train was moving, yet it would all the time be carried onward by the train.

So is it with many individuals connected with the Order. Therefore, they should not be discouraged if they cannot remain in as close touch with the Order as they would like. Neither should they be upset by the many changes that may come into their lives, nor at the many changes that have come to the Order and that will come in the future. They are simply turning in the orbit of their own personal evolution, their own individual wheel of life, which apparently turns in a different direction from that of the Order. But if they are living not merely in the outer life but are striving to live consciously in the Inner Life of their Real or Divine Self, and if the personal touch they have made with the Order and its Teachings has lighted the spark of the Inner or Soul-life within them or has blown its embers into a glowing Flame of Love that brings an illumination into their lives, then that Flame, being one with the Universal Flame of the One Life, has united itself with the greater and wider evolution of all life. Hence, they have touched and correlated with the Inner Center around which the Order is sweeping and can never be separated from it in their hearts. Their heart's love will go with its Founders wherever they are directed to carry the message, and that devotion and ardor will be continually sending them streams of love, strength and inspiration; for all such have identified themselves to some extent with all humanity and desire that everyone shall hear the glad tidings and have the same opportunity for help which they have had. Hence, like the fly in the train, while they may have to walk in their personal orbit of life seemingly in an opposite direction, the Real Self of them is all the time rushing onward and upward, one in heart and Soul with the work of the Order.

There are many factors to be considered in connection with
this idea of the Spiral of Evolution. First of all, when things go
a little differently from the way our limited outlook leads us to
expect, we are apt to cry out and say: "Why are there so many
changes in my life? Why do I seem to be left behind and alone?
How am I to know that this thing that I have held so close to my
heart, these Teachings that have so far answered my heart-cry for
Light and explained my problems, how shall I know that they are
the thing for me when the Order seems to be sweeping on and
leaving me still turning round and round in my own little orbit?"

The answer is easily found. Are we realizing in our inmost Soul
the vital fact that this Order is a manifestation of cosmic law and
cosmic force? That it is a universal and world-wide movement?
Have we not only consecrated our lives to the higher ideals, but
have we realized the part this Order plays in our lives and is
destined to play in the world's evolution? Have we realized its
importance, its immensity, its inexhaustible power to conquer all
difficulties and surmount all obstacles the world may place in its
path and steadfastly press on to its ultimate destiny in the greater
spiral of human evolution when its appointed time arrives? If we
have realized only a little of all these ideas we will know that its
onward sweep includes all mankind and hence no little orbit of
one condition, one little wheel of life, one little city or country can
encompass it and hold it fast. If we understand this we will say:
"Go on! Go on! If my feet seem tied, then give me the strength, O
Divine Law, to do my duty in my own little orbit until I am ready
for the next step, yet let me travel onward one in heart and mind
with the Order, giving my love, my strength, my understanding
and support to the Great Work it is destined to accomplish."

There is another question that has been voiced in the
hearts of many students, a question which has often puzzled

them, namely, "How shall I know who the Teacher is and when the Teacher is speaking? How shall I know when to believe the lessons and the personal letters I receive?" The answer is that whether we know or not makes little difference, life itself is really our Teacher. As we learn our lessons of life which the Great Law places before us; as we become aware of and respond to the Great Love that is overshadowing and striving to guide us, so will we know the truth and prove the words of the Teachings, whether they be words of truth and wisdom or not, no matter who speaks them.

We are not required to believe that they come from a Master of Wisdom. Our own heart's conviction must tell us that; for no claims are made. Neither do we have to believe that they are the result of inspiration and direct teaching from the higher worlds. The substance of life and help in the message itself must decide that. Neither are we given the name of a particular Master as authority, for truth is its own authority. For every Great Soul who has reached Mastery has mastered personality first of all and does not proclaim a name that can become a stumbling-block to undeveloped students; for either such a name tends to arouse their spiritual pride, because they are in personal touch with Master So-and-So, or by the indiscriminate use of the name they drag it in the mire of criticism and ridicule and involve themselves in controversies which divert their minds from meditation, peace, harmony and spiritual things.

The Masters have also conquered the desire for personal recognition, admiration or even gratitude. Their only desire is "to do the will of Him who sent me," and to do it silently and impersonally through the agency of truly humble disciples who are willing to work impersonally. The names of the Masters may be revealed to us within when we have correlated our hearts with them and so identified our lives with their Teachings as to warrant it. If, however, we find greater satisfaction in these Teachings than in the many others presented to us; if they sink deep into the hidden chambers of our hearts and bring light, comfort, peace, joy and wisdom, what matters it whence they come? All Light, love, wisdom and comfort is of God, and the channel through which they come is of little importance. "Verily, by their fruits shall ye know them." If the Teachings help us over the hard places in life and explain its many perplexing problems, then accept and follow them, asking not for authority. That which is said and the vital help it gives is the important thing, not who said it.

Again some have asked, "How are we to judge the Teachings? How are we to know that they are not merely the personal opinions of the Founders and have no cosmic truth or force back of them?" The answer is that they must be judged simply by the vital life of the ideas expressed, not by the imperfect personalities of the servants through whom they are presented, any more than we would judge physical food by the appearance of the waiter who presented it. We must ask ourselves, Have the Teachings rung true? How have they affected the lives of those who have endeavored to follow them? How have they helped to change the thoughts and influence the teachings of the world? Leave all personality out of it. The question is, Have we proved the truth of the Teachings, either in our own lives or in the lives of others? Has our own heart responded to them and given us the inner assurance and confirmation of their truth? That should be sufficient.

St. Paul left a monument of truth to point the way when he said: "Quench not the Spirit. Despise not prophesyings. Prove all things; hold fast that which is good."[3] In other words, we are to hold fast that which endures in spite of human mistakes and the imperfections of those who are striving to do the will of Him who sent them, even tho they are not perfected. Again he told us to "Try the spirits whether they are of God: because many false prophets are

---

[3] *I Thessalonians*, V, 19-21.

gone out into the world." By this he did not mean to confine his injunction to the challenging and testing of the disembodied so-called dead, but included a far wider and deeper meaning. He meant that in everything with which we are confronted in life we must seek for the Spirit of Truth back of it. Try the spirit animating it and see whether it be of Good. And this is what we ask each student of this Order and its Teachings to do: try out its Spirit.

Every Order, Movement or Society has its body, mind, Soul and Spirit. The body of these Teachings is that which gives them form—the printed page, the written letter, the spoken word. The mind of the Teachings is the concrete thought back of them, which to help us must awaken a similar conception in our own minds. The Soul of the Teachings is that force within them which gives them life, which holds them together, which makes them harmonize with and express the Great Law of Manifestation which is back of all evolution. But they also have a Spirit, that Divine Spark from the Central Flame of Life, the fiery core around which they evolve, the animating Principle of all Life.

Therefore to try the Spirit of a movement and its Teachings means that we are to consider each idea presented, and then if it receives the inner confirmation of our own Souls, put it into practice in our lives. If it be of God it will bless our lives and help on our spiritual evolution. If it be not of God it will soon come to naught; for the Spirit is Divine Life and without the Spirit of Truth there can be no enduring life, only a short period of apparent life which is but a galvanized activity simulating life, hence will soon disappear. If we would know the source of the Teachings, follow the Spirit up into the higher realms to its Source.

To know that we are one at heart with the great stream of Divine Life-force that constitutes the Spiral of this Order and to be thankful and grateful that greater light and understanding, more consummate wisdom, more Divine Love and Life is being poured out upon us and all humanity who will accept it—this is the thought that all earnest students of the Order should hold. Then will they be swept onward and upward with the great sweep of the Spiral of the Order, no matter how variously the little spirals of their individual evolution may twist and swirl.

CHAPTER XVII

LIFE WAVES

"All thy waves and thy billows are gone over me. Yet the Lord will command his loving kindness in the daytime, and in the night his song shall be with me, and my prayer unto the God of my life." *Psalms*, XLII, 7-8.

"Old things are passed away; behold, all things are become new." *II Corinthians*, V, 17.

In the previous chapter we considered life in its spiral manifestation; in this we will try to apply a phase of the law of spiral manifestation to life as we see it manifesting in our environment today. Conceive of a number of spirals of various sizes interblending and embracing the universe. It is evident that but a limited part of each spiral can be visible or even manifested at any one given spot or at a given time, yet at that spot there would appear many lines in the form of waves. A study of the higher non-Euclidean geometry reveals the fact that there is no such thing in Nature as a straight line, all lines being parts of greater or lesser curves, hence all lines of force are curved or waved as they manifest in their positive and negative aspects.

Since man is a microcosm or miniature universe, we naturally find the forces of his bodies—physical, astral, mental and spiritual—following the same law of wave-motion, and an understanding and utilization of this law is an important step toward the attainment of self-mastery. If we find ourselves one day riding on the upward curve or crest of a wave of life-force and cry: "All is well! There is no such thing as sickness, suffering, sin or poverty; all are but figments of the imagination, and have no existence!" with what a shock do we find ourselves on the morrow plunged into disillusion and discouragement by the downward sweep of the negative wave! just as the mariner at sea is plunged into the trough of the waves where he is cut off from the sight of other ships and seems to be alone and deserted and on an empty sea.

But if we realize that all Nature's forces work toward ultimate progression, and that the negative wave is of as much importance as the crest, we will endeavor to rule our lives accordingly. For just as we could not sustain our physical life if we breathed ever outward and never inward, so all the forces of Nature must have their rhythmic wave-motion of indrawing as well as outgoing if they are to gather the power, force and momentum for the cycle of expression, just as the ocean wave must indraw or descend into the trough if it is to gather the momentum necessary to rise again into manifestation at the crest. Yet we must ever strive for poise and control; for if we allow the waves to rise too high and become too tempestuous they must sink to a corresponding depth.

Even the physical breath follows a spiral path and is not a straight in and out motion, as many suppose. We can see and appreciate the rhythm of the physical breath, but the rhythm of the innumerable finer forces passing in and out of our bodies from various sources is not so easily observed. The breath, however, being the main vehicle of the life-stream, is the controlling factor. Hence, when the breath of life leaves the body the finer forces which co-ordinate with the breath to make it the Breath of Life are withdrawn, and it and all the other forces are left to work at random, individually and uncoordinated, and thus accomplish the work of dissolution and disintegration; a manifestation of the lowest or negative sweep of the life-wave in the physical body.

We can make our lives flow smoothly, harmoniously and rhythmically only as we understand and work with this law of rhythmic wave-motion. An unbalanced person lives on a tempestuous sea where the waves beat and toss the bark of life and weaken it and hasten it to its end. This might be compared to a tidal wave so great that it lifts the Soul out of the body and then sinks so low as to leave the physical body like an abandoned drifting wreck on the shore of time. Yet Jesus, the Christ-man, was symbolized as walking on the tempestuous sea, the waves of which obeyed his mandate, "Peace be still." Hence, since we are told that He was an example for us in all things, we, too, can follow in His footsteps and speak the word of peace that the tempestuous sea of life shall obey us.

When we find that we no longer maintain the highest crest of a wave of happiness, inspiration and achievement, instead of struggling against its descent or permitting ourselves to grow irritated, discouraged or hopeless, let us make an effort to remain calm and say to ourselves: "This is but the outgoing of some tide in my life. It is running out that it may return to the bosom of the boundless sea and gather greater force and momentum to sweep me higher up the Mount of Attainment at its next incoming cycle. Now is the time to examine myself and make ready for the new incoming wave." If it be the ebb of a wave of life-force—for we have health waves as well as others—much depression and suffering can be avoided by realizing that often periods of ill health are but the spent forces of certain life-waves which are retiring to gather power for a higher manifestation in a new cycle of life, even death being but a more complete retirement of the life-wave preparatory to a new incarnation.

During such periods hold in mind the picture of the ocean beach as the tide goes out. How clean and smooth and pure it is! The debris is washed out to sea and the beach is cleared and made ready for the new inrush from the mighty deep, bringing new and unknown forces and materials from unknown shores. Think, therefore, of the body as having

210 The Message of Aquaria

been swept clean and made ready for a new wave of health. Treat corresponding ebb tides in the mental, psychic and spiritual life in a similar manner.

But, as often happens on the seashore, if the last inrushing tide has been tossed higher than usual by some storm it may have washed up debris and wreckage far beyond the reach of the ordinary tides. Hence, if we are to have a clear beach, we must gather up and burn all the wreckage of the storm. So in our lives. If we permit storms of anger or grief or even of excitement to rush over us while the life-wave is at its height, as we sink into the negative or outgoing tide, we will find much wreckage to dispose of.

Under such conditions, instead of viewing our lives as tho buried in debris, sadly bemoaning our fate and saying, "My life is ruined," "I am consumed with a hopeless grief," "My life can never be joyous again," and so forth, we should use the time of the outgoing wave to gather up the debris. Then we should call down the living fire of the Christ-love and ask that all these things, which seem but wasted opportunities or wrecked and blasted hopes, shall be consumed and utterly transformed that the essence of good, *i.e.*, the lesson, that was in each may be built into our character, and all that was not for our good shall be washed away with the next outgoing tide, leaving our lives like the beach, clean, smooth and shining that they may reflect in all its glory the Spiritual Sun as it arises for a new day.

This planet on which we live also has many cycles or wave-motions. All the forces of the universe are passing around and through it in rhythmic waves. This can easily be verified by the study of an engineer's map of the magnetic variations of the Earth. Altho such a map is a study of but one of the cosmic forces manifesting on Earth, it will show that not only do the currents of magnetic force follow the laws of wave-motion, but are also manifestly a part of an immense spiral, the variations changing constantly as the

Earth passes from one condition to another, yet always in wave form.

In humanity this wave-motion is most marked as we pass from one Age to another, as from the Piscean into the new day of the Aquarian Age. The swirling and upset conditions resulting from the World War are but currents in the undertow of the ebb tide or negative swing of the life-forces of a great cycle of humanity sweeping out the debris of the past cycle that the incoming wave may be unobstructed and again the tremendous momentum necessary to swing mankind and the planet higher in the scale of evolution and spiritual expression than ever before.

As humanity experiences the ebb tide after the high and stormy wave of war, which in its long and incessant beating on the shore of life has strewn its wreckage far up on the beach, there is work for all to do, especially all advanced students and thinkers who realize the significance of the events through which mankind is passing. We must gather up the wreckage and make proper disposition of it that all its lessons may be learned, its good preserved and its mistakes corrected, that the incoming of the next tidal wave may but intensify the good and wash away all that is evil. This is already being sensed by thoughtful students; for already we see many bulwarks of the past being swept away—old modes of life, old ideas, old forms of government, of social order and of religion—and the wonderful promise of the New Day is beginning to dawn.

Can we not conceive that back of the terrible destruction we so deplore on Earth during the close of the Piscean cycle there is gathering a mighty force which will be poured out upon mankind in the wonderful New Era which is to follow? The wave of destruction was but a manifestation of the ebbing tide of the old cycle sweeping away many of the old mediaeval conceptions and making possible new and greater memorials which shall be raised to our God, expressed in forms better suited to our new and higher conceptions of the tender Love and absolute Justice of the Father-Mother God than were possible while mankind was floundering in the deep trough of the cycle of the Dark Ages.

Many of the most cherished treasures of religious art whose destruction is so deeply regretted expressed much of the old religious misconception of the grand and eternal Plan of Salvation; many perpetuated the literal, materialistic and narrow views held in the days when God was worshiped as an anthropomorphic Being; when salvation was regarded as the result of the literal pouring out of the human blood of an innocent victim as a propitiation for the sins which man was and still is creating; the days when man was taught the doctrine of "original sin," that he was vile and impure and condemned from birth; that he was a miserable sinner instead of a Son and heir of God and "joint-heir with Christ," having all the attributes and powers of God latent within him only awaiting unfoldment and expression.

In fact, even the continual repetition of "Lord have mercy upon us miserable sinners" in the service of thousands of churches throughout the Christian world for ages has peopled the mental and astral worlds with powerful thought-forms which, as they manifest through their creators, could not do otherwise than tend to make them the miserable beings they had claimed to be.

In those days man was taught to believe in God as a Being who could become jealous and give way to unreasoning anger; also in a hell of literal and unquenchable fire of brimstone, and in a mysterious worm which forever gnawed at the vitals of the damned. Man was taught that the punishment must last forever and ever, be the sorrow and repentance ever so sincere, and that this everlasting punishment was administered even to those who merely refused to believe in such doctrinal precepts. Even ignorance of the law was said to be no excuse, nor did it mitigate in any way the unthinkable punishment, so that the millions upon millions of human beings who had lived and passed away before such teachings were formulated, as well as the many millions who were living happily under other forms of religion, were all condemned to eternal damnation! With such monstrous doctrines taught in the name of the God of Love is it any wonder that man grew cruel, bloodthirsty and pitiless to his brother man? for no nation can ever rise higher than its conception of God.

Today mankind is beginning to understand that civilization is measured by its conception of God and the working out of its highest ideals. But in those days it was quite conceivable that to punish our fellow man here on Earth for a brief period that he might repent and be "saved" was far less horrible than that he should be punished forever and ever in a burning hell. Hence this teaching was considered the best way to bring man to a realization of the enormity of his sins, or more correctly to an understanding of the inharmony resulting from his own wrong way of thinking and acting, just as many parents even today think that the best way to correct and secure obedience of their children is to punish them. But we see that that false idea was the outgrowth of mistaken religious interpretation and teaching, just as parents are learning that corporeal punishment is not the best way to train children and secure their confidence and love.

Therefore, as the New Age dawns we are awakening to a higher conception of God; not as a stern parent, but of God as Divine Love; that "God is Love;" that "God so loved the world that He gave his only begotten Son, that whosoever believeth in him (the Christ) should not perish, but have everlasting life." And just as the former teaching tended to develop fear—the fear of a possible hell fire—and selfishness—the necessity of saving our own Soul first of all from a possible wrath—as we awaken to the new world-thought it tends to foster our love and trust in a tender, compassionate and ever-present Father-Mother God who knows that all children must be trained and wisely taught to understand the results of their disobedience and to assume their personal responsibility for it, yet who ever waits in love and compassion to forgive and show the children how to meet the results of their disobedience once they have learned their lessons from it.

Shall not the inrushing wave of new spiritual realization and religious conception lift us above talking and thinking of ourselves as miserable sinners? stop representing in literature and art a cruel, angry God and a mutilated Savior? The new realization must depict God as Divine Love, the sustaining power of the universe, whose beloved Son is the spiritual outshining of that Love—the Sun of Righteousness—sent to Earth, not to be cruelly murdered, but like the physical Sun—the physical manifestation of its prototype, the Spiritual Sun—to shine into the hearts of all God's children, and in this way pour out or sacrifice His life—give His spiritual life-force—that the seed of the Divine in man may sprout and come forth into manifestation in the daily life.

This does not involve the cruel death of a mortal, however godlike and divine, but is a glorious and a joyous sacrifice of the Greater that the lesser may have life and manifest in perfection. For the Sun does not die, altho it sacrifices its life-force—periodically sheds its symbolic "blood"—that all Nature may rise with it in a new and glorious springtime, or period of manifestation. Neither does the Son of God, the Christos, die, but sits down at the right hand of the Father, from whence He shall come again in His glory at each new springtime or Era in human evolution, bringing all His holy angels with Him, *i.e.*, bringing to humanity His holy Messengers (angels) who will unfold the true meaning of the symbology of these misunderstood truths. "For God, who commanded the Light to shine out of darkness, hath shined in our hearts, to give the Light of the knowledge of the glory of God in the face of Jesus Christ". "For I delight in the law of God after the inward man."

We are therefore *not inherently vile*, nor are we essentially miserable sinners, but are joyous children of God who, when properly taught, delight to do His will; "joint heirs with Christ" to the Divine Love, which is the manifestation of God in and to us. We are the negative expression or wave of God, the positive wave touching Earth that humanity, made in His image, might rise higher and higher until the great wave of humanity reaches its crest and breaks upon the shore of eternity, one with the Father.

The beloved Son (Sun of God) descended and became embodied in flesh and dwelt among us that those whose eyes were opened might behold his glory, "the glory as of the only begotten of the Father, full of grace and truth . . . . . . And of his fullness have we all received." Plain language this! And we wonder at the darkness of the minds of men who could make literal the blood sacrifice of the personified outpouring of Divine Love—poured out into the hearts of His ignorant, willful and misguided children—and believe that such a crime would be an acceptable sacrifice to the heart of Divine Love, especially as it has proved so inadequate to save the world from sin! The Redeemer of man and the universe is indeed the mystical Christ-force which is shed abroad like the physical Sun that none perish but all have eternal life; that Force whose spiritual pressure for expression enables even the lowest trough of the sea of humanity to gain the power and momentum to rise to its highest expression. For without this Christ-force that is inherent in every Soul, nothing can be accomplished. This is the Way, the Truth and the Life; no man cometh unto the Father but by and through this cosmic Christ-force.

Ever since those Dark Ages the great body of humanity, as powerful in its God-given strength as Samson, has, like Samson, been bound as with willow withes; so bound mentally and spiritually that it has been forced to accept the literal interpretation of the Scriptures as determined by a small group of men during the darkest period of man's intellectual conceptions. The Christian Church—a mighty force if it were spiritually awake and its inner mysteries fully understood and taught, indeed, a chosen vehicle for the Christ-force—has grown comfortably and lazily fat, fed upon the authority and interpretations of bygone ages.

It has become much easier to follow in the footsteps and accept the precepts of modern commentators and textbooks than to strive to enter into the spiritual understanding and realization of the sainted early Church Fathers who understood the symbolic and esoteric nature of the Gospels and who breathed into the symbols and ritual of the Church the mysticism of their illumined consciousness resulting from personal communion with the Spirit of Truth or the Christ-consciousness. In the symbols, sacraments and ritual and teachings of the early Church there can be found all the instruction needed to satisfy every inquiring mind and all the spiritual food needed to feed humanity *if it is mystically understood and spiritually interpreted and taught.* Yet, alas, it is a common thing to find ordained ministers who dare not give to their flocks the golden grains of spiritual truth concerning the Mysteries which the Christ-light has revealed to them, lest they lose their positions, and others who have left the ministry because they were not permitted to give voice to the revelations of Truth given by the Light Within; for unless they feed their flocks with the outer husk of accepted exoteric doctrines and stereotyped interpretations, they are made to feel that the sacred calling of the ministry to "feed my sheep" holds no place for them, no latitude being allowed for advances in interpretation in harmony with the advances in world knowledge or for the illumination of the Spirit.

St. Augustine, one of the greatest of the early Church Fathers, tells us plainly that: "What is now called the Christian religion has existed among the ancients, *and was not absent from the beginning of the human race* until Christ came in the flesh, from which time true religion, which existed already, *began to be called Christian*."[1] Yet the ancient and universal symbols are now either covered with dust of accumulated traditions and explanations, settled and fixed as their ultimate and only meaning during the most benighted period of human development, or they are put aside as being too precious to permit of expert inspection, interpretation and valuation; and one who dares to question further is told that "such things belong to the mysteries of God and are not meant to be inquired into!"

Can we wonder, then, why so many churches are sparsely filled? Why sensationalism and outside and secular attractions of all kinds—even concerts and moving pictures—are resorted to that crowds may be attracted and the Church appear seemingly to be accomplishing its mission? Yet just as there has never been a time—even in the darkest ages of ignorance—when the spiritual understanding of some great Soul has not shone forth as a star of brilliant light and glory, so today God has not left His children comfortless, in darkness and without a prophet—meaning "one who speaks for God," or reveals the esoteric wisdom. Those who watch through the night have seen the heavens open and have seen the Angels reveal the glory of the hidden Mysteries of God to mankind, altho few there be who follow them.

But we are told that "There is nothing hid that shall not be revealed. . . . Because it is given unto you to know the mysteries of the kingdom of heaven." The symbols and their true interpretation may be likened to the ancient Temple of the Sphinx buried in the drifting sands of the desert with only the image on its roof visible to man. Altho even the image is not understood, we are told that the same winds (breath of God) that buried it beneath the sand—really that it might be preserved for man when he was able to understand its mystical message—shall, in due

---

[1] *Retractions*, St. Augustine, 1, 13.

time blow away the sand, that its wonderful mystic lessons may once more be revealed to mankind.

As the New Age gradually dawns and the incoming tide of the New Cycle rises, and as the New Humanity awakens in its illumined consciousness and the strong man stretches, like Samson awakening from his sleep, the withes of tradition with which man's religious conceptions have been bound will be broken "as a thread of tow is broken when it toucheth the fire." Indeed, they are already breaking rapidly, one after the other, as the Fire of the Lord descends to "thoroughly purge his floor, and gather his wheat into the garner." Even tho the ignorance of priestcraft has put out Samson's eyes, yet today the "little child" is leading him between the pillars of the churchly temple, and when he has lifted up his voice to God and stretched forth his hands three times, need we be surprised if the whole man-made structure of misconception and misinterpretation crumbles and leaves standing only the original, true and beautiful foundations? that the incoming wave of the true priesthood—prophet, priest and king—shall have room unmolested to erect its altar to the living God!

But we must not overlook the fact that religion is the God-given vital heart organ of humanity, through which the spiritual life-blood is meant to flow that the whole body of mankind may be full of life. *Religion is therefore absolutely necessary* to the spiritual health and welfare and progress of mankind. This is amply proved by history, for when a people or nation loses "faith in the gods" or spiritual ideals, in the reality of the invisible worlds and of spiritual Beings, Teachers, etc., and no longer makes religion a part of its consciousness and daily life, such a people soon degenerates and passes away; witness the fall of Babylon, Egypt, Greece, Rome, etc. Therefore, religion must never be destroyed, but corrected or healed, when infected with materialism. And its healing must come from a conscious realization by the brain (the thinking portion of humanity) that "the blood of Christ" does indeed cleanse us from all sin or redeems all our mistakes; from a realization that it is the duty of all the cells (persons) in the body of humanity to give their force to build into the heart of mankind living vital cells, to make straight the paths through which the spiritual life-force (the Christ-force) or mystical "blood" can flow.

Yet those who still remain under the shadow of the old cycle scarcely realize that they are bound and are slaves in the hands of the Philistines. Therefore, they deplore the passing of the old and, like the child who builds its tiny house upon the beach when the tide is out, they are enthused with the beauty of that which is and are in despair when the inrushing tide of a New Era threatens to sweep away their old creations.

The Piscean cycle, which is now passing, was an intellectual cycle, and during the two thousand-odd years of its sway, mankind has been perfecting the lowest aspect (feet) of his understanding. Intellect and reason have been the ruling factors, and because of this it has been a cycle of materialism; for intellect demands only that which it can see, handle and classify. But it has been a very important cycle in the unfoldment and progression of this planet and of man's relation to it. Therefore, do not get the idea that because the physical universe represents the lowest and most dense vibration of manifested Spirit and the lowest arc of the life-wave, and materialism represents the lowest and most dense phase of intellectual development, that the intellectual and material attainments of man are of little importance. The cycle of materialism was indeed the negative expression of a great racial life-wave, but one that was necessary to gain the momentum that shall make the wave of the New Age reach its destined height in the attainment of spiritual development and realization.

The phase of mind which the Piscean cycle has developed is the rational mind of the intellectual man, or what in the

Eastern teachings is called *Lower Manas*, but the coming
Aquarian Cycle must develop the superconscious mind or *Buddhi
Manas*. The subconscious mind, or man's consciousness of the
elemental forces operating through him in common with the
lower kingdoms, was developed in long previous Ages, when
the relation between animal man and the material universe was
established. The rational mind occupies the middle region, the
lowest sweep of its vibratory waves almost touching, yet seldom
making full conscious contact with the subconscious mind, and
its highest crest of attainment reaching up to but seldom making
complete contact with the superconscious mind of the Higher Self.
Yet some day this rational mind when stimulated by a different
wave of force coming from the heart, will touch the lowest waves
of the spiritual mind, then in its lowest sweep it will touch the
highest waves from the subconscious mind. Then will man be
able to fulfill the edict, "Man, know thyself." It is only the Christ-
consciousness manifesting through the heart, and crucified by the
rational mind or nailed to the cross of materiality, that can descend
into the lower regions (subconscious) and preach to the Souls
imprisoned there or subjugate and control the forces of the lower
mind and through the consciousness thus illumined, make man,
in very truth, Lord of Creation and the image of God the Father.

Just as man's body, during the short period of gestation of
the fetus, passes through all the phases of evolution—vegetable,
animal and human—so in man's mind can be found all grades
of elemental consciousness, whose essence has been left behind
as man passed through the lower elemental forms. It also contains the consciousness of the four elemental kingdoms, earth, air,
fire and water. But the rational mind has no link with that great
store of lower consciousness until, through having learned the
desirability of correlating his consciousness with that of the spiritual or superconscious mind, man learns to build up a bridge of

spiritual conceptions over which the higher consciousness can flow to enlighten him.

Only when the Spiritual Sun has shot down a Ray of itself into the darkness of that vast field of lower consciousness and the door of man's understanding is opened by his correlation with the spiritual mind can a full consciousness of all the kingdoms of Nature be possible. This will be one of the attainments the New Age will make possible for man. But with it will come the mighty and inevitable test as to what he will do with his new-found powers. Will he use them as a means of helping on the unification of man and Nature and aiding the uplift of the lower kingdoms, or will he use them for his own selfish aggrandizement and power?

As the inrushing tide of the New Day sweeps over humanity there must be those who are duly qualified and prepared to help their less evolved brethren to learn the wonderful lessons of the New Age. Many have come in His name, claiming to be prophets of the New Day, yet each emphasizing but one phase of the Great Law so that much confusion results and hungry hearts cannot hear the gospel "in their own tongue," so that instead of a baptism of pentecostal fire, it is more like a severe storm of lightning and thunder.

The Great Masters of Wisdom have stored up the entire philosophy of the Wisdom Religion so greatly needed in the coming age, ready to be given to mankind. But it cannot be given like rain on a rock, lest it fail in its mission. It must be given out through agents who have learned the lessons of the past Age in the cultivation of the rational mind, and who have illumined it with the rays of the Spiritual Sun and hence are ready to reach up understandingly into the Divine Mind and consciously carry their illumination down to the lowest point of the wave. For if we are to have a reconstructed religion, which shall meet the needs of the New Age, it must be all-inclusive; must be both philosophical and devotional, rational and inspirational.

To place such a system fittingly before the world a new order of
ideas in education, specialization and efficiency must be grasped.
As long as men are content to be tied with the old withes of
prejudice and continue to hold to the mediaeval idea of beggary
for spiritual teachers; that such teachers must be freaks or beggars,
gladly living on the pittances the more worldly throw into their
laps, just so long must the world expect to go hungry for spiritual
food or be fed by the unsatisfying scraps found here and there as
today; be puzzled by the many contradictory partial statements
of Truth rife today, or be led astray by every teacher who can
produce phenomena sufficiently startling.

As to the support of spiritual teachings there should be but
one question. Is the spiritual food I am receiving worth having?
Does it help me in the daily living of my life in the world? Does
it satisfy my reason as well as my heart hunger? If so, then it will
help others in a similar way, hence, is worthy of the best support I
can give it. How, then, can I best help to make it possible for such
teachings to be spread broadcast to mankind? For until spiritual
teachers can be properly supported and be left free from either the
necessity of spending the best part of their time earning a living
or the great mental anxiety, or even the time and effort given
to so-called "demonstrating supply," the world need not expect
fully equipped spiritual teachers. Those fitted to give the world
such specialized help must be enabled to devote all their time and
attention to such work.

As to spiritual teachers "demonstrating supply," a phrase so
glibly used in such cases, there is no doubt but that the Great Law
could amply support all who devoted their lives to its promulgation
and expounding. It could even feed, clothe and support in idleness
all the children of men if it so desired, but that is not the order of life.
The plan has always been, "If any would not work, neither should
he eat." And since man's higher development requires spiritual
food as truly as his physical development requires physical food,

and since those capable of obtaining and preparing such food have to exercise the highest of talents and spend many hours of concentrated application to present such food, one of the important lessons that humanity needs to learn in the New Age is that humanity itself must supply ample support to those capable of giving them the best, else humanity must be satisfied with that which can be supplied at odd moments. If this ideal is held by each student, then the inrushing new wave of spiritual revelation, will find channels, flumes and conduits already prepared, by means of which its foaming crest, filled with dynamic spiritual power, will not merely break on the narrow shores of advanced humanity, but will be carried far inland to water and refresh the thirsty multitudes and cause their latent seeds of Christhood to put forth, sprout and grow and bring forth fruit unto the salvation of mankind. The harvest is at hand, but the laborers are few.

Chapter XVIII

THE MESSAGE OF THE SPHINX

The whole essence of truth *cannot be transmitted from mouth to ear*. Nor can any pen describe it, not even that of the Recording Angel, unless man finds the answer in the sanctuary of his own heart, in the innermost depths of his divine intuition. It is the great *Seventh Mystery* of Creation, the first and the last. . . . It can be represented only in its apparent objective form, like the eternal riddle of the Sphinx. *The Secret Doctrine*, Blavatsky, II, 543.

As it has been, so is it; and so shall it be forever more. Far back in the beginning of recorded history the same world-old truths that this present Aquarian Age must express were symbolized in imperishable stone. This New Age was alluded to later by Jesus as "the Sign of the Son of Man in heaven." The Age when a new manifestation of the "Lord of Light" should again "declare the things which are hidden" was symbolized and foretold in the majestic image of the Sphinx. This image was carved during an age when our solar system was passing through the same zodiacal conditions it is now facing, altho at that time on a lower arc of the Spiral of Evolution. Age after age has rolled by. Race after race has come and gazed and gone, ever seeking to answer the mysterious questions expressed in that mighty recumbent figure. Yet the great riddle of the Sphinx is still mutely propounded: "Man, whence? Why? Whither? What is the meaning of evolution? What the promise of the Great Day to come? What wait I for?"

The true Sphinx is double-sexed and has wings, either folded or raised, altho in some cases and for special reasons the sexes are separated. In such case the two images, male and female, usually face each other with a growing tree between them, the male being bearded and the female having wings. They thus point out the eternal truth that it is only through the combined power of the two—the mother-love fructified by the wisdom of the father—that the Tree of Life can bring forth its fruit or that humanity can learn to spread its wings and lift up the Scorpion into the Bird of Life.

But the characteristic Sphinx is double-sexed just as is Aquarius, in which the Man falls on his knees in his ardent desire to pour out the Water of Life (feminine) to quicken the seeds of future powers and faculties in man. As the Egyptian *Ritual* describes it: "Praise be to thee, O Ra (the Sun-god) . . . . . Thou art the two bodies of the Double Sphinx god."

Altho at present buried so deeply in the sand that little more than its head and fore paws are visible, the Great Sphinx of Giza at one time stood upon a high hill and formed the roof of a sacred temple. Even today, between its paws, a shrine has been found dedicated to the Sun-god Harmachis (Horus), the "Great Light of the World." But ere the Aquarian Age has entered upon its second decanate, the sand that now so nearly buries it will be removed and many wonders and facts confirming the truths destined to be brought to light in this New Age will be found, as predicted by Madame Blavatsky in *The Secret Doctrine*[1] many years ago.

What then is the fundamental idea symbolized by that mighty image? What but the dawn of the new Age of Light, the great Aquarian Age, when the Sign of the Son of Man shall reign in heaven; when the ancient priesthood shall be gathered from the Four Winds again to receive the ancient wisdom of the Spiritual Sun direct from its Infinite Source and give it forth that its rays of Divine Truth may again illumine the minds and warm the hearts of mankind. The very name of the Sphinx identifies it as a Bearer of

---

[1] Vol. III, 95.

Light, for in the Egyptian tongue its name is Hu or Hu-piter, meaning the Hu-father, or Father of Light, being identical with the Greek Hu, or Ju-piter, the Father of the Gods. As the *Ritual* says, "Hu-iti. Thou art the Lord of Light, and declarest the things which are hidden."

In this mighty figure we see symbolized the Foundation Stone of the Universe, the cosmic cross, composed of the four signs of the zodiac of which Aquarius the Man is the head and ruler, *i.e.*, its hind quarters are those of the Ox (Taurus); its fore quarters those of the Lion (Leo); its head and breasts those of a human being (Aquarius); its wings those of the Eagle, and its tail that of the Scorpion.[2]

That this figure was meant to prophesy an Age when these four zodiacal signs should occupy the place they do in the heavens today and point to the true man, the Aquarian, as the one who could read the riddle of the Sphinx, is indicated in the many little comprehended legends of the Sphinx in which it is represented as devouring men, and in many examples of Egyptian and Greek art, in which the Sphinx is seen either seizing, standing upon or tearing man to pieces. For so must these eternal truths seize man and through the ages tear from him his lower propensities that the true Man may come forth. The reply of Edipus to the riddle of the Sphinx, "What animal is it that walks on four legs in the morning, on two at noon and on three in the evening?" shows that only man can solve the riddle; for his reply was that man crawls upon all fours in his childhood, walks upright during maturity and with a cane in old age. Thus ever does the riddle of the Sphinx have man for its solution.

In the Egyptian Sphinx the wings are folded, for the learned priests knew well the length of time that must elapse ere humanity as a whole could open the dense *elytra* which encased its wings, unfold the wings and rise into the higher realms of consciousness. Similarly in another favorite

---

[2] See Pages 26, 90.

Egyptian symbol, the scarab, the folded wing-cases indicate the dense covering that has been placed over all that is symbolized by the uplifting and transmuting of the Scorpion into the Eagle. They also signified that mankind must pass through its beetle stage, during which, while possessing wings with which to soar, he is still slowly crawling upon the Earth and bringing forth through the lower aspect of his creative powers, verily a scorpion biting the heel of the Rider.

This stupendous symbol of the Sphinx was carved out of a single rock 189 feet long, at a time so remote that in an inscription of the Fourth Dynasty (4700 B.C.), it is mentioned as a monument that was only "found by chance" during that reign, and whose origin was *even then* lost in the night of time, altho it is usually assigned to Cheops by exoteric scholars. It rises out of the pyramid field and faces due East, gazing steadfastly through the ages out over the Nile valley toward the Source of light.

In those long past ages *The Order of Christian Mystics*[3] had its birth. It was then that the mighty mystic teachings were given to the Race and the meaning of the symbol foretold to those Souls who were entrusted with its manifestation in that Age; for it was then as now an expression of the Great Work for the enlightenment of humanity founded on definite lines by those Divine Masters whose work throughout the ages is to unfold to man the sacredness of all that this mighty image of the Sphinx symbolizes.

And the seed of those teachings then sown in mystery and secrecy has been watered and nurtured through the ages until they are now beginning to blossom forth in the sunlight for all who are attracted to them. For in every Age at least some few have incarnated who in those early days had been taught these Mysteries and vowed themselves to their promulgation. Even during the darkest days of ignorance and persecution the light of these Great Truths has been cher-

---

[3] See *The Key of Destiny*, Curtiss, 202-5.

ished by the few, for the Masters of Wisdom have never lost their touch with mankind nor been without their illumined disciples on Earth. *The Order of Christian Mystics* is again put forth in this present Age as one more link in the golden chain of truth which connects mankind with the Divine Teachers.

And today, as this great Aquarian Age begins its cycle, those same Souls must once more gather together their reincarnated students and followers that that which was symbolized in stone may be manifested in the world today in living flesh, this time erected in the hearts and lives of men. But in that far off time, seeing the end from the beginning and knowing the impossibility of preserving unmixed with error and misconception the mighty esoteric truths for which this Order stands, they were preserved for those who knew, for those who could understand, in the majestic figure of the Sphinx. Therefore, each one who is today strongly drawn in heart and mind to the Teachings of *The Order of Christian Mystics* was no doubt a follower of these mystical truths in those ancient days, when the Celestial Teachers descended and gave directions how this sacred Order and its principles should forever be preserved intact until the day of their complete manifestation.

As the new Aquarian Age dawns, the Great Teachers realize only too well that it is not sufficiently helpful to force mankind to delve into the musty records of the past for its spiritual food, for in those past ages of general ignorance and intellectual darkness many vital truths had to be hidden or at least veiled from the ignorant which today, at the dawn of the day of fulfillment, must be revealed. For their teachings form a *living* philosophy which will always be expressed in every age in a way to meet the needs of each age. They are eternally old yet, like the Sun which remains the same, yet rises anew for each new day, they are forever new. For they contain the Wisdom of Life, symbolized by the Tree of life which grows by the River of Life and bears its fruit each month for the healing of the nations.

Hence it is fitting, as the Great Day draws near when the many scattered ones are to be assembled, that there should be at least a few gathered together whose hearts and minds are attuned in perfect harmony, united in love and illumined by understanding, and once more have the Riddle of the Sphinx in its spiritual aspect elucidated for the betterment of mankind.[4]

Just as that stony figure, with its imperishable message to humanity, has stood upon the border of the desert, enduring the fierce heat, the storms and the forces of the ages without disintegration, so has this Order endured throughout the ages and its message been given to man in each succeeding cycle, under various names suited to the times. Again and again have the terrific sand storms of worldly criticism and opposition beat upon it until it seemed almost extinct and its message distorted and lost to sight. Yet as its day dawns in each cycle the winds of heaven blow away the accumulated sand and those who belong to its tribe are gathered under its banner and are once more thrilled and enlightened and fed by its mystic message, presenting the world-old truths in language suited to the age. For no movement that is under the active present-day inspiration of the Great Ones will attempt to present the great truths of life in the obscure jargon which may have been necessary in the Dark Ages of physical persecution and possible physical death. For Their object now is not to obscure truth, but to reveal it in such a way as to help present-day humanity.

And just as none can look into the eyes of that great stone image, with their human gaze piercing the desert depths, without feeling a thrill of awakened inner sight, so today none who were once its followers can look into the Eye of the Order (the center of its symbol)[5] without feeling a thrill as its rays pierce the darkness of their understanding and bring to them the Light of their ancient wisdom.

---

[4] See *Realms of the Living Dead*, Curtiss, 283.
[5] See *The Voice of Isis*, Curtiss, Chapter XXXIV.

As we stand upon the threshold of this New Age, the cruel blasts of sand and the hot scorching winds of the desert may sweep over us. Yet we wait, resting like the Sphinx in powerful strength. The patient endurance of the Sphinx is needed to win the crown. Many hearts have cried out in the agony of their waiting, "How long, O Lord? How long?" Many litle ones have groped their blind way through the things of the outer life, seeking Truth. To all these we bring the message of the Sphinx. The storms of ignorance, sectarianism and priestcraft have piled the sands of misconception up around the Mystery of Truth until it seems to stand today with but its head above the sands. And yet its countenance is filled with unutterable longing, love and patience.

Like the Sphinx, deep in our hearts we know that the incarnation has never dawned when we have not stood in the midst of life; when our hearts have not beat in response to the roll call of the living, even tho we have forgotten whence we came and whither we are going. We, too, have stood on Egypt's sands; have given up our life for this Great Cause. We, too, have been born again and again; have struggled and hoped and despaired and laid down our lives with trust in the Great Law. Yet always, as life departed, the vision of the Reality has been held before us.

We know that incarnation after incarnation the misinterpretation of divine symbols and scriptures has erected dense, heavy slabs of misconception around our mind and heart, so that forgetfulness—the price of Earth existence—has covered over or blotted out the memory of the past. Yet, as in the carvings of the Sphinx, there has been impressed upon our Soul-consciousness a dim understanding of the mystery concealed within our heart, in which we will find the answer to the riddle of our life and the work we must perform. Many put their hands to the plow, yet look back and are fixed to the spot until a new incarnation. But there are a few who never can go back, because the look in their eyes is compounded of the imperishable qualities of the four signs composing the Sphinx, to *Know*; to *Dare*; to *Do* and to *Keep Silent*.

Let us for a moment disregard the passage of time and once more see ourselves assembled in that ancient Egyptian crypt beneath the Sphinx. Let us once more hear the thunderous tones of the Celestial Teacher as He comes again to tell us that the task then outlined is now almost accomplished; that the thing then symbolized in stone is almost ready to be expressed by a statue of living flesh and blood; in a united body of faithful followers of the Law, which shall fulfill in its every detail that which was foreshadowed then in stone. Let us examine this mighty symbol and see the message it holds for us.

The flanks of the Ox give us the power to Do. Is not this Order resting upon those flanks, its power to Do? Has it not toiled and labored through the ages? Has it not been bowed with burdens to the Earth, the burdens of the hearts of its children? Has it not crouched on the edge of the desert of life, buffeted by storms, ignored by the multitude, almost buried in the sands of outer conditions, as it bore the burdens of the many who look to it for help? Yet through it all never has it forgotten that even tho a very Ox indeed, it is nevertheless yoked with the Divine Christ, whose command ever is, "Take my yoke upon you, and learn of me; and ye shall find rest unto your souls. For my yoke is easy and my burden is light."

Its fore quarters give us the power to Love and to Dare. Are they not those of the Lion? Has it not had the courage to use its fore quarters to seek out Wisdom and tear the acquired knowledge of the ages to shreds that it might feed on its inner meaning? Has not the Lion aspect of the Order manifested itself? Has not the great and powerful Love the support and balance that has made this Order endure, that is symbolized by the higher aspects of the Lion been resting in powerful strength? Has not this Love emanated

from the very heart of the Order since its beginning, as the
perfume emanates from the Rose?

Has not the eternal stillness in which the Eagle soars given it
the power to Keep Silent? Humanity has for ages looked with
wonder upon that which is symbolized by the wings, *i.e.*, the
transmutation of the Scorpion into the Eagle. Too long in past
ages has the Order kept its wings closely folded, veiling the
mysteries of the creative life-force. Too long has it struggled to
teach mankind obscurely how to unfold its wings, how to spread
and rely upon them to soar into the higher realms with the power
and freedom of the Eagle, far above the sting of the Scorpion.
But today its wings are lifted up from its shoulders. Are not its
mighty talons conquering the force of the Scorpion, heeding not
its sting, and crying aloud for the breath of the New Age to bear
it into the higher realms? Again and again have the cutting sand-
storms beaten down these wings until they seemed almost broken,
yet today we see them lifted with the power of the Aquarian, the
Man Who Conquers.

The world has brought accusation after accusation and sting
after sting, saying: "How dare this Order unveil the Mystery of the
Ages and show mankind how to open its wings through the power
of sex uplifted, teaching that it must be pure and holy and used as
a manifestation of the Christ-life!" Yet these storms have rolled
from it, as the feathers of the Eagle shed the raindrops as it flies
fearlessly through the passing storms, and have left it unscathed.
Is it any wonder then that today we see the question of sex being
lifted up throughout the world as the ideas concerning its innate
purity and holiness gradually spread and permeate all classes of
thought and all advanced teachings?

Its human head gives us the power of the Aquarian to
Know. See how the normal human livable aspect of the
Teachings it promulgates are always presented to the world.
See how the breasts of the Mother are always filled with
nourishment for her children, always giving, giving, giving

of her spiritual food to all. And look you! Upon her brow sits the kingly cap, the Ureus, which vandal hands have tried to tear from her,[6] the crown of Man triumphant. It crowns only the Man Who Conquers, the Knower, the Aquarian, who is (a) Lord of the beast, (b) Tamer of the Lion, (c) Ruler of the Ox, (d) Transmuter and Uplifter of the Scorpion.

Thus is the Sphinx a symbol of this Order. And altho the desert of the outer life and its materialistic conceptions and consciousness seems barren and forbidding, and the scorching sands still whirl about it in fitful gusts at times, as we are passing through the reconstruction period of the ages, let us nevertheless realize how many ages we have waited for this day of freedom and upliftment, and not grow weary.

Try to understand the symbol of the Order.[7] Meditate upon it and realize the greatness of the work, the greatness of our privilege. For the time is at hand when it will be necessary for us to know and understand what is symbolized and what is meant by this Great Work. And it will not be many years, as Earth counts time, ere we will realize why we are connected with the great Celestial Hierarchy that is manifesting through this *Order of Christian Mystics*. Therefore, help spread its Teachings, so that they will no longer be merely symbolized by an image of stone, but shall be a living, vital factor in the upliftment of the race. We must *Know*, we must experience, we must *Dare* and we must *Labor* that the Silence of the ages may be broken and the Truth be revealed to the children of men.

Do not be impatient if the world does not respond at once; if it runs after other gods or congregates where the drums beat loudest. Do not blame it if at first it is afraid of the heights to which the wings of the Sphinx can bear it.

---

[6] Although the stones that complete the upper part of the *pallà* have been pried off, the forehead still shows part of the *Ureus*, the king's sign of Divine Wisdom—the Serpent (Wisdom)—coming from out the Head.

[7] See *The Voice of Isis*, Curtiss, Chapter XXXIV.

It takes time to learn spiritual aviation just as it does its physical counterpart. Wait patiently. Rest in peace, relying upon the imperishable foundation, the Temple of Truth that supports the Sphinx; for it is carved out of the solid "Rock of Ages."

Let us learn from our symbol the attitude of mind that shall give us endurance. Like the Sphinx, we will patiently bide our time. Let not despair or even impatience appear in the steady look of our eyes, no servility in our attitude, no droop to our uplifted wings. Rest in the infinite knowledge and calm confidence that tho nations rise and fall the Great Law moves ever on toward its fulfillment. Trust in the power of our symbol, for it has the brain that Knows, and within it is beating as one heart the hearts of all its children. In its nostrils is the breath of the Life Everlasting.

Chapter XIX

THE SECOND WOE

"One woe is past, and, behold, there come two woes more hereafter." *Revelation*, IX, 12.

"And he shall send his angels with a great sound of a trumpet, and they shall gather together his elect from the four winds, from one end of heaven to the other." *St. Matthew*, XXIV, 31.

"As for these things which ye behold, the days will come, in which there shall not be left one stone upon another, that shall not be thrown down." *St. Luke*, XXI, 86.

By all who listen with the inner ear of understanding there can be heard today "a great sound of a trumpet." It is sounding from the Four Winds in thunderous waves of heart-searching melody unheard as yet amid the strife of Earth. Yet the Elect, or every ear attuned to the overtones of life, can discern beneath the great unrest of the peoples of all lands the rhythmic beat of angel's wings; can feel as never man has felt before the urge to gather together, to stand shoulder to shoulder, sinking all differences of opinion, creed and politics in a united effort to prepare for the second woe, the second phase of the great war drama which closes this cycle, the first phase of which was the World War which has been fought out on the physical plane. "One woe is past; behold, there come two woes more hereafter."

The second woe will just as surely come as did the first; in fact it is now upon us. And if we are to learn wisdom from the bitter experiences of the past years it behooves us to preach continually the "doctrine of preparedness" for that which is sure to follow. This second woe will be the testing, cleansing and proving of the ideals and teachings of the religious and moral world and their natural consequences in the industrial, political and social fabric of the nations. We may say that the war drama must be again fought out, but now in the mental world with thoughts, arguments and ideals for weapons, unless we should so far forget the principles of *liberty of thought* and *freedom of religious expression* upon which this country was founded, as to permit physical conflict.

Just as the World War involved all the nations of the world, so that even those who called themselves neutrals nevertheless had to suffer from it, so this mental phase of the drama of the ages will involve every phase or presentation of religious thought or expression in all lands. And because our social fabric, our laws, politics and government are all supposedly built upon the religious conceptions of the people, the testing, scouring and purifying process must embrace every institution of man's building. Just as the physical war reached down into and altered the foundations of the society of nations, so shall the coming mental war reach down to and alter the very foundations on which our liberty of thought and our freedom of religious expression are based.

The religious conceptions, beliefs and thoughts of all humanity have built up a mighty temple composed of many, many "goodly stones." Each nation has builded its part of this temple, hence no division of mankind can entirely escape from the responsibility and the consequences which it entails; for it was this Temple of Humanity to which Jesus alluded when he said: "Not one stone shall be left upon another that shall not be thrown down."

"And the sixth Angel sounded, and I heard a voice from the four horns of the golden altar which is before God, saying to the sixth angel which had the trumpet. Loose the four angels which are bound in the great river Euphrates."[1] The trumpet sounded by the Sixth Angel announced the close of the fifth sub-race and the beginning of the sixth, over which he is to preside, as this sub-race is to foreshadow that which will be fully manifested in the Sixth Great Race.

[1] Revelation, IX, 13-14.

The meaning of the word Euphrates is "generation; to increase; the creative power," and the four angels which have been bound by man's misunderstanding and misuse of generation and his creative powers are the forces symbolized by the four beasts, the Ox, the Lion, the Eagle (Scorpion) and the Man. Until the present time only the very lowest aspect of generation has been recognized by humanity, but as the Sixth Angel—the Angel of the Sixth Great Race, sounding his call to our sixth sub-race—sounds his trumpet the Ox (labor) must learn to toil not merely for wages, but to bring forth perfect and helpful things for the good of all. The Lion must give us the courage to face our creations and through purified love redeem them. From the experiences of the Scorpion, whose sting has poisoned the springs of life, we must bring about the regeneration of sex that it may rise up like the Eagle. And the Man (Aquarius) must give us the wisdom of self-knowledge. With these forces we must lay the foundation upon which we are to erect our spiritual temple.

The river Euphrates is referred to in many places in the *Bible* as a bringer forth, a fruitful river, symbolizing the creative powers of man, and it was upon the bank of this river that the Tower of Babel (confusion) was built. It was confusion because only one aspect was recognized, hence the Tower of Babel symbolizes the limited perverted aspect of the true Temple of the Sun which must ultimately be built upon the banks of this great river. This points to the fact that in the coming New Age the spiritual or angelic aspects of the Divine Creative Force shall be released from the stream of pollution (the trail of the serpent) in which they have been bound for so many ages. Hence, one of the outcomes of the coming struggle must be a greater purity of thought in regard to all man's creative functions.

The name "Babel" also means "The Gate of the Lord" (Law) and the city was founded by Nimrod, the "mighty hunter before the Lord," or that force of evolution which founds or brings forth new manifestations of the Law. The

confusion of languages and the scattering of the people over all
the Earth symbolized the development of personal and intellectual
conceptions of the Law which were not in harmony with those
given humanity by its Divine Teachers upon which to build
its civilization. And only as humanity returns once more to a
common understanding of the universal spiritual principles of
the Wisdom Religion can the confusion of thought and teaching
be transformed into harmony and humanity be enabled to build
a Spiritual Temple which shall reach into heaven. The confusion
also symbolized the many individual aspects of concept and
creation which the great River of Life brings to man ere he can
build his individual Temple.

The angels referred to in the text represent the messengers
of the Lord (Law) whose trumpet call is finding response in the
hearts of the Elect; those who have elected to follow the Divine
Guidance. The Elect are those who are being gathered together
from the Four Winds to form the advance guard of the coming
Great Teacher, the Avatar. But the four angels loosed by the Sixth
Angel at the command of the Voice[2] are those who shall bring
about the cleansing of humanity's temple; who shall bring forth
into the clear searching light of truth every hidden idol, be it
enshrined in ever so sacred a niche, worshiped with ever so sacred
a ceremony or guarded and upheld by ever so plausible priestly
sophistries. In fact, everything that demands man's worship and
his spiritual or even his mental allegiance, must now stand forth
naked in the searchlight of truth which the coming Great Angel
(Avatar) is turning upon men's minds and hearts. For verily we
are living in the days in which it is decreed that: "There is nothing
covered, that shall not be revealed; neither hid, that shall not be
known."

The Voice which gave the command to release the four
angels came "from the four horns of the golden altar which
is before God." Horns symbolize powers—the perfect bal-

---

[2] Ibid., IX, 14-15.

ance of love, faith, trust and patience—hence the horns of the altar would mean the powers which are conferred upon one who lays hold of the horns of the altar, the superhuman powers which would be available to a true Priest of the Most High who, as an Initiate, was a true Prophet, Priest and King unto God. The Voice was the voice of all that should be held most sacred and holy, protesting against the materialization and desecration of the Holy of Holies by many of those who stand before the world as priests, but are not.

Besides the personal meaning of this allegory there is also a universal application as pertaining to humanity. The altar of any temple is that portion in or upon which the worship is focused; that place where the incense of prayer, devotion and aspiration continually ascends; where the true Priest offers daily sacrifices, *i.e.*, the sacrifice of his human personality, of a pure heart and of a life devoted to enlightening, guiding and helping his people toward a personal realization of and correlation with the Divine. In the great Temple of Humanity man has erected for himself an altar or that upon which his devotion and worship of the Divine is focused, namely, religion. Before this altar today, however, we seldom find the Initiate Priest, the Super-man, fully conscious of his oneness with Divinity and endued with Wisdom and an understanding of the "Mysteries of the Kingdom of God," hence, able to direct and use the powers which come from the horns of the altar.

Owing to this lack of wisdom, understanding and power, the four angels of humanity's temple have been imprisoned in the Euphrates, but must now be released from the bondage of misconception and materialization under which they have been held for centuries; the bondage created by man's misconception of religion. They have been called forth by the Voice crying from out the altar, appealing to the Sixth Angel and his children—the more enlightened humanity of the sixth sub-race—demanding freedom from the autoc-

racy of the church, and for liberty of worship. They have been
commanded to go forth and purify the Temple of Humanity of
its accumulated evils.

One interpretation of these four angels in this cycle may be
called Service, Enthusiasm, Righteousness and Unity. The false
manifestations into which they have been perverted by man are
(1) the power of unselfish service to mankind which, through
selfishness and ignorance, has degenerated into priestcraft; (2)
ardor for the spread of spiritual Light and Truth, which has
degenerated into hypocrisy; (3) the desire that rightness, or
harmony with Divine Law, should guide mankind, now turned
into intolerance and the persecution of those whose conceptions
of right differ, and (4) that sense of oneness or the gathering of
all into universal truth, which has been turned into separation of
sectarianism. All these aspects of the four angels, which have been
perverted by man, *i.e.*, either overwhelmed by the waves of sex
temptation or stranded in the midst of the river on the rock of sex
misconceptions, must now be let loose and have their sway over
him until he recognizes his mistakes; recognizes them for what
they are; until he repents and purges his religion from them and
redeems them from their bondage and enables them to manifest
their true nature.

Thus does the Lord often use as his messengers or angels the
very evils he is correcting; for only as man is permitted to eat of
the bitter bread of his own kneading or suffer from the perverted
aspect of the four angels which he has enshrined upon the altar
of his temple, will he recognize their falsity, drive them out and
bring back the true. Man has enthroned them and man only can
dethrone them.

"And the four angels were loosed, which were prepared
for an hour, and a day, and a month, and a year, for to
slay a third part of men. And the number of the army of the
horsemen were two hundred thousand thousand."[3] The

---

[3] Ibid., IX, 15-16

ciphers in the number of the "two hundred thousand thousand horsemen," which are called forth by the angels, symbolize an almost unlimited number, while the figure two shows that this army will be composed of both sexes, men and women. That this war will be a mental war, or conflict of ideas, is clearly shown, since horses always symbolize intellectual conceptions or powers, also "their power is in their mouth." "Them who sat thereon" symbolize all the awakened thinkers, both men and women, who must be the ones to bring this woe to an end by purging the minds of men of their misconceptions "by the fire which issued out of their mouths," altho this is done in love, yet with great power and courage, symbolized by their having "the heads of lions," or Leo, the sign of the heart.

The second woe will have four distinct periods, during which the foundation of the New Age will be laid, for we are told that the four angels will prevail "for an hour, and a day, and a month, and a year." Although we are also told that "of that day and hour knoweth no man, no, not the angels of heaven," still, we can gain an approximate idea if we remember that the first woe was allotted "five months," or five short periods for its duration. These periods are not literal, but symbolic, and we note that the first period of the World War lasted nearly five years, with a considerable overlapping, before all the fighting ceased and peace reigned.

With this working out in mind we can apply the same standard to the second woe, but in doing so we must remember one great factor, which must always be taken into consideration, namely, that man has free-will within certain wide limits. While he has a fixed destiny—his ultimate spiritual perfection—which is not fate, until "he becomes as one of us," the gods, yet he is free to choose both how soon and in what manner he will work out that destiny. He can resist the Divine Guidance, break the Law, suffer and greatly retard his advance along the Path of Attainment, or he can follow the Guidance, work with the Law and in peace and harmony greatly accelerate his spiritual unfoldment.

The exercise of his free-will affects not only individual man, but also communities, nations, Races and the entire evolution of the planet. Therefore, every event that is foreshadowed or prophesied, no matter how definitely, is subject to this variable factor of man's free-will. Its hour of manifestation depends upon how man reacts to it. Does he learn his lesson quickly or must he suffer a long time ere he is ready to repent (turn around)?

From the present outlook (1921) of world conditions we may calculate that the first period of readjustment, "an hour," will see the readjustment of capital and labor, which is quite likely to come to a tremendous crisis soon, but which should be as quickly settled, altho doubtless leaving many tangled ends to be unraveled later. The second phase, "a day," may well be the struggle for the political and social readjustments now taking place. Naturally, it will take many times as long as the first phase for its working out. The third phase, "a month," will embrace the great upheaval, and the consequent strife and struggle which is unavoidable in the overturning and readjustment of religious conceptions, teachings and thoughts on spiritual subjects. It must also bring about a readjustment of political, social, industrial, educational and financial organizations and methods, looking toward greater co-operation, freedom of exchange and uniform administration of justice between organizations, classes and nations.

All these three phases may be experienced within the space of four or five years, while the fourth phase, "a year," we may expect to last from twelve to fifteen years. This period must necessarily be somewhat extensive since time must be given within it for the trying out of all the new conceptions presented as a solution of the world conflict; for testing all the new standards of thought and conduct; the weeding out of the false from the true, of sophistries from true and comprehensive philosophies, and the beginning of the establishment of the practical manifestation of real brotherhood among men and nations. All this will not be accomplished except through much intolerance, conflict, tribulation and bitter woe.

While at the present writing (1921), all these four aspects are seething together as in a cauldron, yet each should reach its focal point and settlement within the approximate time and in the same order as mentioned in the prophecy. It is this struggle of the forces of adjustment that is causing the great unrest in the minds of mankind, much like the swirling currents of a great river which through some cataclysmic change has had its old channel dammed up and must seek a new bed. Yet one mind after another will find its new outlet and will settle down just as some of the waters find their way past the obstacle and flow peacefully on while others still seethe and boil until the new channel is entirely formed.

"All these are the beginnings of sorrows. Then shall they deliver you up to be afflicted, and shall kill you: and ye shall be hated of all nations for my name's sake."[4] Those who are delivered up to be afflicted and to "be hated of all nations for my name's sake" are all those who recognize the Light of the Christ within; who stand for the *absolute liberty of each heart* to interpret the Divine *as it is revealed to him* and who also stand for *freedom from persecution*—whether religious, social, political or industrial—because of their beliefs. It embraces all who are working sincerely for the enlightenment, the uplift, the independence, the self-reliance, the purification and the inspiration of mankind through his recognition of the Divinity within himself; who are therefore working for the overthrow of autocracy or compulsion of any kind in thought and religion. Jesus, in describing this Second Woe, said: "And then shall many be offended, and shall betray one another, and shall hate one

---

[4] *St. Matthew,* XXIV, 8-9.

another. And many false prophets shall arise and shall deceive many. And because iniquity shall abound, the love of many shall wax cold. But he that shall endure unto the end, the same shall be saved."[5]

There will be a tendency to go to extremes, to pull down all established institutions just because they were established under the old regime. As is always the case before equilibrium is attained, the pendulum of popular opinion will tend to swing to the opposite extreme. Ignorance and blind obedience through compulsion, when driven to desperation by lack of sympathy and understanding, ever tends to end its sufferings by plunging into an orgy of so-called "liberty" which, uncontrolled, quickly becomes license to express its selfishness, greed and animal lusts in horrors of injustice, tyranny, cruelty and bloodshed quite as frightful as those against which it revolted. Many ignorant ones seek to rectify their wrongs, yet only make their ignorance more dense, by seeking to eliminate the educated and enlightened in an endeavor to attain their goal. Such an ideal persistently maintained makes humanity stand aghast. Does it mean that civilization has failed? and that all the results of culture, refinement, invention and progress the twentieth century has attained are to be wiped off the face of the Earth and man be reduced to a state of savagery and the reign of brute force? No, it does not. It is but the confusion due to the overlapping of great cycles of evolution, and the length of this period depends upon how mankind reacts to it.

While the last phase of the Second Woe seems to follow after the others, in truth, it is but a part of them, for we have but to look around us today to see and hear of many false prophets who work wonders for a time and deceive many. This phase exists with the other phases, yet will last far longer.

---

[5] *St. Matthew*, XXIV, 10-13.

CHAPTER XX

THE DAY OF JUDGEMENT

"Then if any man shall say unto you, Lo, here is Christ, or there; believe it not. For there shall rise false Christs, and false prophets, and shall show great signs and wonders; insomuch that, if it were possible, they shall deceive the very elect. Behold, I have told you before. Wherefore if they shall say unto you, Behold, he is in the desert; go not forth; Behold, he is in the secret chambers; believe it not" *St. Matthew*, XXIV, 23-26.

The conditions mentioned in the previous chapter are but the natural working out of the Law of Manifestation. If during the long cycle of the fifth sub-race now closing it has created the conditions which generate the horrors which we see in its closing days, then those creations must have their manifestation on Earth that man may be brought face to face with his creations and see them in their awful hideousness; that he may realize what results may be expected when wrong ideals and wrong thinking find expression in action. These are among the things that were covered, but which must be revealed to those who covered them up, for only so can they be recognized and redeemed. To cover up and refuse to face conditions; to smugly cry "There is no evil. All is good!" while evil is rampant around and within us for the very reason that we refuse to recognize and uproot it, is to court disaster sooner or later. This is amply proved in the case of those who preached that doctrine in national affairs before the World War, as all such have found out to the sorrow and undoing, not only of themselves, but of their nations.

What is the cure? There is just one cure, truth, honesty, justice and righteousness; only truth can set us free. While

God never created anything evil, yet man, with his free-will, in choosing to disobey, did create all the terrible evils in the world today, and the wild beasts of his passion are prowling through the jungle of life ready to devour any lamb that is tied by the cord of sophistry or authority and with eyes fast shut is blandly bleating, "All is good." In the future let us build our temple upon the Rock of Truth, which does not camouflage life or refuse to see the mud in the gutter because the sky is blue and the Sun is shining.

Following the revolt against autocracy in government we must expect a similar revolt against autocracy in religion. No longer can the old mediaeval interpretations of religion impose their autocratic creeds and dogmas on men's minds through fear, the fear of hell-fire; for today millions of men have been through fires worse than any ever pictured of hell and worse gases than brimstone. As one young veteran said: "If there is any hell worse than we've been through, show it to us and well clean it up!" Neither can the church any longer appeal to the selfishness in man to submit to its decrees to save his own Soul, for he has already given his life for humanity—for an ideal—and has realized that the Soul is immortal and needs no "saving" in the theological sense. Therefore, just as governments are being readjusted on a more democratic basis, so must religion be reorganized if it is to survive the coming tests and searching inspections of the awakened thought of the New Day.

Already there are a number of churches, movements and sects which, seeing the vision of the coming Great Teacher and the inevitable reconstruction of religion, yet, either not having adjusted their minds to an understanding of true freedom or being incapable of expanding their consciousness to take in the broader conception of the absolute guidance of each Soul from the God-consciousness within, they are even now sending out literature which calls upon all who desire to work for the coming New Era to accept unquestioningly their interpretation of the prophecies and join their society or church, offering to all who do so that they shall be numbered among the Elect and threatening with dire consequences all who refuse to see as they see. It scarcely needs to be pointed out that all such efforts are but new attempts to coerce through fear or through promise of special rewards, in other words, the old autocracy in religion in a new dress.

The doctrine of hell fire and "lost" Souls has now been tried, tested and rejected, and if such seed is again sown in this New Era it must inevitably bring forth the same crop of selfishness, spiritual pride, intolerance, persecution and unbrotherliness that the world has been reaping and wiping out today. It is as tho a farmer, whose field has brought forth a large crop of tares among the wheat, should plow and plant the same seeds merely because they had a new label and then expect better results.

The text which heads this lesson warns us that just such conditions must be expected at this period. But how emphatic yet terse is the warning: "Behold, I have told you before!" Many, however, instead of feeling comforted and helped by this warning are puzzled to know just how to take it, and like so many warnings, permit it to generate only alarm and suspicion, so they fear to look anywhere for help, like frightened children they cry out: "How shall we know?" Yet the language is so simple that if we stop seeking for some learned earthly teacher to give his opinion and ask from within for guidance, we cannot fail to know.

Firstly, if we hear any person, church, or society saying, "Lo, here only, in my person, in my church, or in my society you will find the coming Christ," believe it not! Evidently it was preordained that He shall not be announced in that way, else we would not be warned so specifically against it. There can be no exclusive claim on His appearance. "For as the lightning cometh out of the east, and shineth even unto the west: so shall also the coming of the Son of man be." It is to be universal among all who do His works, feel His tender love and manifest His humility in service, rather than in making great claims about being His Elect. Of those whose love, wisdom, service and understanding of true spiritual freedom, opens a path of Light direct to Him through which He can pour into their hearts and lives His own Divine Love, we are told: "He calleth his own sheep by name . . . . and the sheep follow him, and He saith: I am the good shepherd and know my sheep and am known of mine."

Secondly, to know Him when He comes we must overcome the natural tendency to follow after signs and wonders; for even the Elect, if over credulous, may be deceived. Hence, discretion, an understanding of the Law and wise judgment are necessary factors. The tares have been allowed to grow with the wheat until the harvest, which now has come, and now we must carefully separate one from the other. But we must judge lovingly, yet wisely, for, "As ye judge, so shall ye be judged," *i.e.*, with what amount of enlightened judgment we display will we be judged. In these last days of the old dispensation—for these are the days of judgment, the end of an era, not the Day of Judgment or end of the world—every person and every form of religious thought will be brought to judgment, not by God, but by their own works and by mankind. And every tree—form of thought and teaching—that brings not forth good fruit shall be cut down, and "By their fruits ye shall know them."

If taken literally, the parable of the barren fig tree[1] is a stumbling block to many, for they cannot reconcile the thought of the gentle and loving Jesus cursing anything, much less a fig tree because, forsooth, He was hungry for figs and found none, especially as the parable tells us that "the time for figs was not yet." Yet if this symbolic incident is properly interpreted it becomes quite reasonable. The fig tree is used to symbolize a class of persons who, because

---

[1] St. Mark, XI, 13, 20.

of religious training and association, are expected to be very fruitful, yet when the Lord of Life comes seeking their fruits—their works—he finds nothing but leaves. And if a cultivated tree has an abundance of leaves it is only natural to expect fruit, or at least find buds, if the time for the ripened fruit is not yet.

Another version of this same parable is found in *St. Luke.*[2] There we are told that a certain man—the Divine Self—had a fig tree, and for three years he had come seeking fruit and had found none. Then he ordered it cut down, but the caretaker—the personal self—asked that he be given one more chance, one more season in which to further cultivate it, or a total of four seasons—the number of the physical plane—in which to establish it before being cut off from recognition and contact with the master of the vineyard. Similarly in these days of testing, many may be found covered with beautiful leaves of outward pretension and lip-service, which attract the attention of the superficial, yet have no fruit for the spiritually hungry. The four years of cultivation mean four periods or incarnations, in which every opportunity has been given to understand and learn how to bring forth fruit. If, however, in spite of all this, they do not bring forth fruit, in the succeeding incarnation they will find that even their outer pretense fails them or is withered or dried up; for we are told that it was the next "day" or incarnation, that the disciples—the spiritually advanced who had known us in the past—who passed that way, saw that the leaves were withered and the tree dried up.

And thus will it be with all who neglect or abuse their opportunities. No loving Lord of Life will curse them, but the Karma of their own indolence and pretentious show of leaves which formerly deceived the multitude will be their undoing. In other words, in the succeeding incarnation they will find themselves born into an environment in which despite their great hunger for spiritual food and spiritual

---

[2] *St. Luke*, XIII, 6-9.

attainments, they will be cut off from their realization, perhaps so poor that they cannot buy helpful books, or living far from anyone who can speak their spiritual language and with their spiritual faculties blunted, etc.

Almost every form of religious teaching formulates many good ideas and lays down many helpful precepts, and by these, rather than by their fruits, have they been judged in the past. Now, however, conditions have changed. The harvest is now at hand and we see the tares choking the wheat and we judge each field only by the good wheat it has brought forth, not by the good intentions planted. How do the teachings manifest in the lives of their followers? What is their effect on the moral and social structure of mankind? What amount of evil, selfishness, sin, sorrow, suffering and inefficiency have they eradicated from the community? These are the tests now to be applied.

The New Age, being the Sign of the Son of Man in Heaven, is pouring out upon mankind a real and highly spiritualized force—the Water of Life—which must germinate in the world the seeds of spiritual thought. The past age was called the Intellectual Age, during which humanity markedly developed its intellectual faculties, in many instances to the depletion of its heart qualities, and much misery and many vile weeds have sprung up in consequence. Today the thinking world stands aghast at the result and is earnestly seeking a remedy, while the ignorant conclude that intellectual development is responsible, hence are apt to advocate the stamping out, in blood if necessary, of all that man has gained during the Intellectual Era.

The intellect may be likened to the stalk and leaves of the growing wheat, which must be strongly developed if it is to bring into manifestation at its apex the nutritious grains of spiritual realization and expression. Hence, if we refuse to cultivate the intellect in this cycle or summer period we will have to pass through a long cycle of bleak and wintry conditions ere we can bring forth a new crop of nourishing grain. We must therefore cultivate the intellect as the farmer cultivates his wheat, *i.e.*, not to bring forth a great show of wonderful stalks and leaves to sway in the breeze and attract attention, yet only to make straw and chaff at the harvest, but with the one end in view, to bring forth as much grain (spiritual manifestation) as possible, to do which there must be healthy straw. The intellect is not truly developed, no matter how full it may be of the ideas of others, until it has been trained to respond to and express the consciousness of the Divine Indweller, the Real Self. The wheels of progress move relentlessly on and all who try to stop them, either by refusing to accept the new advanced ideas and spiritual conceptions, or by trying to blot out all education, refinement and scientific advance are sooner or later but crushed themselves.

We must face conditions as we find them and recognize that the Water of Life now being poured out upon us will and must bring forth the seeds of the New Age, and that those who choose can—for there is no compulsion—correct conditions by refusing longer to accept the old conceptions, and by planting new seeds of higher and more spiritual ideals. In this New Age man can and must learn to see his mistakes and correct them. He can, if he will, learn the highest use of mind and realize that only as intellect is made the servant of the Higher Self can it reach its ultimate perfection.

Thirdly, we must remember that if we hear, "Behold, he is in the desert," *i.e.*, if we hear that to find the Christ we must get away from our duties in life, reject all the advances of science, refuse to train and develop the intellect and ignore all the higher intellectual pursuits or make them subservient to manual labor, or if we refuse all creature comforts and go back to savagery, or what is almost the same thing, live away from contact with mankind, where we endeavor to seek our own salvation without fear of contamination from the less evolved, all this we are distinctly told: "Believe it not!"

Or if we are told: "Behold, he is in the secret chambers," *i.e.*, that only by entering the secret section of certain societies or lodges or by following certain secret formulas we can find the Christ, "Believe it not!" Nor are we to be misled by those who say that in the secret place of the heart alone can we find Him; for there are many today preaching that the Christ will come only in the hearts of His true followers. He must, indeed, come in the hearts of a large number ere a place can be prepared for His bodily manifestation on Earth, but when such conditions are prepared He "Shall so come in like manner as ye have seen him go into heaven." This time He will not come unto His own and find them so unprepared that they will receive Him not. His own will be gathered out of every land, every tongue and every form of religious teachings, and they will know Him and prepare for His coming.

Jesus tells us that He is Alpha and Omega, the beginning and the end. Hence, at the beginning of the Piscean Age He answered in advance every question that might arise in the minds of men as to His coming again at the end of the Age and the beginning of the Aquarian Age. We will, therefore, have little excuse for not knowing Him when He comes.

He also promised to send us the Holy Ghost, the Comforter,[3] to remain with us even unto the end, and to bring all things to our remembrance whatsoever He had told us. That promise has been fulfilled, for the Comforter is the force of the Great Mother, the Water of Life, which is being poured forth so abundantly for the New Age for a deeper understanding of truths so familiar to the ear that they have in a great measure ceased to mean much to the heart. But the Comforter is here, and as this Order repeats the words pertaining to His coming and strives to awaken in us a

---

[3] See *The Divine Mother*, Curtiss, Chapter IV.

memory of their significance, it is the Comforter, the Holy Ghost who is with us all even to the end, who speaks from the printed page, and the Water of Life that will bring them to fruition in our hearts. It is the descent of the Holy Ghost in a far more tangible and definite way than ever before, for during these terrible days of the Second Woe the comfort and tender Love of the Divine Mother are more sadly needed, and have been more definitely felt, than in any previous era. And it is only this cherishing Love that can bring to our remembrance the many promises of the preparations made for these awful days. And if we ask humbly and sincerely it will surely bring the real meaning of all His words to our remembrance.

CHAPTER XXI

THE LAW OF SACRIFICE

"Present your bodies a living sacrifice, holy, acceptable unto God, which is your reasonable service." *Romans*, XII, 1.

All religious teachings are based upon the Law of Sacrifice. And since all religions spring from the same source, *i.e.*, are given to humanity by the Spiritual Teachers of the Race, the Law of Sacrifice must be a principle of divine manifestation. It is the law of the descent of Spirit into matter. Form involves limitation, and all limitation involves sacrifice. As the Creative Ray is sent forth into manifestation from the Divine, something of its divinity, purity and power is of necessity sacrificed by the limitations of every successive form through which it expresses, from the ideal thought-forms in the Universal Mind down through their manifestations in ethereal substance, until they reach their densest expression in physical matter. Each step of the descent is a sacrifice of a higher state and consciousness that a lower form may manifest. God sends forth his Son that all forms may have their life or expression. "I am come that they may have life, and that they may have it more abundantly." The Heavenly Man sacrifices Himself that the daytime of the universe may be brought forth.

In Nature we see an illustration of this phase of sacrifice when the Sun pours forth or sacrifices its Light, heat and life-force that the day-period of the year—the summer time—may manifest, evolve and bring to fruitage all the myriad forms or expressions of the One Life. This is the sacrifice of the descent, of *involution*, the conscious sacrifice of the greater that the lesser may evolve.

The sacrifice of the ascent, or evolution, must follow the same law, but in reverse order and, until the higher stages are reached, without a full comprehension of the workings of the Law. Thus, we find the rocks crumbling under the influence of the elements, frost, erosion, etc., and being washed down the mountains to form the rich alluvial soil of the plains. The mineral thus sacrifices its *form* of the One Life to a greater; is killed and eaten that a higher *form* of life—the vegetable—may evolve. The vegetable sacrifices its *form*, is killed and eaten and its life-forces absorbed that a still higher and less limiting *form* of life—the animal—may evolve. The animal, in turn, gives up its *form* of life that man may express the One Life in still greater fullness and perfection. In each case all that is eaten loses its *form* and all its particles and forces are extracted and raised to a higher rate of vibration and built into the higher form, each element being absorbed by those parts of the body or those tissues which need it. The waste and the broken down tissues eliminated by the higher forms of life pass into the air, water and soil, and from them are again absorbed by the lower forms of life and start out on a new cycle of evolution, carrying with them the impress of the higher vibrations received while in the higher form.

In a similar way the waste thrown off from the previous chain of globes (the Moon-chain)[1] composed the chaotic materials from which our present Earth-chain was formed. And we in turn are today throwing off materials which will be used to fashion the future globe-chain on which we must redeem those materials; for nothing which has ever belonged to man but must be redeemed by him. The lower personal man also ultimately sacrifices his life that the Divine Man within may be enabled to rise above the limitations of the flesh and manifest the perfection of man's oneness with his Father-in-heaven, thus completing the three-fold cycle of unfoldment; expression—sacrifice—at-one-ment; of out-breathing, manifestation and in-breathing.

---

[1] For particulars see *The Voice of Isis*, Curtiss, XIII and XV.

Until evolution had developed man, all seemed automatically
to follow the Law of Evolution, but as the forces are focused
in man he must learn to guide and rule them; for the Lord God
literally brings to man, as the allegory of Adam so plainly shows,
all things to be named. Note well the wording, "Out *of the ground*
the Lord God formed every beast of the field, and every fowl of
the air, and brought them to Adam to see what he would call them.
* * * Behold, I have given you every herb bearing seed, which
is upon the face of all the earth, and every tree* * * to you it shall
be for meat. And to every beast of the Earth and to every fowl of
the air, and to everything that creepeth upon the Earth, wherein
there is life, I have given every green herb for meat. And God
saw everything that He had made, and behold, it was very good."
Hence, man contains in his physical body the materials and life-
forces from all the lower kingdoms. Also, during its intra-uterine
life the human fetus passes through the characteristic forms of
the lower kingdoms and embodies the sum total of all those
life-forces. Hence, in his body, man has fulfilled the allegory of
Genesis in one aspect; for in this form he has all the kingdoms
brought to him to be named.

This is a most significant fact, for a name in occult parlance
means a word which exactly describes the meaning and function
of the thing named, hence the significance of the text, "I know
my own sheep by name." The *Bible* to a very great degree uses
names in this way. The names given to biblical characters, such as
Noah for instance, "furnish in the very names the records of the
causes and effects which led to the event."[2] The biblical deluge
and all stories of the deluge in other records are connected with
a name of the same significance as Noah. Therefore, to interpret,
through the Science of Logography, the story of the naming of
the animals, means that man must take all the materials and
animal forces to be found in his body, recognize and under-

---

[2] *The Secret Doctrine*, Blavatsky, Vol II, 350.

stand them, and gather up their true essence of life and build it into his higher Soul-life. Herein lies one of the greatest mysteries of life, for not only is man given dominion over all these kingdoms, but he assumes his dominion only as he "names," *i.e.*, recognizes, controls and gives them their true place in the Garden or uplifts them in his own organism. Hence the Hermetic axiom, "Man, know thyself," is carved over the entrance of every gate along the Path of life.

We who are studying life and the healing of the body from the more advanced standpoint know well that whatsoever we call or name anything that we find in our body, so is it. If we say we are hopelessly ill or are a worm of the dust, or destined to be poor or desolate, so are we; for we have misnamed the substances that God has brought to us for our harmonious manifestation, and we must experience the results of our misnaming. Therefore, we must have the same things brought to us life after life and literally built into our bodies, until we awaken to our duty and realize that they have been brought to us by the Lord God (Law of our Good) to be named as they really are.

In ancient times when a place of worship was to be established, a more or less conscious recognition of the Law of Sacrifice was made, for the first stone to be laid was the Stone of Sacrifice. Around this at some distance walls were erected and later a temple was built over it, and around the temple a center of civilization gathered. The laying of a corner-stone is a modification of this same idea. This law is also illustrated in the ceremonies of Initiation into the Mysteries, during which the Neophyte must sacrifice the lower, personal man; must allow it to be dead and buried, ere the resurrection into the higher spiritual consciousness can take place. Among the ancient Druids a priest cast himself, with arms outstretched in the form of a cross, upon the Stone of Sacrifice as a propitiation for the sins of the multitude, a symbol of the sacrifice of the lower, personal man to the Divine Man. Also, when the Sibyl or High Priestess of the Temple was to be consulted, she stretched herself upon the Stone of Sacrifice in the presence of the priests in the same posture, as a symbol that she had completely sacrificed her own personality and given herself up as an oracle of the God who spoke through her.

These ceremonies, like all others when the inner, symbolic meaning is lost, became materialized and degraded into the sacrifice of human victims upon an altar of stone. This is held against the Druids to this day as a proof of their barbarism, altho at one time they were the most learned, refined and cultured of all the people of Europe. And well may we expect, in ages to come, that scientists who unearth statues of a crucified Jesus will accuse modern Christians of being savages who believed in a literal blood sacrifice.

The Stone of Sacrifice must be symbolically formed and voluntarily laid by the Neophyte in the Holy of Holies of his life, and must be able to withstand the fires built upon it. The stones which go into its making—the imperfections and hard faults of the personality—must be ground to powder to form the cement from which it is made. Every stone of stumbling in the personality, every hard, unyielding, selfish trait in the lower man must be placed beneath the millstones of the Law and ground to dust, and then, by the power of Divine Love, transmuted into the Stone of Sacrifice.

Some, alas, find that the Law of Sacrifice grinds too fine. Their stones have been carved into talismans to cherish or into idols to be worshiped, and they cannot give them up. They cannot stand still and allow the Law to grind from them all that holds them back. Is it any wonder, then, that the foundation of the spiritual life requires a Stone of Sacrifice? Every grain composing it represents a living sacrifice, something of the lower self given up, sacrificed, overcome, that its essence may be transmuted into spiritual growth. This was symbolized among the ancients by the sacrifice of animals and the fruits of the Earth. Therefore, we must plant our feet firmly upon the Stone of Sacrifice and realize that through every sacrifice the Divine Life-force is released from selfish and personal, perhaps perverted, manifestations, and is poured out that our understanding may be illumined and our growth promoted.

One of the treasures of the ocean is coral, which by its formation illustrates the Law of Sacrifice. The coral reefs are built up literally by the life sacrifice of the polyps which compose them. Each generation lays down its life and deposits its limestone skeleton as a foundation upon which the next generation can build. To the countless millions of tiny creatures in each generation the sacrifice of their lives might seem of little moment, useless; yet without them the protecting reefs and the beautiful atolls and islands of the sea could never rise.

Comparing humanity to the ocean, coral aptly illustrates the Law of Sacrifice in humanity. The apparently useless sacrifice of countless millions of human lives, while seemingly for no reason, for no purpose, has nevertheless laid the foundation upon which humanity is slowly rising above the waves of adversity into a more perfect manifestation. It is not alone the Sacrifice of those who have willingly given up their lives in war, or for the advancement of science, or that they may be teachers and leaders, but also the unknown lives that are laid down in ignorance, ceaseless toil, poverty and despair; the great mass of common people who seem born but to toil, suffer, sacrifice and pass away leaving no trace, no memory. Yet, woe to the individual or the social, political or industrial system which demands such sacrifices; for such are stones of stumbling which the Great Law will grind to powder. Not one shackled or industrial slave who has given up his life to minister to the selfishness, greed or self-indulgence of his master but is noted by the Great Law and marked for suitable compensation in some future incarnation. Since not one sparrow falleth to the ground without the Father's notice, so not one of those obscure sacrifices is valueless or forgotten.

If we could look down upon humanity from the spiritual heights, as we look upon the coral in the ocean's depths, we would see that the sacrifice of all those obscure, unknown lives has built up in humanity a great structure, has brought about conditions upon which a new humanity—the reincarnation of those who thus sacrificed—can take up a more advanced evolution, because of the lessons learned through sacrifice, just as the islands built up by the coral polyps support a new and luxuriant form of vegetation. Even the coral polyps evolve and change the character of their formation as the reefs rise to the surface. The sacrifice of mankind has thus built up a great and beautiful island in the sea of humanity, a fit foundation upon which the New Jerusalem, with its Temple of the Living Christ, shall be built.

Those who today are ready and desirous of taking up the work of erecting this great Temple of helping humanity, or providing a home or Center in which the coming Avatar may manifest, and where humanity may find shelter, instruction and love, must remember that it is not they alone who can make this possible. Think of those who have suffered martyrdom, who have been ridiculed, reviled, persecuted and crucified for their efforts to express truth as revealed to them; for their efforts to bring enlightenment to humanity! Think of the millions and millions of humble toilers who have laid down their lives without the vision, without hope! These have formed stratum after stratum of the Coral Rock of Truth, truly a foundation of sacrifice.

It matters little whether the sacrifice be of physical life, as in former ages, or today in the mental world, the sacrifice is but on a higher step of evolution. Each life of sacrifice has left behind its grain of truth to make up the foundation upon which we are today erecting the Temple of Humanity. To us is given the great privilege of becoming active factors in the work of erecting the walls of the Temple upon the foundation which has now risen above the waves. We need no longer labor in the depths, but can now lay stone upon stone above the surface in the Light with the knowledge that each is being laid according to the Grand Plan.

This is equally true in the life of every individual. For each Soul must erect the Temple of the living Christ in his or her own heart and life. But he must first lay its foundations beneath the surface, within the turbulent depths of his lower nature, and through sacrifice gain the wisdom to lift it step by step into the glorious light of the Spiritual Sun, his immortal oneness with the Divine.

The ocean's depths contain many jewels. Each has its meaning and symbology and represents a force at work both in Nature and in humanity. While coral stands for self-sacrifice and devotion, the pearl stands for accumulated wisdom. Hence, it is not enough merely to sacrifice. We must sacrifice wisely. We must gather our pearls of wisdom and with them beautify the structure which we are erecting. The pearl is primarily but a grain of sand around which is gathered layer after layer of material poured out by the oyster, which is giving its life-force to transmute the grain of sand into the pearl. So wisdom overlays the common experiences of life until they are transmuted into pearls of great price. Let each Soul take the little grains of experience in his or her nature, learn the lessons from them and build round them layer after layer of love and devotion, until they become pearls of wisdom.

Coral can be made into a useful talisman, provided we let our consciousness correlate with its forces; for each jewel contains a living force which has entered into its formation, and which it can impart to man if he but correlate with it. But no talisman should be used as a fetish. Coral should awaken in our minds and hearts a sense of oneness with all who have gone before; with all who toil and sacrifice. It should make us realize that even tho we may be but the humblest of human creatures, still we have our lives to live, our places to fill, our records to make and our grains of truth to leave behind. Even tho the waves beat fiercely upon us, take courage, for it is in the most turbulent seas that the coral takes upon itself the greatest perfection of form and beauty of color. Coral should also awaken in us a sense of our responsibility, the responsibility for the right use of the wonderful opportunities to help humanity offered us today, be we ever so humble. It is not that we are to think of ourselves as greater, higher, better than those who toiled beneath the waves, who blindly sacrificed that we might emerge into the Light of Divine Wisdom, but that we may realize that because we are in the Light, because we can see the Grand Plan, we are responsible for building more intelligently and more perfectly.

Many today are still looking at truth as a lamp of ancient design, shielding a great light held aloft by some ancient Patriarch. Such a conception was a true and fitting one during the period when the foundations of the mighty Temple of Truth were forming beneath the waves; when the Light of Truth could manifest only as a lamp fed by the oil of midnight conclave and secret vigil, and carefully guarded from the cold blasts of ignorance and the storms of prejudice, criticism and persecution. But as the foundations rise above the sea, many such persons are seeing their old conceptions overturned and sacrificed by the advance of the present day, until in sadness those who are still looking backward into the past for their authority for Truth, find their hands empty and their hearts hungry; and they cry out bitterly at the death of their old ideas. But if they open their eyes they will find that it is not the Light of Truth that has been taken from them; only a past incarnation of half Truths which have had their day and laid down their lives as a sacrifice that upon them may be builded the structure of a greater conception.

Today we see, instead of an oil-fed lamp, the Sun of a New Age flooding the world with a new and mystical Light.

Instead of an ancient Patriarch or Initiate holding high his individual lamp, we see that God Himself now lets the glory of His countenance shine for all who will to behold it. In fact, the outpouring of the Light of Truth to man has kept pace with the development of artificial light: in the first place a rush light above a secret shrine, then a candle in the home, then oil lamps, gas, carbon electric lights, mazda lamps and the enclosed electric arc. And so will it ever continue until there shall be no more darkness in the minds of men, "for the Lord God giveth them Light." For that which transpires in the development or evolution of man is always paralleled and symbolized by inventions and advances in the outer conditions of the world and humanity.

The foundation of the Great Temple is laid in the heart's blood of humanity. It is red like coral, symbolizing love and sacrifice. It is white like coral, symbolizing purity and truth and it is also red like coral, symbolizing the blood of the heart poured out in sacrifice. It is remarkable that the bright, vivid red coral, at one time so greatly prized, has now become practically exhausted, being found only upon certain parts of the African coast, while the coral of commerce is now the beautiful pink coral. Red raised in vibration to pink is the lower red lightened by the white of the One Life and transmuted into the pink, which symbolizes purified love.

But coral is not a mere symbol. It contains an actual, living force. The same force which gives the coral polyp the instinct to build a structure that is beautiful is the same force that has sustained the masses of humanity through their ages of sacrifice; the same force which has sustained the pupils of this Order in the sacrifices which have advanced the work of this Order to the position it occupies in the world today. For with few exceptions, its Teachings are now sent to nearly every country and people in the world. And, as its foundations emerge from the waters of adversity, the same force will sustain it in the sacrifices which are necessary to enable its walls to rise and to establish upon the Earth-plane a Center commensurate with the greatness of its mission.

As the time approaches when, according to cyclic law, such a Center must be established—a quiet lagoon wherein love and peace reign—the cry goes forth more powerfully for an awakening to the great opportunities now before us of putting into concrete form the ideals presented by the Teachings of the Order. To accomplish this there must be established a place of refuge and retreat where, out of every Center now established upon Earth, there may be gathered these Souls who have proved faithful, loving and devoted, whether of this Order or not, that they may come into personal touch with the Elder Brothers of humanity—the coral reef which holds back the waves of evil that would engulf the Race—and be trained to become the teachers of mankind, and form a nucleus for the coming sub-race, each in his appointed place.

Nothing worth having can be obtained without sacrifice. If this be true of the lesser things of life, how much more true is it of the greater, and especially of the spiritual Teachings now being given to humanity through this Order! But the more love and wisdom with which the sacrifice is made the greater will be its accomplishments. These Teachings come freely to those who are ready for them, but their real inner force cannot enter in, be digested and bring forth in their lives the fruits of the Spirit until they have sacrificed something for them—be it their time, thought, love, wealth, whatever they have to give—that there may be erected in humanity the great Temple of Truth into which the heart-hungry, the discouraged and those who lack an understanding of the Law, may be drawn and fed with spiritual food. The success of the movement rests not alone upon those who are giving their lives that the Teachings may reach humanity, but with every loving heart who receives them. Only by co-operation and sacrifice of each and all can these great truths rise higher and higher, until they become a great barrier reef round about a still lagoon or Center where, no matter how much the sea of humanity may be lashed to fury, there will always be a safe and peaceful anchorage for all storm-tossed mariners on the ocean of experience, and into which all the weary hearts of humanity may come for refuge, and where the Great Ones may teach them face to face.

Just to the degree that we lend our aid to build up this great reef of truth to protect humanity, just to that extent will we find our own lives encircled and protected by the power of the Spirit, and will find within our hearts and lives the great Center of love and peace, the Christ-consciousness, where our wildest waves of emotion shall find peace, and our stormy thoughts shall respond to the decree of the Master: "Peace; be still."

What shall be your part in this great work?

CHAPTER XXII

THE SHEEP AND THE GOATS

"When the Son of man shall come in his glory, and all the holy angels with him, then shall he sit upon the throne of his glory: and before him shall be gathered all nations: and he shall separate them one from another, as a shepherd divideth his sheep from the goats: and he shall set the sheep on his right hand, but the goats on the left." *St. Matthew*, XXV, 31-3.

From time immemorial the sheep and the goats have been the symbol of good and evil, just as in occultism the terms right hand and left hand have indicated white and black magic. Yet we find man created with two hands, and were we to say that since the left hand is a sign of evil we will cut it off, such a mutilation would deter rather than help us onward in our evolution. Instead we must recognize that man is created to be the master over both good and evil until he becomes "as one of us" knowing both, as the Elohim said in the beginning. For he must conquer not only the dangers of self-aggrandizement, self-deception and spiritual pride which lurk in that which is called good, but he must also extract or turn to useful and constructive ends the power and force which manifests in that which is called evil, so that by the blending of both forces he can rule his life, even as by the use of his two hands he accomplishes his work in the physical world.

In the larger cosmic sense good and evil are but the opposite poles of a mighty magnet, the magnetism of which is the outpouring of the creative Life or Christ Principle, the Son of the Godhead. In this sense what is called darkness and evil is but the absence of Light and Life. There is also the passive resistance which the dense vibrations of matter offer to the quickening vibrations of Spirit. For the personal aspects of evil—as being not merely this negative absence of Light and Good, but a *positive creation* of inharmony *made by man* through the misuse of the God-given materials and the perversion of the God-given forces of the universe—is not the sense in which the word evil is used in this chapter. We are using the word here only in its cosmic sense of the opposite pole of Good.

The two ends of a magnet are charged with what appear to be two antagonistic forces, or forces working in diametrically opposite ways. At one end they attract, at the other they repel, yet all the time each end is attracting and polarizing the forces from its opposite until in the middle we find the peace and calm of perfect balance and equilibrium. So with good and evil, the sheep and the goats. Since the days when the assembled Elohim pronounced the fiat, "Let there be light," and sent down this mighty Magnet of Duality—positive and negative, active and passive, good and evil, right and left, sheep and goats—man and woman have struggled with their destiny, each apparently along opposite lines. Yet, to the careful thinker there is so great an interblending of the two that one of the greatest problems of the age is to untangle them. Therefore, let us try to decipher the meaning of the allegory quoted at the head of this lesson.

Since we are taught that the book of Nature holds for us the solution of all our problems, let us go to her as to a mother and learn of her. We find that the sheep was domesticated before the dawn of history, and since the earliest days sheep, flocks and herds have represented wealth and good living. The sheep has supplied man with clothing, its wool being among the earliest fibers to be woven into cloth. It has also fed him by giving up its life for him; for because of its gentleness and docility the sheep was probably the first animal killed for food by primitive man. In this it exemplified the great drama of sacrifice, *i.e.*, the laying down of its lower form of life that a higher form (man) might manifest, just as animal man or the lower personality gives up its life that the Divine Man may manifest through him. The goat, too, has served man generously from the earliest ages, for the remains of the Asiatic goat have been found in the Pliocene fossil beds of India. The Angora and Kashmir goats produce the finest quality of hair, as well as highly prized milk. In fact, in the Vale of Kashmir, the weaving of rugs and cloth from the wool of these goats forms the principal industry, at one time there being over 16,000 looms at work in a comparatively small area. But the goat, while feeding and clothing man, does not ordinarily lay down its life for him, altho of late goat meat is being used extensively in the South. This is an important point of difference between the use of the sheep and the goats. In reality both belong to the same family, in fact, are but the two ends of one magnet as it were, and like all magnets, blend into each other in the middle, where the good points of each are separated from the evil and balanced.

The *Encyclopedia Britannica* thus describes the goat: "Altho the more typical goats are markedly distinct from sheep, there is, both as regards wild and domesticated forms, an almost complete gradation from goats to sheep, so that it is exceedingly difficult to define either group." Again, while we are apt to think that the *Bible* utterly condemns the goat, nevertheless in the *Proverbs* of Solomon the Wise we find the goat catalogued among the four animals that are excellent, the four being the lion, the greyhound, the goat and "the king who has no rising up" or who knows how to govern. Also in the Hermetic philosophy we find the goat among the three animals used in its sacred symbology, the goat representing fire, while the bull stands for earth or salt, and the dog for mercury or fluid (air and water).

On the great Day of Expiation the Elders of Israel presented two goats to the High Priest, one to be slain for the sacrifice and the other to be driven into the wilderness, the name Azazel being given to the latter. This ceremony of the scape-goat was followed by many ancient peoples, but in Israel the custom was as follows: Two goats were led into the Inner Temple and presented to the High Priest on the north side of the altar, one being placed on his right and the other on his left. An urn was then set down between them and two lots were cast into it, made either of wood, silver or gold. On one lot was engraved "For the Lord," on the other "For Azazel." After the urn had been well shaken the Priest put both hands in at the same time and drew forth a lot in each; the one in his right hand decided the fate of the goat on his right, while that in his left hand decided the fate of the one on his left. After the drawing the Priest fastened a long piece of narrow scarlet ribbon to the horns of Azazel as a sign that it was to become the scape-goat.

After the sacrifice of the goat set aside for the Lord the scape-goat was brought to the High Priest, who then placed his hands upon its head and confessed his sins and those of the people. The goat was then driven out into the wilderness, and if possible was left near the brink of a precipice, carrying the sins of the people, the sins being symbolized by the scarlet ribbon. It is to this symbology that the text refers: "Though your sins be as scarlet, they shall be as white as snow; though they be red like crimson, they shall be as wool."[1] For the goat dedicated to the Lord was washed pure and white before the sacrifice.

Under the name of Baphomet the goat is used as a symbol of black magic and the devil;[2] yet a deeper understanding of the figure as it is pictured[101] reveals a high symbolism and indicates that even that which is evil is ultimately used to bring about some measure of good, altho *that end might have and should have been attained without the manifestation of the evil.* For on the forehead of this image, which is a

---

[1] Isaiah, I, 18.
[2] *The Key of Destiny*, Curtiss, 256, 208.

composite embodying the figure of a goat, we see the pentacle with its point up, the unqualified and universal sign of Light and humanity. His two arms are in the position of occultism: with his right hand he points up, in this case symbolizing man's ability to soar into the heavens and draw from on high the power to complete the development of his God-powers (his destiny), while with his left hand he points down, symbolizing his power to reach down and help his fellow men and the kingdoms below him (his work); for man must ultimately learn that to make his work most effective, esoteric truth or Soul wisdom from on high must be the foundation of all his efforts to uplift humanity. This position of the hands is called that of Justice and Mercy.

Between the horns of the figure burns the torch of Intelligence, the magical Light of which shall bring about equilibrium; or the Soul exalted above and illuminating matter even while manifesting within it; the Flame of Divine Love, which shows man the Path to Mastery. The head and face of this monster, which have earned for him the name of the devil, in reality express but the horror of sin and the realization of man that he alone is responsible for whatever results from his misuse of the forces of Nature.

Over the navel is the globe, showing that through that center he is in touch with the lower worlds, while the generative organs are replaced by the Caduceus, the symbol of transmutation and eternal life, also of the two opposite poles of the magnet becoming balanced and blended and passing up the central staff. His breasts symbolize that humanity is fed spiritually from the breasts of the Great Mother. Over his right shoulder is a light crescent Moon, symbolizing the overshadowing power of Intuition given for his guidance, while beneath his left hand is a dark crescent Moon, symbolizing the astral powers of the Moon used in black magic.[3]

---

[3] This is a different interpretation from that given in *The Key of Destiny*, because considered from a different aspect, yet both are equally true.

The Moon is a dead planet and yet a living body, for while the planet itself is dead, yet like a decaying corpse its particles are full of active destructive life-forces. Hence, during the dark of the Moon it is the force of these corpselike emanations which lends its aid to all black magical practices. Necromancy and sorcery seek to utilize these forces, much as they seek to call up the forms of the dead, to do their bidding. But when the Moon is full-orbed it not only reflects the light of the Sun to the Earth, but back of the Moon as well as back of the Sun are situated two of the three Sacred Orbs or Secret Planets, known to the Masters from all time, yet absolutely unknown as yet to modern science.

When the Moon is full a ray of the light from its Sacred Orb is blended with a ray from the Sacred Orb back of the Sun and a force called the "Sushumna Ray" is transmitted to the Earth. From this blended light are many and wonderful occult properties accredited to the full-orbed Moon. It has been called the "Mystery of Mysteries," and by the Egyptians was identified both with Isis and Osiris. In *The Book of the Dead* Osiris was said to inhabit the Moon and is represented as saying: "I will issue by day (the full of the Moon) to do that I have to do amongst the living." The Egyptians held a festival at the time of full Moon to celebrate the ingress of Osiris (the God of Life) into the Moon, which they called the symbol of the renewal of life to the Earth, and reincarnation to the Soul of man. Yet the Moon in Egypt was also made the ruler over magic and enchantments, and during its dark period, as was fully understood by all the ancient teachers, it sends forth an unholy emanation. The concealed or secret side of the Moon was called the infernal regions and named "Teaou, the path of the night Sun." In very truth the concealed side of the Moon is that which has been called the eighth sphere of our Earth-chain, and when during the sixth and seventh sub-races of the Seventh Great Race the now visible Moon disappears from our sight, this dark repository of Earth's left-overs will begin its preparation for a new spiral of evolution. Hence, today light and darkness are struggling within its womb. Those of us who can understand this mystery can do much to help on evolution by correlating with this mystic Light and letting the separation of the evil in the seething melting-pot of time fulfill its work. As a whole, therefore, Baphomet symbolizes black magic only when interpreted negatively; in other words, only as man perverts the very powers given him by which to climb to the gods.

The celestial sign of the zodiac (Capricorn) symbolized by the goat, is the most mystical of all the signs, and altho much has been written of its meanings and potencies, still little is really explained as to its esoteric significance, and even now only hints as to its deeper meanings can be given out. In the Hindu zodiac this sign is known as Makara and is referred to the crocodile. In reality its meaning is the same as the goat, which is usually pictured as a half aquatic monster. This sign was formerly the eighth sign of the zodiac, instead of being the tenth as at present,[4] but it always had the same mystical meaning and was always represented by a monster that was half terrene and half aquatic, with a dual nature representing the dual forces of fire and water and, like Baphomet, symbolizing both the microcosm and the macrocosm or man and the universe.

It is, therefore, not at all remarkable that this most mystical and little understood sign and its symbols should be relegated to black magic; for what man does not understand he fears, and what he fears he endows with sinister motives and evil powers, then tries to propitiate through fear instead of understanding through love. This is and ever has been the true origin of devil worship. Even the most revered and adored of Christian symbols, the crucifix, if turned upside

<hr/>

[4] See *The Voice of Isis*, Curtiss, 347-8.

down becomes a black magic symbol, and is so used in certain cults. The dread Baphomet, or the "Goat of Mendes" as he is sometimes called, in his true meaning, therefore, represents Man in his highest attainment of power, becoming, to the extent that he rules over the beast within himself, the Aspirant to Godhood.

This symbol also indicates man's oneness with the whole created universe, and further points out that it is only through correlation with the One life, through the ruling of the positive and negative phases of the creative force or lifting up of the two serpents upon the Rod of Power, that the Christ can be born in man and bring forth in him as it has already done in the universe.

During the reign of this mystical Sign of the Goat (Capricorn, December 21 to January 20), the birthday of the Christ is celebrated. This again indicates the transmutation of gold from dross or the separation of the sheep from the goats, for out of the very Throne of Satan (Saturn, which rules the first decanate of Capricorn) the Christ-child is brought into the world. Since Jesus is represented as being born in this Sign of the Tester we need not wonder that He says: "Think not that I am come to send peace on earth: I came not to send peace, but a sword."[5]

From the above we can gain some understanding of the great mystery set forth in the few cryptic sentences of the passage quoted as applied to the birth of the Christ in man. "When the Son of man shall come in his glory, and all the holy angels with him, then shall he sit upon the throne of his glory," the glory of victory, of perfect equilibrium. His throne of glory is the point of blending, where all the opposing manifestations of forces are gathered up, indrawn and the full experience of both extremes is balanced and registered. At this point man, as the Lord of Creation, must blend himself with the universe. "His holy angels" are the divine spiritual forces and Helpers with which man

---

[5] *St. Matthew*, X, 34.

has correlated and whose help has enabled him to garner the golden grains of wisdom from all his experiences in the fields of the outer life, where the tares and the wheat have been allowed to grow side by side until this time of harvest.

"Before him shall be gathered all nations," *i.e.*, all the manifestations of the great evolutionary force expressing as good and evil, and the Christ-man standing at the point of balance shall separate the conflicting elements one from another. All that is good; all that has yielded its positive qualities toward strengthening and perfecting humanity; all that has been transmuted into pure gold and given of its innate riches for the betterment of the world; all that has been put to its highest use; in short, all that has been separated from its dross and purified, he will put on his right hand that it may lend its positive creative force to the reconstruction, first of his life, then of society and all mankind; that it may point man to his highest ideal and help to unfold his God-powers. All that remains; the dross, the weak, negative and hampering qualities that have for so long prevented or hindered the Christ from manifesting in the life, he will put on his left hand which he points down as a sign of his dominion over all negative aspects, instead of permitting them to have dominion over him.

He will then say to these left-overs, this dross out of which he has extracted the gold of experience, these husks out of which he has garnered their kernel of Truth: "Depart from me ye workers of iniquity. I have no longer need of you. I know you have served your purpose, hence I will see that you also have an opportunity to pass through the fire of transmutation; the everlasting fire prepared from the beginning, not for anything that is good—for all that has been separated and I have gathered it in my right hand; I have gathered it out of the burning and have forged with it my Staff of Life, my Rod of Power—but for the devil (the man-created thought-forms of evil) and his angels (the thought-forms created by the superstitious practices and the perversions of force and orgies which prolong the devil's life and give him power to become the Great Adversary),[6] unto all those forces and conditions I say: Depart from me into the everlasting fire of purification, the fire that remains unquenchable as long as man creates fuel to feed its flames, yet which is the only element that can overcome the resistance and transmute that which we call evil into good."

This fire is raging even in the physical world today. Its full fury was let loose on the battlefields of Europe. Yet in its very midst and from out the heart of its lurid flames the Christ-man is being born for the world; the Christ who shall sit on His throne of glory and separate the sheep from the goats, the good from the evil. For both are a part of the great Magnet of Life and each must lend its true force and substance to blend with the other that a perfect balance and equilibrium may be prepared as a Throne of Glory against His coming.

Not only in the world is this Throne of Glory being set up, but in every heart which is preparing Him room. All must prepare for His coming by separating the sheep from the goats, and while standing still in the center balance the two forces, calling their sheep by name and also recognizing the work the goats can accomplish. Therefore, in our personal lives we must recognize that the goats are but the "other sheep," for "Other sheep I have, which are not of this fold; them also I must bring, and they shall hear my voice; and there shall be one fold, and one shepherd."[7]

The everlasting Fire is the manifestation of the Divine Law: that which is forever changing the outer forms of expression that the vital life may be released and take on new and more glorious expressions. Could we have consciously watched the formation of this globe when it was but a mass of fire mist which writhed and swirled in space, or later on when as a denser but molten mass it seethed and

---

[6] See *The Key of Destiny*, Curtiss, 174.

[7] *St. John*, X, 16.

bubbled and belched forth disaster, would we not say, What an awful hell God has made for man to dwell in! Yet those stages were a necessary preparation for the world of life and beauty we see all around us today.

Man in his evolution must follow the same law. First, separateness; each man apparently a separate atom striving to find his own place, drawn by the irresistible attraction of something he scarce knows what, all scurrying round and round. Then come burning and harrowing disasters in the conditions of the outer life which make it a veritable melting-pot, all engulfed in an apparently molten-mass of sickening sorrow and death. Yet out of it there shall finally arise a new and beautiful humanity; each man and woman, like each flower, tree, bird and animal, perfect in its own way, yet all working harmoniously together to make life for all a perfect whole. Then there will be no jealous effort to compel a violet to become an oak or a sunflower a rose, but all will lend of their God-given powers toward a mighty manifestation of the Christ who has come in His glory to sit on His throne and rule forever.

The beautiful picture given us in the twenty-third *Psalm* is not mere poetic imagery, but a deep mystical truth expressed in the most beautiful symbology: "The Lord is my shepherd; I shall not want. He maketh me to lie down in green pastures; he leadeth me beside the still waters." The divine Law of Love is indeed a Shepherd of Souls. And once a Soul has heard its voice and has followed, that is, has become one with the Law, he finds this loving guidance a deep and abiding reality, hence that Soul wants nothing but to follow on wheresoever the Voice leads.

He maketh His followers to lie down in the green pastures of abundant Earth conditions, where the supply is no longer scanty and hard to obtain. For once having learned that the Law of Love is the fullness of plenty, we find the pastures green, yet we are contented to lie down at His command, no longer running to and fro bleating plaintively for food or for worldly things, but resting quietly on the Law. Then doth it lead us beside the waters of life that are no longer turbulent; that no longer gush forth from the eyes as tears, for the eyes now see clearly the glory of the Shepherd who leadeth us. Then no longer is the Great Mother-force or the mystical Water of Life by which we evolve godward wasted in emotional storms, for in following the loving Shepherd, so still do we find all the earthly desires and emotions that in a moment, by turning our attention inward with a loving thought of our oneness with the Great Law, we seem to be lying down like contented sheep in deep, green grass beside a still mountain lake, and upon the surface of our tranquil mind the reflection of our Shepherd's face is imaged, even as are the clouds upon the bosom of the lake.

Another application of the allegory of the sheep and the goats is to the two types we find among the followers of the Christ-life. The sheep are those gentle and docile Souls who follow unthinkingly in flocks wherever they are led; who must have a Shepherd and a sheep-fold wherein they are carefully protected from the wolves; who follow their Shepherd lovingly, yet who will follow just as blindly one who would lead them to the verge of a precipice, or one who would fly and leave the sheep to their fate when the wolves appear.

The other class, represented by the goats, think for themselves. They wander forth from the sheep-fold of church, creed, dogma and organization, courageously and independently seeking sustenance from the sparse herbage which they find on the rocky mountain side as they climb. They are always ready to face whatever comes, for they are well armed with two strong horns — symbol of power — upon their heads and are quite able to keep the wolves at bay. Both these types are followers of the Great Law, hence somehow, sometime, instead of either one fearing or despising the other, they must find that they both belong to the one family and each has the same Shepherd. Therefore, they must find the point of balance where each can partake of the virtues of the other and eliminate their weaknesses.

The idea is not that some people are to be considered as sheep and are elected to stand at the right hand of God, while others are to be looked upon as goats which are to be cast out into the wilderness or into the burning, but that each one must reach that at-one-ment with the Great Law where we not only recognize that we have within us both the qualities symbolized, but must wisely separate the one from the other and yet use the good from each. And since with our right hand we accomplish on Earth, the right hand needs as helpers and servants to express its forces only the sheep; those faculties and forces which will follow faithfully and docilely wherever they are bidden by the Shepherd; which will lie down at his command, even in the midst of Earth's greenest pastures; which will tranquilly rest beside the still waters in that quiet yet exalted state of meditation which feeds the Soul abundantly, even as the green pastures feed the sheep.

But after we have learned to make the differentiation we must not forget that we need the help of the goats as well; for we must use the power of our left hand to dominate the inner forces. These cannot so easily be led and made to lie down tranquilly. In fact, we must go forth and seek them, even in the clefts of the rocks where herbage is scarce. We must often climb high mountains of intellectuality and material conditions and call the goats to us. And only as we seek them with the love of the Christ will they trust and obey us for they naturally tend to wander at will and despise the seduction of soft places. Hence, we need these forces to dominate Earth conditions if we are to accomplish our work in the world in the face of its hard, rocky conditions and the sparseness of its spiritual herbage.

We must, therefore, resolutely face the conditions surrounding us and do our full duty in the world and to the world, correlating with our fellows against the aggression of the human wolves who would fatten on the flock. This we must do by displaying the valiant courage of our convictions, the tenacity of our purpose and the warmth and radiance of the Spirit derived from our inner nourishment. For all this we need the force of the goats or all those qualities and mystical ideals which make for strength and endurance and which give us the ability to climb over all obstacles, even tho we can see no clearly marked sheep trail to follow, so that in spite of yawning chasms and the treacherous footing, we can find our way to the very top of the Mount of Attainment. Hence, only he who can stand at the point of balance and use both these forces can sit on the Throne of His Glory.

CHAPTER XXIII

THE MYSTIC OAK

"And there came an angel of the Lord, and sat under an oak which was in Ophrah." *Judges*, VI, 11.

"Let them praise his name in the dance. . . . Praise him with timbrel and dance." *Psalms*, CXLIX, 3. cl, 4.

The dance in some form was connected with the religion and worship of every ancient nation, from the dances performed by King David before the Ark of the Lord,[1] down through the serpent-circle and sun-dances of various tribes to the May-pole dance which survives today, even tho its original significance has been almost obliterated by the mists of time. The dance as a sacred ceremony was performed by those who were set apart and trained for that service and who lived either in the temples or closely connected with them. "The Hebrew Kadeshim, or Galli, lived 'by the house of the Lord, where the women wove hangings for the grove,'[2] . . . . . . and were identical, as to the duties of their office, with the Nautch-girls of the later Hindu pagodas."[3]

Rhythmic motion is the second syllable of the creative Word. The first syllable, Light, sets in motion all the particles contained in the Chaos, whose evolution begins with the words, "Let there be Light," and each particle vibrates with a certain rhythm which is the producer of form, while the last syllable is color. Hence, without Light, motion, color and form, there is no creation in the objective world. The knowledge of this law formed the basis of all sacred dances, for they consisted largely of postures and rhythmic movements of the entire body involving every muscle, emphasized by the color of the costumes and lights, rather than merely

---

[1] *II Samuel*, VI, 16.
[2] *II Kings*, XXIII, 7.
[3] *The Secret Doctrine*, Blavatsky, Vol. II, 482.

the continuous movement of the feet, as in modern social dances. The basic idea was that since Light creates motion, color and form, conversely proper rhythmic motion, color and form would produce Light, spiritual illumination and ecstasy, according to the psychological axiom that going through the motions which express an emotion will tend to induce the emotion again. For example, stand before a mirror and make the facial muscles go through the expressions of some emotion, such as joy or sorrow, and a corresponding state will temporarily be induced. Indeed, it is often helpful when in a depressed mood to stand before a mirror and make the features wrinkle into the expression of laughter and a more cheerful frame of mind will speedily be induced.

Even today a branch (*asana*) of the Hindu *Yoga* system seeks illumination and liberation for the Spirit through the assuming of certain postures which, when combined with color, music and also the breath in directing the life-currents of the body, tend to bring about, not real spiritual illumination, but certain psychic states, varying from trance to ecstasy or, on the other hand, to catalepsy or frenzy. We find similar methods still employed today for the same purpose in the Sun- snake- and other dances of the American Indians, also among the Whirling Dervishes of Arabia and the Shakers of America.

At an early date, however, sacred dances became corrupted by the misuse of the forces generated, and became identified almost exclusively with phallic worship, and hence were eliminated from the more solemn and sacred forms of worship. Consequently dancing took on an undeserved odium, which did not properly belong to the dance itself; for harmonious, rhythmic motion, performed both to induce and to express the feelings of joy and ecstasy arising from religious experience, should have its place in religious ceremonials. It is well, however, for sensitive persons not to dance with those who are not in harmony with their ideals, for the change in vibrations contacted in dancing first with one person and then another, when they are not in mental and spiritual harmony with the same ideals, is very disturbing to the vibrations of one's aura and very depleting to the nervous system. Had religious worship retained the graceful and joyous forms of expression in their purity, religion would never have descended to the narrow, cold, austere and unlovely forms of expression through which it passed during the days of the Puritans, when all expressions of beauty, pleasure and joy were looked upon as sins and punished.

The chief sacred dances were performed in a circle and in honor of the nation's Sun or Fire-god, and were intended to symbolize both the circling of the planets around the sun and the descent of the Divine Light, or the creative potencies of the Christ-force— by whatever name it was called—into the Earth that darkness, winter, death and the inertia of matter might give place to growth, expression and evolution, as the result of the quickening power of the Spirit. The ceremony from which the modern May-pole dance descended was originally performed around a bonfire. It was instituted by the ancient Druids before the British Isles were separated from the mainland.

The very meaning of the word Druid, *i.e.*, "the very knowing, the wise," shows that they were not the ignorant idolaters which uninformed and superficial modern writers have supposed, and their original teachings were far from being the superstitious practices into which they later degenerated.[4] For the coming of the English invaders (Angles, Saxons, etc.) took away the simplicity of the people and degraded their ceremonials by literal interpretations of the symbols, until there came a time when human victims were sacrificed upon their altars. The ancient rite in which the priest cast himself upon the Stone of Sacrifice symbolized the sacrifice of the lower nature of man to the spiritual, the

---

[4] The mystery veiling the origin and the religion of the Druids is as great as that of their supposed fanes to the modern Symbologist, but not to the initiated Occultists. Their priests were the descendants of the last Atlanteans." *The Secret Doctrine*, Blavatsky, II, 799.

human to the Divine. Thus the sacrifice of the personality to the Higher Self became degraded, just as later the mystic crucifixion of the personality that the Christ might rise, gradually became materialized into the literal death and human sacrifice of Jesus.

Caesar, returning from his conquest of Gaul, reported that the Druids constituted the learned and priestly class and were the chief expounders of the law. They taught the immortality of the Soul, believed in reincarnation and had for their favorite studies astrology, geography, physical science and theology, long before written works were known to the common people. In fact, the earlier Druid priests were Initiates from the Lodge of Masters who, in the degenerate days of Atlantis, taught all the people who would listen the true religion, and before the final sinking of the continent, led all their followers out of the country into Europe, over the peninsula which at that time made the Mediterranean an inland sea. Later they sent out missionaries to the younger and more childlike peoples in Gaul, Ireland, Wales and elsewhere, to establish the one true Wisdom Religion. Among them were the legendary semi-divine Kings from whom many Irishmen believe in their hearts they have descended.

"History shows the populations of Central Gaul revolting against the Roman yoke. . . . Bibractis . . . perished. Bibractis, the mother of sciences, the soul of the earlier nations (in Europe, a town equally famous for its sacred college of Druids, its civilization, its schools, in which 40,000 students were taught philosophy, literature, grammar, jurisprudence, medicine, astrology, occult sciences, architecture, etc. Rival of Thebes, of Memphis, of Athens and of Rome. . . . Such was the last city in Gaul wherein died for Europe the secrets of the Initiations of the Great Mysteries . . . . Pliny devotes many a chapter to the wisdom of the leaders of the Celts. The Semothees—the Druids of the Gauls—expounded the physical as well as the spiritual sciences. They taught the secrets of the universe, the harmonious progress of the heavenly bodies, the formation of the earth, and above all, the immortality of the Soul."[5] "In religious literature they are almost exclusively represented as magicians and diviners opposing the Christian missionaries, tho we find two of them acting as tutors to the daughters of Laegaire, the high-king, at the coming of St. Patrick. . . . The word *drui* is always used to render the Latin *magus*, and in one passage St. Columba speaks of Christ as his Druid."[6] *Dru* also means an oak.

The great fundamental truths as to the inter-relations of God, Nature and man, instead of being indicated by symbols and by printed explanations as today, were in those days illustrated by symbolic customs and ceremonials in which large numbers of people in every village took part, thus impressing the meaning of the symbol more forcefully upon the minds of the people.

In the days when the dance was performed around the bonfires, the Fire Signal, which symbolized the consent of the Deity to another cycle of life and evolution on Earth, was not given until the constellation of the Pleiades in the neck of the Bull—the sign Taurus, the Thunder-god of England—was exactly overhead in the night sky. "The Druids, then, understood the meaning of the Sun in Taurus, when, all other fires being extinguished on the first of November, their sacred and inextinguishable fires alone remained to illumine the horizon."[7] This is evidence that it was the Spiritual and not the physical Sun that was worshiped, for the Pleiades contain the central star, Alcyone, around which our universe circles. But as this required exact astronomical calculation and varied from year to year, later on the first day of May was fixed as exoterically approximating correct season.

The ceremony was conducted by seven priests, representing the powers of the seven Sacred Planets and the seven

[5] *Ibid.*, Vol. III, 199, 312.
[6] *Encyclopedia Britannica*, Vol. VIII, 598.
[7] *The Secret Doctrine*, Blavatsky, II, 802.

Pleiades, while the dance itself was performed by twelve maidens, symbolizing the circling of the twelve signs of the zodiac and the twelve months of the year around the Sun. In the later symbolism the dance was performed around the Sacred Oak and still later, if an oak were not available, the masculine principle of Fire or the Sun was symbolized by the upright May-pole, while the feminine principle was indicated by the circle drawn on the ground, the two having the same significance, forming a creative symbol, like the dot within the circle or the *Lingam* and the *Yoni*, all of which later became degraded into objects of phallic worship.

The fact that the Druids looked upon the oak as a sacred tree again proves their knowledge of occult lore, for the oak is the highest type among trees or has reached mastery in that kingdom. And like all types which reach mastery in their respective kingdoms — gold among metals, the diamond among earths, the rose among flowers, etc., — the oak sends out a force of perfection, strength and mastery. Because of these emanations it was used in the May-dance of the Druids and was also planted in groves around their centers of worship and their dwelling places. Therefore, just as the Christian ceremonies of Easter bring to our minds the great cosmic fact of the resurrection of the Sun from the southern hemisphere, or the renewal or resurrection of the life-force (the Christ-force) of Nature from the tomb of winter, as well as the personal significance of the resurrection of the Christ in each heart, so the bonfires and Maypoles, with their attendant dances and ceremonials, had the same double significance and symbolized the same grand truths to the early inhabitants of Ireland, Britain and Gaul, *i.e.*, that the masculine Principle of Fire had again descended to fructify Mother Earth that she might bring forth her increase in the new cycle of manifestation.

One of the ceremonies of the ancient May festival was the planting of an oak by the Druid priests in the center of the plot set aside for the dance. This tree was planted with

certain magical rites which invoked or which, through the
enlightened will of the priests, so concentrated the life-forces of
the elements that the spot became a focus for the Earth-currents to
such an extent that the oaks thus consecrated lived and flourished
for centuries. Even today many of the trees thus planted survive
where not devastated by the hand of man.[8] Among the Hawaiians
of today a tree-planting ceremony closely resembling the ancient
druidic rite is still occasionally performed by the older *Kuhunas*
or priests, by means of which exceptionally long life and great
fruitfulness is imparted to the trees.

The reason for the results is easily understood by the occultist,
for it is well known that the elementals and Nature-sprites obey
the will of one who knows how to invoke them through the use
of the symbols, sounds and colors to which they must respond.
"The Elementals, the Nature-Forces, are the acting, tho invisible,
or rather imperceptible, secondary causes, and in themselves
the effects of primary causes behind the veil of all terrestrial
phenomena."[9] The primary cause in the above instances lay in the
trained will of the initiated priests. But woe to him who dares to
invoke Nature's forces for selfish purposes, for they obey blindly
the inner desire of the heart and can disintegrate and destroy as
well as create.

It is common for the hearts of ancient oaks to turn dark and
decay while the tree grows on. This leaves a hollow interior,
blackened as tho burned with fire. Hence, the oak is said to have
a "Heart of fire," and the blackened cavity is cited to prove it.

All true symbology and ceremonial is but the outward
picture of a Divine Reality, an inner Truth, which is of vital
importance to the unfoldment of the Soul. This *Order of*

---

[8] The Newland Oak in Gloucestershire, called "the Great Oak," is said to date from
the second century. Its girth is now 47½ ft. at a point 5 ft. from the ground. The
Cawthorpe Oak (38½ ft.) near Wetherby in Yorkshire, is said to date back to early
Saxon times or earlier.
[9] *The Secret Doctrine*, Blavatsky, I, 170.

Christian Mystics is also likened to a sacred oak and its successor the May-pole, in that it is another effort of the missionaries of the same Great Lodge to call down the Divine Fire of the Christ into the hearts of humanity. Recognize, therefore, its significance and make it a living Oak with a true "heart of fire," not a blackened and empty hollow. And as we circle round it through the twelve months of the year as the followers of the Sun of Righteousness, let us call down the forces of the Planetary Deities and the lesser influences of the zodiacal signs, that this Mystic Oak, or Spiritual May-pole of the Order, may be the vehicle for the downpouring of the creative Christ-force which shall warm and fructify the germs of spiritual life within the hearts of all mankind; that it may be firmly rooted and that as it grows its branches shall spread far and wide and furnish shelter and grateful shade for many weary hearts and nesting places for the birds of the air, *i.e.*, helpful, unselfish thoughts for the betterment of mankind.

Let the twelve streamers attached to this Mystic May-pole remind us of the twelve monthly lessons sent out from the "heart of fire" of this Spiritual Oak. Think of them as streamers transmitting to us the spiritual forces of the twelve zodiacal signs, and recognize that the power of the Planetary Deity ruling each month can be transmitted to us in and through each lesson if we will correlate with it.

Realize that just as the forces of the Central Sun go out to all the planets and intertwine as the planets weave their courses through the heavenly spaces, so must there be established on Earth a universal Center of Spiritual Light which shall be the Universal Oak from which there shall go forth the twelve expressions of the Spiritual Sun to illumine the minds and warm the hearts and vivify the lives of all mankind, each a distinct streamer, yet interblending and working in harmony with all. Therefore, let each student who is sincerely striving to follow the spiritual Light seek out and take hold of one of these streamers from the Universal Oak or Center of Spiritual Light and realize that it is a live wire connecting him with a great dynamic force, whose power comes from the spiritual Flame of Divine Love and Wisdom.

To make this symbology practical we will find that by concentrating upon the thought that the Heart Center of this Order is in direct touch with the Spiritual Sun, in very truth, all who touch one of its streamers will find the radiance of that Sun illuminating their Path and its warmth and spiritual life-force filling their veins and rippling through their bodies. Then shall all gladly join hands and joyously dance, so intertwining their forces that the world will see the change in their lives and will recognize that they have united themselves with something that is vital and life-giving. In other words, that they have found the Angel (messenger) of the Lord sitting beneath this Mystic Oak, and that He has placed His mark upon their foreheads, the mark being the shining forth of the Christ-light.

Among the May-day festivities there were feats of strength and endurance. The pole was greased, and he who was strong and persevering and able to climb to the top, became the village hero of the year. So is it today with this Mystic May-pole planted in humanity. Let him who can climb to the very top, the center whence all the streamers radiate, lift up his hands unto the heavens and invoke the glory of the Spiritual Sun to shed its benison on all who are not far enough evolved or not strong enough to climb the slippery Path to the top.

As an Order its students have all been climbing, but there have been many slips. Many have started up the pole or Path and have found it difficult to maintain their hold. But, thanks be to the Great Law, they have held on, for they have said: "In the might and strength and power of the Christ I will reach the top." There are others who are climbing fitfully, going up a little way today and slipping back tomorrow; picking themselves up and essaying it again. Of such materials are heroes made. By the power of the Divine manifesting through the human, we can all become heroes of the Mystic May-pole, once we have found our Sacred Oak; once we have grasped its streamers; once we have joined the circle of the consecrated dancers; once we have called upon the powers of heaven to aid us. Then we can stand around the Oak and with clasped hands and blending hearts ask that the Fire of the Christ, the Divine Flame and the Sun of Righteousness, shall descend like tongues of flame in a fiery baptism upon this Oak and fill its heart with Divine Fire. And verily, according to the creative forces we bring to it, according to the support we accord it, shall the miracle be accomplished; but to grow and put forth it must have its human as well as angelic support in Earth conditions.

It is said that many miracles were performed under the sacred oaks. It was taught that at noon and at midnight the consecrated oaks sent forth mysterious powers, especially during the full Moon, and that everyone on whom their shadows fell was healed, comforted or relieved of his distress. Also the devotee who prayed beneath the oaks had his spiritual sight opened and saw beautiful visions of the life eternal.

The days of miracles and magic are not over. In fact, there is no magic, only manifestations of Nature's laws. That which the initiated Druids, through a knowledge of the inner workings of the Great Law, could accomplish in the ancient days; that which the childlike Hawaiians, by believing in and following implicitly their Divine Instructors, [10] can accomplish today with physical trees destined for food, that shall we also do, but in the spiritual realm. Every day at noon a Healing Service is held by its priests under the Mystic Oak of the Order,[11] during which many miracles have been performed, many sick healed, much bitter sorrow comforted

---

[10] A Hawaiian legend relates that their Divine Instructors were white men who came from the East in a ship and who will return to them again; another evidence that all nations originally received their spiritual teachings from the same source, the great Lodge of Masters, through their messengers.

[11] See *The Temple of Silence*, Curtiss, Chapter IV, for details.

and much distress relieved, in every land where the shadow of this Mystic Oak has fallen, for it is an Oak planted by the River of Life under whose grateful shade all who will may rest. Yet, in our lighter moments it can also stand just as surely as our May-pole and inspire us with joy and gladness, thus making life colorful and happy, for May is the month dedicated to the Divine Mother, who ever provides cheer and gladness for her children, just as she provides the many-hued flowers which grow around the oak.

Those who have found this Order to be the May-pole of their choice and have danced and prayed and poured out their offerings around it, who have believed and trusted and loved, how much more shall their fulfillment be from their spiritual planting! How much more shall their spiritual eyes be opened! For, like the physical oaks, this Mystic Oak, under whose branches we are praying, shall endure throughout the ages and bring forth twelve manners of fruit, yielding its fruit each month.

Let us then lift up our hearts in dancing and thanksgiving and join our voices in praise, for the days of miracles are not past. For we see before us the fruits of a tiny acorn planted in darkness and discouragement, watered with tears and tended as a tiny sapling through the years of hardship and suffering, yet today, amidst all the adverse conditions, it is putting forth firm, strong roots, upward reaching limbs and outspreading branches which reach into every country and nation and people.

Is there one among us who is fearful or faint-hearted? Is there one who thinks that the arm of the Lord is shortened; that He is not able to save His own? Behold, before us this miracle! Is there one among us who cries out: "Life is too difficult. There is nothing but toil and poverty and misery, I am crushed!" Let him behold the miracle of this Mystic Oak! For out of poverty, out of ignorance, out of darkness and obscurity has this young Oak come forth, forcing its way up through the crevices of the hard rocks of Earth conditions, far up on the mountain side. And in spite of all opposition it is still growing sturdily, because it draws its Light from the Spiritual Sun, and its roots are planted and nourished in the bosom of the Divine Mother.

In the sacred groves of the Druids each tree was said to have its dryad or spirit, which transmitted the mystic powers of the oak to the priests. This dryad was an ethereal elemental, half Nature-sprite and half a thought-form created by the worship of the devotees, yet able to interpret to the priests the counsels of the gods. This belief is not the mere superstition into which it has degenerated, for most old legends which today read like pure fairy-tales are expressions of an underlying Divine Truth. Today that which was foreshadowed in the ancient ceremonies is fulfilled in our midst. For this Mystic Oak of the Order also has its Dryad. Today it is not a mere elemental, sprite and thought-form, but a living Soul, a living embodiment through which the Masters of Wisdom and the powers of the zodiac can transmit to us their words of encouragement, guidance and wisdom.

Let each of us begin then today to invoke the forces of the Spiritual Sun, not only in our own lives, but in the Heart of the Mystic Oak, that its priests may have the power to perform their magical rites; that its Dryad may be freed from all hampering conditions and be able to bring to us more perfectly the wisdom of the ages. Let us gather close then around our Mystic Oak and protect it by our love, devotion and support from all untoward conditions and forces, that its life and fruitfulness may be prolonged throughout the ages!

Let each one ask his own heart, each one of us, why he has joined himself to the band of devotees gathered round this Mystic Oak. Has he come merely as a critical spectator? Has he come merely for a passing May-dance, merely to be entertained? Or has he come that he might grasp fast hold of one of its streamers of force and become an active worker in spreading the dance of joy and peace and love of the resurrection day in the hearts of those who surround him? because he recognizes that in his life the resurrection from the old habits, thoughts and ideals has really taken place and he wishes to join hands with those who understand and worship round the Mystic Oak, that the coming cycle of his life may be filled to greater measure with the perfume of new blossoms unfolded, kind words spoken, loving deeds performed, and with the satisfaction that comes from bringing forth in his life the mystic "fruits of the Spirit?"

If it is this mystic bond of love and unity which holds us close and fills us, can we not understand that as we send the return current of our forces into this Center, into this Mystic Oak, that we are helping the whole world to share our joy and ultimately join us in the sacred dance? Let the world see live, glowing hearts, willing sacrifices and unselfish lives, and it will soon seek the source of our power. Some of us have tried to give it up. Some have said: "It is too much to ask. I cannot give up the old thoughts, the old point of view, the old life. It is too advanced. I cannot go so far as actually to live it." And yet the streamer of living force from this Mystic Oak which has entered and twined itself around their hearts draws them back to the Order once more. Believe, therefore, that if the divine powers brought to Earth through the Mystic Oak can help us to lift up the Light of the Christ in our lives, the promise shall be fulfilled: "And I, if I be lifted up from the earth will draw all men unto me."

There is but one question for us to ask. Answer that truthfully and we will know where we stand and what our next step must be. We must ask ourselves, "Am I a sincere follower of the Christ? Am I letting that mystic Light abide in me?" If not, then pray for a greater realization of the fullness of the love and power of the Mystic Christ. For this Power is life and love and immortality. And it must work out in us when invoked as it has worked out in the universe since the invocation, "Let there be light," was pronounced.

If we have identified ourselves with this special aspect of the creative power of the Spiritual Sun, each effort we make, each step we take is creative and is not taken for ourselves alone. Each thought and act is creative for the good of all. Our very life becomes creative and each thing that comes to us will be filled with the Christ-force and will go forth into humanity with a germ of redemption in it.

Not only can we invoke these divine powers to focus and manifest in our own lives, but we can invoke them to focus and manifest through the Mystic Oak of this Order that all mankind may benefit. Just as the Druids focused in their saplings the life-forces of the Sun and Earth, so can we call down the spiritual life-forces that the Mystic Oak may have the power and substance on all planes necessary to accomplish its great mission. We can call down the power of the Sun and it shall obey us. We can invoke the spiritual forces of the universe to become our servants. But not merely to enrich our personal life, not to give power and aggrandizement to the personal self, but for the help of all. For to be a true Magician or Druid, we must unselfishly use our Rod of Power to perform miracles for the good of all.

CHAPTER XXIV

THE DIAMOND HEART

Fire is the most perfect and unadulterated reflection in Heaven as on Earth, of the One Flame. It is Life and Death, the origin and end of every material thing. It is Divine Substance." *The Secret Doctrine*, Blavatsky, I, 146.

"O hidden mystery of the Flame! Thou art the very eye of the Eternal One. Thou reignest in the heights of Heaven: thou dwellest deep in the heart of Earth. Thy warmth and light and mystic powers make of the orb of day an open door into the eternal bosom of the Father who, through the purifying Flame of Divine Love, hath brought forth all flames; for all are parts of the Eternal Life, Love and Perfection."

"Thou, O Flame, art one with Divine Love, which floweth like a River of Life into the depths of the heart of Nature and bringeth forth after the fashion of the Divine Imagining! Thou piercest deep into the mystic depths of each human heart and bringest forth as bubbles upon the surface, every hidden thing. O purifier of our inmost hearts! O searcher of our thoughts! We Thy servants and disciples bow before Thee, O Divine Power sent forth from the Ever-living One!" Invocation to the Flame by the *Teacher of the Order of Christian Mystics*.

Nearly all ancient names for God include in their meaning the idea of fire. Hence, a universal belief in the sacredness of fire, and its connection with the manifestation of a mysterious power greater and more incomprehensible than all other manifestations in Nature, is older than recorded history. It is common to all religions, from the dumb adoration of primitive man, awed and mystified by its power, down through the ages in every clime and in every form of worship. The Christian religion is no exception; in fact, so full of references to fire and the Flame are the Christian scriptures that well might they be classed by a foreign investigator with the religion of the Parsees and other Fire Worshipers. But it must not be concluded that, either in the

Christian religion or any other form of so-called "fire-worship," the physical fire itself is worshiped any more than the cross can be said to be worshiped by Christians. And a symbol so universal to all mankind must have a vital spiritual significance. It is the recognition of fire as the most awe-inspiring manifestation of Deity, or, speaking metaphorically, fire and Flame are an outer garment of the Divine.

We are told that "Our God is a consuming fire,"[1] and of the Ancient of Days it is said: "His Throne was like the fiery name, and his wheels as burning fire. A fiery stream issued and came forth from before him."[2] Job, in speaking of the Great Initiator, says: "Out of his mouth go burning lamps and sparks of fire leap out . . . . . .His breath kindleth coals, and a flame goeth out of his mouth."[3] "The light of Israel shall be for a fire and his Holy One for a flame."[4] David tells us that "The Voice of the Lord divideth the flames of fire." [5] Jesus said: "I am come to send fire on earth,"[6] and of Him John the Baptist said: "He shall baptize you with the Holy Ghost, and with fire."[7] Hundreds of other references to fire and the Flame make it very plain that the inspired writers of both the Old and New Testaments were fully aware that the Mystery of the Flame is the Mystery of God and of all creation.

Just as the Light and heat of the Sun bring to Nature God's divine power as a manifestation of Cosmic Light and Life, so hidden in the symbol of the Flame is the secret of man's spiritual quickening; his spiritual growth and unfoldment; his testings and purifying burnings, which are so necessary until his heart has become like a diamond, pure and limpid, yet firm and unswerving, a Sun in miniature. But only through contact with the fiery Flame of Divine Love can man transmute the particles of earth which compose his physical body into a matrix in which the pure Spir-

[1] *Heb*, XII, 29
[2] *Dan*, VII, 9.
[3] *Job*, XLI, 19, 21.
[4] *Isaiah*, X, 17.
[5] *Psalms*, XXIX, 7.
[6] *Luke*, XII, 49.
[7] *Matt.*, III, 11.

itual Flame can be focused and all else excluded, so that like
the ingredients from which the diamond is slowly formed when
mysteriously incased in its matrix, the earthly desires and selfish
thoughts may be consumed in the glowing Flame of Divine Love
until the heart becomes a jewel of great price, pure and colorless,
holding in its depths the pure White Light, yet shedding forth
every colored ray of manifestation.

Humanity is now entering into a wonderful new era where it
is being subjected to tremendous pressure and great heat,[8] for
humanity as a whole must have its Diamond Heart perfected.
We are now passing through definite stages of this testing of the
ages and we are hearing with no uncertain ear the herald angel
proclaim: "Behold, we count them happy which endure . . . . . . He
that endureth unto the end, the same shall be saved." Also "Blessed
are they that have not seen, yet have believed." Throughout all the
ages this Diamond Heart has been slowly forming in the matrix of
the world, at first only a few tiny crystals, in the earth yet not of
it, buried deep in the rocks—the hard, oppressive forces of ages
of materialism and worldly conditions—and covered over with
sand and gravel—the sordid cares, the misunderstandings and the
ridicule and persecutions of men.

In previous chapters we have dwelt much upon the power of
the Living Flame, as it has swept and is still sweeping through all
earthly and human conditions. We have seen it in its lowest and
most destructive form on the field of battle where the flower of the
world's manhood has been mowed down like grass, where women
have been violated, children enslaved and homes made desolate or
utterly destroyed. Yet all this has been but the retort seven times
heated to melt the matrix in the stony heart of humanity out of
which must come its jewel. The time is approaching when this
matrix must open and reveal its many diamonds, for the rock of

[8] Diamonds are formed by the coalescing of many tiny crystals in a matrix under the
influence of tremendous pressure and the great heat of volcanic action.

Earth conditions and materialism has been exposed to the elements and has begun to disintegrate[9] because it has felt the great heat of Divine Love from the Sun of Righteousness as He draws close to Earth to gather His jewels.

We have also seen this Divine Flame manifesting in great power in all Nature, bursting the seeds, pushing up the tender sprouts through the resisting soil and bringing about the new springtime which covers even the devastated battlefields with the verdure of the new season. Just so will the Flame of the Spiritual Sun cover and make beautiful the stricken hearts of humanity with the verdure of new hope, courage and the power to push on through all obstacles and face the new era with trust and confidence in the power of the Divine to manifest in all conditions; for the Diamond Heart of the world is now rapidly being freed from its dense hard matrix of materialism.

This same Divine Flame is today in action in a greater and fuller measure than in many ages, searching out the inmost secrets of our hearts and lives,[10] burning in the very depths of our being, purifying, eliminating flaws, testing and proving each crystal, preparing the children of men to receive the announcement: "Behold, the Bridegroom cometh; go ye out to meet him." Thy Bridegroom, whose breath of Flame is upon thy cheek; whose encircling arms surround thee; whose life-giving power is sweeping through thee, consuming-renewing, destroying-upbuilding, that out of the union of Divine and human love "that holy thing which shall be born of thee" shall be the Child of the New Age, the Diamond Heart of Humanity. Only truth and pure love can endure the burning and bring forth: all else will fall away and disintegrate like the artificial, man-made

---

[9] In 1875, at the diamond mines of Kimberley, South Africa, it was discovered that if the hard earth forming the matrix of the diamonds was exposed to the air and the Sun's rays it would crumble and fall apart: a far more perfect and natural method of freeing the diamonds than the former method of breaking open the matrix with a mallet.

[10] *I Samuel*, II, 6, 7.

diamond, which crumbles and turns to black carbon dust when subjected to over-much heat.

Altho the artificial diamond yields the same chemical elements as the true diamond when analyzed, yet the true diamond is found to contain a mysterious something, a fire, a life-principle or soul impossible to impart to the artificial diamond, and it is this fire or soul, which science is unable to discover, *yet whose presence it recognizes*, which characterizes the true diamond. Even the smallest particle of the diamond adds its quota to the world's work and accomplishes that which no other substance can, such as its use in engraving, cutting glass, wire drawing, rock drills, accurate turning points in instruments of precision, watches, etc. Just so will every heart that responds in spirit and in truth to the burning of the Flame of Divine Love as the Sun of Righteousness draws close to Earth, find its own work to do; for there is work for every tiniest crystal of true diamond.

The Diamond Heart of the World has been slowly gathering its crystalline atoms (individuals) and perfecting them from the very foundation of humanity, but in this culminating cosmic era they are being drawn closer and closer together and consolidated into facets. Just as the one White Light contains and is the source of all colors,[11] so all mankind with their differing conceptions of truth are all God's children. And out of each colored reflection of the Light—each church, movement or conception of truth— if it be sincere and constructive and really seeking to know and do God's will on Earth, even as it is done in heaven, will He make a pathway direct to the serene heights of Christ-consciousness that all may hear His message in their own tongue or way of thinking and receive from Him direct. And when each

---

[11] Diamond matrix is found in varying conditions in river gravels embedded in a conglomerate called *cascalho (white)*; in terraces in a similar conglomerate *(yellow)*; in surface deposits of *red* clay in a conglomerate known as *gurgulko*; in *blue* earth occurring in pipes or funnels extending to unknown depths but connected with volcanic eruptions; also in meteorites. They therefore occur in matrices of red, yellow and blue, the three primary colors from which all other colors are formed.

pathway has been tested and proved able to stand the burning of the Flame it will be found to be a polished facet in the Diamond Heart of the World.

The crystals that shall compose this great Diamond are being gathered out of every people, kindred, tongue and country, both the civilized and the so-called uncivilized, for all are God's children. No church, society or order dare claim that unto it alone will the Bridegroom come or out of its limited ranks alone shall be gathered the atoms to compose the crystal facets; for it must be a universal ingathering of all pure, true crystals wherever found, without regard to race, color, creed, stage of civilization or intellectual advancement. Indeed, while there are many especially prepared avenues through which the Spiritual Sun is shining and many especially prepared matrices in which tiny separate diamonds are maturing and being polished, nevertheless, every Soul that is aspiring and crying out for the light in ever so obscure and humble a way, shall feel the quickening power of that Sun, and the rocks of Earth conditions, materialistic thoughts and intellectual limitations that have shut them in and separated them from one another shall crumble in its warmth, so that out of the most narrow and sectarian limitations all the crystals that truly reflect the Light shall be gathered to make up His jewels. But only those who have been perfected in their own limiting individual matrix and *have been released from it* can be gathered together to form the Diamond Heart of the World.

The time has now come when there must be such an ingathering into one great Brotherhood of Truth, each facet retaining its individuality and shedding forth its color, and all colors flashing and blending each with the others, yet all recognizing each other and working together to manifest perfectly the Light to every type of mind and condition of mankind. Already His angels—literally meaning Messengers of God and including human, as well as celestial messengers—are giving forth His message in every nation.

They are also recognizing each other as co-workers and fellow servants in the vineyard of the Great Master, Jesus.

These Messengers are humble human beings who have received their illumination and message direct from the coming Lord of Life and who have been consecrated to their individual missions by having His hands (powers to accomplish) laid upon their heads, yet all need to know the spiritual principles and the scientific aspect of the laws of manifestation which it is the special mission of this Order to furnish them that they may do their own portion of the Great Work more intelligently and efficiently and work in harmony with their fellow Messengers. For there are certain fundamental cosmic principles which all must follow.

All constructive teaching, like the diamond, is the result of the action of definite lines of force and consciousness which in their outward seeming may appear different, yet which are nevertheless from the same source, just as the sapphire, amethyst, ruby, topaz and Oriental emerald are all jewels composed of corundum (oxide of aluminum) variously colored, and follow the same law as to their formation. Just so spiritual teachings may differ in their presentation or coloring, due to the tint given by the race thought, training or bias of the mind through which they are given out, yet if they are true they can be traced back to the same fundamental principles as a common source.

In many churches and temples such enlightened ones are giving forth the Message through inspired sermons, giving to their flocks the truth in the way best suited to their understanding. In many societies and movements inspired Messengers are setting forth in language best suited to the comprehension of their followers the news of His coming and the necessity of preparing themselves and the world for it. In the Orient, in Australia, in South Africa, as well as in America, we have already recognized those Messengers who have been "called of God," who have been consecrated and sealed with the unmistakable seal of His per-

sonal touch that they may carry His message to the people of
their own land, wherever there are childlike hearts—those who
are teachable, eager to learn and not so bound by too great
intellectual and preconceived ideas that they cannot receive His
simple message. But during this time of formation let no one be
deceived, for the forces of natural selection will put each particle
in its rightful place.

There are many precepts laid down for those of us who,
because we have felt the Christ-light quickening our hearts,
ardently desire to be a part of this Diamond Heart. First we must
cultivate discrimination. "Learn to discern the real from the
false, the ever-fleeting from the everlasting . . . . . . The mind
needs breadth and depth and points to draw it to the Diamond
Soul . . . . . Seek, O Beginner, to blend thy mind and Soul."[12]
Therefore we must realize our great responsibility to weigh and
by the light of Soul-wisdom discriminate between true and false
teachings before giving them our support; for while the one giving
out false teachings is held responsible, yet if each Soul used the
God-given power of discrimination and read the signs along the
Path and obeyed the plainly marked rules of the road, as well as
asked for inner guidance, false teachings could do little harm.

One of the most strongly emphasized of these rules is not to
be carried away by great personal claims, for humility is the first
and one of the most essential of all characteristics for a teacher
of the Great Law. We are told "Self-gratulation, O Disciple, is
like unto a lofty tower, up which a haughty fool has climbed" and
yet only too often such a self-gratulating teacher is followed and
encouraged by the world until the lofty tower of self-praise has
grown to alarming heights. Hence when the Divine Fire of the
Lord (Law) flashes forth and the thunder of divine adjustment
rolls, the tower falls and engulfs all who have gathered at its base,
gazing up in admiration.

---

[12] *The Voice of the Silence*, Blavatsky, 25-6.

The Diamond Heart must be formed either in a matrix of living rock (Rock of Ages) or in the sand and gravel which because of their hardness and geometrical formation have only polished and perfected it. Hence all who would be a part of that Heart must look deep into their own hearts and by the wisdom thus gained be enabled to look deep into the heart of all things.

Here in America many have long recognized that *The Order of Christian Mystics* is such a Messenger. Its mission is to prepare for His coming by presenting the principles and philosophy of divine manifestation. These have been sent forth from the beginning of its ministry in 1908, when its commission was given direct from on high. And His hands have ever upheld its agents through all the trials, testings, persecutions, burnings and purifications through which the Order has passed. And His everlasting arms have been outstretched to bless and comfort all who have responded to the special call given through this Order. Hence, in spite of the natural human weaknesses of its messengers, they have never doubted the success of the message nor hesitated to obey in the face of the greatest opposition and discouragement, for they have ever remained humble and teachable. The Great Ones can give to their messengers everything except an humble, loving heart, a teachable mind and a determination that nothing can daunt; these are qualities the messengers themselves must furnish. And they have been amply rewarded by the knowledge that through their efforts many, many beautiful crystals have been freed from their confining matrices and many facets of the Diamond Heart have been polished.

But the messengers of the Order have received a new and more impressive and urgent message, which they must now transmit to you. They are bidden to proclaim to you the near approach of His advent on Earth[13] among His true

---

[13] See Chapters XXIII and XL herein, also *The Voice of Isis*, Curtiss, Chapter X.

and devoted followers in all lands. To prepare for this He bids all draw close in faith, devotion and love to their fellow men and to their chosen messengers, and help to spread the Teachings wherever a mind and heart is found open to them.

It is not that this Order is the only facet of the Diamond Heart, but it is the facet to which many hearts respond; the facet which sends forth the Light in the way that is most illuminating to their minds and most satisfying to their hearts. Therefore, all such will wish to help to bring this same Light, comfort and satisfaction to those who are spiritually hungry and are groping for the clear Light. Their love and devotion and help will make this Order a true, perfect and unsullied jewel, universal and beautiful, because made up of many, many particles in all lands, all true in themselves to the Christ within, yet all drawn together to the very heart of the Flame—which is the manifestation of the Christ in the Order—because their hearts respond to the outpouring of His Divine Love and because they have consecrated themselves to His work through this avenue of Light.

(To be concluded)

Chapter XXV

THE DIAMOND HEART
(Concluded)

"Light is cold Flame, and Flame is Fire, and Fire produces Heat, which yields Water—the Water of Life in the Great Mother." *The Stanzas of Dzyan*, Stanza III, Sloka IX.

While the Order of Christian Mystics is destined to be drawn into the Diamond Heart of the World, yet it must develop a Diamond Heart of its own within the matrix of the outer conditions in which its Diamond must be perfected.

A diamond grows because of the living Flame that focuses upon and flows through it, yet it could never crystallize into an individualized spark of that Flame unless the mother (matrix) held it close within her heart and covered and encased it within her living tissues. Its great brilliancy is caused by the fact that owing to its form the light or flame is reflected back into the stone instead of passing through it as in most gems. The diamond, while belonging to the cubic system, generally assumes the form of the octahedron (eight-sided), but it may take other forms embracing from twelve to forty-eight faces (rhombic-dodecahedron, hexakis-octahedron) and combinations of these geometrical figures. It is the Light playing on the angles formed by these variously formed facets which produces the wonderful play of colors.

While the diamond is not born in a hard rock matrix, as are most other gems, nevertheless it is literally born of the Flame. The Earth Mother has prepared the conditions, has gathered the materials and held them close, so that when the great eruptive volcanic flames sweep up from the very foundation of the globe these materials are transmuted into the transparent globules which go to make up the diamond,[1] a process similar to that which goes on in the mother's womb while the child is taking form. Yet were the materials not there, had the Earth Mother not gathered together and held close in her bosom the special materials that were the essence of the diamond, the cataclysmic eruption of the Flame would have swept through her and left behind only volcanic ash and debris, as it does in so many instances.

Thus is the Diamond Heart of each Soul and of this Order born. Laboriously we gather to us the lessons of life and hold them close in the matrix of our hearts, shielded from the outer world, and when the fiery blasts of upheaval, sorrow or disruption come, we recognize in them but the quickening breath of our Father and lo! our Diamond Heart is born (our Christ-child). Hence, always can it be said of each one who has passed through this experience, "That holy thing which is born of thee, shall be called the Son of God," for God quickeneth His Son in our hearts by the power of the Holy Ghost, *i.e.*, the Flame of Divine Love, just as the volcanic flame brings to birth the diamond in Nature. The diamond, which represents mastery in the kingdom of chemical earths, has many remarkable qualities little known to the modern world; nor will they ever be known as long as the diamond is only valued at a commercial rating. Yet its intrinsic value was and is known by the initiated Adepts and was guessed at by the ancient peoples. Were we versed in the symbology of Nature and had more than a superficial knowledge of geometry its very formation could reveal much to us. To quote: "This indicates that the apparently simple crystal may really consist of eight individuals meeting at the center (*i.e.*, a group Soul) or, what

---

[1] A great diamond is formed by the coalescing of many tiny crystals. But it is pure and flawless only when the coalescence is so perfect that the strongest magnifying glass cannot detect the slightest trace of separation between the individual crystals.

comes to the same thing, of two individuals interpenetrating and projecting through each other,"[2] corresponding to the blending of the individual Soul with the Over Soul, or man and woman merging the separate personalities into oneness in the Higher Self. A pure diamond will radiate in a dark room if it has been subjected to sunlight or radium. Also, it reflects the aura of the wearer if the aura be pure enough to give forth light, and it is said that through it a Master can read the inner life of the wearer. Also, by its color flashes and its shadows events to come can be foretold. If understood and correlated with, it will warn of danger and prove a faithful mentor, for evil thoughts and impure desires will dim its luster. By the ancient Greeks it was called the "invincible," and is credited with the power of averting insanity, and of rendering poison harmless. In the Middle Ages it was known as the "*pietra della reconciliazione*," as the peace maker between husband and wife. All these and many more qualities surely inhere in that which it symbolizes, if not in the stone itself, yet every gem has its special qualities and radio-activity which influence the wearer in accordance with his degree of sensitiveness.

From the above it will be seen that we cannot form and manifest the Diamond Heart of the Order—which is its point of contact with the Divine Flame manifesting through all true spiritual inspiration—and the Order cannot take its place in the Diamond Heart of the World unless a proper matrix is formed of living Souls, each one in his or her own place, each one gathering and transmitting to the Heart Center the various ingredients necessary for its formation, and each one standing close and firm as a part of a protective matrix, yet like the matrix, open to the inflow of all the inner and higher forces.

It is through its rocks that the Earth breathes and sends forth her magnetic forces to sustain all life upon the planet.[3]

---

[2] *Encyclopedia Britannica*, Vol. VIII, 158.
[3] See *The Voice of Isis*, Curtiss, 311.

And by the melting and fusion of her rocks through volcanic eruptions (the breath of the Flame) the vital life is distributed to the planet; for only through the action of fire was the Earth herself given her separate birth. This is one reason why every city built upon a rock foundation is more apt to grow great and endure than one built upon sand or soil. Altho sand is disintegrated rock, and soil is a later process in the preparation of the planet for man's habitation, they do not transmit the forces as do the rocks.

This law is the esoteric basis for the biblical parable of the man who built his house upon the rock and he who built upon the sand. This is also one of the occult reasons why New York is the greatest city in the world today, for it is built upon solid rock. Hence, while the lower end may be inundated in the coming cataclysms, the city as a whole will not be destroyed, for it has a great work to do in the world for the coming New Age and a duty to accomplish to the many alien peoples within its gates; and because it is founded on rock it must become the exponent or foundation of American principles to all the children of other Races who contact this country through its doors.

There is work for each sincere student to do, if we are to have this Order so securely founded upon the Rock of Ages that it may become a nucleus of the New Age. We must determinedly gather the strength and the forces from the lessons of patience, tolerance, brotherhood, cheerfulness, faith and perseverance which we have learned in the environment (matrix) where the Great Law has placed us because of our past activities, that we may build those forces either into the matrix which supports and helps to bring forth the Diamond Heart of the Order, or perhaps into the very Diamond itself; for without the matrix the Diamond cannot be produced. Let us build these forces firmly into our own lives that we may also automatically become necessary particles that must be drawn into the Living Flame to become a part of the Diamond Heart, firstly of the Order and then of the World. For not one particle of diamond substance can be wasted.

It is well, however, for none of us to waste time in trying to impress on the world the fact that we as individuals may be a part of the Diamond itself, for only those particles which have endured the force of the Flame for ages are so prepared that they can be thus used, while all particles can be used for the matrix. Let us be content to be built in wherever the Great Law needs the materials which we can furnish. For suppose a wonderful child is to be born, would the mother refuse to carry the child and give it her life-forces and protection lest she be of less importance than the child when born? Only as the Order forms such a matrix and holds up the hands of the messengers through whom the Flame of Inspiration is flowing can it form a glowing facet in the Diamond Heart of the World. The hands symbolize the power of the Order to accomplish, hence to hold up the hands of the Order means to form a matrix which shall make it possible for the Order to carry on and broaden the work and spread the Teachings more widely throughout the world.

It will be remembered that when the Children of Israel, while in the wilderness, questioned: "Is the Lord among us or not?" they at once had to fight Amalek, who symbolized doubt. Amalek and his tribe originally inhabited the shores of the Dead Sea, where earlier they were met and defeated by Abram. But when Moses (the Law) led the Children of Israel out of Egypt these same Amalekites were encountered all the way from the boundaries of Egypt even to the Promised Land. Both Saul and David defeated, yet did not annihilate them. So does the Aspirant encounter doubt from the moment he turns away from following selfish desire (Pharaoh) and begins to follow the Divine Law (Moses) until he reaches the Promised Land, continually gaining victories yet never quite annihilating doubt.

The moment the Israelites began to question and doubt their leader, Amalek came upon them and the Great Law said to them: "Go out, fight with Amalek: tomorrow I will stand on the top of the hill with the rod of God (power of the Law) in mine hand * * * And it came to pass, when Moses held up his hand, that Israel prevailed; and when he let down his hand, Amalek prevailed."[4] When Moses became weary and could no longer hold up his hands, his faithful helpers put a stone under him that he might sit or rest on the Rock of Truth. And Aaron and Hur stood one on either side and held up his hands until the going down of the Sun, so that Israel prevailed over their doubts and lack of faith in the power of the Divine Law to lead them out of the Wilderness into the Promised Land and to give them the power to conquer all obstacles on the way.

How often, like Moses, after assuaging the thirst of its followers by cleaving the Rock of Spiritual Understanding that its waters might flow forth, the hands of the Order grow heavy and weary because of the doubts and fears and lack of faith in the hearts of those whom it has led out of Egypt! Often the hands grow weary and droop because the physical means is lacking to support the hands and carry on the work as it should be done; to publish the books, to answer the personal letters promptly, to translate the Teachings into other languages' for which there is such a crying need, and to accomplish the many other things which the students recognize as important and complain about when not done. Hence, like the Children of Israel, some of the students begin to ask: "Is the Lord among us or not?" Even a printer's error or a slight grammatical mistake in the transmission and expression of the message is sufficient to call out the forces of Amalek in the minds of a few. If at such times, when Amalek seems to prevail, the close, devoted and understanding ones would step forward and place a stone or form a matrix of the Rock of Faith under

---

[4] *Exodus*, XVII, 9-11.

the Order and, standing like Aaron and Hur on either side, hold up the hands of the Order, Israel (the followers) would continue to prevail.

The hands of the Order being its power to accomplish, the right hand symbolizes the exoteric work to be accomplished in the world by transmitting the lessons, spreading the Teachings, publishing the books, lecturing, forming study-classes, etc. The left hand is the esoteric or personal work accomplished by the private correspondence and teachings of the true and devoted followers, helping them with their personal problems, answering their letters, transmitting the healing love and the personal advice of the Teacher to them, etc. All this requires so much patience, time and strength, that the left hand often becomes utterly weary and needs to be upheld by understanding and love; for it is the students of the Order, standing as Israel or "the chosen people" — those who have chosen to follow the Law Giver — who must stand close and fight Amalek for the good of all, for his army is legion.

Who is the enemy? All those forces in the world that influence the minds of men — even the consciousness of those who have found their Soul-home in this Order — and persuade them that all this talk of a new and better era for mankind and of the near approach of the Great Teacher to Earth is but imagination or a fantastic dream; that even the personal experience and spiritual realization they have had in their hearts and lives are but the hallucinations of the neurasthenic! These are easily recognized as the same forces of Amalek that manifested at the beginning of the former eras. "And as it was in the days of Noe, so shall it be also in the days of the Son of Man. * * * Likewise also as it was in the days of Lot. * * * Even thus shall it be in the day when the Son of Man is revealed."[5]

The time is drawing near when the Lord of Life shall again appear on Earth. Those who have waited and

---

[5] *St. Luke*, XVII, 26-30.

watched; those whose hearts have gone forth in love and longing in many incarnations, such have now the opportunity to do something definite to prepare for His coming. If they cannot hold the burning force of the Divine Flame close and still in their own hearts, they at least can gather round and stand firm on the Rock of Spiritual Understanding, hold up the hands which contain the Rod of the Law and help to form a loving matrix which, like the womb of the Divine Mother, shall shield from all inimical influences and nourish the Christ-child within with all the life-essences necessary to bring it to birth.

Only those who have lain in the dark matrix of Earth conditions and have felt the burning of the Flame of His Love through many long years, growing warmer and clearer of insight; whose hearts have been transmuted into a gemlike substance embodying within it in crystalline clearness the same fiery Flame of Divine Love, the same depths of limpid stillness which mirror undistorted the higher ideals from the realms above, only such can understand the hearts of others and know how to help them wisely. Only those who have become more responsive to the burning of the Love poured out, whose hearts have thrilled with the same ideals and who desire to help on His work—to feed His lambs—by uniting the diamond spark in their own hearts to the Diamond Heart of the Order and of the World, can furnish the qualities which will enable the Order to flash forth the many colors or aspects of Truth—which in the heart of humanity symbolize the diversity in unity of all hearts—with which the Order feeds, comforts and satisfies all whose hearts are drawn to it.

There is, therefore, work for all to do. No particle of the Diamond, even the chips and the dust which result from its cutting and polishing, are useless or wasted. Each can play an important part when wisely used. Let the Great Law, then, cut deep. Let the polishing storms and trials of life sweep over us strongly and fiercely if they must for our polishing; for we fear not as long as the burning Love of the Master's heart throbs close to ours. Let us unite our efforts first to respond to the Divine Flame within, then to stand firm and uphold the hands of the Order, that the Teachings may be spread abroad and lived out; for only as the Order, through its messengers, holds up the hands (powers) given it to accomplish for the Master and humanity can the Children of Israel (the diamond globules) prevail over the opposing forces of Amalek.

Beloved of the Flame! do you love your Lord who alone can fulfill the Law of your destiny? Do you realize and reckon with the mightiness of His power? Believe you in the absolutely unconquerable force of His oncoming? Like true diamonds are you ready to bear the burning of His love until the dust and gravel—the earthiness of your personality—have been transmuted into a tiny crystal of diamond, ready and able to coalesce with others of like substance to form a facet in the Diamond Heart of Humanity?

All through the ages the little crystals have been drawing their life from the Divine Flame of the Sun of Righteousness and have clung together for sympathy and protection, but now the Diamond Heart is gathering them together to consolidate them into one Jewel of Truth, yet with many facets, through which the one Divine White Light can flash forth its many brilliant color rays so that every type of mind may be reached from the one great Source of all Light; for all colors draw their light from the one Flame in the heart of the jewel. It is such a great flawless, flaming Jewel of Universal Truth that all, through love, devotion and service, should help this Order to become, so that "when He cometh to make up His jewels" He will find it ready and fit to be the central Jewel of His Crown.

Upon the threshold of the New Age we stand with bated breath and trembling feet, with eager eyes strained toward the mystic East to catch the first glimmerings of the coming dawn, scarce knowing whether the Earth will open and swallow us or whether an Angel shall suddenly throw wide the doors of the Temple of Light and reveal our Lord coming forth "in power and great glory." Yet, once we understand the Law of Manifestations, we will work unceasingly to prepare the way and make straight His paths in our own lives and in the world, while we confidently await the Coming with quiet faith and serene joy.

CHAPTER XXVI

FAITH AND WORKS

"Ye shall know them by their fruits. Do men gather grapes of thorns, or figs of thistles?" *St. Matthew*, VII, 16.

"What doth it profit, my brethren, though a man say he has faith, and have not works? Can faith save him? . . . Even so faith, if it hath not works, is dead, being alone." *James*, II, 14-17.

The word faith has been variously interpreted as being belief, or mere credulity, even superstition; as confidence in a person or thing; and more commonly to designate a particular religion, such as the Christian faith, the Buddhistic faith, etc. We, however, prefer to use St. Paul's definition: "Faith is the substance of things hoped for, the evidence of things not seen."[1]

Faith and works are like the two ends of a magnet; faith the unseen, negative or attracting end; works the seen, positive or manifested end. The substance of a thing is its soul; that which makes it alive or essentially distinguishes it. Therefore, we "hope" not for the temporal outer manifestation of things, but to find the reality back of them, back of all manifested life. And by faith we pierce the enshrouding outer seeming and with our inner senses gain evidence of that which, altho not seen, really exists, just as the psychologist seeks for the motive back of every art. The motive may be unseen, yet it is potent to produce the result noted.

A thing hoped for, if that hope is to be more than a hope, if it is to be manifested, must be worked for and must find a channel. That which is unseen can be evidenced outwardly only by the works which it brings forth in the realm of the seen. For instance, a young tree is planted in the dark,

---

[1] *Hebrew*, XI, 1.

cold earth. We see only a sapling with bare twigs, yet we are told it is a fig tree and that it is alive. We have faith that the unseen forces of life within the earth, air, water and fire (Sun), will so fill those bare and leafless branches that in the fullness of time they shall bring forth fruit. Yet we know that it requires something more than faith in those unseen forces if the tree is to bear perfect fruit; for the forces of Nature unaided by man will produce only wild fruit; small, imperfect, bitter and with little nourishment. Therefore, if the unseen works of God are to come into evidence in perfection, man must provide adequate channels for the expression of his faith or all that is hoped for cannot be evidenced. He must add to his faith, works; must dig around the tree, must prepare the soil, must fertilize it, must protect it from rodents, from insects, from blights, etc. So with the manifesting of our Tree of Life within. Only as we perform the works necessary can the forces of its life make our faith manifest in perfection. Only so can our Tree bring forth in our lives the things hoped for. Yet, since we have compared faith to the Soul or Real Substance, we must not merely hope some day to realize the inner life or substance of that which we believe, but we must realize that since the Soul of man is the Substance or Real Self and the outer personality but a manifestation in Earth conditions, if we are to prove to ourselves that our faith is really a living factor and true, we must definitely seek to correlate with its substance, the Soul or Real Self. For if we plant a sapling as a fig tree and it is not, no matter how many people tell us it is a fig tree, it cannot become one, nor can all our faith or the powers of heaven force it to bring forth figs. Therefore, we must go deeper than merely to believe all that we are told. We must use our God-given intuition to know the true nature of that which is offered to us as a fig tree. This will be the realization of a living faith, *i.e.*, faith in the power of the Divine Self within us to discriminate and recognize the essential nature or Soul or "the substance of things hoped for" in all things.

Conversely, if we see a tree bringing forth certain fruit we know that it is that particular kind of a tree and no other, no matter what other name the nurseryman may attach to it or how it has been misrepresented by those who have an interest in so doing. In other words, we judge the tree by its works or fruits, for the fruits are the acme of the tree's expression and prove the tree, even tho some of its leaves may be imperfect or may wilt and fall. The same is true of ourselves. Our fruits or our works are the best expression of the unseen Self we have been able to manifest, even tho they are far from that which we hoped for. Not what we think, not what we intend, but what we do, what we accomplish, what we express, is the *manifested us*; for the world can know us only by our fruits, our works. And conversely, the works of a man, society, movement or Order represent that man, society, movement or Order, no matter what anyone may say about them and no matter how many imperfections or limitations they may have. "Do men gather grapes of thorns, or figs of thistles?" "Then he shall reward every man *according to his works*. * * * To every man *according to his deeds*."[2]

As we have continually pointed out, every law that we see manifesting in Nature we may expect to see manifesting in man; for man is a part of the grand chorus singing the great Psalm of Life which has been sung by all creation since the morning stars sang together to greet the dawn of our present day of manifestation. But because man is the highest "evidence of things not seen" which evolution has unfolded and manifested on Earth, it is possible for him to sing his part in the paean of divine manifestation more perfectly, for he can sing understandingly and by note that which Nature sings only instinctively by ear.

Man may be likened to the musical staff on which a sym-

[2] *St. Matthew*, XVI, 27. *Romans*, II, 6.

phony is written. His five senses may be compared to the five lines
of the staff, while the four spaces between the lines may be likened
to the four elements: fire, air, water, earth. These elements are
continually playing their unseen part in the melody, yet man must
learn to use his five senses to listen to, understand and interpret
the notes that fall in the spaces as well as those that fall upon the
lines. Above the five lines (senses) is the infinite ether of space,
which is forever impinging upon man's senses, but of which he is
usually aware only as vague yearnings, because it transcends his
physical senses. Below the staff there are also many notes written
in the deep emotions of longings unspeakable, of experiences
garnered, of suffering and pain. But if man endeavors to interpret
the Symphony of Life through faith, through aspiration, he may
reach up to notes of infinite harmony, joy and ecstasy and join in
the angelic chorus forever singing around the great white throne.
But he must also learn that the notes below the staff are necessary
to complete the melody. Therefore, to express the melody aright
man must learn to listen to all the notes and sound them clear, true
and understandingly. But, alas, many hear only the notes that fall
upon the lines (senses) and all the other notes remain unheard.
To them the Psalm of Life seems imperfect or even discordant,
yet all the notes can be heard by faith and expressed in the life
through works.

   While we are all singing the same grand symphony, yet each
has his or her own part. And each has implanted within exactly
the ability needed to fit him to perfect and express his part. The
Great Law never expects us to gather grapes from thorns, nor figs
from thistles. And just as surely must each one bring forth the fruit
of his own perfected life. If we try to imitate another we fail to
bring forth our own fruit. And when the Lord of Life passes by,
seeking figs and finding none, He will command that the barren
fig tree be cut down, not as a punishment or a curse, but because—
as the parable illustrates—of a manifest law, that unless each

individual gathers the forces of life and puts forth all possible
effort to utilize his powers to grow and bring forth the fruit that
is the natural result of his stage of evolution, he is not only failing
himself, but is encumbering the ground, *i.e.*, is so misapplying the
forces of the great evolutionary urge within him that all mankind
is held back.

The parable of the barren fig tree[3] is frequently misunderstood.
It was not cursed in the way which the faulty interpretation seems
to imply, for we are told "the time of figs was not yet" and it would
surely be most unjust to curse a tree because it did not bear fruit
out of season. The true interpretation is revealed in the thirteenth
verse of the passage,[4] where we are told that the tree had plenty of
leaves and yet there was no sign of fruit. When a fig tree is full of
leaves there should in the natural course of events be figs forming,
or at least blossoms, even if the full time for ripe figs was not at
hand; for the buds must come first, then the leaves, the blossoms
and later the fruit, one of the functions of the leaves being to
protect the ripening fruit. Hence, the symbology of the parable
is that each Soul who is planted in the vineyard of the Lord and
is enriched and tended for three seasons, or three periods during
which the body, mind and Spirit have been given special attention
or special opportunities for unfoldment and advance, and yet fails
to advance, when the Lord of Life comes to that Soul seeking figs
and finds none, because that Soul has used all its forces in making
a great show that will attract the attention or the admiration of
the world—mere leaves, be they never so beautiful—the Great
Law as Karma will surely entail upon that Soul what may seem
to be a curse, namely, that it shall not be able to bear fruit and
meet the requirements of the Lord of Life when it desires to do
so. That is, in the next incarnation such a one will greatly desire

---

[3] *St. Luke*, XIII, 6-9. See also Pages 248-9 herein.
[4] *St. Mark*, XI, 13.

spiritual development, but will find himself so environed that it will be almost impossible to attain it or manifest it.

Moreover, whenever or wherever the life-forces are not used to create and bring forth, the three-fold Law of Life (creation—preservation—disintegration) naturally removes the thing that cannot or will not use the forces to bring forth. It must die out, for disintegration is just as surely a part of the Law of Life as creation and preservation. A study of all Nature will confirm this, and also the wonderful interactions of the three-fold life stream. In southern climates, where life is luxuriant and riotous, we see many buzzards hovering in the air, keeping watch for every animal that may die that its carcass may be consumed lest it spread disease and death. Hence, a little thought will show how these three threads of life are interwoven, for that which removes the dead and decaying carcass preserves the pure life atmosphere, and from the carcass new creative life springs forth; while in more northerly climates the carcass can more safely be left to enrich the soil and thus create new life and preserve the equilibrium.

"Inquire of the earth, the air, and the water, of the secrets they hold for you." The earth corresponds to the physical senses which take cognizance of only those things which impinge upon them; the air represents the aspirations of the heart which reach up in longing to the throne of God; the water is the symbol to us of Love, ever changing and unstable on Earth, yet in its divine aspect ever constant and unfathomable as the ocean; the fire is the Flame of the Spirit in our hearts, that which warms our hearts and without which the melody of life will ever be flat and lifeless.

The world is today passing through an era in which greater power is given unto Satan, under the opprobrious and ignominious title of the devil. This is an era, therefore, in which evil has great power for a short time, because it is working out its own extinction. Satan, who in reality is Saturn—

one of the Sons of light manifesting as stern justice[5]—must and does lead and marshal these powers of darkness and guides them to their own destruction. Yet he leads them in love, for it requires a Divine Love for one of the Sons of God to accept a task involving so much misunderstanding, ignominy and contumely as the guidance of evil to its own destruction; for love is God and is the consuming buddhic fire for all that is not in harmony with it. The tree of evil planted by man in the soil of Earth has reached its harvest time, and only as it bears its characteristic fruit and the mass of mankind who do not follow their intuitions eat of it, can they prove that its fruit brings suffering and death instead of joy and life. The whole world must taste of this harvest in a measure, for everyone has had something to do with the planting and nourishing of its baneful growth. Even if one has merely stood by and permitted evils to go on unchecked he must in a measure suffer, just as one must who sees the harvest of his neighbor ravished by insects, yet does nothing to check their spread until they overrun his own field.

Saturn is the Great Tester. It is his part in the Divine Plan to further the redemption of man by helping him to eat of the fruits of his own sowing and experience the bitter results that he may be ready the sooner to turn from them and learn to seek the fruits of the Tree of Life, knowing only too well that man will use his God-given free-will to eat first of the forbidden fruit, and will only turn to the Tree of Life when he needs healing and saving from himself. Hence, at the end of every Great Race and sub-race, all that has been planted, both of weeds and golden grain (the tares and the wheat), which has grown together until the close of the season (cycle), must be made ready for the sickles of the Angels who are the reapers; for only by their fruits (works) can we surely know them.

Saturn is, therefore, not the devil. The devil[6] is the

[5] *Job*, I, 6. Also Chapter XXXII herein.
[6] See *The Key of Destiny*, Curtiss, 174.

synthesis of the evil created by man which Saturn is helping man
to reap; and his testing is in absolute justice. "The Sons of God
came to present themselves before the Lord, and Satan (Saturn)
was among them."[7] The Sons of God are the Planetary Deities
or the seven expressions of the one white Light, each with his
own work to do toward the evolution of man and the Cosmos.
Only this understanding of Them can keep the words quoted
from clashing with the oft-repeated statement that Jesus was the
only begotten Son of God. While the Planetary Deities are the
seven-fold expression of the one Godhead, just as love, justice,
etc., may be expressions of one man, the Christ as manifested by
Jesus is the "only begotten Son" of this one Godhead, "begotten
not made, being of one substance with the Father by whom all
things are made."

If we consider the planetary Rulers as manifestations of
the one God, working His will, and gathered before the Lord,
i.e., manifesting each in his appointed time and manner before
the Lord or in accordance with the Great Law, we will understand
why they were Sons of God and why Saturn was one of them.
Today we are reaping under Saturn the harvest of all that man has
sown during the long period of Saturn's reign, because his cycle
is now ended and we are passing out of his influence and coming
under the reign of the occult planet, Uranus.

Saturn comes, therefore,—just as he came in the story of Job—
from "going to and fro on the earth," and each Soul who has
professed the name of Christ and called himself a follower of
Christ, must be specially tested. No one can say that he is one with
the Divine Law as long as, like Job, he is hedged about on every
side and blessed in the works of his hand.[8] Therefore, ere he has
completed his redemption and is ready for the great Sun Initiation—
symbolized by the story of Job—he must pass through the testings of

[7] *Job*, I, 6.
[8] *Job*, I, 10, 12.

Saturn; "For behold, all that he hath is in thy (Saturn's) power." [8]
This testing comes in love and in perfect justice. It is the Fire of
Divine Love which, while it consumes all that is evil, nevertheless
quickens every seed of good. It is justice because each one is
tested according to the work he was expected to accomplish.

Man does the same thing in his physical works. He tests every
so-called inanimate thing needed to accomplish a work. If he
builds a bridge, every span is tested to bear a strain far greater
than any it will probably be subjected to; every beam, every rivet,
has its severe test, according to the work it is expected to do. We
do not test a knife that is made to cut bread for the hungry in the
same way that we test a bridge span destined to carry much traffic
over the river that separates us from the Promised Land, yet each
will and must pass through the fire and be fitted for its own work.
If we conceive of all these materials as sentient lives, with little
understanding of what structure they are to be a part, and hence
unable to grasp the reasons why they should thus be tested and
be subjected to almost unbearable strains, we will see that they
differ but little from man, except in degree. Perhaps we will then
cease to murmur and blame God or Saturn for our seemingly
unjust treatment, for "Blessed is the man whom thou chastenest,
O Lord, and teachest him out of thy law."

When the passing conditions of the world today are over and
the nations, the leaders, the churches, societies, religions, orders
and individuals have passed through the great testings of Saturn,
that which remains will be pure gold, the grains of Truth gathered
for the planting of the New Era. All that was good and wholesome
will have been stored up to feed the new race, and those trees
which have borne good fruit, no matter if during the testing
heat and drought some of their leaves have faded, will take their
places as food-producers for the new humanity, just as the famous
horticulturist, Luther Burbank, has gathered from every country

in the world thousands of wild trees and plants and is cultivating and testing them and endeavoring to bring them to such perfection that they shall add to the food supply of future generations. If we have helped and fed the spiritually hungry and the food has nourished their Souls, then our tree will stand. If, on the other hand, we have wasted our time shaking from other trees their ripening fruit and trampling it in the mire, and have brought forth little of our own, and that little is acrid and unnourishing, even tho we conscientiously believed the fruit we destroyed was not as good as it might have been, we must confront the new day hungry and lacking.

The fruit that this Order is bearing season after season has been bitterly attacked on several occasions, yet the tree still stands and flourishes and brings forth increasing crops each year. But as Saturn's cycle closes and the gates of the new day are opening and we have an opportunity to establish the Order in a permanent way, all the force of opposition to Light and Freedom is stirred up afresh. Therefore, let no one be dismayed if he finds it again and again attacked by those who stand for autocracy in religious thought and against the spiritual freedom and liberty of conscience and the individual guidance from within which this Order advocates. It will be but another testing of Saturn. But it need have but little effect if every one who has eaten and been nourished by its fruits will give of his love, gratitude and devotion to protect it. We ask all who wish to help thus to repeat the *Protecting Invocation*,[9] morning, noon and night and put around the Order, its Founders and its students a rampart of Divine Love, realizing that since Divine Love is also Divine Fire, no human mind need decide whether the tree be good or evil, for the Fire will consume all that is evil, quicken all that is good and cause it to put forth more abundantly, and also protect it from the vicious insects that would destroy it.

---

[9] See *Appendix*.

This Divine Fire is the spiritual force which alone can purify and redeem the world in these troublous times. The use of the *Protecting Invocation* is therefore constructive in the highest sense. We do not have to fight evil or think of the personalities through whom evil is manifesting, or of those who are inharmonious, who persecute us or even of our so-called enemies, if we have any. All we have to do is to use this *Invocation* and see ourselves and the Order surrounded by Living Flame, and rest assured that it will consume all the evil it contacts and at the same time will stimulate and bring forth all the germs of good that exist, even in the hearts of evil doers, also in ourselves. Only when the days of testing are over—Saturn's reign—can there be peace on Earth, goodwill toward men, under the influence of the mystical planet, Uranus.

The planetary configuration which some time since alarmed so many, namely, the position of Uranus on one side of the Sun and all the other planets on the other side pulling against it, announced not a physical cataclysm, as some feared—altho many minor disasters have resulted—but the terrific and united opposition of all that pertains to the old order of things, the old cycle under Saturn, to the manifestation of the deeper occult, spiritual and mystical forces and teachings of the new day, all of which are ruled by Uranus and which at this time are already finding themselves entangled in the last testings of Saturn. In other words, all teachings, societies, orders—especially all pertaining to the occult or spiritual—must stand or fall according to their fruits, for the mighty whirlwind of earthly opposition to all things belonging to the new day is already shaking the branches of the various trees. And only those whose roots are sunk deep in the soil of spiritual realities, in faith in the power of things not seen and anchored round the Rock of Truth can stand the testing.

CHAPTER XXVII

CROSSING JORDAN

"Now after the death of Moses the servant of the Lord it came to pass, that the Lord spake unto Joshua the son of Nun, Moses' minister, saying, Moses my servant is dead; now therefore arise, go over this Jordan, thou, and all this people, unto the land which I do give to them, even to the children of Israel . . . within three days ye shall pass over this Jordan." *Joshua*, I, 1-2-11.

The crossing of the river Jordan is one of the most important and final events in the great allegory[1] of the wandering of the children of Israel ere they reached the Promised Land. And in these days of physical and psychical unrest it is well to explain more fully than we have already done elsewhere[2] the spiritual meaning of its universal symbology and its application to the personal experiences of those chosen people who are about to enter the Promised Land of the higher spiritual consciousness.

The wandering in the wilderness for forty years[3] symbolizes that period in the life of each awakened Soul when it is being taught by the Great Law to cull the lessons out of its wanderings in the wilderness of outer conditions by following the guidance of the pillar of cloud by day and the pillar of fire by night as it is led to the brink of Jordan where it must take its next great step.

It will be remembered that Moses, who represents the Law Giver who led the Children of Israel out of Egypt,

---

[1] "The book of Joshua has ascribed to one man conquests which *are not confirmed by history.* . . . From a careful consideration of all the evidence, both internal and external, biblical scholars are now almost unanimous that the more finished picture of the Israelitish invasion and settlement *cannot be accepted as historical* for the age." *Encyclopedia Britannica*, vol. XV, Article on Joshua.

[2] See *Realms of the Living Dead*, Curtiss, II.

[3] See *The Key to the Universe*, Curtiss, 151.

was not permitted to cross over Jordan and enter the Promised Land; for we are told that after having been shown the fair land of promise from the top of Mt. Pisgah (meaning prayer and a boundary), his bones were laid in the wilderness. The symbology of this incident is that we are led out of the bondage of the land of ignorance and spiritual darkness (Egypt), where we were slaves to King Desire, by recognizing and following the word of the Lord (Law) given us through the Law Giver. In other words, at that stage of our unfoldment it is necessary for us to follow the written or spoken word, the letter of the Law interpreted and laid down for us by someone in authority, whom we can see, know and follow, who like Moses constantly chides, directs and teaches us; who permits us to go three days without water, the love-aspect of the Law, (*i.e.*, expounds the Law intellectually but fails to give the refreshing water of love and sympathy), but when this is demanded insistently he strikes the Rock of Truth and the love gushes forth to refresh us. Such a leader may feed us with bread from heaven (manna), teach us to conquer the enemies we meet in our journey, *i.e.*, the temptations we encounter in life and the evils of our own creation; instill faith and courage when we murmur from fatigue or lack of faith; he may even punish us with fire or bring a plague upon us when we seem ungrateful or careless, yet he leads us ever on until we reach the Jordan.

But when we have learned the lessons of the wilderness and no longer rebel or murmur, and through prayer and aspiration have climbed the height which separates the Law given from without from the Law intuitively perceived by us, or the Law graven on tables of stone from the Law graven in our hearts, we must look to Joshua, the Christ-man within, as our Law Giver.

Another interpretation is that even tho we go through life thoughtlessly, we are nevertheless guided broadly or in a general way by the great Divine Law, a Law of Life leading us step by step in development through our wanderings in the wilderness, bringing us manna from heaven when we hunger, and when we thirst striking the rock of hard conditions until the Water of Life (Divine Love) flows forth to us. It also brings to us all our bitter karmic chidings when we go astray or murmur, and guides us ultimately within the borders of the Promised Land.

When we reach the Jordan the former phase of our unfoldment must be left behind and like Moses must be buried in the valley of Moab, the resting place given us ere we cross the Jordan, so that "no man knoweth his sepulchre unto this day." This indicates that the burial of Moses was not a physical fact nor a historical incident; for the Law Giver must always exist, ready to lead unending companies of God's chosen ones out of Egypt and through the wilderness. Yet, as we cross Jordan, we must leave him behind; recognizing all that he has done for us in the earlier stages of our great pilgrimage and giving him our loving remembrance and gratitude. In occult studies a lack of gratitude for each help along the Path is one of the greatest hindrances the student can develop; for the Masters teach that every help along the journey, every word spoken or law interpreted for the advancing Soul, is like a jewel of great price: hence, to accept it and refuse gratitude and love in return creates a Karma for the unfolding Soul similar to that created by undeveloped persons through robbery.

Moses is buried in the sense that life is so pressing that as we advance spiritually Earth conditions seem to cover over and bury out of sight many things which were most helpful and which in our earlier stages of growth we thought would be forever essential. Our spiritual life follows the same law as Nature, and we find the analogy in the burial of the plants, herbs and flowers, which were so beautiful and helpful during the summer yet which, when winter comes, can no longer manifest to us, yet are ready to spring up full of life and vigor at the next season; ready again to make the summer months glad and happy for the many other children who will need just the help they can bring. So when we have reached the end of our wanderings in certain fields of consciousness and are ready to follow our Divine Leader we do not condemn any of the helps we have received by the way; for heartfelt gratitude must be given the Law Giver who was so patient with us when we were but children in spiritual things, and often rebellious and disobedient. Just as the Lord made the flowers and sends the sunshine and the rain, so did He send Moses, and so will He send Joshua in due season.

We are told that "Moses was an hundred and twenty years old when he died: his eye was not dim, nor his natural force abated." The figures 120 show plainly that ere we bury our Law Giver he must have taught us the wisdom of a completed expression of the Divine Law, as symbolized by a complete multiple of 12, 10x12=120. When the followers of the Law have reached the point in their development where they can be taught directly through intuition (tuition from within) and inspiration (inbreathing of the Spirit), they have reached the symbolic Jordan, but to cross this mysterious river they must have a new leader. For even tho Moses was divinely appointed for his work, when that work was accomplished another divinely appointed one is ready to take us the next step onward. "When the pupil is ready the Teacher appears."

The name Joshua comes from the Hebrew Jehoshua, later Jeshua, from which root the name Jesus is also derived, Joshua meaning "salvation with us," or "Jehovah saves," while Jesus means "God with us." The word Nun means "a fish" and symbolizes the Mysteries, a "son of Nun" meaning one initiated into the "Mysteries of the Kingdom of God"; hence "Joshua, the son of Nun."

As we already know, Jesus was the Avatar for the Piscean or Age of Fishes, and a fish was the symbol used to identify His followers, hence Joshua, who leads all God's chosen ones—not merely the Hebrews—and Jesus, who completes their salvation, esoterically and symbolically considered are the two fishes of the sign Pisces, the Alpha and the Omega aspects of the same Christ-power personified. The Lord sent Joshua to open the way through the waters of Jordan and lead His chosen ones into the Promised Land where Jesus could perfect their evolution and complete their cycle of salvation until, like Him, they could walk on the sea of life and no longer merely swim in it like fishes.

The river Jordan, while sometimes used to symbolize the River of Death,[4] like all true symbols, has many meanings. But in connection with the narrative we are considering, it refers to the beginning of a definite period in the spiritual life of the Aspirant. When the Soul has awakened and has earnestly determined to find the way to the Promised Land, each Soul finds some avenue of Truth which leads it out of Egypt. This avenue of Truth, if it be a true Law Giver, is to that Soul its Moses. Yet we find it hard always to follow and accept the Law as laid down for us by our chosen leader. We cavil and rebel and lose our way in the vast stretches of the intellectual wilderness and have to retrace many steps. We are sometimes turned aside from following the one God to worship false gods. We even set up for ourselves a golden calf, and after giving up our most precious jewels of thought to be melted and molded into this false god, we bow down and worship it. For every false god is made up of man's most precious jewels and valuable possessions, *i.e.*, his jewels of thought, aspiration and desire, which are melted up and used to form a god which will express that which he conceives to be God. It has, therefore, been said that the idea of God expressed by each person can be only as great as the individual's consciousness can grasp and as high as his imagination can soar. Yet there must be times when we are left to stand

---

[4] See *Realms of the Living Dead*, Curtiss, 27.

alone; when our Law Giver must ascend Mt. Sinai and be bidden from our sight amidst the lightnings and thick clouds while he receives the Law upon the two tablets of stone[5] and brings them down to us. This is a period of testing as to whether we will continue to follow the Law or will be led astray by false gods of our own fashioning.

But there finally comes a time in our spiritual life when we have learned the lessons out of all our weary wanderings; when even our Law Giver seems incapable of leading us further, and we cry out for personal knowledge gained through personal experience. No longer are we content to drink of the stream that flows from the rock our leader has struck. We pray that the stream of Living Waters gush forth at our own command. We realize that we have reached the end of the wilderness, yet between us and the Promised Land there flows a swift, deep, turbulent, muddy and treacherous river. For just as the River of Death marks a definite boundary between our mortal life and the life beyond, so does the mystical River Jordan mark a definite boundary between the life of a seeker, which we have led as wanderers in the wilderness — to which life we must die as we cross the Jordan — and the new life into which we are born when we cross the mystical river and begin the life of a Neophyte.

At this step our astral senses begin to unfold and we are confronted with strange happenings and experiences which we do not understand, and which often frighten us. And because these new faculties are beginning to unfold we are subjected to the trials and temptations of that world of insidious desire and delusion. The swift eddies of the astral forces toss us this way and that, often undermining our footing and carrying us beyond our depth, just as would happen were we to attempt to wade the physical river Jordan at the season of its flood.

As we have said before, one aspect of this mystic river is

---

[5] See "Two Tables of Stone" in *The Voice of Isis*, Curtiss, 331.

the great stream of astral force which surrounds mankind as the
amniotic waters surround the unborn fetus, and through which
we must pass ere we can reach our spiritual birth. There are many
psychic practices which enable the seeker to launch out upon this
river, but if we are to cross, not by battling with its treacherous
currents, but "dry shod," we require a divinely appointed leader,
a Joshua to roll back its waters and allow us to pass in safety. We
have crossed *over* this river many times ere this, but never *through*
its waters; for we cross it during sleep and at the death of the
physical body, but always unconsciously, altho we may bring back
a confused memory of its swirling and bewildering forces. Just
as the restless and unstable mass of humanity is called the sea of
humanity, so is this stream of turbulent astral force called a river.
But because in its waters the pure River of life flowing to humanity
from the higher worlds is mingled with the mud and slime and
debris from all the lower worlds, it is fittingly symbolized by the
River Jordan in Canaan, for its physical features correspond most
marvelously with those of this river of astral force.

The River Jordan is the only river in Palestine, and is one of the
most remarkable in the world. "It has never been navigable, no
important town has ever been built upon its banks, and it runs into an
inland sea, which has no port and is destitute of aquatic life . . . . . .
On the whole, it is an unpleasant, foul stream, running between
poisonous banks, and as such it seems to have been regarded by
the Jews and other Syrians."[6] It rises from two springs in the valley
between Lebanon and Hermon, gushing forth from a deep hollow.
For twelve miles it flows through the valley and then enters a dark
defile for six or seven miles, after which it spreads out into a marsh
ten miles long which terminates in a lake. From the lake it flows
on for another twelve miles and empties into the Sea of Galilee,
where its muddy course through the clear waters of the sea can be

---

[6] *Encyclopedia Britannica*, XV, 509.

distinctly traced. Issuing from the Sea of Galilee, it flows on with ever increasing force until it finally falls into the Dead Sea. Its entire length is but 120 miles in a straight line—the same figures as are given for the age of Moses—altho if all its many twists and turns are followed it measures 240 miles.

The river of astral forces also rises from two springs; first, from the clear, pure Waters of Life that flow down from the higher worlds and, second, from the offscourings and debris of the lower worlds. It gushes forth from that which is called "the outer darkness," quite comparable to the "deep hollow" from which the Jordan rises. It flows for a complete period or Cycle of Manifestation (12) through a quiet valley between the two worlds. It is in this portion of its course that we cross it during sleep or on certain psychic stepping stones, for here it is shallow, quiet and restful and has many fords. Here many little children from both sides meet and play together. Children often talk of and to little playmates unseen by the grown-ups, yet from the words and actions of such children it is plain that an actual playmate is present and very real to their senses and consciousness. When this phase of its course is ended, the river enters a dark defile between the physical and astral worlds where it flows through a six-mile period of struggle in which the Christ-force (6) is striving to express, on to the seventh or period of rest (7). Here it receives the name of the River of Death. Here its waters are dark and deep and mysterious. Those Souls who cross at this point have closed their eyes in death and are either ferried over by the symbolic Charon or are borne on the wings of angels.

The river then has another period of perfecting, (10) in which it is spread out and almost lost in a vast marsh. It is in this viscid and polluting quagmire that the astral monsters have their abode. All who essay to cross at this point get lost in the treacherous bogs and slimy pools, and are often not only befouled by its impurities, but are engulfed in the putrid mud which swarms with every evil form of astral life. It is from this region also that the black magician draws his powers and the necromancer evokes his shades, through the horrible practices in which blood is used. But even here many beautiful yet baleful flowers grow to tempt the untrained or unwary venturer into the unseen, yet around each is the serpent of seduction coiled. Hence, he who would cross at this point must have an enlightened and experienced guide, and must beware lest he be overcome by its miasmic emanations or be stupefied by the perfume of its swamp-like flowers or be seduced by its monsters of lust and evil.

When the marsh has completed its work of disintegration and transmutation or runs its 10 miles, it terminates in a beautiful lake of clear, pellucid waters. Upon the banks of this beautiful lake, in contemplation we often walk in dreams and hold sweet converse with our friends and our Divine Helpers from the other shore. It is often this converse which we remember vaguely as spiritual instruction given us in dreams, but the substance of which is built into our consciousness, even tho not remembered clearly on waking, yet which works out in our lives as intuitional guidance, so that finally we are ready for our next stop.

Again this stream completes a cycle of 12 ere it empties into the Sea of Galilee. This is the sea of consciousness which we touch in deep meditation when we enter a certain phase of the Silence, corresponding to the limpid, smooth and bowl-like physical sea surrounded by lofty mountains. The Sea of Galilee is almost free from storms and buffeting winds and mirrors the mountains on its calm, silent surface, while the flow of the river across the center is quite distinguishable. Upon the shore of the astral Galilee is the astral counterpart of the Temple of Silence.[7]

Like the physical Jordan, this astral stream ultimately

---

[7] See *The Temple of Silence*, Curtiss.

empties into the Dead Sea of humanity, far below sea level (the Dead Sea is 1300 feet below) where the density of its salt causes extremely rapid evaporation, thus lifting its essence up in the form of vapor until it is lost in the higher realms. This sea is a fitting symbol of the great sea of humanity which, altho dead to the consciousness of the spiritual world, is ever releasing its higher essence to ascend into the realms of spirit, purified by its salt tears of suffering and repentance. It must be remembered that the phases of the river here mentioned are not sharp divisions, but are used as mystical symbols of states of consciousness.

When we have reached this mysterious river in the course of our search for the Promised Land, the only way in which we can cross it "dry shod" and in full consciousness is by following our Christ-leader, Joshua, yet walking alone and through our own personal efforts. There is now no Charon to ferry us and no angel band to waft us across in unconsciousness. We die to the old conditions and have a conscious realization of the continuity of life. Here on the margin of this river we bury our Moses, reverently giving him the full loving gratitude for the help he has given us on our journey.

We remain on the bank of this river for a period of three days, as did the Children of Israel, a period of preparation, which may last for a long time, as reckoned by months and years; a period which corresponds to the three days in the tomb. We could not recognize a manifestation of the Christ-man in Moses, the Law Giver, and we must wait until we do recognize him in Joshua, the servant of Moses, and in whom Moses may be said to have arisen. We forget that the Christ has proclaimed that "Whosoever will be chief among you, let him be your servant" Joshua was surely the servant of Moses, working humbly for him, and through him performing miracles. Yet, like "the servant in the house," we heed him not, nor are we at once ready to let him take the lead in our lives; not until Moses is dead and buried for some time.

Joshua was in the camp all the time, living in their very midst, yet the Children of Israel neither listened to nor took any special notice of him, altho he was the only one who accompanied Moses up Mt. Sinai when the Lord gave him the two tables of the Law. During their wanderings they had followed Moses exclusively, just as each of us, while still wandering in the wilderness, followed the Law as given to us through our accepted channel. Even tho the Christ is already in our midst and living in close daily contact with and speaking to us daily long ere we reach the banks of Jordan, we either do not recognize Him or we fear to listen or depart from the Law of Moses. But when the three days of preparation are completed, Joshua orders the officers to go through the camp and proclaim through all our faculties, like a voice from heaven, which we must obey—"When ye see the ark of the covenant of the Lord your God, and the priests, the Levites bearing it, then ye shall remove from your place, and go after it." And when we hear the Divine Voice thus unmistakably summoning us we must obey.

(To be continued)

Chapter XXVIII

CROSSING JORDAN
(Concluded)

"And Joshua said unto the people, Sanctify yourselves: for tomorrow the Lord will do wonders among you. . . . And it came to pass . . . that the waters which came down from above stood and rose up upon an heap . . . and those that came down toward the sea of the plain, even the salt sea, failed, and were cut off: and the people passed over right against Jericho." *Joshua*, III, 5-16.

The Law of Creation demands that we either confirm and perfect or else redeem all our creations. One aspect of this Law requires us to fulfill and prove our words or retract them in humiliation. Therefore, the practical mystic will be careful in the use of words and especially about making definite promises, agreements and vows, unless he has carefully considered them, is ready to be called strictly to account and is quite sure he is able and ready to fulfill them. It is far better to say that we will do the best we can concerning a certain matter than to give a definite promise, for once our word is given, we must either fulfill it or take the consequences.

In accordance with this Law the course of events was so arranged that through the fulfilling of his words, Joshua would give to the Children of Israel a positive proof of his divine authority. Since this is a spiritual principle, it endures throughout the ages, hence, can be applied today to the words of leaders and teachers, as well as to our own words, and its fulfillment will never fail to convince the thinking mind that a teacher who can thus prove the words and teachings is indeed a Joshua chosen of the Lord, *i.e.*, chosen and confirmed by the Divine Law.

First of all, the Children of Israel had to be tested as to their readiness to obey Joshua. This test was a simple one: they were told to remain in their tents quietly waiting until they saw the Ark of the Covenant borne by the priests into the Jordan, then they were to arise and follow after it. Jesus gave similar directions to His disciples after His resurrection, telling them that they were to remain quietly in one place in Jerusalem until He came. While we must be willing to take our steps alone, we are never left to decide through our own unaided reasoning where to look for truth. But we must obey and remain in our tents, *i.e.*, our own intellectual, altho temporary shelter, and follow the directions of the Leader who appeals to our intuition, remaining quietly in one place "until he come" or until we see the Ark of the Covenant enter Jordan.

As long as we wonder and worry over and fear to trust our new-found Leader, or seek for some bridge or boat to carry us over this river which seems to bar our further progress, or as long as we waste time and effort in vain prayer and supplication for some miracle to be vouchsafed to us; that we be given illumination or some great psychic experience to convince us beyond all doubt that the Living God is indeed with us, we are still camping on the bank of the Jordan. We have already buried our Moses in the wilderness, and we feel very much alone and forsaken. But as soon as we truly sanctify ourselves we will recognize and follow those priests who prove they are divinely appointed by their ability to take the Ark of the Covenant and carry it into the midst of the swirling muddy waters and cause them to divide, even tho the river has overflowed its banks, as we are told the Jordan does at every harvest-time.

This period in our unfoldment is truly a harvest-time of the Soul. The waters which come down from above, *i.e.*, the spiritual outpouring of love and understanding from within—will rise up in a mighty wall upon our right hand, a wall which will shut us safely in the fold with a realization that we have found our spiritual home, while "those that came down toward the sea of the plain, even the salt sea, failed, and are cut off," and we are commanded to pass over against Jericho.

The Ark of the Covenant represents the Presence of the Lord God; the holy mysteries of our faith; that which embodies to us the purest and highest interpretation of God's truth; that which brings to us the most comfort and help and the greatest realization and assurance of God's presence with us. When we reach this point in our unfoldment, the point where the letter of the written word can no longer lead us, because we are standing on the brink of Jordan and the experiences symbolized by its mixed waters (astral and spiritual forces) are laving our feet (understanding), we are to wait patiently in our tents until we see that the priests who represent our faith have actually been able to carry the sacred Ark into the midst of the stream and set it down on solid ground, thus proving their ability to divide the waters.

At this point in our unfoldment we may have been told that we must prove our faith in the leaders of our chosen representation of truth by stepping alone into the swirling waters of Jordan, *i.e.*, by letting the astral experiences that are pressing upon us at this step mingle with the spiritual teachings we have learned to love and trust and with the spiritual experiences that we are having. This, indeed, at first sight, might seem to be the supreme test of our faith. But this we are not asked to do. The crossing must be prepared for us by the priests. The great Divine Love never asks us to do anything that is so unreasonable, for to go on into the astral world (truly symbolized by a swift, turbulent and muddy river), unprepared or without a competent guide, is quite as dangerous as it would be to start to wade across the Jordan at full flood. When the mixed sensations from the astral realms begin to mingle in our consciousness and impinge upon our minds they are just as difficult to understand and as appalling as would be the problem of crossing the turbulent Jordan dry shod.

Since we are not asked to enter the water alone, to cross Jordan dry shod means that we must face these new experiences and problems and in a measure meet them, relying entirely upon the Christ-man within, and learn to understand and cull from each its lessons without allowing our understanding (feet) to become saturated with the astral waters. And if we obey the command and rest quietly in our tents, one will come to prepare the way who will prove his leadership by his ability to explain to us all our odd and mixed experiences and point out their significance. He will not tell us, as so many ministers do, that our experiences are of the devil or are neurasthenic vagaries, wandering imagination, subconscious suggestion or else are among the mysteries of God which are not to be inquired into. He will prove by his ability to carry the Ark of the Covenant into the midst of the waters that he is a safe and reliable guide.

Here we must learn to discriminate for ourselves and not continually run to some Moses for explanation, for he, being but the Law Giver, can expound only the written law, and necessarily, it being impersonal and all-inclusive, the written law may not satisfy and comfort us in our new and personal experiences, hence, Moses may not be able to satisfy us. At his command the Red Sea—symbol of the sea of humanity, red with passion, anger and war—can be divided and a path made for us through its waters; but even here Pharaoh and his hosts follow after, altho the Divine Law causes the waters to engulf and drown them. But Jordan is not the great sea of humanity: it is something much more personal, as described in the previous chapter. Therefore, we need a more intimate and personal guide for its crossing, one whose name—mystically, a name always signifies that which a thing really is—springs from the same root as Jesus, the Savior and Redeemer. But we must remain

quietly in our tents until this Leader justifies his credentials and
proves his power and authority.

During this period Joshua, or the Christ in us which we are
now learning to trust and obey, sends out two spies to view the
land over across Jordan, for we must be cautious and use common
sense or "Prove all things; hold fast that which is good." These
two spies are our *aspiration*, which we send out to pierce the
mists which hide from us the distant land of our inheritance, and
our *reason*, which we command to bring to us some reasonable
evidence that that which we are seeking is the truth. These two
always return laden with the fruits of the new land, even if
perchance they may have had to escape at night from the many
misleading and terrifying illusions with which the inhabitants
of the land have assailed them. These inhabitants, however, we
are destined to drive out ere we possess the land. Therefore, we
must not allow any unfavorable features of the spies' report to
discourage us; for when we enter the land we will be given the
necessary courage and strength with which to face and conquer
the inhabitants. We are never given the strength with which to
face a danger before it comes, hence the fear with which we often
anticipate that which is coming, but we are given strength and
courage to wait quietly in our tents until the word comes to move
forward, hence, the occult truth back of the old adage, "Never
cross a stream before you reach it."

Altho our path may seem to lie straight ahead, yet this river
Jordan bars our ongoing, and we have had so many warnings as
to the dangers of its snags and whirlpools that we dare not venture
in. At this point in our unfoldment we are not to run wildly from
teacher to teacher, or to various mediums, asking for messages,
guidance, etc., growing more and more confused at the seeming
contradiction of the teachings; nor should we become discouraged
as one after the other fails us and proves to be but a priest of Baal,
repaying our blind faith and devotion with selfishness, deceit

and impure or false living. We are to do just what Joshua required of the Children of Israel, namely, remain quietly in our tents until we see the Ark of the Covenant carried into the midst of the turbulent waters. Then, and then only, are we to follow after it.

When we see the priests lift up the Ark and see the waters divide before it so that the pure Waters of Life—the inspiration, teaching and guidance given us by our divine Higher Self—make a wall upon our right hand and the mud-laden waters of misleading experiences, flatteries and temptations from the lower astral, together with those that come down toward the sea—even the salt sea of the bitter tears shed over sorrows, hurts and disillusions, the sea into which all deceiving astral waters empty—flow away on our left hand, then we must rise up and follow the Ark. For the priests have proved their obedience to the guidance of Joshua and also their ability to accomplish, hence have proved that they can be trusted.

Then will the Christ in our hearts speak as did Joshua, saying: "Sanctify yourselves: for tomorrow the Lord will do wonders among you." How many of us have heard this command, yet have grown tired of waiting for the morrow, which seems never to come because we have neglected to sanctify ourselves. The meaning of sanctify is "to make sacred," hence no mere outward ceremony or profession can sanctify us. Only after a night of vigil, which must be spent alone in the Holy of Holies of our own hearts, can this take place. And to accomplish this we must cast out of our tent (mind) all that is unholy, meeting our Christ in purity of heart and mind and receiving from Him the sanctifying grace or Oil of Consecration. It is only when we have thus purified our minds and consecrated our lives to the Christ that we can enter the treacherous waters of the astral world with any hope of crossing over dry shod.

As true today as from the beginning is the assurance of Joshua. "Hereby shall ye know that the Living God is

among you, and that he will without fail drive out from before
you the Canaanites, and the Hittites, and the Hivites, and the
Perizzites, and the Girgashites, and the Amorites, and the
Jebusites. Behold, the Ark of the Covenant of the Lord of all the
earth passeth over before you into Jordan." The mention of all
these seven heathen nations which are to be driven out of our
Promised Land, refers not to the historical peoples whose homes
and lands were apparently to be taken from them and confiscated
without compensation—a most unjust, cruel and bloodthirsty
proceeding, if taken literally—but to the heathen usurpers of our
own lives; those things which are possessing our Land of Promise
and which must either be driven out or made our servants that
we may retain for our further growth all that is good in them, but
make them subservient to the rule of our Joshua.

Twelve men were selected by Joshua, one from each tribe,
each to take a stone out of the bed of Jordan with which to erect
a memorial. This refers to the complete consecration of all our
faculties (tribes) with which we must find and take out of the
bed of Jordan—out of the very spot where the Ark rested—the
twelve stones for our memorial. This means that every Soul who
has passed through the experiences symbolized by following the
Ark into Jordan must gather out of those experiences a strength
of character which can be built into the foundation of his spiritual
life as stones. For only as each of our faculties and powers—a
man symbolizing a positive aspect and a tribe a faculty—takes
up a stone from the midst of this divided river and all are built
into character as a firm memorial which nothing can shake, can
we bear evidence to those who come after that we have really
passed over Jordan dry shod and have not been carried away or
overwhelmed in its floods.

Every true psychic or spiritual experience which we
have understood and been able to retain quickens all our
faculties, builds character and helps us lay the foundations
for our New Jerusalem. The New Jerusalem must have its

counterpart on Earth in the life of each perfected individual, built on its twelve foundation stones, ere it can come down from God out of heaven for all humanity.

The gathering of these twelve stones while consisting of spiritual experiences will, nevertheless, make its mark in the foundation of our character. They will not consist of great physical or psychic events, which all our friends and neighbors can see and appreciate, for we pass over Jordan in spiritual consciousness. Hence, it is useless to try to tell anyone of it who has not had a similar experience, and much talking of it wastes its force. The only way we can truly testify to having passed over is by the presence of the Stones of Truth we have brought with us from the midst of the river and used to build a cairn or a sacred testimonial in our character, which shall be so solid and firm and fundamental, that it is like the everlasting rocks on which the Earth's crust is laid.

For no matter how much philosophy we have grasped; no matter if we have sat at the feet of a Master and been taught from his lips; no matter if our psychic faculties are developed and we can speak with the tongues of men and angels, unless our lives show evidence of a greater poise, common-sense, patience and consideration for others, and unless we have that "charity," or that love which is more than love, as it is generally understood, we have not gathered our twelve stones from Jordan and built our memorial. For charity is that unselfish and clear-seeing love which discerns clearly the shortcomings and weaknesses of others, yet makes allowance for them, because it is so clear-seeing that a knowledge of the ultimate overcoming of all evil is the guerdon which this love brings to all who manifest it.

It is in the little everyday affairs of life that we must prove that our house is built upon the rock. Long before the winds blow and the rains descend and the floods beat upon our house we will know, and most of our acquaintances will know, if we have not built upon our twelve stones.

For, if we have not, at every little disturbance we go to pieces or grow discouraged; cannot bear disapproval; must be flattered and admired; in short, demand and suffer acutely if we do not receive great consideration from others. But having gathered our twelve stones and built our memorial upon them, we are ready to give all the glory of the achievement to the Lord, whose power enabled us to cross over dry shod. Then, when our children or our friends ask, What mean these stones? we can answer that they are a testimonial that we have passed over Jordan dry shod, for the Lord dried up the waters from before us "That all the people of the earth may know that the hand of the Lord is mighty."

Another important point is that "The priests that bare the ark of the covenant of the Lord stood firm on dry ground, in the midst of Jordan, and all the Israelites passed over on dry ground, until all the people were passed clean over Jordan." This does not mean that those who have been chosen as priests to carry the Ark, *i.e.*, those who preserve for us and reveal the sacred mysteries, will, therefore, be miraculously shielded from all harm and find their lives free from excitement and filled with nothing but quiet experiences, peace, harmony and joy. Not so. They must bear the Ark boldly into the very midst of Jordan, thus proving their courage, faith and ability. And there they must stand, not only until all their own immediate following (tribe) have crossed over, but until "all the people have passed clean over Jordan." This means that all chosen leaders of men who have sincerely taken up the Ark of the Covenant must stand firm in the midst of Jordan as a help, comfort and example to all the people who, seeing their stand, will follow them, no matter how they may be compassed about by the restless waters seeking to resume their old channel, no matter how they may be taunted, even by some of their own followers, who may say: "We have passed over, yet you who presume to be our leaders, still remain in the midst of the water."

The three-days' waiting on the banks of Jordan agree

in their symbology with the three days spent by Jonah in the belly of the great fish and with the three days spent by Jesus in the tomb. These refer to three periods, during which certain changes must be accomplished within ourselves. During these three days Joshua had commanded the Children of Israel to prepare victuals for the journey. If taken literally, this command was absurd, for if God could feed them with manna daily during their forty years of wandering in the wilderness and was about to show them a most remarkable proof of His power, surely He could sustain them during the few moments required to cross the divided Jordan! For this stream averages not more than a quarter of a mile in width, two miles being its greatest width for a short distance, and has more than fifty fords between the Sea of Gallilee and the Dead Sea, all of which can be crossed by caravans today in less than an hour, in spite of the fact that they must battle with its swift current. Therefore, we must conclude that the three days given in which to prepare victuals for the journey were three periods or phases of unfoldment, in each of which certain spiritual food was to be prepared.

In other words, while we wait beside Jordan for the Ark to enter, we must prepare our spiritual sustenance. Firstly, the Bread of Obedience. For, not until we have gathered the Grain of Trust and Confidence and it has been ground to flour in the mills of testing experiences and we have kneaded it assiduously with the Water of Patience and the Leaven of Love, can we prepare that Bread to eat which the world knows not of. Secondly, we must produce the Wine of Joy, which can only be prepared when the Soul has gathered the ripened grapes which grow on that Vine to which Jesus alluded when he said: "I am the vine and ye are the branches." Hence, the grapes are brought forth on the branches by the same divine Christ-sap that feeds the vine. These grapes must be gathered and pressed out in the winepress of the bitter experiences of life. "I have trodden the

winepress alone; and of the people there was none with me."
Thus cries out each Soul in bitterness during that period, yet
the Wine of Joy and Life must be pressed out in just such a
winepress. Thirdly, we must prepare the oil. Oil (or fat) is not
only a necessary constituent of our dietary, without which the
bread and wine will not completely nourish, but it is also that
which is used in the consecration of a priest. Hence, at this step we
must prepare within ourselves that rich sustaining realization and
intimate knowing of the Christ which will enable us to assimilate,
i.e., incorporate into our spiritual life, all that is meant by the
Bread and the Wine, together with that Joy of Life which will
give the sustaining quality to our spiritual food, so that even in
the midst of the swirling waters of Jordan we can "feed on him
in our hearts with praise and thanksgiving."

We must also let this Oil of Consecration be poured out upon
our heads until it runs down and anoints our feet (understanding)
that we may be wholly consecrated. In short, at this step we must
permit the Godhead, the Three-in-one, to take possession of us,
firstly, as a realization of what the triune God really means, and
secondly, why God must always manifest as a Trinity[1] in all His
works, and thirdly, as a growth manifesting in our lives.

For manifestation must follow realization. Only that which we
can impress upon the personality and make it manifest, is of vital
importance to us now.

This Trinity, variously expressed as Father, Son and Holy
Ghost; Father, Mother, Son, and in other religions in various terms,
always means the same thing and should convey the idea of the
actuality and the completeness of the Godhead. There must be the
power of the Progenitor; that which plants the seed containing the
germ of that which is to be. There must be the Mother-force; that
power of the Holy Ghost which broods over, nourishes and in the
fullness of time brings forth and cherishes the offspring. Then there

---

[1] See *The Key to the Universe*, Curtiss, 102.

must be the power of the Christ-force; that vivifying power back of all life; that growing, pushing, evolving and perfecting force; that which is called the Divine Urge, and which we call the Christ-force, because it is ever with us, even unto the end, unfolding, expanding and perfecting us; that force which draws all things back into the bosom of the Father through unfolding, perfecting and completing their cycle of life expression. God must manifest in all these aspects, else it would not be God. Therefore, we must prepare the three kinds of food for the nourishment of our spiritual body ere we can cross Jordan: the Wine which circulates within us as the sap of the One Life and inspires us; the Bread which feeds and sustains and the Oil which consecrates and blends all and produces the spiritual development needed ere we can cross Jordan dry shod and enter the Promised Land.

All this cannot be accomplished at once, but requires three periods. Yet it must at least have been begun ere we can enter Jordan and expect to take up the twelve stones from the spot on which the Ark rested and build our memorial.

Chapter XXIX

TAKING JERICHO

"And ye shall compass the city, all ye men of war, and go round about the city once. Thus shalt thou do six days. And seven priests shall bear before the ark seven trumpets of rams' horns: and the seventh day ye shall compass the city seven times, and the priests shall blow with the trumpets. . . . And Joshua saved Rahab the harlot alive, and her father's household, and all that she had; and she dwelleth in Israel even unto this day." *Joshua*, VI, 3-25.

Jericho is a historical city, situated five miles north of the Dead Sea. At one time it was quite extensive and was considered the most fruitful spot on Earth, being described by historians as "a tropical oasis, set down in a temperate zone." It has been partially devastated a number of times, but never entirely destroyed, nor is there any historical evidence to corroborate the extraordinary and spectacular siege described in the biblical narrative. The story of its capture by Joshua we must, therefore, take as purely symbolical. Today Jericho consists of but a small hamlet in the midst of an important fruit-growing center. This is further evidence that it was never "utterly destroyed and its place left desolate." The biblical story of that enterprise is so full of unnecessary and wanton cruelty and also so full of mystical metaphor and marvelous spiritual truths that its symbolical and mystical intent is beyond question; for only divine inspiration could tell so bloody a tale in so simple a way that every incident, almost every word, held a wealth of spiritual teaching.

We may well ask why, in the symbology of spiritual ideals, bloodshed and cruelty should be used? The answer is that the spiritual ideals to be expressed were given to the

Prophet, but were expressed, as such ideals always are, in the metaphor of the race thought, and as at that time the Hebrew civilization was crude and cruel, the only way to express the overcoming and conquering was through fighting and killing. Similar metaphor would be necessary even today to express similar ideas, altho perhaps not so crudely expressed and using modern terms and illustrations.

It must be remembered that all true inspiration is not given in words. The overshadowing consciousness illumines (inspires) the mind of the Seer so that a realization of Divine Truth or the ideal is grasped. This realization must then be given out or uttered by the inspired one in the best language he can command to express or at least symbolize the essence of the realization attained. This explains the difference between inspiration and astral dictation, even from advanced teachers in the invisible realms. Inspiration is by no means a word for word recording of information given by some Divine Being or by some spiritual Teacher or Master; for were it so, instead of being inspired we would become mere puppets, automata or automatic writers, with no need to think for ourselves and without responsibility for what we wrote.

In the Divine Mind there is stored up the ideals of all that is to be manifested, as well as all the truth that has been grasped and expressed by man since the beginning. To the degree that he can raise his consciousness to correlate with the Divine Mind or Reservoir of Wisdom, the Seer can draw upon it and grasp those phases of truth which the great Custodians of Truth deem it wise to have revealed by him at that time; for an impenetrable veil is drawn over all else. Therefore, it depends upon the intellectual and philosophic, as well as the spiritual and psychic, training of the Seer how those truths are expressed, even after further explanation by his Spiritual Teacher. This accounts for the differences in the way various trained Seers express truths in regard to the same subject.

This is the method, together with theopneusty and theophany, by which the books of the *Bible*, and all other great Scriptures, were revealed and later compiled. These are also the methods by which the *Teachings of The Order of Christian Mystics* are received. They are then expressed in the best terms the Agents can use, interpreted, explained and corroborated by examples from science and Nature. The interpretations are further corroborated by quotations from various Scriptures and other recognized and authoritative sources or expressions of the same truths.

This explains, as nothing else can, much of the blood curdling metaphor of the Old Testament, as well as many symbolic teachings of the New Testament, couched in what seems today to be gross and repellent language.

Jericho was chosen to symbolize that city which each and every Soul must conquer when he has built into his life the strength of the twelve stones taken from the Jordan and has stood in their midst; that sacred spot concerning which the Captain of the Lord's hosts said to Joshua: "Put off thy shoes from off thy feet; for the place whereon thou standest is holy ground." Only as we take from off our understanding (feet) all hampering coverings (shoes) can we see the vision of this mighty Angel, our Higher Self, standing in the center of our circle of life.

The meaning of the name Gilgal is "a circle," hence the twelve stones which Joshua had taken from Jordan and pitched in Gilgal were arranged in a circle, as the Druid stones were later arranged, *i.e.*, the circle of the zodiac. At once we see that the mystical meaning of these stones, which must be gathered one by one from the midst of Jordan, and whose forces must be built into the character of each Soul who passes over that river dry shod, is the balancing and conquering of the forces which come from the twelve signs of the zodiac. Symbolically, each perfected Soul is represented as a Sun Initiate, standing in the midst of a circle where all the forces are focused, not being ruled by, but ruling his stars. We read that "when Joshua was by Jericho," or when he had taken his place as a Sun Initiate, "he lifted up his eyes and looked, and, behold, there stood a man . . . with his sword drawn in his hand," the sword of the Spirit of Truth. When challenged by Joshua, he answered: "As captain of the host of the Lord am I now come." In other words, when he had attained this step, Joshua both recognized and gave obedience to his Higher or Divine Self, who henceforth dwelt within the personality, and he became one with his Father-in-heaven.

The Captain of the Host, or the Higher or Divine Self, merely overshadows and strives to inspire and guide the personality of human self until, through the initiation and realization of the personal self, the Divine Self is invited to enter into His earthly temple—the body—when it has been properly purified and prepared, and dwell therein. Then will He come, as He did to Joshua, with His sword drawn—the sword of Truth, whose two edges cut both ways—to drive out the polluting forces which have been dwelling in the personality—selfish or impure thoughts and desires, perversity, inharmony and sickness—and also to cut clean and true the line between good and evil, that there may no longer be excuse for ignorance. When this attainment is reached, Joshua can then proceed to take Jericho, not merely in his strength as a man, but as a mystical Son of God, a Sun Initiate. Even tho he had already led the Children of Israel—all his faculties and creations—dry-shod over Jordan, and had gathered the forces from all the zodiacal signs, yet only when he stood in the center and had been baptized by the Holy Ghost and become a Sun Initiate could he complete the task of taking Jericho.

One meaning of Jericho is "a fruitful place." By some it is called "the Moon God City" and the "City of Palm Trees." Most varieties of palm trees, while beautiful and stately, bear no edible fruit and give but little shade, hence they symbolize pride, well-being and contentment with physical conditions and with little spiritual food. But the fundamental meaning of Jericho is the City of Desire, a place of pleasure and the fruitfulness of our thoughts, acts and desires for physical well-being, in which we dwell contentedly until our Joshua demolishes the wall which shuts us away from the larger life.

Jericho is also the home of the Moon, the symbol of intuition. The Moon goddess represents that aspect of the Divine Knower corresponding to one aspect of the Great Mother, the fruitful Bringerforth of all things, both good and evil. For as the Moon shines only by the light it receives from the Sun, so the Great Mother brings forth only that which is implanted by the Father or, as Karma, that which is implanted by man. Therefore, in man as in Nature, Jericho would symbolize the manifestation of that stream of creative force which brings forth, through thought and act as well as sex, that which man either ignorantly or foolishly has sown.

It is because man has the power both to modify his creations through thought and literally to create thought-forms that he is a *creator* rather than merely a *procreator*, like the animals, which can bring forth only after their kind or the pattern set for them. Hence, to take Jericho is to master this force, purify it with Divine Fire and make it subservient to the will of the Higher Self, destroying all but "the silver and the gold, and the vessels of brass and of iron," *i.e.*, all those phases of desire and pleasure *save those that are true and pure*, and those which, altho as common as iron and brass, are needful as vessels of service, all of which we must consecrate and place "in the treasury of the house of the Lord."

The esoteric teachings tell us that the Moon is the mother of the Earth and not a satellite cast off from the Earth, and that it was while man was evolving on the Moon-chain of *globes*[1] that he set up the Karma which necessitated many

---

[1] See *The Voice of Isis*, Curtiss, 204.

of the experiences of the separated sexes, altho the separation of the sexes was a necessary experience destined in the course of man's manifestation on Earth. The seeds of that Karma were planted in the then embryonic planet which was destined to become the Earth. It was because of these karmic seeds that a planet, producing man in separated sexes, was evolved, that upon it this problem could be given expression and be worked out and the wisdom of the experience gained. Hence, this Earth is the only planet where the problem of separated sexes exists, yet which, by the solution and victory of all that is implied in that problem, will become the Sun of a new system. For through the proper solution of this great problem we will change the condition, first of ourselves, then of all humanity and finally of the planet itself. Through the many experiences this question has brought us and the suffering it has entailed, when we learn all its lessons we will have become as gods, knowing the good as well as the evil. The deeply mystical teaching, symbolized in the story of Jericho, would, of itself, stamp the *Bible* as a most marvelous book of occult wisdom, one in which so few words and symbols indicate and include so much.

Only when, like Joshua, we have taken off our shoes or bared our understanding and have recognized the Captain of the Hosts of the Lord and have bowed before Him, become one with Him and have been endowed with His power, as Jesus was endowed with power at His baptism, willing to follow whithersoever He leadeth, are we ready to take Jericho. Only as we recognize our Divine Leader standing in the midst of our zodiac and have become one with Him, realizing that He has brought us out of the wilderness and across Jordan dry shod, and we have proved our willingness to follow His commands, can we really capture Jericho and ultimately possess the Promised Land. But once we have had this experience we can depend upon our Leader to show us how to take the city.

Since the great lesson of this planet is that of the mastery of sex, the control of the sex force and magnetism and the use rather than abuse of all the forces of this wonderfully fruitful city in the valley of the Jordan is the great task before us. For all its fertility must be utilized and its fruits consecrated to the feeding of the Children of Israel; all its poisonous waters made sweet; its streets cleansed from impurity and depravity, so that sickness and disease and death may no longer result from the miasma that arises from the decaying fruit thrown out and let to rot upon the ground. The Neophyte must begin then with this first city in the Promised Land. But his task will be fully completed only when he reaches the New Jerusalem, where the Tree of Life brings forth its twelve manner of fruits for the healing of the nations, also for the healing of all the sorrows and the wounds we have received in the many battles fought while gaining the victory over Jericho and conquering the Promised Land.

Therefore, let it be plainly understood that the taking of Jericho means conquering, subjugating and *putting to proper use* all the creative forces and functions of the body and mind, whether they manifest through sex, thought, word or deed.

We must indeed capture this City of Desire and rule it. But because in the course of our evolution we have sown seeds of bitter weeds in this fruitful city, as we come into our spiritual majority and begin our Soul's work in earnest we must recognize our weeds, pull them up and begin to make the Earth a better place to live in; an advanced theater of action; a stepping-stone to ever higher fields of evolution. And one of the first steps is capturing from the King of this World, King Desire, the city which we have only too long permitted him to surround with a wall, that the debauchery he calls pleasure may be hidden from the world's gaze.

Let us consider how the Christ-man captures the City of Desire. There are many misguided teachings on this subject, and students confronting this important task are often told that once they have stepped into the stream (Jordan) and taken the vows or adopted the resolutions necessary to lead the truly mystic life of a Neophyte, they must avoid Jericho altogether, must even deny its existence; must not at all interfere with the rule of its king, even tho he bids fair to subjugate the entire world; must utterly ignore all its fruits and pleasures, calling them only temptations and seductions. But Joshua, even while still in the wilderness, sends out two men, as scouts, to investigate Jericho. These two we have said[2] symbolize two of our positive faculties, which we will call aspiration and reason, or intuition and judgment. While he is passing through that which is symbolized by the Jordan, the Neophyte must send forth his newly unfolding intuition and judgment into the City of Desire that he may understand it. In other words, he must face *himself and take cognizance of all the forces he finds within*, find out how to conquer them and see if much of the wonderful fruitfulness of the city cannot serve in the house of the Lord as vessels of gold and silver and of brass and iron.

This, however, does not mean that we should indulge in the debaucheries of Jericho; for while some maintain that we can never know and understand the temptations of the flesh until we have experienced them, until we have eaten of their fruits and have proven that they bring only suffering and death, such teaching is but sophistry. For we sow the seed of suffering and death and fulfill the prophecy: "In the day ye eat thereof ye shall surely die," just as inevitably if we eat merely for experience as if we eat to gratify the flesh. Hence, by such an act we are kept out of Eden, lest we eat of the Tree of Life and live forever in our unregenerate state.

When the scouts came to the city they found its inhabitants very antagonistic to the approaching hosts of Israel. And just so do intuition and judgment find little to encour-

[2] See Page 340.

age them when they begin to explore the City of Desire, for the desires of the flesh ever seek to capture and kill the messengers of the Spirit. But the scouts at last find a dwelling-place upon the wall and are given lodging by Rahab, a woman who was a harlot. Surely a most astonishing place for the messengers of the Lord to dwell! Yet she took them into her home and hid them and thus saved their lives. Who can this harlot be? She is Love dressed in the habiliments of King Desire.

When the City of fruitfulness, provided for her children by the Divine Mother, becomes the vassal of King Desire, Love establishes her dwelling upon the wall; for altho she has fallen from her high estate and has forgotten that she is the destined Bride of the Christ, she still waits and watches upon the wall, ready to help and cheer all who come to her sick of living on the husks or needing her touch to start them on their long journey back to their Father's home. Even tho she has played the harlot with many lovers; yet she will ultimately return unto the Lord.[3] And even tho "Their mother hath played the harlot: she that conceived them hath done shamefully,"[4] yet since their mother is Love, when we take the city she must be saved. And even tho when clothed in mere animal desire, she seduces all who come seeking only pleasure and animal gratification, yet in reality she is divine, for God is her Father and her Mother is the great Bringerforth of all Good.

All whose intuition and judgment can penetrate her disguise in their search for truth and who are willing to accept it and do not seek to contaminate it with preconceived opinions, find her an immortal goddess, often turning the seeming pleasures of lust into gall and wormwood and bringing forth from such illicit union only the cankering worm that dieth not. Let all who send out their scouts guard well against her wiles lest, in the livery of desire, she lull them

---

[3] *Jeremiah*, III, 1.
[4] *Hosea*, II, 5.

to sleep with her seductiveness and ensnare both intuition and reason in the nets of mere animal indulgence.

She is represented as having her house upon the wall, firstly, because her real dwelling-place is above the mere animal pleasures of the City, even tho she descends to them from time to time at the command of King Desire; and secondly, because those who are bringing forth merely through the pleasures of the senses, when they find true Love, even tho it be not yet purified and ideal, have scaled the wall of the City of Desire or have risen above the limits of sensual pleasures and have reached a point where they can at least glimpse the Promised Land that lies beyond. Yet, because her real name is Love and Love is immortal, if the scouts are wise, fearless and strong of will and do not yield to flattery and seduction, she will hide them from the enemies who would take their lives. Even today we find a remnant of this Divine immortal Love in the heart of many a harlot who wears the livery of King Desire and is forced to do his bidding.

It is a fact well known in esoteric teachings that as long as a true love for anything outside of self is in the heart of the personality the Higher Self will not be fully separated from the personality, even if that love be but a vibration of affection for an animal or a flower. For love is a cord, no matter how fragile, by which communion with the Divine can be set up and over which the Higher Self can pour its force into the personality to redeem it.

We are told that Rahab let the scouts down from the wall at night by a cord, and that she made a covenant with them that as a reward she and her mother and father and all her household should be saved when the Israelites took the city. Thus are intuition and reason often saved by Love and, in return, Love and her household are recognized and saved by the scarlet thread. Many there be who play the harlot, but those who are truly of the household of Love wear the scarlet thread made up of many twisted strands of loving thoughts and kind deeds, dyed scarlet with the force of unselfishness and self-sacrifice. That which is generally called scarlet in the *Bible* is today called royal purple, the color supposed to be worn only by kings and queens. Hence, the scarlet thread symbolizes the livery of the King of Kings, the royal garment of sincerity and truth.

Rahab may not have the entire robe of the Divine King, only a scarlet thread or cord, but enough of an insignia to proclaim that true love is of the King's household. We are told Rahab "Dwelleth in Israel even unto this day." Hence, wherever we find the scarlet thread we must recognize and save Rahab and all her household, for her scarlet thread proclaims that her true household is the household of the King of Kings and Lord of Lords, and that her father is the Father-in-heaven, and her mother is Divine Love. But to thus save her we must take her out of the City of Desire and see that she dwells thereafter in Israel.

How plainly is indicated the way we are to capture the City of Desire! For six days, the six periods or cycles of the creative week, must we quietly and yet steadfastly follow the priests who carry the Ark of the Covenant around the city, making one complete, round each day. All this time we must follow silently; for "Joshua had commanded the people, saying, Ye shall not shout, nor make any noise with your voice, neither shall any word proceed out of your mouth, until the day I bid you shout; then shall ye shout."[5] This applies as truly to the followers of the Christ in these days. How often do we hear some, when they have scarcely compassed the city for the first cycle—in which they recognize the tawdriness of the pleasures of the world and feel quite superior because they fancy they have grown away from such things—shout loudly of the foolishness and wickedness of it all, making such noise with their voices in what they think is an effort to bring the inhabitants of the city to a realization that all they hold most dear and can see

---

[5] *Joshua*, VI, 10.

no harm in it is utterly wrong, and madly calling to them to leave their pursuits, even their duties, to break away from their families and all they love and join the procession outside the City.

Again, in the second day or cycle, many do much shouting and proclaiming to the citizens of the City concerning their own superiority and godliness and boasting of the greater city that Joshua shall build upon the ruins of the one they are about to destroy. On later days, when they see that their individual shoutings do not cause the walls to fall, many loudly criticize the priests who bear the Ark as to how they bear it, how they walk, how they blow the trumpets and so forth, quite sure that had they themselves been chosen to bear the Ark they could have made a much more impressive appearance.

Also often the notes of the ram's horns displease many who are nevertheless determinedly following Joshua around the City. A ram's horn symbolizes both power and intellectual leadership, hence the seven priests who bear seven trumpets of rams' horns correspond to "the seven churches which were in Asia," spoken of in *Revelation*, namely, seven, or more correctly speaking, a perfect number of spiritual leaders, each marching before the Ark of the Covenant, each blowing continually on his own horn, or giving out the message of the Mysteries, of the Kingdom of God—symbolized by the Ark—each in his own way and to the best of his ability.

If we remember that only as the hosts march silently in their own places can the mystic potency of the blasts of the horns make the walls of the City totter, we will understand that as a host we have not yet compassed the City even once, for we have not yet learned to listen to, let alone obey, the first command of Joshua to keep silent. Many who have been called and chosen to march in the lead, instead of keeping silent until Joshua bids them shout, are now talking and boasting loudly of all the inner teachings and promises given them by Joshua conditionally as a guerdon if they prove worthy. They are thus distracting the attention of the people from Joshua, and because of such orations the hearers stand still instead of marching steadily and quietly around the City. The moment even a few stand still they break the rhythm which many marching feet create, hence, instead of helping to make the walls of Jericho weaken, they stimulate the curiosity of the inhabitants who come forth from the City to listen to and argue with them, and often accuse such leaders of being but one of themselves.

While many as individuals have obeyed and have journeyed safely through Jericho and onward over the rugged hills until they may almost be in sight of the heavenly city, the New Jerusalem, yet we look around the world sadly and are dismayed to see the Gay White Way of Jericho still in full blast, and see how apparently futile are the efforts of the hosts of the Lord to demolish its walls. Yet all we can do as individuals is to go on obeying the command of Joshua, marching each in his place and keeping silent until we are told to shout.

We may not personally like the priests who blow on the horns, and we may feel that were we in their places we could do much better, or we may have a ram's horn of our own we seek to blow and may believe that we can cheer the marching hosts if we blow upon it, but only when all obey the chosen Joshua and follow the lead of the armed men—those who have put on the whole armor of God—and the great mass of followers rearward follow on, all keeping silent until Joshua bids them shout, will Jericho be taken.

When the seventh day comes, the Sabbath day of the Lord, *i.e.*, when the perfect number of God's chosen priests are commanded all to blow together the one note, only then shall the people shout the shout of Victory! And the one note shall be the Grand Amen. For while the seven priests are marching and leading the people through the six periods of unrest and struggle, each blows his horn in his own key or gives his teachings in his own language, thus helping those who are naturally affinitized to his keynote. But if he has been the true priest and has given of his best he will in time reach the seventh period and will then be able to sound his note so true and harmoniously that it will vibrate to the chord of universal harmony. And when each of the seven strikes that chord all will be attuned and bring about the victory. For all differences will have vanished. Each will realize that all the others have been blowing but a part of the one chord, and only when this perfect harmony and at-one-ment among those who are priests has been attained, will the walls of Jericho fall. This does not mean any loss of personality for the priests. Each will still sound his own note, but will sound it in such perfect accord with the others, that they will blend into the one note of Victory.

So must we as individuals gather together all our higher faculties and march at least once around Jericho every time its temptations and allurements are presented to us, but silently, without talk and without fighting, merely marching valiantly and allowing the vibrations of the trumpets to accomplish the work; for the time of utter destruction of the wall has not yet come. Thus shall we ultimately conquer.

Also the priests in us, the radio-activity of our seven sacred centers and our higher ideals and aspirations which lead us Godward, must sound in our lives their notes of victory over the City of Desire if it is to be captured and made a useful servant of the Christ. For, individually, we each must conquer our personal City of Desire and preserve all its good vessels ere we can march in the great procession of the Hosts of the Lord, who shall conquer it for the world.

Chapter XXX

THE VAIN SHOW

"Surely every man walketh in a vain shew: surely they are disquieted in vain: he heapeth up riches, and knoweth not who shall gather them."*Psalms*, XXXIX, 6.

"Vanity of vanities, saith the Preacher, vanity of vanities, all is vanity. . . . Behold all is vanity and vexation of spirit." *Ecclesiastes*, I, 2-14.

"Beloved, *now* are we the Sons of God, and it doth not yet appear what we shall be: but we know that when he shall appear, we shall be like him; for we shall see him as he is." *I John*, III, 2.

"As for me, I will behold thy face in righteousness: I shall be satisfied, when I awake, with thy likeness." *Psalms*, XVII, 15.

The above texts seemingly contain two conflicting ideas, and yet we find in them a true picture of life and evolution; for each Soul evolves through the periods of time and through the experiences expressed by both ideas.

Let us consider the word "vanity," and analyze its meaning from a deeper and more inclusive point of view than the superficial one generally accepted. Vanity is not merely shallow pride, frivolity, ambitious display, something ephemeral, something that belongs to the surface of life, that does not go deep or touch on the realities of life, but vanity in reality is everything that is in vain, that hinders instead of hastens on the true purpose of life. It is everything that helps to make the black shadow of personality throw its darkened length between the Soul's eye and the divine likeness of God to which we must ultimately awaken; for to unfold that likeness in the flesh is the aim of evolution.

From this standpoint, how many things of this life over which we are disquieting ourselves are in vain! Indeed, we have but to look with the eye of the Soul at our daily lives to realize that we are walking largely in a vain show. We strive to make an ambitious display of outer things, heaping up riches that we may enhance the show. Yet, in the very struggle to attain them, we are losing much that makes life worth living, and are forgetting why we are passing through this expression of life in a physical embodiment in a physical world.

We are not told that riches in themselves are the vain thing, for, like the physical body and its functions, wealth is necessary and holds great lessons for humanity. And only when it ceases to lend its glamour to the vain show of selfishness and ostentation, and we learn to see in it a gift of God, a talent which we must not bury in a napkin, but use for humanity, to help all of God's children, yea, and the Cosmos itself, to unfold the true likeness of God, only then will it cease to be a vanity.

"He heapeth up riches and knoweth not who shall gather them." We should realize that in the very striving thus to heap up worldly possessions against "a rainy day," old age and death, we are planting in our consciousness and in the Race the seeds of death and are fulfilling the scriptural statement that "by man came death into the world." We assure ourselves that wealth is a good thing, and that if we should pass away, as pass we all must, someone will get the benefit and all will be well, quite forgetting that all wealth, be it money, possessions, position or power, or any other thing in this vain show for which we toil and disquiet ourselves to attain, is impregnated with the seed-thought by which it was attained. Hence, it will go on and on perpetuating that thought in a vain show and enslaving the Race more and more. Yet, since all these things, in our present stage of evolution, are things which, like the Tree in the midst of the Garden, are "pleasant to the eyes, and to be desired to make one wise," and since we believe in the unceasing care and all-powerful love of the divine Christ that would not that any perish, we must also believe that these gifts of God were not given to us to tempt us; that we were not sent into this far country of physical embodiment, and surrounded by temptations which seem almost too great to be resisted, as a punishment, but rather that we were sent here as Ambassadors of Divine Grace[1] with all the faculties and equipment necessary to perform a mission for our King, namely, to use all the resources of this far country, not only to unfold in it the likeness of our heavenly Father, but also to uplift the very substances of the planet itself and awaken in them their divine patterns, and to use all the riches thereof to the several ends for which they were destined.

When we realize this great mission we will no longer heap up riches for self and know not who shall gather them, but we will gladly receive all the Father gives us and use it for the awakening to a new and better day of manifestation or dispensation. Then we will know who shall gather all the treasures of Earth, all the gifts of the Father, *i.e.*, the Angels, who are the Reapers; for they will gather them as golden grain and sow them abroad in the soul of Earth conditions where they shall bring forth for all humanity an hundred fold in blessings to the Race.

The more fully we digest and express this thought, *i.e.*, that every form of wealth is a power or talent entrusted to us, not only to help us "do our bit," but also to help in the Great Work of uplifting the world, and prove our ability thus to use it, the more will be entrusted to us thus to use. But if we strive to hoard up for our own vanity that which the Great Law brings to us to use—for, remember, "all is vanity and vexation of spirit"—the less we will have in the end, altho for a season we may have much, but with it increasing vexation of spirit. And this law will be increasingly manifest more and more on Earth, in this new cycle.

Indeed, we have seen today[2] many of the hoards of wealth which have been heaped up in selfishness and vain show, even now in the very beginning of the end of the old dis-

---

[1] Grace, "the inspiration of love which prompts us to practice according to what we know, out of a religious affection and compliance." *Austin.*
[2] Written in 1917.

pensation, being either swept away by the exigencies of war or being at least temporarily taken over and administered by governmental commissions. And this will continue in one way or another until a means is found by which the stored up wealth, in spite of man's vain desire, is used to bring about better conditions for humanity and the whole world. And ere the end of this great upheaval and readjustment of conditions there will be brought about, among many other changes, a much fairer distribution of wealth and a much more equable sharing of the products of labor.

Again, the law that like creates like is eternally operative. If we heap up wealth or even disquiet ourselves to skimp and save and devote the best years of our lives to putting away a so-called "nest egg" for our old age, verily out of that egg will come only that which was put into it, namely, vanity. Instead of relying absolutely and confidently in perfect faith and trust upon the Great Law, we have lived in the vain hope that we shall have at least provided for ourselves no matter what happens. Therefore, that is all we will have to rely upon and all we have a right to expect in time of need.

The very stimulus to such hoarding is the thought that we both fear and expect some dire thing to happen. Also, since our mind is all the time fixed upon oncoming old age and incapacity to take care of ourselves, we are planting a seed-thought which is sure to grow and bear fruit, so that when old age comes, we will either be unable to take care of ourselves or will have to exist on the pittance we have saved up for that time. For in the saving and skimping we have smothered out much of the beauty and expression of love and enjoyment in life, hence have estranged our friends. We have so feared poverty that this fear has been built into our flesh in deep lines of care and anxiety, etc.

If we have not laid up a store of love, sympathy and companionship for our fellowmen we should not be surprised in our old age to find that none of these things manifest to us.

For if in our selfish "saving up" we have ignored the rights or
needs of others, others will be apt to ignore us and our needs at a
time when we will need their sympathy most, or they will expect
to be paid for everything they do for us.

On the other hand, we should recognize that all that is given
us, is a sacred trust to be used wisely, hence we should not, as
is so often done, turn over all our possessions to our children
or to some one who we think will use it as we desire, saying,
"The Lord will provide for me in my declining days." For the
very fact of such unwisdom calls for a lesson, even to the most
loving Soul, hence we may find ingratitude where we expected
love, and find at most a forced doling out of the necessities of
life and a grinding surveillance most difficult to bear. We must
learn to use wisely all that is entrusted to us, and as we prove our
wisdom in so using it, more will be entrusted to us to administer.
The fairy tale of the magic purse which, like the widow's cruse
of oil, was always replenished no matter how much was drawn
from it, illustrates a vital truth.

Even the money we may accumulate may be swept away, for
the bank may fail, the stock go down, the property burn up, the
land be inundated or lost through some flaw in the title, etc. "Lay
not up for yourselves treasures upon earth, where moth and rust
doth corrupt, and where thieves break through and steal." On
the other hand, if we see in wealth only a means to an end, only
a book out of which we may learn great Soul-lessons, and use
it as it comes, not foolishly or in self-indulgence or for vanity
or in vain, but with love and wisdom for the better unfoldment
of God's likeness in ourselves and in the world, then the supply
is not limited to what we can hoard, but it is exhaustless. We
have tapped the well-spring of an inexhaustible supply. We
are working with the Law, becoming channels through which
it can express for greater good. And as soon as this phase of
the Law—the right use of wealth—has been fulfilled and the
lesson learned by the Race, there will no longer be any use

for money, and hence we will pass on to other lessons to be learned through other channels.

Some day each Soul will awaken to its true mission on Earth, and when the awakening comes it will find in itself the likeness of God. Then, as it begins to strive to unfold this likeness, it will impress the likeness so strongly upon the thought forces of the Race that more and more Souls will rapidly awaken, until the morning of a New Era dawns for all humanity, and the Soul of humanity finds itself and manifests the true likeness of Divinity.

What are we to understand when we say, "I shall be satisfied when I awake in thy likeness?" Alas, that the orthodox teachings have for centuries conveyed the idea that this awakening could only come after the sleep called death! If this were all then it has been proved false, for it has been scientifically proved—as was taught by the mystics of all ages—that after the change called death we awaken in the likeness of the personality we developed or unfolded while on Earth and not in the likeness of the Divine Self.[3] We may see a little more clearly the vanity of it all and suffer because we have walked so many years in a vain show, and may gain vivid conceptions of life which shall be impressed upon us so strongly that they will manifest in our next life as the results of our repentance, but the mere passing from one phase of life to a still more vivid phase, not of death but of life, will not unfold in us a new likeness. We must awaken *here and now* and then strive with all our powers truly to unfold the Divine Likeness, to whose presence within us we have awakened.

The Divine Likeness! How shall we manifest it? We go on perfecting our physical bodies, seeking to unfold a god-like stature and mighty intellectual and psychic powers. But even after this is accomplished, how dare we say of even this perfected body, "This is God's likeness. This is my highest ideal of God the Unknowable, the Omnipotent, from

[3] See *Realms of the Living Dead*, Curtiss, 59.

everlasting to everlasting the I am?" For if we leave out our spiritual unfoldment, realization and manifestation we must answer with the Preacher—that great Power back of all evolution, that which is forever preaching and teaching the human heart through experience and intuitive perception of the Divine—that all is vanity. For no matter how perfectly we have developed our body, our intellect or even our psychic powers, if we have failed to unfold and manifest our spiritual nature *we have lived in vain*.

Our first step in this unfoldment is a realization of the disquieting and unsatisfying result of this living in a vain show. Then we must strive for a deep realization of the power of the likeness of God that is striving to manifest within us. This is not a mere picture of the Almighty seen as though through a telescope reversed or as the sunlight is reflected on the waves of the sea. It is far more than this. It is an essential likeness in that the attributes of Divinity are striving for expression through us. It is the struggle for manifestation of the image projected from the consciousness of God when we were sent forth on our cycle of evolution, destined to unfold the perfect pattern and fill a certain place in the Grand Plan, a place which, if left unfilled, would leave the Plan imperfect, a place which no other Soul in the universe can perfectly fill. It would be as tho a great artist had painted a masterpiece, with every figure, line and shading perfect save one which was left false, imperfect or out of proportion, or like a grand symphony in which one bar was discordant.

The image of God is not an outward resemblance, but a shining forth of the perfect ideal which we were intended to express. A tree grows in the image of God as it manifests the ideal of the tree God intended it to express; when it is as perfect as that kind of a tree can be. God's image includes a perfected universe with everything in it perfect after its kind, hence all reflecting and outpicturing God or made in God's image.

To manifest this likeness we must put away the vanities of life. And all things are in vain which do not contribute, first to the unfolding within our hearts and then to the manifesting in our lives, of the attributes of Divinity, the likeness which we each individually are destined to unfold, knowing well that the moment we manifest the perfected likeness the Great Law will place us in our true position in the cosmic picture.

We are wont to call men and women vain when they are overwhelmingly in love with themselves. We are wont to confine the term vanity to an admiration of personal qualities or physical possessions. We say she is vain of her looks, he is vain of his intellect, she is vain of her unfolding psychic powers, he is vain of his struggle to overcome his defects or both are disquieting themselves because the world fails to appreciate them at their own valuation or because others seem to attain spiritually who do not make half the struggle, but just go on growing as the flower grows; trusting and loving and living and doing for others instead of disquieting themselves with outer practices, such as fastings, refusal to eat certain foods, breathing exercises, and various yoga practices, etc., but this is not its full meaning.

We can give no technical directions here how to "behold thy face in righteousness," the face being the manifestation of the likeness that is expressed to the world. But we are assured that the likeness of God is within us—the image He intended us to manifest—and that if we meditate upon and dwell in the consciousness of the Divine that is within us, the image we are destined to unfold will gradually open in our lives like the petals of a rose and radiate the perfume, of His presence. It makes no difference what we have been in the past. Today we are the synthesized embodiment of all that we have even been. Even our mistakes and failures and the suffering they have entailed and the struggle to overcome them have all had their part to play in our unfoldment, hence are registered in the composite picture we are today and mark the degree to which the likeness has been unfolded.

That likeness has unfolded just to the extent that we do or do not walk in the vain show of the outer life or of mere psychic attainments without corresponding spirituality. Many in previous lives have held high positions in society, yet in this incarnation find themselves in obscurity and often poverty, while they still feel stirring within them all the tendencies and ambitions and desire for recognition as of old. They spend much time disquieting themselves and bemoaning a sad "fate" that has given them the almost irresistible desire for worldly grandeur and adulation, yet which has placed them in such humble positions that their desires cannot be gratified. All this is but the mathematical and inevitable result of the vain show in the past. We are placed in our present positions in life, not by an arbitrary fate nor by a jealous or revengeful Deity, as so frequently allegorically pictured in the *Bible*, but by the degree of our own unfoldment, by the causes we ourselves set up; because we allowed the vain show of the past to hide from us the likeness of God, the Image within, to the realization of which our present positions perchance may awaken us. Yet poverty and obscurity have their vain show also if their lessons are not learned, just as surely as have pomp and greatness in the world's eye. Only the awakened Soul can refuse to walk in the vain show of personality and seek to unfold the Divine Image of His likeness.

There are many today, alas, who because they find that they have developed a very sensitive nature, are disquieting themselves a great deal, either because their sensitiveness is not recognized by others, or because life presents to them so many commonplace problems. One may be very sensitive to sound yet may be compelled to live amid the grinding noises of street traffic or the blare of jazz music from neighboring phonographs. Others may be sensitive to color and yet be compelled to wear clothing that is not the exact shade they

love, etc. All such conditions, however, must be met and overcome.
If, through our higher development, we have made our nerves
more sensitive than others, we must remember that with this
increased sensitiveness there should also have come greater
power to conquer, greater poise and a closer touch with and
understanding of our great supply. Hence, we should refuse to
disquiet ourselves over such vain things, for we know that when
we bravely learn our lessons and determine to do the best we can
to unfold the Divine Image within us, our heavenly Father will
bring to us better conditions, for which we will then be ready.
But we must do our best to change undesirable conditions, not sit
down under them in a negative spirit and wait for a supernatural
deliverance.

In the late summer in some localities we see the hillsides and
meadows covered with the bloom of the wild carrot, a common
weed, yet a beautiful plant. Its white, lacy flowers beautify the
waste places and rejoice the eye, yet to the farmer it is but a
noxious weed. For before he can properly till the soil he must
eradicate its long, tough roots, so hard and woody, so tenacious,
and which so deplete the soil of its nutriment, yet which are so
devoid of nourishment in themselves, many lands being even
poisonous. But this same wild carrot, after a few generations of
cultivation, corresponding to a number of incarnations, can be
completely changed and its true image expressed. What is the
result of this cultivation? No more beautiful flowers. No more
attractive, spreading stalks nodding in the breeze. No more tough,
gnarled root, but instead a large and succulent root, something
that is of value instead of a nuisance, something that affords both
food and medicine for man and beast. And within this common
vegetable there are even greater possibilities. For carrots, as their
color indicates to the occultist, contain substances which penetrate
into the innermost tissues of man's body, helping to supply the vital

force which knits together his finer bodies and nourishing those faculties which shall help him to unfold the image of God more perfectly, such as will, persistence and tenacity of purpose. Everything we eat or drink not only nourishes our physical body, but also our finer bodies by imparting to them the finer essences which the food has developed and made its own during its period of cultivation or its long cycle of unfolding its true image of God, and contributing its forces to the manifestation of a more perfect universe. It is the same plant, but what a difference in its manifestation!

Yet, even in its uncultivated state, as the carrot grows in the wild places it not only helps to loosen the soil and add to its humus, but it also beautifies the landscape. For every blossom is a flower when in its right place, but a weed when in its wrong place. Thus is it often with the undeveloped Soul. It has its part to play in the world; to bloom in gladness and freedom in its own place, where it will be a beautiful flower, but if it tries to manifest where it does not belong it is but a weed. But when it has grown in its proper place and developed a succulent nourishing root, it must begin to feed the world and bring to it the help needed to unfold the image of God. Therefore, even the wild blossoms covering an uncultivated field are not a vain show, but are calling to man to do his part as faithfully as they do theirs.

The history of the wild carrot is the history of the Self. In the course of evolution there are three lines of unfoldment, each evolving toward its own perfection. Yet each of these threads of destiny must be interblended like a cord made up of three strands. The cord is strong and durable in proportion to the smooth and even blending of the strands. Even so must the Self evolve and blend its three strands or avenues of manifestation, *i.e.*, the physical body, the mind (including the psychic and mental bodies), and Spirit. And according to the individual trend or, let us say, the individual variation in the likeness of God breathed into each Self as it was sent forth into this far country of Earth life, do we unfold more rapidly and easily one or the other of the three threads.

Many attain great perfection of bodily development, strength and beauty, or great development of intellect and power of mind. Such are placed in positions in life in which their physical and mental perfections find recognition and emphasis. But without a corresponding spiritual unfoldment, like the wild carrot, they flaunt their blossoms to the wind. They attract attention, are admired and become great in the world's estimation. But the roots of their lives are gnarled, tough, woody and devoid of spiritual nourishment.

Then come many lives of pruning and cultivation, life after life the beautiful flowers of outer attainments that have attracted and pleased the eye of the superficial observer—for the wild carrot is without perfume and has an acrid odor which causes it to be rejected by those who give it more than superficial attention—all these flowers have to be cut away so that the life-force which formerly expended itself in outer show is forced to manifest beneath the surface, making the carrot grow and develop under ground. The result is, for the Self as well as for the carrot, that its root becomes succulent, wholesome and nutritious. We are then developing our inner possibilities and will, therefore, be able to feed humanity.

Some may ask, Has then this common garden vegetable the likeness of God within it? We answer that it has its aspect of that likeness, and it has taken its second step toward its unfoldment. Its third step will be attained when there has been developed within it the substances which nourish man's finer bodies in as great abundance, and to as great a degree, as its present nourishing qualities excel those of the wild root. In like manner must the Self develop its higher and finer possibilities. To awaken, then, in His likeness, we must correlate body, mind and Spirit; for to manifest the Image of the triune God the three must become one.

We know not what we shall be, but we shall be satisfied when we awake in His likeness. We can only go on doing the duty that lies nearest, unfolding those buds of our nature which the Great Gardener has not pruned away, be they above ground as leaves, stems or blossoms in the world's eye, or underground and in obscurity as inner and spiritual qualities which shall make our roots succulent and nourishing to mankind. Only as we take up each task in earnest, weaving the threads of our three-fold life into a strong cord that shall bind us to the Master-soul can He, our Lord, appear. But to hasten this great day we can each of us here and now say in sincerity and truth, "As for me, I will behold thy face in righteousness. I will no longer walk in a vain show. For the vanity of vanities is everything that hides from my consciousness the likeness of God that is within me and that is striving for expression."

Each one of us is today in the place which the Great Gardener sees is the best for our development and where the qualities in which we are lacking are undergoing cultivation. The three Fates—Clotho, Lachesis and Atropos—are each spinning a thread of destiny or guiding the evolution of our three-fold lives. Let us rest patiently then in the assurance that even tho the threads are seemingly tangled and the weaving of our spiritual Seamless Robe sometimes seems wearisome, yet over and above all is the divine Law of Love which is ever unfolding within us the likeness of God which we are destined to express in its three-fold perfection.

CHAPTER XXXI

LUCIFER

"How art thou fallen from heaven, O Lucifer, son of the morning!
how art thou cut down to the ground, which didst weaken the nations."
Isaiah, XIV, 12.

"It is a favorite popular delusion that the scientific inquirer is
under a sort of moral obligation to abstain from going beyond that
generalization of observed facts which is absurdly called a 'Baconian'
induction. But anyone who is practically acquainted with scientific
work is aware that those who refuse to go beyond (demonstrated)
fact, rarely get as far as fact; and anyone who has studied the history
of science knows that almost every step therein has been made by
the 'Anticipation of Nature'; that is, by the invention of hypotheses
which, though verifiable, often had very little foundation to start with."
Collected Essays, Huxley, I, 62.

In these wondrous times, when every day brings to light new
conceptions of universal laws, and the discoveries of science
border so closely on the miraculous that in some cases the
supposedly ridiculous claims of the early philosophers, occultists
and alchemists are being reproduced in our scientific laboratories
and are openly taught as scientific verities; when science herself
is finding it necessary to change her text-books every few years;
when the minds of men are constantly expanding to embrace
a wider and more comprehensive conception of the universe,
there is an ever increasing number who refuse to accept former
religious teachings unless they are given not merely dogma
and creed, but a rational and scientific explanation of the basis
of their claims. Such persons feel instinctively that while the
Bible may be a truly inspired book, whose teachings can be
corroborated by their agreement, in most fundamental points,
with the teachings of the other and older scriptures of the
world, yet that the dogmatic exposition of its truths, fastened

The Message of Aquaria

like a mill-stone around the neck of Christendom during the Dark Ages by minds of limited outlook and understanding, has undoubtedly hampered, if not prevented, the development of freedom of thought, and hence has delayed any great and wide-spread advance in our conceptions of spiritual truth.

The old explanations, not fitting in with the new discoveries of science, have little place in this age of enlightenment and great advance, hence among thoughtful minds there is a growing tendency either to discredit or to be apathetic toward all religious teachings, and to look upon the *Bible* as a mere collection of myths pertaining to past and primitive ages. Especially is this true of the old dogma which makes Lucifer, Satan, and the devil a trinity of evil which usually triumphs over the Trinity of Good. The interpretation of the Christian church alone stands sponsor for this dogma, for a careful study of the *Bible* fails to corroborate it convincingly. Indeed, in every place where either Lucifer, Satan or the devil is mentioned a little thought can separate them and give to each his proper place, yet all three have their part to play in the unfolding, purifying, illuminating and expressing of the one Divine Consciousness of the Real Man. In this chapter we will endeavor to correct some misconceptions by presenting the cosmic principles upon which this important subject is based, and to point out some of the truths concealed in its wonderful symbology.

As students of a Cosmic Philosophy we should not be confused by the old church dogma, but should clearly distinguish between Lucifer, Satan and the devil. Lucifer is called Son or Star of the Morning, the Shining One, also the Day Star. Indeed, many years ago in the earlier editions of the *Bible* the passage which now reads, "Until the day dawn, and the day star arise in your hearts"[1] was more correctly translated, "Until the day dawn, and the Divine

---

[1] *II Peter*, 1, 19.

Lucifer rise in your hearts." And this is the translation used today in the Greek church. Lucifer is, therefore, regarded as a Divine Being, an Arch Angel, a Son of God.

Satan, or Saturn, is referred to by Job as one of the Sons of God (Arch Angels) who, because of his office, becomes the Tester, the Adversary, the Accuser and the Initiator. This office is one which requires great devotion, for it means the conscious and willing taking upon himself (a great Planetary Angel) all the ignominy, hatred and censure of the world's misconception. Think what it would mean to such a Being to stand as the devil, Satan, etc! Yet, as Tester his office is a most important one, for "Whom the Lord (Law) loveth he chasteneth, and scourgeth every Son whom he receiveth."[2] Furthermore, we have human fathers who correct us and we give them reverence; and shall we not much rather be in subjection to a Divine Father?[3]

David recognizes this office of Tester when, in speaking of his enemy, he says: "Set thou a wicked man over him; and let Satan stand at his right hand,"[4] *i.e.*, to test him. It was Saturn who tempted (tested) Jesus when in the wilderness, the reply of Jesus being: "Get thee hence, Satan," for Jesus had met the test and conquered. Also, when Peter was influenced to tempt Jesus to put forth His power that He might avoid the persecution, trial and crucifixion, Jesus again recognized the Tester and replied: "Get thee behind me, Satan." In fact, in nearly all texts where Satan is represented as tempting, the word should be translated "testing."

That the devil was not looked upon as an individual expression of evil is quite plain, for in most places the devil is represented as the manifestation of *many* evil forces or oppositions to Good or God. This is especially noticeable in the several instances in which Jesus cast out *devils*. In fact, the

---

[2] *Hebrews*, XII, 6.
[3] See Saturn in *The Key of Destiny*, Curtiss.
[4] *Psalms*, CIX, 6.

devil is generally spoken of in the plural, altho like all forces, it is supposed to have an entitized ruling intelligence or prince, in this case Beelzebub (meaning "Lord of Flies, or Insects").

According to the esoteric teachings we find the seven Sacred Planets with their Rulers marshaled by the Divine Spirit, the Rulers being individualized divine manifestations or aspects of the One God. We can readily understand this if we remember that every one of us has many aspects or expressions. For instance, in the bosom of his family a man expresses love, affection, tenderness, etc.; in business he expresses the impersonal business code; in recreation he seems but an overgrown boy, while on other occasions he may have to express stern and impersonal justice, without regard to his personal feelings, yet all the time he is the same man, but expressing or showing the world different aspects. In a similar, altho to a far more entitized degree, the Rulers of the seven Sacred Planets are aspects of the One God. The Church calls them "the seven Spirits of the Presence," and Thomas Aquinas says that "God never works but through them." They are also called the Hosts of Heaven, and, by the Ancients, the Kabiri. "The Kabiri were always the seven planets as known in antiquity, who, together with their Father, the Sun—referred to elsewhere as their 'elder brother'—composed a powerful ogdoad."[5]

As we have pointed out more fully elsewhere,[6] every active power, principle and attribute of the Earth—the latest born of the planets—as well as of man, is derived from or through one of these Kabiri or Regents. "Each gets its specific quality from its Primary (the Planetary Spirit); therefore, every man is a septenate (or a combination of principles, each having its origin in a quality of that special Dhyani). * * * Light comes through Venus, who receives a triple supply, and gives one-third of it to the Earth. Therefore the two are called 'Twin-sisters.'"[7]

---

[5] *The Secret Doctrine*, Blavatsky, III, 316.
[6] *The Key to the Universe*, Curtiss, 221.

Not only is this the teaching of occultism, but astronomers confirm the fact that the Earth gets one-third of its light from Venus, altho just how they do not know, nor do they know the occult significance of this fact.

"Every world has its parent Star and sister Planet. This Earth is the adopted child and younger brother of Venus, but its inhabitants are of their own kind. * * * The Regent loved his adopted child so well that he incarnated as Ushanas and gave it perfect laws, which were disregarded and rejected in later ages."[7] "Thus the Kabiri are said to have appeared as the benefactors of men, and as such they lived for ages in the memory of nations."

Each of these forces is presided over and manipulated by the Regent of the planet whence it comes. In other words, God has given these great angelic Beings charge of the evolution of their youngest brother and its inhabitants, each bringing to him a definite gift over which he must watch and for whose use by mankind he is responsible. Indeed, it is upon this great cosmic truth—so well taught in all ancient religions in symbol and allegory, yet so overlooked by modern schools—that the many fairy-tales are founded, in which a child is visited at its birth by its Fairy-Godmother, who gives it a magical gift, the use of which will bring good or ill according to its use, and a magical call which the Fairy will always obey. Thus, when mankind disregarded the law given it by Lucifer-Ushanas, the allegory tells us that Ushanas "performed a Yoga rite, imbibing the smoke of their chaff with his *head downwards* for 1,000 years."[8] In other words, he had to partake of the results of mankind's misuse of the light of Mind he had conferred upon it, because man had allowed the mind, which should be above (higher *Manas*) or always in touch with the Divine, to be turned downward (lower *Manas*) and there become entirely enmeshed in matter and be dominated by it (*Kama Manas*).

---

[7] *The Secret Doctrine*, Blavatsky, II, 32-3-6.
[8] *Ibid*, II, 36.

While "Man derives his Spiritual Soul (*Buddhi*) from the essence of the Sons of Wisdom, who are the Divine Beings (or *Angels*) ruling and presiding over the planet Mercury,"[9] and while his Ray of Divine Life, Light and Immortality (*Atma*) comes from the Sun or its substitute, the higher and lower aspects of Mind (*Manas*) are derived from the essence of the Hierarchy ruling Venus.

Venus is called the morning and evening star, and the Hierarchy of Venus rules the higher and lower *Manas*. The color of Venus is indigo, while those of higher and lower *Manas* respectively are indigo and green. Indigo is obtained principally from the *genus Indigofera*, a group of plants of the highest occult properties, well known in India and much used in white magic "Eastern symbologists, from the earliest ages, have connected the spiritual and the animal minds of man, the one with dark blue (Newton's indigo), or true blue, free from green, and the other with pure green."[10] The higher or spiritual mind continually aspires to the Divine and is represented by the blue vault of heaven, while the lower mind tends toward and is represented by the Earth, where green in all its endless variety of tints prevails and forms a beautiful setting for flowers of every hue. Just so man's mind must be cultivated and developed to form a background or setting for every thought, if we are to get the full understanding of truth. And, like the green of the grass and the trees, a cultivated mind, or one which has been trained to think constructively, enhances every color and shade of thought. Therefore, the lower mind when put to its highest development, like the beautiful green of Nature, makes a perfect blending of Earth and heaven or of the lower mind and the spiritual mind. And since the Divine Mind holds for us many mystic truths, and only waits to shower them upon us, so the color indigo holds many occult and mystical potencies. Indeed, by the ancients

---

[9] *Ibid*, III, 458.
[10] *The Secret Doctrine*, Blavatsky, III, 462.

this color was held to be sacred, and the names India, Indus, India (the God of the firmament) are derived from the same root.

One name for the Regent of Venus is Anael, but he is represented by two great complementary Arch Angels, Lucifer (masculine) and Uriel (feminine), which in essence are one. Of these, only the masculine or Luciferian aspect has manifested on Earth as yet. For the feminine Ray, under the rulership of Uriel, is so far in advance of the Earth's present evolution that it has not as yet been manifested through mortal teachers. At one time an inspirational message was received from Uriel by *The Order of Christian Mystics* in which, among many other things, she said: "If I could find but one spot on Earth where I could touch but the toe of my foot (*i.e.*, awaken but a slight understanding), the impress of that touch would remain forever and the understanding of what Uriel could bring to the children of men would grow and grow in the hearts of mankind. And all the pollution of man could never hide it, for pollution would melt away like snow on a summer day. Nor could the salt waters of tears and sorrow wash it out. I whisper dreams of an ideal, heavenly love, but they alas! are misunderstood, and only too often are degraded and overlaid with lust and passion. Therefore, when I try to speak to mortals the Planetary Gods place their mighty hands on my lips; and alas! language is inadequate, and man has not yet evolved to the point where he can properly interpret my vibrations. A realization of this divinely-human and humanly-divine love is the bridge of swords which crosses the abyss of perverted human love, and the feet (understanding) of those who would cross it must be wounded and their heart's blood must flow until the purified hearts of a majority of mankind can see and grasp a ray of this divine love. * * * Try to learn the lesson now, O mortals! Learn it now if ye can, and save all the sorrow and pain, the anguish and bitter regrets through which you are now slowly being taught it."

"But do not try to learn it alone. There must always be another to join hands. This great force of love and wisdom (higher *Manas*), which comes from the planet Venus must ever come as a dual ray because this Earth is the planet of duality, hence it can only reach mankind through the 'twain who shall be made one,' not one in bodily structure, but one in mind and spirit. Love without wisdom works evil, and wisdom without love works coldness and selfishness, but together they become the 'golden apples,' or perfect sphere of life. To manifest this the force between the two must be exchanged in a way now unknown to man, to be understood only as the present crude exchange is purified and consecrated until the Angel of Life can say 'Come up higher.' When the Earth children misinterpret my whisperings my veil falls to my feet and I am obliged to return to the gods with bowed head and in disgrace. Then they push me to the rear, altho they know well that some day I will be crowned Queen of them all. And in that day the humanity of this dark star will receive my message and rise eagerly to the heights."

Intellect alone is cold and selfish, being devoid of the warmth of its love-aspect (Uriel). Therefore, most highly intellectual people who are ruled by Venus, *i.e.*, born in the signs Taurus or Libra or having Venus powerfully placed in their horoscopes, find it difficult to understand or correlate with the true love nature, for altho they are strongly sexed its expression tends largely toward mere animal passion. Therefore, if such persons are at all advanced and are earnestly seeking the higher life, they are very apt to denounce all use of the sex forces, call them evil and strenuously try to kill them out. And since this is impossible as long as the sex forces have not yet been brought to their very highest manifestation and truly consecrated or made holy to the Lord (Divine Law of Life), the result is frequently either suppression of those forces, or else the sex force that should be and is called forth as a creator by Divine Love, is perverted; hence creates instead abnormal self-love, and greatly clouds the ability to judge, so that all things seem to be but caterers to and builders up of this self-love. And we find persons claiming, and even truly believing, that they are superhuman beings because they have apparently killed out or put from them the principal lesson given to the humanity of this planet by Venus, and have turned their backs upon Divine Love and Wisdom and in their own judgment have improved on the Divine Law of Manifestation.

Lucifer is one of the Cherubim of Venus, while Uriel is one of the Seraphim. "The Seraphim loved most, while the Cherubim knew most," hence they combine as Love and Wisdom. The Cherubim aid and guide the evolution of mankind through love, while the Seraphim guide through knowledge. And because of this intimate tie between the currents of mind and love from Venus, every sin and every misuse of mind, as well as every perversion of or refusal to express love on Earth, is said to be felt on Venus, and vice versa. In fact, one of the greatest reasons why Uriel has not been able to manifest on Earth (as Muriel)[11] is because the mind of man is still so stained with thoughts of impurity in regard to love that the near approach of her auric vibrations only stimulates the average mind to lust. Only when Lucifer has been able so to purify the mind of man through knowledge of the law that it can bear the vibrations of love without perversion can he accomplish his true mission, but he cannot fully accomplish it without the help of his complementary manifestation, Uriel.

While Saturn is the first of the Kabiri to go forth at the command: "Let there be light," that a boundary to

[11] The letters U and M have similar symbology, but the M primarily represents Divine Love or mother love poured forth, while the U represents the esoteric or hidden side of Love or that mystery of the Love of the Divine Mother which is incomprehensible to humanity in its present state of evolution.

the system may be set and inertia and stability given to its substance, it was Lucifer, Star of the Morning or the Light Bearer, who "fell" or descended to give mankind the light of mind. In other words, it may be said that Saturn established the boundary and gave stability to the dwelling, and Lucifer put in the lights when the "builders" had made it sufficiently ready. Hence, Venus is often referred to as Venus-Lucifer.

Altho "Venus is the most Occult, powerful, and mysterious of all the planets; the one whose influence upon and relation to the Earth is most prominent" its influence is the least known and understood, both because of the mystery of Lucifer and Uriel and because, from a purely astronomical point of view, Venus is the most difficult of all the planets of this system to study; for altho it comes very close to the Earth, yet at those times when it does so it hides behind the Earth. In fact, Venus comes so close to the Earth that for many generations astronomers thought that she was but a satellite of the Earth. But in occult lore Venus is known to be the sister of the Earth, and is said to have "adopted the progeny of the Moon," referring to the fact that the humanity of this globe passed an earlier phase of its evolution on the Moon-chain.[12]

A transit of Venus can be seen astronomically only when the Earth and Venus pass a node of their orbits at the same time. The Earth passes the line of nodes about the 7th of June and the 7th of December, while Venus passes a node near enough to these dates to be seen against the Sun only four times in 243 years, the next such transit being June 8th, 2004. This will be a period of great enlightenment on this mysterious subject, and will bring a great advance to the mind of man.

The light that came from Venus when the animal man was evolved to a point where he was ready to begin the evolution of mind, was the Luciferian Ray, which completed the

---

[12] See *The Voice of Isis*, Curtiss, Chapter XV.

manifestation of the Trinity in man, that which makes him more than an animal; for this three-fold Ray constitutes his Higher Self or Immortal Soul—*Atma* (from the Sun), *Buddhi* (from Mercury) and *Manas* (from Venus).

Being dual, the light of mind can reach both upward and downward, but when it entered into man it became so enmeshed in the sensations of the physical world and the desires of the animal soul that it forgot its Divine origin and its spiritual complement (love), and thus developed as mere intellect, ignoring its two co-workers, love and spiritual life. The Luciferian influence, therefore, made man proud and arrogant, filling him with ambition, self-aggrandizement and all that selfishness and pride of intellect which reached such an extraordinary development in the Atlanteans, and which was largely responsible for the degradation of woman (love) and the relegating of her to the position of slave, or mere puppet of man.

(To be concluded)

Chapter XXXII

LUCIFER
CONCLUDED

"I beheld Satan as lightning fall from heaven." *St. Luke*, X, 18.

Among the nations composing the earlier sub-races of the Atlanteans, woman held a high and exalted place, not only in the family life but in the nation, similar to the place she held in later ages among the early Egyptians, namely, the priestess of the home. But as die Light of Mind reached its extraordinary development in the later sub-races it gradually became concentrated upon the development of mere intellectuality and will power, with the resulting subjugation to it of the gentler and more feminine qualities of the heart. This kept pace with the great development of psychic powers which made the Atlanteans the greatest magicians the world has ever known, and finally divided the Race into two main schools of teachings, the majority, who more or less degraded their powers for selfish ends, and the minority, who followed their Divine Instructors and strove to counteract the evil effects of the other school.

In the course of these two great developments—selfish intellectualism and psychism—the tender, softening influence of love and the purifying and uplifting influence of spiritual aspiration, together with the proper use of the life-forces, were more and more ignored by the majority, until finally woman was relegated by them to the background and even degraded merely to minister to the lusts of the intellectually and psychicly over-developed man, while the creative powers were horribly perverted, even to the extent of compelling female captives and slaves to cohabit with huge, ape-like animals (now extinct) to breed super-intelligent, semi-human animals to perform all the manual labor and menial tasks of their masters, just as today a jack is bred to a mare to produce a sterile, hybrid work-animal, the mule.

This perverted sex-force, together with their practices of black magic and their evil thought forces were responsible for the bringing forth of swarms of destructive insect life inimical to man; for man, being a creator through thought, word and deed, is responsible for all the perverted forms of life which prey upon or work against him. Hence, the bacteria, protozoa, insects and all such lower forms of life, which should be beneficial to man and live and work with him in symbiosis, among the Atlanteans were perverted into manifesting as pathogenic bacteria, death-dealing parasites, plant blights, disease carrying rodents, poisonous reptiles and other plagues which so overwhelmed and devastated the flora and fauna of Atlantis that only a submersion beneath the cleansing salt waters[1] of the ocean could stop the scourges and purify the very soil of the continent. In fact, the majority of the later sub-races of the Atlanteans perverted the forces of mind and their psychic and creative powers to such an extent that the terrible vibrations of inharmony and evil thus engendered upset the normal currents of magnetic force which sustain the equilibrium of the Earth's crust and thus caused the ultimate collapse and subsidence of the entire continent of Atlantis.

It was, therefore, the perversion of the Luciferian Ray, ignoring and working without its complementary ray (Uriel)—mind separated from love—which resisted the spiritualizing influence of Michael (Sun) who, through spiritual illumination, would have united Lucifer with his Divine Spouse (Uriel). Hence, Lucifer taught mankind to fight against the influence of Michael and his human followers, and thus transferred one aspect of the so-called "war in heaven" to Earth. Therefore, well might the prophet Isaiah exclaim:

---

[1] See *The Voice of Isis*, Curtiss, 386.

"How art thou fallen from heaven, O Lucifer, son of the morning! how art thou cut down to the ground, which didst weaken the nations?"

When these conditions had reached the climax of iniquity, to Saturn, "one of the Sons of God," was given the thankless task of ending the evil and bringing man back to his high estate of spiritual consciousness through the testing and suffering resulting from his own creations, even to the extinction of the majority of the Race which had failed so lamentably to follow its higher and divine guidance. This illustrates how far the use of free-will, granted man (within certain wide limits) in the beginning, can carry him away from his spiritual destiny. Man is not compelled to do right, altho all the Higher Powers and his own Higher Self do all they can, short of compulsion, to influence him toward a harmonious and constructive life; yet he can choose to do evil if he wishes, but if he so chooses he must suffer the consequences of broken law.

But through repeated and unspeakable sufferings throughout the ages, those of the Luciferian Ray will ultimately learn the lesson and, as we enter the coming sixth sub-race, will no longer fight against the messengers of Love (Uriel), Soul (Mercury) and Life (Sun), but will turn all the powers of their purified intellect and their indomitable will toward co-operating with them in presenting the three-fold expression of the Divine Law to mankind, and thus strive to teach humanity how to use its intellectual and magnetic powers to redeem both its bodily inharmonies (diseases), and to redeem the Karma of its past mistakes; thus helping to place its feet one step higher on the upward Path of Attainment.

Today many of the same Souls who failed so lamentably in old Atlantis who are of the Luciferian Ray, as well as those who strove to counteract their pernicious teachings, are incarnating in America. Hence, we may expect to see an important phase of the old struggle between good and evil or between the teachers of spiritual Light and Truth and those opposed, or those teachers of mere intellectual or magnetic forces, worked out in this country in the near future.

The devil is a generic term for all opposition to God's perfect law; is the D-evil or deification of evil. It has been created and given power through the ages by man's own choice.[2] For man, being made in the image of the Divine, has conferred upon him the power of choice and the gift of free-will. God could have made him a perfect automaton which would always have acted exactly right. He could have appointed some great Arch-Angel to pull the strings and man would mechanically have obeyed. But He did not. He gave man liberty either to follow the three-fold Ray of Light, Love and Life and have it work constructively in all his affairs, comforting him, illuminating, guiding and vitalizing all his efforts, or to separate the Light as expressed through Mind and place it on the throne, worship it as God and use it for selfish ends. In the latter case, man must learn through bitter suffering that mind is only one-third of his true illumination, and that through mind alone he can never pass the tests of the Angel of the Flaming Sword (Saturn) and enter the Eden of the higher consciousness.

It is Saturn who sets a limit to man's evil — after a certain point has been reached — by precipitating upon him the accumulated results of his own creations. In some cases this is more than the physical body can bear, and man is thus compelled to cease his life of evil. Many in their ignorance have called this great Tester the devil, forgetting that were man in his present stage of evolution to find the Tree of Life and be able to prolong his physical existence he would indeed be cursed, not by the devil, but by the continual accumulation of his own evil creations, thus making for himself a veritable hell. Therefore, until man has reached a far higher stage of purification and advancement than at present,

---

[2] See *The Key of Destiny*, Curtiss, Chapter XXV.

death is a great blessing, for it stops his further creation of evil, affords him a chance to rest and look back over his past life and see the results of his activities and learn therefrom the needed lessons. Altho he may for a time continue his evil ways in the astral world, even that must cease sooner or later and bring home to him its results.

We find this same law of testing and the disintegration of that which has ended its usefulness expressed in Nature. The power of the Sun, descending as heat, light and magnetism, is poured out upon and absorbed by the Earth, testing and proving it. Every seed in the dark Earth will be quickened by the Sun's force and be aided toward a constructive expression, but everything that cannot manifest constructively, will be decomposed; every dead and useless thing will putrefy and permit the manifestation of lower and destructive forms of life (molds, bacteria, etc.), while those contaminated by man's evil emanations will be brought to festering disintegration. Yet the Sun's force is not sent to Earth to bring forth evil, but to transmute evil into good; for without the testing and disintegration of that which can no longer work with the constructive aspect of the Law the evil conditions or forms would not be broken up and allow their forces to be turned around to fructify the good seed, manuring it and giving to it the life-force that was manifesting negatively as evil, thus making the good seed better fitted to feed mankind.

Some day man will learn that Saturn is one of the "Sons of God," one of the "Dragons of Wisdom," and that only through his testings and provings can the Light of Mind become the Light of Wisdom. Then man will realize that the Flaming Sword is Divine Love, which must separate the good from the evil. Then, too, will man be able to enter the New Jerusalem and find the Tree of Life and eat of the fruits thereof.

At the dawn of each new era the three-fold Ray of Divine

Light is sent forth—for Mind, Soul and Spirit—even as the rays of the physical Sun proclaim each new physical day, the Mind and Love-light from Venus, the Soul-light from Mercury and the life and Spiritual Light from the Sun. And as the world is now entering upon the new Aquarian Age we may expect to see all that is symbolized in the wonderful allegory of Lucifer manifested on Earth, modified of course by the limited stage of development reached by the Race. We will see the Mind of man illumined by a new comprehension of old truths, the Soul of man warmed and quickened by a greater outpouring of the Soul of the Universe and the Spirit of man awakened to a deeper and fuller realization and manifestation of Life, conclusively demonstrating that Life is not mere animal existence nor mere mental activity, but the eating and drinking and existing upon the mystic blood of the Cosmic Christ (the Divine Life-force) without which there is no real life in us.

Each of these Rays must ultimately establish a School of Light, composed of the many who belong to the planetary Hierarchy from which each Ray emanates. This will be accomplished through the efforts of illumined complementary Souls who are sufficiently developed to express, to a greater or lesser degree according to their development, the mission of the Ray. As the Solar Light is the most fundamental and embraces all that will later be differentiated into its separate rays, and as it is the first to manifest in each era, it is only natural to find that at the beginning of this new cycle the Solar Ray is as yet the only one manifesting through Agents who are *consciously in touch* with their Hierarchy and who are embodying its teachings in a definite School of Light, *The Order of Christian Mystics*, altho others are evolving toward such conscious touch and realization of their mission.

As the Law of Duality rules all expressions in the physical world, each of these Rays can be perfectly expressed only through man and woman working together in perfect harmony under the influence of the same Ray, altho a Ray may be temporarily, incompletely and less perfectly expressed through only one sex. Yet if one personality alone undertakes to express it without the balancing force of its complementary mate, no matter how sincere or how divinely illumined that personality may be, the expression is bound to be one-sided, and to make up for the lack of natural and normal balance there will be a tendency to pervert the fundamental Law of Manifestation, the Law of Polarity.

At the present time, the Solar School, as represented by *The Order of Christian Mystics*, is giving forth the fundamental principles of the Cosmic Philosophy which each School will later elaborate and emphasize, just as the one white Light is differentiated into its prismatic colors and yet unites all in perfect harmony.

The Solar School will emphasize and explain the principles of the one Divine Source of all, manifesting through a great Cosmic Scheme or Divine Plan in which each manifested life-expression has its place and its part to play. It will, therefore, present a cosmic outline, an all-inclusive philosophy, which will recognize and accord its true place to every expression of Truth. In fact, it is now preparing all who are ready, and is working toward the founding of a Universal Center of Spiritual Light and Truth where an ideal community can be established in which each differentiated School will have its place and co-operate with all the others to manifest the Light and Truth to all types and conditions of men. But first it must find the Souls and prove them ready to enter and dwell harmoniously in such a Center. For only as Love and Wisdom illuminate their understanding, and the broad cosmic principles are clearly grasped by one here and there can they be prepared. And only when a number have proved themselves both worthy and ready can they be gathered into one place to organize a Center and work together toward a common end. In other words, instead of attempting to found a Center and then striving to find persons to fill it—as is so often attempted—the right persons must first be found, tested and proved, and then gradually be gathered together and grow into a Center. Only thus can such a Center be established on a sound, constructive and enduring basis. The Solar School is, therefore, like the tap-root of a tree which gathers together and harmonizes all the varied elements and atoms that are to make up the various differentiated expressions of the tree.

The Solar School will emphasize the all-pervading Spirit of all Truth and will try to bring to mankind a greater realization of the Great Mother aspect of the Godhead; the nourishing Divine Love which brings forth and suckles all things; that spiritualizing and all-enfolding Love, "the Spirit of Truth which shall bring all things to your remembrance" and which shall be with us even unto the end of this day of manifestation. It is this Divine Mother-love which ever hovers with protecting wings over this Earth, where the great Bird of Life has made her nest and where she is calling to her and comforting under her warm feathers all the children of men whose spiritual natures, like nestlings, are being hatched in joy and immortality through the stress of the conditions resulting from the ignorance and sin of the past.

Since Venus is a dual planet and holds for mankind the perfected idea of divine union in its spiritual essence, the perfect pattern of that which is to be, much as the pattern of the ideal oak may be said to be in the acorn, it is from that planet that the seed of perfect duality in union is projected or planted in the Earth. Hence, the most fundamental and characteristic teaching of the Luciferian School will necessarily be the Law of Polarity or the duality or sex of the Soul, and that the Soul's perfect expression can be obtained only through complementary mates united in pure love and working together. Only as this doctrine is recognized and made the essential groundwork of the Luciferian teachings should the assertions of anyone who claims to be of the Luciferian School be recognized or accepted. For the teachings of the separate Schools will not violate the fundamental cosmic principles which have been set forth for all by the Solar School, principles which have stood the test of the ages as being fundamental and which have been reaffirmed by each successive great Light Bearer to mankind.

Indeed, since Venus is the manifestor of both Love and Wisdom, as Uriel has so beautifully told us, when it becomes possible for her to plant even a part of her footprint (understanding) on Earth, a wonderful comprehension of the true spiritual significance and the sanctity of marriage will prevail, not only as the bulwark of the family and national life, but equally the foundation of philosophical conception of life and spiritual unfoldment.

The Luciferian School will also teach how to direct and utilize the magnetic currents of the life-force when they have been properly balanced. For the magnetic currents are the result of the polarization of the two opposite cosmic creative currents, the positive and negative. In this present field of expression, our Earth, the Soul is manifesting in separated sexes to learn the great lessons of the separated manifestations of polarity through pure love and wisdom. And to attempt to use the positive magnetic current or *kundalini* without having it properly balanced by the rightful harmonizer or the helpmate for that work, invariably awakens the negative aspect of the current in the person treated and tends to connect the operator with and precipitate upon his head—be such a one ever so sincere and eager to help suffering humanity—all the stored up negative and destructive power generated by the perverted use of the creative forces by man and woman as a result of the wrong teaching, wrong thinking and wrong use of these forces throughout the ages. Verily, the Lord of Life spoke truly when he said: "It is not good that the man should be alone."

The electro-magnetic force of the *kundalini* is unknowingly being used today in hypnotism and allied practices to implant seed-thoughts in the mind or aura of the subject treated. It is also brought into action in the "laying on of hands" whenever the will or the desire of the operator is added to the flow of the psycho-physical magnetic current; for the dividing line between the electro-magnetic and the psycho-physical currents is so fine that it is only by a clear understanding and the exercise of a strongly developed and spiritualized will that the operator can so guard his thoughts and desires as to send forth the magnetic current untainted. Even his desire that a certain healing or other result should take place as he thinks it should is sufficient to bring into play the *kundalini* and make the procedure hypnotic in its effect. In fact, it is very difficult to use the magnetic current without awakening the *kundalini*, which is both magnetic and electric, and which tends to stimulate all the centers, according to their development. And as the sex centers are the most developed in mankind today, the use of the *kundalini* naturally tends to stimulate them. Therefore, to play with these forces which caused the downfall of Atlantis, or for students who are untrained, inexperienced in psychic matters, and undisciplined in mind and body, to try to apply them is to play with a fire which can corrupt and destroy as readily as make alive.

Since all but a very few of mankind are still subject to the law of the physical plane, the Law of Polarity, no one should allow another to hypnotize him, and, *as a rule*, no one not spiritually illumined, consecrated and specially trained should practice the "laying on of hands" on one of the opposite sex, for sooner or later it is apt to stimulate the sex centers. And average people are not greatly to be blamed if such a result occurs, for they have had no training in controlling and transmuting the vibrations set up by the concentrated magnetism of the opposite sex. Therefore, such forces should not be used without a full understanding of the dangers involved.

While many good and useful fruits of mind and of the *kundalini* discovered by the Atlanteans are preserved in the higher realms, they cannot be properly understood or rightly used until man has again reached the same stage of mental development, but this time with the spiritual growth added which will enable him to re-enter the Garden of Eden and bring forth its fruits for the whole of humanity. Then the Tree of life will grow on both sides of the River of Life and will bring forth its fruits each month for the healing of the nations.

The Luciferian School will also emphasize the power of mind, the development of will, the creative power of thought and all the problems of mental science, as well as the force of spiritual aspiration, in bringing about harmony in the student's own body and in those who may apply for healing. It will also teach that mere intellect without love is sterile and one-sided; also that mind is not all, but must be used to reach up into higher realms and become united with the spiritual consciousness of the Higher Self and receive the baptism of the Spirit. "Intellect by itself alone will make a Black Magician. For intellect alone is accompanied with pride and selfishness: it is the intellect *plus* the spiritual that raises man. For spirituality prevents pride and vanity."[3]

The exaltation of intellect and the effort to subserve the spiritual forces within to bring temporal domination and gratification of the lower senses, passions and desires was the "Original Sin" of the early Races, not the use of the creative powers themselves. This is clearly shown by the fact that the creative powers were given to man by his Maker and he was told to use them, to "Be fruitful and multiply and replenish the earth" long before he misused

---

[3] *The Secret Doctrine*, Blavatsky, III, 539.

these powers and was cast out of the Garden. Man was first turned out of his Garden individually and as a Race out of his temporal home (Atlantis), not by God, but his own misuse of his opportunities, forces and materials which brought death, with all its attendant ills and miseries, first into his own body and then into the body politic. But even in those terrible days there were in Atlantis many who did not bring death upon themselves, because they used their forces according to the Law of Good (Lord God). These later evolved into the class of spiritual Masters who are called "Sons of Light." "The Lemurians, and also the early Atlanteans, were divided into two distinct classes — the 'Sons of Night' and darkness and the 'Sons of the Sun' or the Light.'"[4] These Sons of Light have never died, but remain in the higher realms, yet are able to appear in the flesh whenever humanity needs such a manifestation.

Only when man has learned that mind is but a gift of God to be used for His glory; that the Holy Ghost can be bestowed upon him only by a power outside of and above mind, through spiritual development and initiation into a higher state of consciousness, can he return to his Garden. Only when we learn that mind is merely the servant of the Real Self or the superintendent of our Garden unto whom is given the wise direction of all its forces, yet who must be responsible to the Lord of Life, who is the real Indweller, can the Flaming Sword be turned into the Rod of Power at whose knock the gates of Eden shall fly open and admit us to our heritage.

The Mercurian School will emphasize the necessity for personal union with the Divine (Soul), the Fatherhood of God and therefore the essential Brotherhood of Man. This School will proclaim an era of peace and harmony among nations and the necessity — as man's greatest need — of harmonious co-operation for the good of all. Its emphasis will be on the principle that because the Soul has its roots in

---

[4] *Ibid*, II, 816.

the Divine, the Soul of the Universe flows like a mystical River of Life from the Throne of God outward through every manifested form of life in all the worlds.

These three types of Teachers or Agents, symbolized in the various allegories of the Three Wise Men from the East—the source of Light—have each their characteristic mission, and representative exponents of each must ultimately arise and recognize each of the others and work together in perfect harmony. Just as the planets Venus and Mercury, each receiving their light from the Sun, yet sounding their own creative notes and playing their own peculiar part in the mighty scheme of evolution, unite to bring about the predestined salvation of the physical Earth, so will the chosen Agents of these Rays recognize the part each must play, and together lay their gifts—gold, frankincense and myrrh—at the feet of the Cosmic Christ now preparing an individualized manifestation on Earth; the spiritual gold of Light and Truth from the Solar Ray; frankincense, the aspiration and the guidance resulting from a personal realization of the Divine, emphasized by the Mercurian Ray; and myrrh, the bitter yet cleansing and healing experience of pride and self-sufficiency overcome, of the oneness and equality of man and woman, the necessity of Love (feminine) to guide, and Wisdom (masculine) to illumine and bring about the perfect Soul-marriage of humanity, which is the work of the Luciferian Ray.

Yet there is no one so humble and seemingly insignificant who cannot help to gather up and express the forces which these three Rays are now pouring out so lavishly for manifestation on Earth. If anyone feels the urge to thus be about his Father's business, let him know and realize that all the powers of the three-fold Ray will help him and work through him to the extent he makes it possible, both for his own perfection and unfoldment and to make him a more helpful focus of harmony and enlightenment in his environment.

None who find interest in this chapter can say that they are too ignorant, too weak or too selfish to do their humble part, for the Great Law has placed them in just the positions where they have the ability to do their work. Seek out, then, the avenue of illumination and helpfulness which most appeals to your heart's desire and seek to make of yourself an understanding and willing worker for the Great Ones in Their efforts to enlighten, uplift and benefit all.

Use the Prayer for Light daily and hourly and ask for Divine Guidance in all things.

CHAPTER XXXIII

MARS

"The Globe, propelled onward by the Spirit of the Earth and his six Assistants, gets all its vital forces, life and powers through the medium of the seven planetary Dhyanis from the Spirit of the Sun. They are his messengers of Light and Life." *The Secret Doctrine*, Blavatsky, II, 32.

"Innocence cannot be virtue nor simplicity merit. Man is only that which he has conquered." *Prophecy of the Zodiac*.

In beginning the study of the planet Mars, or in fact any other planet, it must be understood that it is not the physical planet known to astronomers and physical science, but the Spiritual Ruler, whose abode or seat or whose force is focused in the planet, to which we refer.

As we have explained elsewhere,[1] the seven sacred planets of this system are each the abode of one of "the seven Spirits of God" which are before his throne. This is made very plain in the *Revelation of St. John*, where, in his opening address, he says: "Grace be unto you, and peace, from him which is, and which was, and which is to come; and from the seven Spirits which are before his throne."[2] Why should "Him which is, and which was, and which is to come," *i.e.*, the Lord of Life, include the seven Spirits if they were not an essential part of the manifestation of the One God? We therefore allude to the seven Spirits or Planetary Deities in the universally accepted terminology of the ancients as the Administrators of God's decrees, as the Projectors of God's attributes or the Manifestors of the Divine Plan; the same Elohim who said: "Let *us* make man

---

[1] *The Key to the Universe*, Curtiss, 219
[2] I, 4.

in *our* Image, after *our* likeness," *i.e.*, embodying all the planetary forces of this system.

The ancient Syrians and Chaldeans defined the Planetary or World Rulers thus: (1) the Earth, the lowest sub-luminary, is watched over by *Angels* of the first or lower order; (2) Mercury is ruled by *Archangels*; (3) Venus by *Principalities*; (4) the Sun, the domain of the highest and mightiest gods of our system, by the Solar Gods; (5) Mars by *Virtues*; (6) Jupiter or Bel by *Dominions*; (7) Saturn by *Thrones*.[3] "The ancients had, in their Kyriel of Gods, seven chief Mystery-Gods, whose leader was, *exoterically*, the visible Sun."[4] They are also called "The seven eyes of the Lord" by the early Christian writers.

These seven great Spirits also rule the seven-fold powers of Nature, the forces of the universe evolving Nature through seven tones, called the seven creative notes of the cosmic scale, and through the seven color rays, etc. "Through Hippolytus, an early Church Father, we learn what Marcus—a Pythagorean rather than a Christian Gnostic, and a Kabalist most certainly—had received in mysterious revelation. . . . . .The seven heavens (Angels of the Planets) sounded each one vowel, which, all combined together, formed a single doxology, 'the sound whereof being carried down (from these seven heavens) to earth, becomes the creator and parent of all things that be on earth.'"[5] Thus the ancients never considered the planets in any other light than as the abodes of Deities, altho—modern thought to the contrary—they were fully aware of seven physical globes connected with the cosmogony of our solar system.

Among the ancient Egyptians Mars was recognized under the name of Artes, and was worshiped not as god, but as an attribute of the One God, namely, as the dispenser of primitive or initial powers for the purpose of human pro-

---

[3] *The Secret Doctrine*, Blavatsky, I, 469.
[4] *Ibid*, II, 25.
[5] *Ibid*, II, 594.

creation. And in almost every ancient religion these powers are attributed to Mars under various names.

The color of Mars is said to be red, not only because the planet appears red as seen from the Earth or because of any peculiar red formations upon the planet, or because connected with bloodshed, but because the chief function of Mars is the focusing of the life-force into individualized expression through generation. Incidentally, Mars is called the God of War, but far more generally the Lord of Birth and Death, also of Generation and Destruction. The esoteric force deified in Mars is the primal Principle of Life being differentiated into its opposite poles for the purpose of procreation. This is always associated with both water and blood, but with water only in the sense that water is the "blood" of the Earth or the carrier of the universal life-force to Nature. And as the blood carries the individualized physical life-force, so the color red in the spectrum carries the vital life-principle to all the other color rays. And as the color rays manifest in a circle or spiral, rather than one above the other, so in each ascending cycle the red grows lighter and brighter until it becomes the beautiful rose pink of spiritual life-force or Divine Love.

While water is the "blood" of Nature, blood in man and animals is water plus fire. The lower forms of life having little or no red blood—fish, reptiles, etc.,—have little of the life-fire, hence are called "cold blooded," as they do not maintain a continuous body temperature, but take on the temperature of their surroundings. Hence, Mars rules blood and water in the sense that it is through the guiding Hierarchies and forces of that planet that the fleshly bodies of human Souls inhabiting the Earth are produced and also reproduced and maintained in health and vigor.

Therefore, while Mars is the God of War in one sense and is properly associated with the shedding of blood, yet the shedding of blood referred to is primarily that which is shed in connection with the functions of generation. The real "warfare" of Mars is not inciting the nations of mankind to war but the overcoming of the natural resistance of the Soul to the descent into physical generation and all that it entails ere generation is lifted up into regeneration and the experiences garnered into wisdom and power.

Mars is represented as having been born without a mother, one way of expressing the important esoteric truth that it is only the potential forces of generation that come to us from Mars, or we might say *generation in potentiality* ere the sexes were separated, and actually expressed on Earth in separated sexes. While from Venus is sent to the Earth the potential seed-thought of a perfect and purified union of the sexes and the guiding force to bring it into actuality. On the other hand, the same idea is conveyed by Ovid when he states that Mars was born of his mother, Juno, without a father.

In the zodiac Mars is given the place of strength in the first decanate of the sign Aries (the Ram), in which the Sun is exalted. He is also given the place of death in Scorpio, in which sign the task is given to the Soul to purify, control and uplift all the functions of generation. This is represented in the myth in which Scorpio slays Orion. Now, in mythology Orion was an intrepid hunter of enormous size, the same personage as Minotaur and Nimrod, and symbolizes the lower and uncontrolled aspect of sex. Mars is called Ramah in Egypt, where the skin of a ram (Aries the Ram) covered the Holy of Holies in the temples, a symbol continued by the Hebrews after leaving Egypt by covering their Ark of the Covenant with a ram's skin. From these few references the functions of Mars are plainly indicated.

The planetary Ruler of Mars is closely connected with Venus. From Mars comes the force and the strength and the courage by which man can learn the hard lessons and endure the suffering of sex, and from Venus comes the loving tender care and guidance and the promise of ultimate victory, and both planets are so closely associated with the

Earth and its inhabitants that, in one sense, they may be called the Spiritual Parents of the Earth. In an ancient myth the Mother of the Sun, under the name of Semele, was made to ascend her throne and preside as a balancer and harmonizer between the planets Mars and Venus, where she was henceforth worshiped under the name of the "Queen of the World." And it is from this very ancient idea, because it embodies a vital truth, that most of the Virgin Mothers found in all religions are taken, whether called Divine Mother or Queen of Heaven; whether Isis in Egypt, Sakti in India, Semele in Rome, or Mary in Jerusalem. The meaning is quite plain, for Mars and Venus are the sources of the forces which are finally manifested as the separated sexes in humanity, and will ultimately bring about the perfect balance of the two when in its fullness the promise shall be fulfilled, "Have ye not read, that he which made them at the beginning, made them male and female. Wherefore they are no more twain, but one flesh."[6] These planets are the guardians of the great test of sex. And only as Love, the Divine Mother, is permitted to dwell as balancer and harmonizer between the two opposite expressions can the great lesson yield all its powers and fruits.

That mysterious personage known in the *Bible* as Melchisedec was in reality an avataric manifestation of the planetary Ruler of Mars to the early Races, altho then recognized as the Prince of Peace (Salem), instead of the God of War. And in very truth, if we are to receive the mystical bread and wine from Melchisedec, that exalted "Priest of the most high God," then, like Abram,[7] we must arm our 318 trained servants born in our house, *i.e.*, the forces of the zodiac (3+1+8=12), which we have mastered and brought forth in our personality, and use them to conquer our enemies—the lower appetites and passions which have possessed our land—and "bring back all the goods" or rescue

---

[6] *St. Matthew*, XIX, 4-6.
[7] *Genesis*, XIV, 14.

the misdirected good and its "women" or its power to bring forth. And when this has been accomplished we must not be puffed up over our victory, but must await the coming of our High Priest in the valley of humility ere we can receive the body and blood of the Cosmic Christ shed for us from the beginning, even as the later Avatar, Jesus,—"a Priest forever after the Order of Melchisedec"—offers the same mystic bread and wine that Melchisedec offered Abram to those disciples who meet Him in the mystical "upper chamber," saying: "Take, eat; this is my body. . . . This is my blood of the New Testament. . . . Drink ye all of it." For it is through the outpouring of the mystical "blood" of Mars that man reached the great test of generation, and only as we eat and drink "with love and thanksgiving," or correlate with and assimilate it can we pass its test and be blessed as conquerors.

It will thus be seen that among the early Races, when mankind was childlike and was taught face to face by the great Masters of Wisdom—even by the Planetary Deities themselves—the relation that Mars bore to this Earth was well known, as the *Bible* narratives so plainly indicate. For each of the seven Sacred Planets gives to the Earth, the latest born of this system, a special vibration or force to help on the evolution of both the planet and its humanity. Thus, Jupiter sends us the force of judicial deliberation which gradually evolves us toward omnipotence; Saturn is the Tester, the Initiator; Mars the giver of strength, courage and fortitude; Mercury gives that clear intuitive reasoning whose complete development gives omniscience; Venus gives Love and the ability to endure, also understanding, while the Sun gives spiritual illumination, also the blessings of healing.

Among the Romans Mars was regarded as the most important Deity after Jupiter. That Mars was not considered merely as the God of War, even among that warlike nation, is shown in many ways, for the month of March, when the

forces of generation are gathering in the Earth preparatory to
bringing forth anew in Spring, was held sacred to and named after
Mars, especially the Ides of March. Also, special ceremonies were
performed to Mars during the months from March to October,
while the Earth is generating and producing her increase. Until
the reign of Augustus, there were only two temples at Rome
dedicated to Mars, one on the *Campus Martius* or Field of Mars,
the exercising and reviewing place of the army, the other outside
the *Porta Carpena*, the gate through which the army marched on
its campaigns to the South. But in the heart of the city there was a
sacrarium of Mars in the *regia*, originally the king's house, where
the sacred spears and shields of Mars were kept. Should war be
declared, during a sacred ceremony these spears were taken out
and shaken and the protection and help of Mars invoked with the
cry, *Mars vigila* (Mars, wake up!).

If by any chance these spears were shaken without human
hands, it was looked upon as a dire omen and called for expiation,
for in the *sacrarium* the god Mars was supposed to dwell in a
spiritual sense. From March to October the sacred spears and
shields were carried through the city in a procession on three
separate occasions, preceded by dancing priests, flower girls, etc.,
but in October, when generation and bringing forth had ceased in
Nature, there was a solemn ceremony at which they were purified
and blessed and put away for the winter, thus showing that Mars
was primarily connected with generation and reproduction, both
in Nature and in man, and only later and secondarily with war.

This conception of Mars has survived and is so commonly
known even today that in a recent newspaper[8] article it
was stated that because of the conjunction of Mars and
Venus on January 5th, and Mars passing through Pisces and
coming into conjunction with the new Moon on January

---

[8] San Francisco Chronicle, May 1, 1921.

23, 1921, "mean but one thing. They constitute what is known as a 'fruitful zodiac.' Within the next six years the birth of a single child will be an exception to the rule . . . we are to prepare for the arrival of a harvest of twins and triplets." While we cannot endorse this in its fullness, yet this is a most remarkable prediction to be found in a newspaper, for at the beginning of every Age there are hosts of Souls whose work and Karma connect them with the new Age and who should incarnate at that time, yet who have had to wait, perhaps hundreds of years, for the proper opportunity to incarnate under conditions in which they can accomplish their mission. Hence, many may incarnate as twins.

It is quite natural that at the present point in man's evolution his mind should turn to a study of the planet Mars. This is not only because it is the planet next outside the Earth, being the fourth in distance from the Sun, nor because at opposition it is brighter than a first magnitude star and by its position the most favorably situated of all the planets for observation from the Earth, but because of its close mystical relationship and association with the Earth at this particular time. For Mars is looked upon as the spiritual Father of the Earth, and as a father it has manifested its creative power on Earth, while the Mother-force of Venus has not yet been able to find adequate expression. This is one reason why, in many religions, we find more reference to the aspect of God as a Father than as a Mother. But as we have now entered the sign Aquarius, or the Woman's Age, the Father may be said to be growing old (Mars is now drawing to the close of its last Round, while Venus is only coming into the fullness of her last Round) and must withdraw from active work, and that which he has impregnated and implanted in the Earth and its humanity must be brought forth by the great Mother-force of Venus.

(To be concluded)

CHAPTER XXXIV

MARS
(Concluded)

"Every place that the sole of your foot shall tread upon, that have I given unto you. . . . From the wilderness and this Lebanon even unto the great river, the river Euphrates. . . . There shall not any man be able to stand before thee all the days of thy life. . . .I will be with thee: I will not fail thee, nor forsake thee. Be strong and of a good courage: for unto this people shalt thou divide for an inheritance the land, which I sware unto their fathers to give them. Only be thou strong and very courageous that thou mayest observe to do according to all the law." *Joshua*, I, 3-7.

One of the many evidences that the *Bible* is truly an inspired book and, like all other sacred scriptures, written allegorically that its full meaning might he revealed only to those who so ardently desire truth that they seek for it behind the veil, is the fact that the important esoteric teaching as to the relation of Mars and Venus to the Earth, in their aspects as Progenitors and Guardians, is symbolized in the story of the Ark of the Covenant, as well as in the story of Noah and his Ark, in which he is represented as preserving the Races of mankind to repeople the Earth after the deluge.

That the force of Mars has always been primarily connected with generation and reproduction, and only secondarily with war, is further evidenced by the fact that among the ancients we find the Spirit of Mars represented as gathering the germs of all living things necessary to repeople the Earth into an Ark, the Argha of the Mysteries. Among the Egyptians it was called the *cista mystica*, or Ark of Mystery. It was also used as a sacred chalice in the worship of Astarte the Syrian Venus, and in other forms of worship in which the container of the feminine reproductive power is symbolized. In general, the Ark represented both Venus and the Womb of Nature, in which the germs of all manifestation were pictured as floating upon the waters of the Great Abyss during the interval between two periods of manifestation, until fructified by the Spirit of Mars. The nave (from the Latin *navis*, ship or ark) in Christian churches has the same symbology, for it contains the altar on which are focused all the mystic potencies of the religion necessary for the purification and regeneration of its followers.

This was also symbolized by the Ark of the Covenant, which again was the container of the forces of generation, represented by Aaron's blossoming Rod, symbolizing the rejuvenation of Nature; the two Tables of the Law, the masculine and feminine expressions of the Law; and the omer of Manna, the sustaining power of the One Life. This meaning of the Ark of the Covenant is indicated by its construction. It was built of shittim wood (acacia), which focused the astral forces, and was covered with pure gold, symbol of the Spirit. Around the top was a golden rim or crown, and upon this crown were the cherubim, facing each other with their wings spread in such a manner as to form a perfect *Yoni*, the symbol of the feminine reproductive power. The cherubim represent Mars and Venus, and the "Covenant with man" is that while humanity is learning the great lessons of the separated sexes these two expressions of Divinity, *i.e.*, the strength and courage of Mars and the love and understanding of Venus, will ever watch and guard mankind, and that which is brought forth from their purified use of the creative forces shall be blessed of God. This interpretation of the Ark is further emphasized by the fact that the four mystic letters of Jehovah's name—IHVH or *Yod-Hé Vau-Hé*—are carved upon it, *Yod* meaning the *membrum virile; Hé*, the womb; *Vau*, a hook or nail, and the second *Hé* an opening; the whole forming the perfect bisexual emblem, the male and female symbol.[1]

---

[1] *The Secret Doctrine*, Blavatsky, II, 482.

The Argha or Ark was, therefore, a general and universal symbol and was worshiped as the *sanctum sanctorum* or the center in which the forces of Mars and Venus are focused upon Earth. Remember that the force which comes from each planet is but a particular or specialized aspect of the One God. And knowing that humanity must pass through the experience of the separated sexes if it was to "become as one of us, knowing good and evil," God provided and focused upon the Earth just the forces needed to carry us through this experience, if we will but utilize them aright. Yet, alas, the force of Mars is degraded and regarded merely as the instigator of war; is made a malign planet, catering to man's lowest passions and appetites. Saturn, the divine Tester and Guardian, who would not that any perish, who stands ever near to say to man: "Stand and prove all things and hold fast to that which is good lest ye be lost in the abyss of ignorance," is called the enemy, the tempter and the devil, while Venus, the giver of Divine Love, the tender Watcher in the Night who ever whispers hope amid the deepest degradation and sorrow, is often worshiped with lascivious rites and called the "mother of harlots!" So low have our conceptions of these individualized manifestations of the Divine fallen through materialistic and perverted interpretation! and because the Church is apt to look upon all recognition of these great Star Angels as idolatry instead of manifested aspects of the One God!

Having recognized and fully realized that the seven Sacred Planets, or more correctly speaking the Angels, Spirits or Rulers of those planets, are each but differentiated and individualized expressions of the seven-fold Godhead, the Elohim, we are ready to study, understand and appreciate something of their mysteries, potencies and powers. In a similar way if our spiritual eyes were opened to see our finer bodies we would see that each characteristic or each expression of force makes a definite light or color, or if evil a dark streak, in our aura, yet all the colors are but expressions of the one individual. Similarly the universe may be regarded as the aura of God, and every star and planet as manifesting a special trait or aspect of God, yet all necessary for His perfect expression in matter.

During the present chaotic conditions upon Earth an understanding of the force of Mars is greatly needed, for it brings strength, courage and fortitude; and also the disintegration of that which is evil to such an extent that if this force were concentrated upon the Earth before it was ready to respond to its vibration, the Earth would be volatilized in an instant. This force is called malign and evil by some, just as an untutored savage might call electricity an evil force and seek to propitiate it. Yet, when man is ready consciously to correlate with and regulate this force, he can use it to perform all manner of labor, for it belongs to a lower octave of the dynaspheric force. The dynaspheric force comes from all the planets, but only when man has learned to correlate with the forces of Mars and Venus, and has so advanced that he can add to these the radiant energy of his purified will can he consciously and safely direct and utilize this force aright.

If it were possible to shut off all the other planetary forces and focus the Martian force it could be used to bore a tunnel clear through the Earth. We are told that the Masters have constructed wonderful tunnels under continents and oceans through the help of the elementals, but the elementals and forces so used were not of Earth but of Mars. Engineers say that they could tunnel through the Earth even now if they could remove the debris as the greater depths were reached, but with the use of the Martian force there would be no debris to be taken out, for the sides of the tunnel would be compressed and fused and whatever resisted would be volatilized, and the tunnel, when completed, would endure as long as the planet itself. By the use of this force all the great Centers on Earth can be connected when the time comes.

The force of Mars is such a tremendous force of attraction (desire), that if Mars stood alone in the heavens without the influence of the other planets, the power of attraction would be so great that all the planets would be drawn to it as a center. But the other planetary forces intervene and balance it. Saturn repels, Venus modulates, Neptune counteracts, Uranus intensifies, Jupiter holds in balance and so on, even to the most distant star. If it were not for these counterbalancing forces we would find ourselves on Mars quicker than we could think, for the purified Desire Principle so powerfully manifested on that planet would draw us to it.

It is through correlation with the Martio-Venus force that communication must some day be established between the Earth and Mars. For ages Mars has been trying to communicate with the Earth other than psychicly and subjectively, but the Earth has not as yet manifested sufficient stabilized harmony for it to respond. In other words, the Earth is not clearly sounding her own true key-note. If she were sounding her note perfectly and harmoniously, she would so truly take her place in the Music of the Spheres that it would be easy to catch the note of any other planet, just as when a person is singing in perfect tune in a chorus he has no difficulty in correlating with the rest, but if out of tune or rhythm he may think all the rest are wrong and find it impossible to harmonize with them. Hence, when Mars sends us his forces, they are only partially received and utilized, and are largely dissipated. If we could concentrate upon and sound the note of Mars so clearly that it would cut through the other vibrations, we would have a direct channel of communication.

Humanity is again passing over the point in the spiral of evolution which was symbolized by Noah and his Ark. "The earth also was corrupt before God, and the earth was filled

with violence . . . And God said unto Noah, The end of all flesh
is come before me; for the earth is filled with violence through
them; and behold, I will destroy them with the earth."[2] That "the
end of *all* flesh is come" is not to be taken literally is shown by
the fact that the Lord directed Noah to build an Ark to preserve
the seeds of the future Great Race (Fifth). In its symbolic meaning
an Ark of Safety must once more be built in humanity through
correlation with the force of Mars and the consequent purification
of the blood of the Race, through which the salvation of both
man and the Earth must come. And since these are the forces
given man with which to multiply and repeople the Earth, when
perverted they people the Earth with evil, vileness and disease, as
is the condition so prevalent today, nearly all chronic diseases —
tuberculosis, cancers, tumors, arthritis deformans, as well as
neuroses, hysteria, neurasthenia, etc., — are now considered by
certain advanced scientists[3] as developing only in the presence
of a blood-taint created by the perversions of the creative forces
and either commonly inherited or widely acquired in this life.
Even tho nearly one third of the cases acquire their taint in this
life quite innocently and unknowingly, nevertheless, they are
karmically connected with it from former incarnations. And since
it is through the blood that certain higher forces contact the body,
if the blood is tainted with the toxines of perverted sex forces, it
is impossible to contact certain spiritually creative forces from
the higher realms.

The deluge took place toward the close of the Atlantean
period, while that which is symbolized by the building of
the Ark, *i.e.*, the separation of those who listened to and
followed the Divine Law from among those who clung to
the common practices of black magic, required the sixth and
seventh sub-races to accomplish, during which time there

---

[2] *Genesis*, VI, 11-14.
[3] According to the Abrams' Electronic Method which measures the radio-activity of the
toxines from a drop of blood, and destroys them by destructive vibration.

were many minor cataclysms, but ere the final one, all who followed the Divine Teachers were led in safety to colonies in Egypt, Babylonia and even in Central Asia. In other words, it required most of the sixth and seventh sub-races for Noah to preach his teachings, educate, prepare and call forth his faithful "children," altho the biblical account makes it seem but a short time.

The command has once more been given to man to build an Ark which can float on the turbulent sea of humanity and which shall contain the potencies of the purified creative forces given to mankind from Mars to uplift the Race, to re-create our bodies and regenerate the planet. Those who are ready to listen are metaphorically standing on the verge of Jordan, as indicated in our text, waiting for their Joshua to bid them cross over and enter the Promised Land. To them comes the promise, "Verily every place that the sole of your foot shall tread upon, that have I given unto you." This means all things in the cosmogony of life with which we can correlate, all these has the Lord of Life already given us to possess. We have but to enter in and partake of them, from the lessons and blessings found in the wilderness of life through which we are now passing, from Lebanon—the astral world—and from the powers contained in the great river Euphrates, or the generative force from Mars.

But man cannot live and accomplish these things for himself alone; for no individual can rise high enough to utilize these forces to fulfill the destiny of the Race in any large measure until a large proportion of advanced Souls have reached this point of correlating with Mars. Therefore, all who earnestly desire to help on the fulfillment of man's destiny must first purify themselves and then work together for the purification of the whole of mankind.

Many students say that they do not wish to unite with others in any group or movement, preferring to develop themselves and silently send out their best thoughts for the good of all, yet a uniting of forces and influence by those of advanced thought and development is necessary if the needed ideas are to be widely promulgated among mankind. Even those who have reached the highest stage of Mastery possible on Earth have to remain in the higher realms and work for its purification and man's emancipation, and must suffer with both until man has reached a point of co-operation in the Great Work of regeneration. While those who have made even considerable progress in self-mastery must incarnate again and again as helpers and teachers of the Race until they, too, are ready to unite and work in co-operation with all others for the purification, enlightenment and regeneration of the Race.

Chapter XXXV

THE SPIRITUAL BIRTH

"Marvel not that I said unto thee, Ye must be born again. . . . That which is born of the flesh is flesh; and that which is born of the Spirit is Spirit . . . The wind bloweth where it listeth, and thou hearest the sound thereof, but canst not tell whence it cometh, and whither it goeth: so is everyone that is born of the Spirit" *St. John*, III, 6-8.

"Seeing that ye have put off the old man with his deeds; and have put on the new man, which is renewed in knowledge after the image of him that created him." *Colossians*, III, 9, 10.

In all presentations of religion much is said of a re-birth, a change of heart, a renewed life and so forth, yet little is taught exoterically as to the process or the laws of its attainment. Such a vital change is not a chance occurrence or merely a vague mystical dream, the result of strong emotion, crowd hysteria or even of religious contemplation alone. It comes as the result of definite growth, the working out of a definite law of Nature and in accord with the cyclic law of the individual.

Neither can the above text be classed as a mere allusion to the law of reincarnation, altho it does show a familiarity with that law in those days. The reference in the text to the wind blowing where it listeth is intended to give some conception of how the spiritual birth takes place; for the wind, also the breath in man, is a manifestation of the Spirit. No one has seen the wind, yet its velocity is measured, its effects upon the physical plane scientifically studied and its power harnessed to work for man.

So is it with the Spirit. While it is all-pervading and omnipresent and can be cognized only by the eye of the Spirit, yet its action in the human body is regulated by definite laws and can be studied. When man knows these laws of the Spirit then, as with Jesus, both the wind and the sea will obey him and he can harness them to accomplish in his life.

According to the axiom, "As below, so above," to understand the spiritual birth let us consider the laws of physical birth. During the period of gestation the unborn child is attached to the mother by the placenta from which it is suspended in the amniotic waters by the umbilical cord. This cord is three-fold in its structure, being made up of two arteries and a vein twisted together like the strands of a rope. Through this cord the growing infant receives life, nourishment, magnetism and love from the mother, and all the forces of the universe necessary to bring forth on the physical plane. It is much like the stalk of a plant which transmits the forces and substances from the soil. The characteristic trend of thought of the father, his physical peculiarities and traits, as well as those of the mother, also the karmic influences generated by the Soul in its former incarnations, form the three-fold stalk on which the child must grow, hence all three factors modify the growing body and constitute its *physical* heredity. Heredity, however, has to do with the body and the personality and not with the Soul, for during this period of preparing a body of flesh or "coat of skin," the Soul is but overshadowing and superintending the process.

Only after the body is born does the Soul gradually begin to gain direct influence over it, but it can never fully manifest until a new and spiritual vehicle is built up within the physical or until the seed-pattern of the Real Self which lies dormant in the soil of the flesh for many incarnations begins to develop and ultimately comes to birth; for until the vital Sap of Life can flow unimpeded through the stalk the flower cannot bloom nor the tree bear fruit.

Since the body is literally born of the flesh it naturally must come under and be obedient to the law of the flesh, the law of the physical plane. In fact, that law is implanted in every cell and atom of the body, for nothing can manifest on Earth except under the law. Jesus said: "Think not that I am come to destroy the law, or the prophets: I am come not to destroy, but to fulfill. For verily I say unto you, Till heaven and earth pass, one jot or one tittle shall in no wise pass from the law, until all be fulfilled." This refers to the natural and universal law of physical manifestation, the Law of Polarity or duality, and not as has generally been supposed to the Mosaic law or to guidance through inspiration (prophets).

If it referred to those laws alone it was a false statement, for from both the Mosaic and the Christian law many, many things have "passed away" and have been relegated to the limbo of mistaken ideas or wrong conceptions of truth before the law as a whole has been fulfilled; yet, on the whole, or in its essence, it must be fulfilled. But, in spite of this, there are many sincere persons who believe that because of higher laws, man can evolve above or in disregard to the laws of this life. He can live under higher laws, it is true, but they are laws which help him to become one with and fulfill the physical laws, so that he is scarcely conscious of them, just as we live unconscious of the law against murder and theft when we have no desire to violate it: we are one with it.

Man can live above the laws of the physical plane only when the "heaven and earth" of this physical manifestation have passed away and he finds himself no longer in a physical world, but in a higher world whose laws are different. As well might a child say that it would not obey the laws of the kindergarten and grammar school because, some day, it expected to go to high school and college. Yet in college he will find the same fundamental laws of attention, obedience and diligence required. Instead of transcending and living above those laws and becoming a super-scholar, such a child would merely bring trouble upon itself and make a record for disobedience and failure to learn its lessons, hence, could never pass the examinations for or enter the higher schools. And if even Jesus clothed His immortal Spirit in a garment of flesh and became subject to the law of the flesh, not to destroy it but to fulfill it in its highest, purest, holiest and most perfect way, when those who aspire to be His followers try to do the same they will the quicker prepare themselves in the only way possible for the New Birth.

The main object of each earthly embodiment of the immortal Soul is to take another step in preparing for the manifestation of its Divine Sonship, with all the potencies, powers and capacities which it inherits from its Divine Parents—its spiritual heredity—and to manifest them in harmony with the laws of the physical world. The Spiritual Birth is the most important conscious step toward this great completion of manifestation.

Just as the physical child is attached to the mother by the umbilical cord, so are we attached to the Divine Mother. The whole universe is the product of three mighty streams of force which pass through all realms and are connected with all things in all worlds like a mighty life-line or umbilical cord carrying Life, Love and Light (understanding). This is a twisted cord proceeding from the Divine Mother which sustains all things that are not yet brought forth in the fullness of their perfection.

This cord carries the force of the Divine Trinity. From the Father comes Life, the Will to Be, the Universal One Life from which all manifestations of life proceed, yet which is sterile and unproductive unless joined with the force of the Mother. From the Mother comes Love, immortal Divine Love, the power which cherishes, sustains and brings forth. From the Son comes the Light, the Sun-force or the Christ-force, the offspring of the Father-Mother or Life and Love manifested in the objective universe. Likewise, there is a cord, invisible yet real, which connects each Soul with its Spiritual Parents, and over this cord there is a force continually poured into man that ever seeks to bring

him to the point of Spiritual Birth where he can stand forth truly
as a Son of God.

How then shall we attain to this Spiritual Birth? Must we ask as
did Nicodemus, "How can a man be born when he is old? Can he
enter the second time into his mother's womb and be born?" Even
if we are old, in the sense of being world-weary and no longer
satisfied with the pleasures and diversions of life, we must still
have our Spiritual Birth from the womb of the Divine Mother.
But first we must learn to love our Mother and realize that we
have not been left like forsaken children, lonely, sad and weeping
in the darkness of Earth conditions with no Comforter,[1] but that
we have a loving Spiritual Mother, the great Universal Mother or
the Love-aspect of the Godhead, who is always watching over us
and waiting for our period of gestation to give us Spiritual Birth.

But we have first to grow tired or indifferent to the pleasures
of Earth life, tired of reacting exclusively to the vibrations from
the outer world, and long for a higher life and begin to respond
to it. Then we practically die to the pleasures of Earth or to our
response to them; that is, all that Earth has heretofore given us
either fails to bring happiness or to satisfy the inner craving of
our spiritual hunger, and may even be but gall and wormwood
to us. Then, when we seem hopeless and forsaken, some day we
will suddenly be given a vision, or perhaps but a glimpse of our
Real Self, and there will awaken within us—in our hearts, not our
heads—such a comprehension of Divine Wisdom, such a great
wave of Divine Love and such a Light of Understanding that we
will realize the true nature of our Real Divine Self, a vision which
should be an inspiration for the rest of our life.

But this does not mean that we have already become one
with that Divine Self and that the personality has reached
perfection, as is so often imagined. It means only that for

---

[1] See *The Divine Mother*, Curtiss, Chapter IV.

an instant the Spiritual Eye has opened and we have succeeded in attaining a definite realization of the perfect pattern which we must fill in; have had a conception of that which is to be attained. This realization we should strive to hold in mind continually and ponder it in our hearts, for to talk of it to others dissipates its force. By ascending in consciousness we should then endeavor to identify our outer life with our new realization, striving to do all things so as to meet the approval of the Divine Self, thus aiding it to react upon the atoms of our flesh and manifest through them.

Once the Spiritual Birth has taken place in the heart (Mary) it must be recognized and fathered by the mind (Joseph). Our consciousness must grasp a new idea or concept of our Divine Source and the essential nature of our Higher or Real Spiritual Self. Once this new idea is recognized by the mind, according to the laws of mind there is a modification of the mind in conformity with the idea. And if the idea is held continually or is recurred to frequently and positively, it grows and grows and reacts upon the body with greater and greater power until finally the body is modified in conformity with the new idea, just as was the mind. This is true of the birth of every new conception in proportion to the power we give to it.

But the Spiritual Birth means far more. It means the birth within us of a Spiritual Body, the true pattern of the real Spiritual Self, with all its consciousness and powers, which then begins to grow within the physical body with its flesh as soil, until it finally permeates the flesh and modifies, spiritualizes, redeems and immortalizes it. Therefore, we need not seek this New Birth any more than the human fetus strives for birth. We do not have to pray and ask and struggle; in fact, our struggling but delays it. Our arguing, our introspection, our complaints, our mental anguish, all are like boulders in the stream, damming it up and holding it back. All we have to do is to rest under the heart of the Divine Mother and let her nourish us.

This does not mean that we are to blind ourselves to the faults and mistakes of humanity or refuse to recognize and correct our own faults, for every fault or inharmony creates an opposition to the flow of the forces, produces a kink in the cord, as it were. We must, therefore, seriously face ourselves and *cease our opposition* to the manifestation of the Divine in us; must learn what our Real Self is and what influences come from It and what from the lower personal self. Think of the two great streams from the Father-Mother uniting in us and bringing forth the Son or the Divine Light.

Then through aspiration and the realization of our heritage and meditation upon our divine Higher Self, and an effort to live as a spiritual being instead of as a child of the flesh, we raise our consciousness into the spiritual world where we are open to the impress of the pattern of our Real Self. It is still the same perfect pattern of the Divine Self with which we began our pilgrimage through the lower worlds, but until now, owing to the density of matter and the limitations of the flesh, we have almost lost touch with it, hence it is not easy now to reach up to its realization.

After this first period of ecstatic realization of and union with the Divine Self, the ecstasy of Divine Conception, we will seem to drop back into the old conditions of life and pass a period of spiritual darkness, comparable to the period of gestation, a cycle of nine periods of longer or shorter duration, according to how we react to them and the tests they bring. Yet all the time we must remember and realize that we are sustained and nourished and warmed by the great Divine Mother through the three-fold cord of Life, Love and Light, and that we can draw upon Her for all that we need.

During the periods of darkness of our spiritual gestation, instead of becoming discouraged at the darkness and feeling that we might as well give up, realize that all we have to do is to cease struggling and absorb the forces from the Divine Mother, for it is through Her that we are fed and sustained and all our wants supplied, even tho, like the physical fetus, we seem to be blindly floating in the amniotic waters of the great ocean of life, shut up in the darkness of the womb of the Divine Mother. She feels our every move, responds to our every thought and emotion and in the fullness of time will bring us to our Spiritual Birth; for the same stream of force that swept us into this dark Cave of Initiation must bring us forth in the fullness of time.

A good exercise to aid in absorbing the forces of the Divine Mother is to stand facing the East—so the magnetic currents will flow through us more easily—and holding the left hand over the head, palm up, with the hand in a cup shape, and the right hand over the solar plexus, repeat the following mantram: "Oh Divine Mother! Illumine me with Divine Wisdom, vivify me with Divine Life and purify me with Divine Love, that in all I think and say and do I may be more and more Thy child." We should then hold the position until we feel in our hand the tingle of the forces we have invoked. Do the same with the left hand and repeat twice more with each hand alternately (three times with each hand). We may also repeat our wonderful mantram, "The Prayer for Light,"[2] day after day, and hold its ideal clearly in mind. And then as we give it more and more power each day it will react upon our bodies. Some who have done this, find themselves also repeating the prayers in dreams, especially the Protecting Invocation, when the dream seems threatening.

Let us determine to struggle no longer; to cease opposition, to cease complaining and rest in the peace of realization. Rest in the knowledge that because the Life and Love and Light are universal, and that there is no part of the universe where they are not, there cannot be a cell or atom of

---

[2] See *Appendix*.

our bodies or a faculty of our minds where they are not, hence the Great Life-line unites us with all that is.

Let us also remember that if we are still unborn, spiritually, for that very reason the Divine Mother carries us under her heart and pours out her Love more abundantly and travails in pain with us until the Christ (the Light) be born and manifested in us.

Without the manifestation of Divine Life, Divine Love and Divine Light through us the whole universe is imperfect to that extent. Each Soul is needed and each is beloved of the Divine Father-Mother. Therefore, rest in the Lord (Law), and wait patiently on Him. For this is the Law of our Being, and it cannot pass away until it is fulfilled in our flesh, for in our flesh we must ultimately see and realize God.[3]

---

[3] *Job*, XIX, 26.

CHAPTER XXXVI

THE TRUE PRIESTHOOD

"For the Priest's lips should keep knowledge, and they should seek the law at his mouth: for he is the messenger of the Lord of hosts." *Malachi*, II, 7.

"Behold, I will send my messenger, and he shall prepare the way before me: and the Lord, whom ye seek, shall suddenly come to his temple, even the messenger of the covenant, whom ye delight in: behold, he shall come, said the Lord of hosts." *Malachi*, III, 1.

"For this Melchisedec, king of Salem, priest of the most high God. . . . Without father, without mother, without descent, having neither beginning of days, nor end of life: but made like unto the Son of God; abideth a priest continually." *Hebrews*, VII, 1-3.

The term priest in its various aspects means an elder (*presbyter*), prince (*kohen*), hierophant (*hiereus*), and prophet. All these meanings go back to the early days of the Race when humanity was taught face to face by the Elder Brothers, the Divine Beings who are the spiritual parents of mankind. As humanity grew in intellectual attainment these Divine Teachers withdrew and left in Their stead the more advanced Souls among men who had been selected, gathered together and trained in the secret sciences until they had passed life's great initiation and become one in consciousness with their Divine Progenitors.

Such initiated priests needed no credentials, no apostolic succession, no robes or outward show of authority, for they carried within them the memory of the touch of the hand of the Great Initiator and were able to manifest and demonstrate the power of their priestly office and their right to serve forever before the altar of the Most High. Having been set apart and trained in the laws of the spiritual realms

and the science of consciously communicating (theopneusty) with
the spiritual Progenitors of the Race, the gods, they were able to
point out how the physical manifestations of the Great Law must
be observed to produce harmony on Earth.

True superiority is always recognized and sought, both for
advice and leadership, hence as the High Priests interpreted the
Divine Law, they naturally became the governors or kings of the
people, while the less advanced priests performed various other
functions. This is the basis of truth in the doctrine of the divine
right of kings, but it is true only when the king is also a prophet and
priest before the Lord. In Egypt the Pharaoh was also a High Priest
of the Temple. In many more modern nations—Russia, Japan,
etc.,—the ruler is also the acknowledged head of the Church, his
coronation as king being followed by his consecration as priest.

Since religion is the foundation on which all civilization
is built, if this foundation is laid according to mere human
judgment—even the best—the whole structure is doomed,
sooner or later, to totter and fall. The fact that evolution and
progress have steadily advanced, in spite of the many false notes
of man-made interpretation of Divine Wisdom, shows that the
original foundation was laid by the gods themselves, who came
to Earth for that purpose. True reform does not mean tearing up
the foundations of religion or society, but merely substituting the
Divine Teachings wherever the human has been found wanting.
The rule of the true priest-king is a true kingship in the highest
sense, because he is accomplishing the best good of the people
in seeing that the divine laws are carried out. Such a rule is
always beneficent, since the rules of conduct he lays down are
the reflection on Earth of the laws of harmony operating in the
higher realms.

The commands for the establishment of the priesthood, as

outlined in the Hebrew scriptures, show by their beautiful symbology what a divinely ordained priesthood should be. It is there plainly indicated that the priesthood must be set apart and consecrated by the Most High, for altho the priestly office, functions and dress are described most minutely, there is no earthly ceremony given for the consecration of the priesthood. The account simply says "the Lord filled their hands," symbolizing the divine touch which gave them the power to perform the magical rites pertaining to their office.

When the High Priest desired to consult the Lord he donned the sacred vestment called the Ephod—without which it was said no magical ceremony could be performed, either black or white—entered the Holy of Holies, faced the Ark of the Covenant, and propounded the questions of the people. This vestment bore a breastplate containing the twelve sacred stones upon which were carved the names of the twelve tribes of Israel (the twelve signs of the zodiac), showing the foundation of magical power to be based upon the spiritual forces emanating from the signs of the zodiac.[1] Attached to the Ephod was the mysterious Urim and Thummim, of which the *Bible* speaks so much, yet gives no satisfactory description or explanation. It is said to signify "light and perfection or doctrine and judgment," but in reality it symbolizes the mystic power of gathering the positive and negative potencies of the zodiac and through the power of the will making them accomplish that which the priest directs—a power attained only by one who has passed life's great initiation and reached Mastery.

Such an initiated priesthood was founded by Melchisedec, and only when a priesthood "after the order of Melchisedec" has been re-established and humanity again gladly follows the Divine Law—not as children, but because they recognize its authority—can the problems of mankind be truly solved and the conditions under which humanity is suffering today

---

[1] See *The Key of Destiny*, Curtiss, Chapter VI.

be finally readjusted. For these conditions are the result of following the human rather than the divinely appointed priesthood. Especially in this day do we find religious teachers telling their most advanced followers, who come to them for an explanation of the mysteries their Souls have experienced, that such things must not be questioned or studied, showing plainly that, even tho they are priests, they are not in touch with the Divine, and hence cannot explain the deeper spiritual mysteries. They are not true priests of the Lord, else they could put on the Ephod—the robe of spiritual at-one-ment—and inquire of the Lord direct and receive the answer to any question or problem.

The true or White Magicians are symbolized by Melchisedec, who was "made, not after the law of a carnal commandment, but after the power of an endless life," (*i.e.*, an Avatar), and whose superiority and power was so great that Abram recognized him as a divinely manifested Being and gladly paid tithes unto him.

Perhaps there is no more mysterious personage mentioned in the *Bible* than this great priest-king, Melchisedec. We are told so little concerning him, yet what we are told implies so much, that he has been a mystery to all students. *Bible* scholars tell us that Melchisedec's father was Eraclas, Hercules or Helios, the god of the Sun, while his mother was Asteria, Astaroth or Selene, the goddess of the Moon. This parentage makes him identical with Shem, the eldest son of Noah, while the esoteric teachings identify both Noah and Melchisedec with the Planetary Ruler of Mars. Noah is but another aspect of Jehovah, while the ark or the crescent Moon symbolizes the divine Mother-principle, their son always being the Christ-child. This explains why Jesus was ordained "a priest forever after the order of Melchisedec," for He had the same parentage, "Without father, without mother, without descent, having neither beginning of days, nor end of life," *i.e.*, the power of the Most High (the Father-principle) and Mary or Mare, the Great Deep or

Divine Love (the Mother-principle). Among the Egyptians the crescent or ark is placed beneath the feet of the Divine Mother after the Christ-child has been brought forth, a symbol which the Christian Church has appropriated from the Egyptians without change and presented to its followers as the Virgin Mary.

In the allegory, Melchisedec is said to have founded Salem, which after its capture by the Jebusites was called Jebu-Salem, and after they were driven out by David, became Jerusalem, the Holy City. Applied to the personality, the Holy City is man's divine heritage, his originally pure, spiritual body, ere disobedience to the Law had denied it, which is founded and ruled over by the Divine Self until the Jebusites, or man's lower principles, enter and gradually take possession. This allegory refers to the ancient days when the early sub-races gradually fell away from their Divine Guidance and followed after the human rulers, man's developing reason and intellect. Only when David, the King of Love, conquers the Jebusites, can reason and intellect be illumined by the light of the Christ. Then will the New Jerusalem come down out of heaven, in which "they need no candle, neither light of the sun; for the Lord God giveth them light."

Jerusalem, the city in which the human priesthood (priests and Levites) had their temple, altho a real city upon the physical plane, was and still is used allegorically to symbolize the various stages of the unregenerate human body. It was notorious for the stench that arose from the burning flesh of the animals daily sacrificed, from the stables in which they were kept and the various bloody offerings made for the sins of the people. Just so the sacrifices which the personality offers its gods—worldly position, greed, mammon, animal desire, etc.,—are like the bloody offerings made by the priests and Levites, *i.e.*, able to accomplish nothing but the pollution of the air of the city (the breath of the Spirit) and the degradation of its inhabitants. But just as

the lower aspect of Jerusalem had its concrete expression on
the physical plane, so must its higher aspect—the regenerated
spiritualized human body (*Nirmanakaya*), wherein the Prince
of Peace reigns "a priest forever after the order of Melchisedec"
and offers his sacrifice before the Lord—find concrete expression
on the physical plane. In other words, there must ultimately be
established upon the Earth a great City or Center of Civilization
which will just as perfectly typify the regenerate state of mankind
as Jerusalem does the unregenerate. It shall come down out of
heaven or come through the inspired and illumined minds of those
seers and seeresses who can reach up in consciousness into the
heaven realms or states of spiritual consciousness. And it shall
manifest on Earth when man is able to manifest the Divine more
perfectly through the human.

When the true priesthood serves before the altar there will be
no literal sacrifices of rams and bulls, but only a pouring out of
that which they symbolized. The blood of the ram signifies the
stream of spiritual life-force poured out upon mankind through
the sign Aries. The sacrifice will be accomplished when through
the lessons learned by correlating with the higher aspects of Aries
the intellect gladly sacrifices its ruling power upon the altar of
love and obedience to Divine Law. In other words, man will
bring the first fruits of his mental flocks to the Christ. The blood
of bulls symbolizes the life-essence of the sign Taurus, or the
patient bringing forth on the physical plane through toil, labor
and sacrifice, of the highest that physical life can express, and
laying this also upon the altar of the Christ. In the New Jerusalem,
where the great priest Melchisedec shall reign as prophet, priest
and king, daily sacrifices shall be offered for all the people, but
instead of the stench of literal sacrifices there shall arise the
"sweet smelling savor unto the Lord," so long prophesied. For
it could never be fulfilled by the offering of the literal life-blood
of animal victims.

Melchisedec, being "without father, without mother, without descent," would be debarred from the priesthood, according to the requirements of the priests and Levites, just as was Jesus, because of his non-mortal parentage. The priests and Levites were the humanly ordained priesthood which arose as a result of man's refusal to follow the higher law as delivered by the divinely inspired priesthood. The human priesthood may claim "apostolic succession," or even "direct continuance," but as long as their only claim to the priesthood is a certain amount of intellectual training or the possession of a diploma from earthly teachers, *instead of the power to see behind the veil and consciously commune with the Divine Instructors of the Race*, they can never become true priests before the Lord. And as long as mankind looks to such an earthly priesthood for Divine Guidance—which can be imparted only by the spiritual counterpart of the Ephod and the Urim and Thummim—it is no wonder that humanity goes heart-hungry and receives stones when it asks bread. For only as the High Priest can don the Ephod and through the power of the Urim and Thummim stand before the Ark and receive his guidance direct from the Lord, can he truly minister to the spiritual needs of the people.

An earthly priesthood grows more and more materialistic as it gets farther and farther from the direct guidance of the Divine and further from manifesting the divine standards of love, tolerance and brotherhood. Under such circumstances it is wise that church and state be separated, for such an earthly ordained priesthood has no more ability to rule wisely than have civil rulers.

Melchisedec was King of Righteousness (*Sedek*), and also King of Peace (*Salem*). This further connects him with Jesus, who is called Prince of Peace. In other words, Melchisedec is a term used to symbolize a special outpouring or embodiment of the Christ-principle—an Avatar—to the early Fifth Great (*Aryan*) Race, which was founded by the symbolic Abraham. Jesus was a later manifestation, or Avatar, of the same Christ-principle to the fifth sub-race of the Fifth Great Race. An Avatar is not a mortal, but a great spiritual Being, who voluntarily descends into Earth conditions to help humanity. He must be without earthly parentage, for He is a direct manifestation of the Divine to man. He suddenly appears at the proper cyclic moment to re-establish the divine priesthood and bring mankind back to the true principles of the spiritual life. Hence, Melchisedec symbolized an Avatar who came to the early Aryan Race to found or again give out, as had been done in Atlantis, the one great Wisdom Religion for the new cycle, from the seeds of which have sprung all the great religions now known to man.

An Avatar appears in a body which seems to be mortal, but is not so in reality, for the atoms composing it are spiritualized and immortal, hence have naught to do with death or decay. The matter comprising it is so sensitive that, through the power of will, it can be made to manifest on any plane of consciousness. Hence, when such a Being desires to appear among men, by a single act of will the rate of vibration of His spiritualized body is slowed down to the rate of the physical plane and it becomes objective, apparently a mortal body of a very fine type. In fact, it corresponds to the spiritual (*Nimanakaya*) body to which St. Paul refers: "There is a natural body, and there is a spiritual body. The first was made a living soul; the last . . . . . was made a quickening spirit. . . . . The first man is of the earth, earthy: the second man is the Lord from heaven . . . . . as we have borne the image of the earthy, we shall also bear the image of the heavenly. . . . Behold, I shew you a mystery."[2]

Such a body would transcend the limitations of any one Race and embody the perfection of all Races, hence could not arouse race-prejudice by being assigned to any one people.

---

[2] *I Corinthians*, XV, 44-5-7-9.

Such an appearance is not manifested through a body born of woman, but like Melchisedec, is without parents, as such appearances have always been throughout the ages.

The world is today awaiting the advent of such another Divine Teacher or true Prophet, a personalized embodiment of the great Christos-principle of the universe, the all-pervading, vivifying power which underlies all manifestations of the One Life. He comes again, as of old, as the Sun of Righteousness to re-establish the Divine Priesthood and restore the principles of the ancient Wisdom Religion to the sixth sub-race now just beginning.

As this great spiritual Being approaches the Earth-plane each heart who can respond to the vibrations of His message will come more or less consciously into touch with Him, no matter what organization or movement he may be working in. And according as the rational mind of such a one has been trained in the laws of such manifestations and the true philosophy of the mysteries, will his interpretation be clear or imperfect. There are today many hearts who are responding more or less consciously to this force of Divine Love now being focused upon the Earth-plane in greater measure than ever before.

Just as at certain seasons of the year there is a great outpouring of theological students who have graduated from the seminaries, so in the Divine World there are certain cyclic periods when Divine Love and Wisdom is poured out in greater abundance or when it may be said that many priests are initiated or receive the spiritual illumination which marks them as true priests. Hence, in every organization and society promulgating the true Divine Wisdom there will arise some advanced Soul who is capable of being directly overshadowed by a ray of spiritual consciousness from the coming Avatar and thus become to that society or organization a direct representative of the Avatar. These advanced Souls are called *Avesha*, or partial Avatars, for, while they are not the Avatar—in that they are mortal and have a physical personality to contend with—they are overshadowed at certain periods by His divine consciousness. "Necessarily the messages of the various Avesha Avatars will differ in details, for the ability of such a channel to give out the teaching depends upon such factors as the line of endeavor he is interested in, his race-thought, his mental and spiritual capacity, his habits of life, his knowledge of the laws and philosophy of the higher life and the intellectual training his mind—through which all the teachings must pass—has received. In this way the members of every society and movement shall have the divine truths spoken in their own language wherein they were born, *i.e.*, couched in the terminology, symbols and characteristic methods of expression peculiar to their own avenue of truth."[3]

Keeping this law in mind we see that an Avatar does not come to any one society, order, movement or sect, *but to humanity.* And His teachings will be so divine and perfect, yet so simple, unprejudiced and unbiased by the characteristics of any cult that they will be equally applicable to all and will appeal to all spiritually-minded people, no matter what their Race, creed or special trend of thought.

The memory of the past is beginning to dawn upon mankind today, but how few listen to the cry of the ages! Not one earnest seeker but has heard the echo of something sacred, which may seem to just elude his grasp. This life-period is one more opportunity to remember; not only to remember but to set definitely to work. Once more will there come upon the Earth in our midst the same great Priest-King and Initiator, the Priest of the Most High whom we last knew as Jesus. Pray God that He may find us all waiting; that not one upon whose head He has placed His hands in consecration may be missing.

Remember that our dreams of Divine Love are true; that life is more than it seems; that the day of little things shall

---

[3] For further details see *The Voice of Isis*, Curtiss, Chapter X.

grow into the day of the great things. Today pay attention to the little things. The Avatar must come, but how perfect shall be His work depends upon how many can grasp the Great Plan, how many are ready to sink personality in that perfect obedience which the Law of love, justice, peace and righteousness demands.

There can be no compulsory obedience. Each life must gladly follow the discipline necessary for the accomplishment, not of its own ideas of life and service, but the perfect establishment of the true Priesthood of the Most High, the establishment upon Earth of a reflection of the Hierarchies of Heaven.

The cry of the Great One is now going forth to all who can hear: "Come unto me, my little lambs. The fold is waiting and the heart of the Shepherd yearning. What is this fold? It is the great Priesthood of the Most High, the body of His chosen servants gathered from out the flower of the Races that have passed, and consecrated to the upliftment of humanity, sworn by the most sacred vows to understand, to love, and to give."

"Not one word can return unto me void. Not one thought through all the eternities is lost. Think then of the thoughts that have been shed around you as you journeyed through the wilderness of lives and lives! Think of the words that have been spoken through the mouths of the chosen prophets in your ears, life after life, age after age! Will ye still be deaf and dumb to love? To be sheep of the fold means to know your Shepherd, to follow gladly, to hear His voice and obey. Not to obey because it seems to you reasonable and profitable and according to your worldly judgment, but to obey because you know and love the Voice that speaks; because you have learned through the ages that are past that this is the Shepherd who leadeth you beside the still waters of life; who feedeth you with the green and tender grass; who sheltereth you in the fold of His loving arms."

"This is why you follow and why you obey. This is the great test of the ages. How often have you gone astray seeking for strange gods in new pastures! How long has your return and recognition been awaited! And now the clock of time has struck the hour. Behold the day-star rises high in the heavens. Soon, soon, must He come on Earth clothed in the garment of flesh. Will He find you still waiting for His blessings? Or will He find you indifferent, following after your own reason, doubtful of His voice? Unless the sheep know the voice of the Shepherd they will be blind and will never recognize His face. Unless they learn to love, to recognize and thus obey unquestioningly the divine message they will never be ready to take their places in the Great Temple where the True Priesthood must work out the great scheme of salvation, the reflection upon Earth of the Hierarchies of Heaven."

Chapter XXXVII

A NEW TESTAMENT

"Forasmuch as ye are manifestly declared to be the epistle of Christ ministered by us, written not with ink, but with the Spirit of the living God: not in tables of stone, but in fleshy tables of the heart. . . . Who also hath made us able ministers of the new testament; *not of the letter, but of the spirit*; for the letter killeth, but the spirit giveth life." *II Corinthians*, III, 3-6.

Principles and universal laws are eternal and invariable; their interpretations are transient and variable. Creeds and dogmas—man's efforts to interpret and explain to the masses the mysteries of Divine Manifestation—appear in every age, serve their purpose, pass away and are forgotten. But the principles and the symbols which express them remain.

Whenever a great body of mankind reaches a point where it has either outgrown the symbolic language used to interpret an inspired revelation given to a past generation, or when previous interpretations of the eternal verities have become encrusted with so much that is misconceived and false, or have become so materialized and literal that they no longer reveal the truths they were meant to teach, there is given to the world a new outpouring of truth, inspired by the same Divine Source of all truth, a New Testament for a new dispensation. And invariably those giving forth the New Testament are regarded by those of the old dispensation as heretics and disturbers of the people's minds.

As the old Mosaic dispensation drew to its close, Jesus, the great Avatar for the new dispensation, is represented as gathering His disciples together into an upper chamber and giving them what He designated as a New Testament, *i.e.*,

a new and fuller interpretation of the mystery of the Divine
Sacrifice than was taught in the orthodox and conventional
way in the synagogues. The Mosaic law gave to humanity
ten commandments, revealed to Moses amid thunderings and
lightnings, enumerating the things man should not do, the negative
"Thou shalt not" being the keynote of the admonitions. Jesus gave
to the world but two commandments, which He said contained
all the law and the prophets. "Thou shalt love the Lord thy God
with all thy heart, and with all thy soul, and with all thy mind, and
with all thy strength. . . . Thou shalt love thy neighbor as thyself."

No longer were the things man must not do enumerated, but
the positive things he should do. For if we love with all our hearts
both God and our neighbor, we cannot kill, commit adultery, steal,
bear false witness, etc. The new commandments concerned those
things which we should do to be happy and live at peace with
the world. This was the keynote of the New Testament given by
Jesus. But because Jesus departed from the old negative teaching
of the commandments He was regarded as the greatest heretic of
His day; was called a teacher of heresies and sedition, a stirrer up
of the people and a dangerous man. And so has it ever been with
those who present new ideas and new expressions of old truths,
whether in medicine, science, art or religion.

Truth is like a great King's Highway, built by the Angels or
Messengers in the beginning, by the following of which man
might return to his Father's home. This spiritual Highway extends
throughout the world and has branches in every land. But as it is
traveled by millions upon millions, age after age, it becomes worn
and full of ruts. Those who think they know and those who are
timid, when they find there are steep hills to climb, gorges to pass
through and rivers to ford, put up sectarian sign-boards warning
their followers to beware certain dangers, or telling them to conduct
their journey in a particular manner and with certain observances.
In many places the oldest of these signs have fallen down

or grown so dim that they cannot be deciphered. Other pilgrims, often knowing even less about the way, have tried to repair these signs and in relettering them have changed their wording and caused confusion. Later on these signs have been mistaken for original directions by no means to be overlooked. Still others have built detours which they think will either shorten the journey, make it more pleasant, or will avoid what seem to be dangers ahead. These also, in time, have been considered by later pilgrims as part of the original Highway. But when the road has become so narrow, so rough and so confused by sectarian detours and mental ruts that travel is sadly impeded, the King sends forth his servants to repair, reconstruct, straighten and widen the road. Each such repairing and resurfacing of the Highway we call a New Testament, or a restatement of the Way, the Truth and the Life.

The new interpretation which Jesus presented to His disciples was that, instead of the slaughter of animals and the literal shedding of their blood being used to symbolize the Mystery of Sacrifice, the New Testament should bring a deeper understanding of the world-old truth which the slaughter of animals expressed in but a crude and materialized manner. He did not tear from them entirely the old beliefs in which they had dwelt so long, but He interpreted in a higher way the ideals which the materialized symbols indicated. He did not alter the eternal truths which the symbols sought to express, but He widened and deepened His disciples' comprehension of them and led them into a fuller understanding of the Mystery.

Following the same law, this Order does not seek to tear down and destroy the old beliefs of its students, but to *expand and illumine them* so that they shall have a deeper, broader and more comprehensive understanding of the Mysteries back of the symbols, and hence of the many misconceptions current in regard to them. In other words, its Teachings add to instead of take from. They are broadening and deepening; inclusive of others instead of exclusive; constructive instead of destructive.

In the days of Jesus, as today, the Mysteries could be grasped only by the few; only those who could enter the "upper chamber" of intuition and inspiration where alone the Mysteries can be revealed; only those whose expansion of consciousness enabled them to grasp higher ideals, greater truths; only those who were ready to leave all and follow Him, *i.e.*, who were ready to leave all the literal, revolting and unsatisfying teachings and follow the new and higher interpretation which was to carry them one step beyond the old Mosaic idea as then presented by the slaughter of animals. And yet the slaughter of animals was a true symbol, and to the crude and materialistic understanding of the Race by whom it was practiced, was not wholly evil. It probably awakened in many minds a true understanding of what was symbolized, *i.e.*, the sacrifice of the animal traits and appetites that the higher spiritual man might manifest. So in every age certain customs and practices are not wholly to be condemned if they are the best the people of the age can conceive of as a round of the Ladder of Life on which they can rest their feet (understanding) for a moment as they climb. The rule is that we should live up to the highest that our minds can conceive of and be true to our inner convictions, but condemn not other less developed Souls who cannot see or understand as clearly as we. So is it today. These Teachings will appeal only to those who are ready to turn from another literal blood sacrifice—this time not of animals but of a man, a literal interpretation which the New Testament of Jesus was never meant to teach—and grasp a still higher realization of the meaning of the Mystery of Sacrifice.

The New Testament which Jesus gave was that while "It is the blood that maketh an atonement for the soul" and "Without shedding of blood is no remission," nevertheless "It is not possible that the blood of bulls and goats should take away sins."[1] What is the meaning of this paradox? What is the sacrifice and what is the blood that must atone? The sacrifice is indeed that of man, not Jesus, but the lower man, the animal self, the personality, to the will of the Divine. The blood that is shed is indeed that of man, yet not the literal physical blood, but the spiritual life-force. The physical blood is the carrier of the physical life-force and is, therefore, used to symbolize the spiritual life-force or the Christ-force or the blood of the Christ within man. This was symbolized in the old days by the blood of animals and in Jesus' time by the wine of the Eucharist. When Jesus said of the wine: "This is my blood of the new testament, which is shed for many for the remission of sins,"[2] He obviously referred not to His physical blood, which was not shed, but to the great sacrifice of the Christ-force in man coming down into or being shed in the darkness of his outer life; the pouring out of the spiritual life-force (blood) to redeem that which was "lost" or lacked spiritual life-force.

To symbolize this great Mystery of Sacrifice anew, Jesus took bread and wine instead of the body and blood of animals, and with these symbols summed up His whole life and teaching, namely, that it is not in vain that a man lay down his life for another, whether it be his friend and his country or the sacrificing of the life of the lower man to the higher.

The whole Gospel story is focused in this idea. But as the centuries passed we find that the finite tendency to misinterpret, limit and materialize even the grandest symbols has again materialized the new symbols of the eternal sacrifice and redemption given by Jesus into the literal sacrifice of His physical body and the shedding of His physical blood.

He is also continually represented as "a man of sorrow and acquainted with grief." Alas, how few can differen-

[1] *Hebrews*, X, 4.
[2] *Matthew*, XXVI, 28.

tiate between the godlike acquaintance with and understanding of both sorrow and grief which enabled Him to sympathize with and help mankind under all conditions; to differentiate between the part these experiences must play in man's evolution and the mere stolid helplessness of a human victim to the vicissitudes of earthly existence! In holding this mental picture for ages the Church has lost sight of the glory, of the love, the strength, the courage and the uplifting joy of One who willingly endured the sordid conditions of Earth life that He might leave foot-prints to show all who would follow that those things could not touch or . appall the soul.

Instead of being regarded as a symbol of the descent of the Christ into matter and the pouring forth of the Christ-force, the crucifixion has been so materialized and literally interpreted that it has been used as an excuse for negative submission to suffering and sorrow, so that in time, self-torture was looked upon as meritorious and a doleful countenance was a mark of sanctity. Yet, because back of the misinterpretation of the symbols there was a divine truth, man realized within himself that there was something there which he could not grasp. As he grew spiritually and expanded intellectually, there were many who looked at the materialized idea and revolted at the thought of allowing another to suffer for their sins, especially as they were told that the propitiation was made centuries before they were born! And being unable to accept the literal interpretation they turned away from all religion and were lost either in a slough of indifference or in a mental labyrinth of speculation which brought neither peace nor satisfaction. The New Testament given out through *The Order of Christian Mystics* is an effort to show to all the truth back of the allegory, that they may again sit down at the Master's table and satisfy their spiritual hunger.

In the mystic silence of the "upper chamber;" in the higher understanding of the everlasting truth of the Mystery of

Sacrifice[3] the true disciples again today as of old are bidden by their Lord to sit at meat with Him. And to His disciples of today He has given the task of preparing an "upper chamber," and of extending His invitation to whomsoever will come. Here they may recognize that it is this same Jesus who has come again. He whom they have seen taken out of their sight amidst the clouds of higher criticism, the doubts of a disappointed Christendom and the cynicisms of the world; whose body they have seen broken by the doctrinal warfare over the literal teachings which have divided His followers into many sects; whose life-force (blood) has been wasted in dolorous practices of asceticism by those who refused to accept it in spirit and in truth and allow it to make them more virile, valiant and joyous conquerors; this same Jesus has come again "in like manner" as they saw Him go. He now comes "with power and great glory," and with the Light of spiritual understanding for His faithful ones. They saw Him sadly depart from His houses of worship when emphasis was given to dogma rather than to spiritual understanding; when the world began to worship the symbol as a finite happening; when the minds of men were disturbed because the investigations of higher criticism threw doubt upon the literal actuality of the symbol as an event in physical history; when His followers sought Him historically only to find an empty tomb with its grave-clothes, and cried out in bitter disappointment: "They have taken away my Lord and we know not where they have laid him." Let them now listen to the answer of the Angel: "He is not here: for he is risen . . . . . Why seek ye the living among the dead?"

Never yet has the multitude answered that question, yet the answer is the New Testament given to this Order to proclaim to this generation. We are not to look back to and worship a crucified, dead and buried Jesus, but a risen and ever-present Lord of Light, Life and Love! Not a literal

---

[3] See Chapter XXI herein.

event, past and gone ages ago, but a *living Presence*, who calls us to sup with Him now in the "upper chamber!"

When the world was young and thoughtless, it was perhaps wise to hide the deeper Mysteries from the masses, who could not comprehend and might profane them, yet the truth has always been known to the Elect. Even today in some branches of the Church, a part of the sacrament of the Eucharist is withheld from the congregation. The wafer (body) alone is given to the people while the wine (blood) is drunk by the priests. The hungry but unthinking and uninquisitive populace is fed with the dry wafer and taught to bow in adoration before a dead and crucified Jesus, lest a personal realization of a *risen* and *living* Christ cause them to throw off the bonds of priestly subjection. But the risen Lord now gives to the world a New Testament so that all who are hungry for spiritual food, who are tired of suffering, who are sick of bloodshed, may know the glorious truth of His living Presence. As long as a literal blood sacrifice of one man or many is believed in as a propitiation for sin, man will never wake up to the belief that war can be abolished. For if the physical blood of one man could wipe away the sins of the world, why might not the blood of millions, shed for high ideals on the battle fields, wipe away the sins of the nations? But this it has not and never can accomplish; far from it.

As ambassadors of the risen and ever-living Christ we cry out to the world that the Bread (body of teachings) that is given you is Bread indeed! It is filled with the Wine of living truth. The Great One has come to Earth, not on a cross, but full of Divine Life, in a body which is animated by the spiritual life-blood. To the open eye of Spirit He stands among you. Behold His power to accomplish (hands), then nailed upon the cross of matter by the ignorance of the multitude, but now held out in power and blessing! Behold His understanding (feet), then rendered helpless by the cruel nails of misunderstanding, but now

"How beautiful upon the mountains are the feet of him that bringeth good tidings, that publisheth peace; that publisheth salvation; that saith unto Zion, Thy God reigneth."[4] Behold His side from whose wound flowed both water and blood! From it the softening and nourishing water of mother-love, mingled with the blood of spiritual life-force, still flows forth in a never-ceasing stream until the redemption of man and the planet is accomplished!

Indeed, it is to bring to your consciousness a realization of the presence, power and accessibility of this stream of water and blood or Divine Love and Spiritual Life-force that is the reason for this New Testament of today. Each disciple who bathes in this stream bears witness that the Lord Jesus has not and will not leave the world comfortless, especially in these days of darkness and grief, but will always come again and again to each loving heart and to every age, and through those who can meet Him in the "upper chamber," bring to them a New Testament of love, inspiration and life.

Again His voice echoes throughout the world: "Behold, I bring you a New Testament!" What is the New Testament for this generation? We proclaim that it is no longer animal bodies and clotted blood, no longer bread broken and wine poured out, body crucified and blood shed, but body and blood united *in the living form of the coming Great One*. Behold "the Man," the Prophet, Priest and King! the Redeemer! the Savior!

Another and perhaps more personal application of the New Testament, given out today by this same Jesus through independent inspiration, is that the disciples may be compared to the mind; for the intellectual faculties have to break up the bread of truth and give it forth to the hungry multitude, while the wine or blood may be likened to that inner spiritual life-force without which, no matter how fine

---

[4] *Isaiah*, LII, 7.

the intellect may break the mental bread, it remains mere husks, unable to satisfy the hunger of mankind.

This phase of the symbology is also exemplified by man and wife. The true man corresponds to the nourishing Bread or the outer body, which feeds the world with the intellectual presentation of truth. Yet, unless the Bread has been kneaded with the feminine force or the spiritual Water which has been turned into Wine by the Christ at the marriage feast, it cannot satisfy the spiritual hunger of the world. Again, the true man is the body which stands before the world and proclaims the teachings of the Christ, but unless that body is filled with rich, pure blood, it is but an anemic shadow of a real man. Verily it is not good for man to be alone any more than it is good for him to feed on dry husks. Nor is woman her true self when she stands alone, for then she becomes but as water poured out upon a rock or blood shed in vain. And, alas, how often women uselessly sacrifice themselves without accomplishing their aim! It is, therefore, fitting that this Movement which heralds the New Testament for the New Dispensation should have as its Agents both a man and a woman, body and blood.

The blood is shed in vain if the Christ has not performed the first miracle at the wedding feast. Throughout Christendom during the whole of the long dark night of the old dispensation, altho both the body and the blood have been symbolically partaken of in the bread and the wine in true remembrance of Him until He come again, and the adoration for the crucified Jesus has been religiously performed, the world has never yet found perfect satisfaction. Some have said that the Blood has cleansed them from sin, and others have said that the Bread has fed them, but there has always been a separation. The Christ has always been crucified, the body broken and the blood spilled. If we are to enter upon the work of this New Day and spread this New Testament in earnest we must change this old idea; must teach mankind to gain a realization of the *living* Christ as an actual reality, a power and force in their hearts and minds and lives. Then every eye that has pierced him shall behold him, *i.e.*, everyone who has emphasized the sorrows, suffering and death of Jesus has pierced His body and shed His blood. Had more attention been given to the glorious promise of His resurrection and second coming we would not need a New Testament to enable us to recognize the risen Lord, worship at His feet and see in Him not a crucified, but a *living* Christ.

As the risen Lord comes close to Earth He must first come to His own, *i.e.*, to those who now recognize, know and love Him. To them He will manifest and become the living spiritual force or blood animating their lives. These will slowly be gathered together one by one into the "upper chamber," not because they belong to any church, society or movement, but because in their hearts they have spiritually touched the robe of the Christ and have felt His virtue flow into them, and through them into their environment. And this virtue, which is the life blood of the Christ, has filled their body (intellect) and illumined it so that they no longer simply believe, because now they *know* and cannot be deceived. It is these who will be gathered into an "upper chamber" of the spiritual Jerusalem, the city of spiritual realization which cometh down from heaven, yet "cometh not with observation," but as an inward experience.

We must obey the command: "Tarry ye in the city of Jerusalem, until ye be endued with power from on high." For if we simply have intermittent spells of spiritual upliftment when we realize that we are treading the golden streets of this New Jerusalem, we may not be there when He comes. But He has told us to tarry there or dwell continually in that city of the Soul, that upper chamber of the Christ consciousness.

This does not mean that we are to neglect our duties in the outer life, but it does mean that we are to realize that while the body or outer form of our life—which includes our intellectual activities and conceptions of truth—is performing its work in the world, the blood of spiritual life-force must flow in a steady stream through its veins direct from the River of Life which flows around the throne where dwells the Christ.

Only when enough of those who have washed their robes (bodies) in the blood of the Lamb and made them white have been gathered together into the upper chamber can the Great Teacher and Lord appear to them on Earth in a body apparently of flesh and blood. And herein lies a great mystery, for He can manifest physically only in an "upper chamber," made up of the living sacrifice of the emanations of His true disciples, those who have given up their lives not *for* His service but *to* His service, all animated by the spiritual aspiration and ardent devotion of their hearts which have been poured out for Him in unselfish service for mankind, and all joined together with one heart and one mind in the Christ Consciousness.

The inner mystical meaning of the crucifixion is that, just as the Christ manifested in the man Jesus and gave His spiritual blood to redeem the world, so at His second coming His followers must follow the same example and allow the Christ to animate them to the extent that they can pour out their spiritual life-blood for Him that He may gather spiritualized physical atoms in which to appear. For only in a sanctuary or "upper chamber" thus built up and among those "endued with power from on high" can He be made visible to mortal eye.

The "upper chamber" is a symbolic term, meaning a place of worship sacredly set apart and consecrated to the Divine, in which the worshiper rises in consciousness into the higher spiritual realms to meet his Lord. In the individual the upper chamber would be that state of consciousness called the Silence, or the state in which he realizes his oneness with the Divine; in short, both for the disciples and the individual it might be called "the Temple of Silence,"[5] or the Sanctuary.

This New Testament brings to every heart a blessed privilege and a sacred duty. The crucifixion is over, the resurrection completed and He has come "in like manner as ye saw him go," to appear first to Mary, and then to His inner disciples, and then to the world. Who is Mary? the Mother-love or the developed heart which brings forth the Christ. Who are His inner disciples? All who have made a sacred shrine, an "upper chamber," in their hearts where He can enter; those who are "endued with power from on high"; those who feed daily upon Him in their hearts, not in self-mortification and sorrow, but "with joy and thanksgiving."

This New Testament must bring about an absolutely new way of teaching the world, hence this Order proclaims, even now in the wilderness of the world's darkest hour just before the dawn, as did John the Baptist of old: "Repent ye: for the kingdom of heaven is at hand. . . . . Prepare ye the way of the Lord, make his paths straight."

Each one who reads this message and whose heart responds to these Teachings is given the privilege of entering the "upper chamber" and drinking in the outpouring of this New Testament. It is then their blessed privilege and sacred duty to be a forerunner; one of the heralds of the New Day; an exemplar of the New Testament that the body is no longer pierced, broken and dead that the blood may be poured forth, but that the true blood, the spiritual life-force, which is indeed the life of the world, is to be found in the radiations of the Divine Life from the Coming One; that He has come to Earth in a sacred and immaculate form combining the physical elements of both flesh and blood, overshadowed by the Consciousness and filled with the Divine Life of the Father-Mother-God. Conquering and to conquer He rides forth. Will you be of His train?

---

[5] See *The Temple of Silence*, Curtiss.

Chapter XXXVIII

THE MIGHTY ANGEL

"And I saw another mighty angel come down from heaven, clothed with a cloud: and a rainbow was upon his head, and his face was as it were the sun, and his feet as pillars of fire." *Revelation*, X, 1.

"Our time is just as ripe for a true Messiah as when the Star of Bethlehem appeared, and a new dispensation is just as needed and just as possible as when the Baptist heralded the advent of the greatest of all "presentifiers" . . . In a word, the world is sick and needs again a great physician for its soul just as it does for its body (one-third of our youth being unfit to fight)." *The Message of the Zeitgeist*, Dr. G. Stanley Hall.

"This same Jesus, which is taken up from you into heaven, shall so come *in like manner* as ye have seen him go into heaven." *Acts*, I, 11.

In recent years the world has been in the throes of a crisis such as it has never yet faced to the same degree, for it is travailing in the birth pangs of the sixth sub-race. These disturbed world conditions, however, are but the result of the overlapping of the two cycles and the reaping of the inevitable results of their conflict. Then will come the planting of the seed for the new cycle and the gradual growth of the new, and we trust better, crop to be gathered in its ripened perfection at the ushering in of the next great racial cycle.

During this coming cycle the conditions will at least be outlined or the seeds sown which will blossom and mature in perfection in the Sixth Great Race. "This process of preparation for the Sixth Great Race must last throughout the whole sixth and seventh sub-races"[1] of this our present Fifth (Aryan) Great Race. But as the sixth sub-race lays down or outlines those advances destined to be completely

---

[1] *The Secret Doctrine*, Blavatsky, II, 465.

worked out in the Sixth Great Race, we today find men's minds turned to new ideas, discoveries of new mechanical devices, new interest in man's inner forces, communication between the incarnate and discarnate, etc. In short, there is scarcely a realm of Nature that man today is not beginning to inquire into; not a force he is not studying to utilize or a condition he is not dreaming of improving. All these things are but the signs of the coming Great Age. But only as man conquers his own nature, utilizes the hidden forces within himself and correlates with the Divine Law of Being, will the promise be fulfilled. And as the seventh sub-race will outpicture the Seventh Great Race we will find in it a prophecy of the ultimate rest and fulfillment promised to the children of God.

Hence, this is a critical period, for in this coming era the transition must be made from the old ideals and conditions which predominated in the materialistic cycle of the Fifth Great Race to those which will predominate in the Sixth Great Race in ages to come, and such marked transitions are always periods of great unrest, strife and inharmony between the contending ideals which are seeking manifestation, the old and the new. The new ideals must ultimately prevail, however, and be accepted by the majority of mankind and be put into actual practice, yet the opposition will not be fully overcome until those who are wedded to the old have either accepted the new or have passed on into the higher life, where they may have an opportunity both to rest and also to consider again the truth of the new ideas.

While the Law of Cycles rules all manifestations, it must never be forgotten that man is a free agent and hence, within certain limits, can either retard or accelerate the manifestations of the various cycles. It is well known to occultists that humanity is at least five thousand years behind the point in evolution it should have reached during the past cycle, due to its refusal to work in harmony with the Divine Law. Hence, it is not blind fate or the natural forces of evolution that can make up the deficiency and prepare conditions for the bringing forth of the Christ-consciousness broadcast in humanity; it will be accomplished only when through the free-will choice of man a majority consciously choose and diligently strive to cultivate the Christ-consciousness in their hearts and begin to manifest it in their lives. It is, therefore, well at this time to look deeply into the philosophy of the manifestation of life and try to realize our responsibility and learn how the use of our free-will can either advance or retard the manifestation of the Christ.

Each of the seven Great Races through which humanity finds expression in one great cosmic Day Period or Round is governed by a mighty Celestial Being called its Progenitor who is one of the seven Angels of the Presence "sent forth into all the earth," the Regents of the seven Sacred Planets of our system, while each of the seven sub-races of each Great Race also has the special guidance of its own Divine Ruler or Angel.[2]

In the Fourth Great Race the physical foundations of mankind were laid. In the Fifth Great Race, especially in its fifth sub-race, man reached the most objective expression of number 5, the greatest development of material advance through his wonderful inventions, physical appliances, etc. So in the sixth sub-race must he manifest the forces of number 6, the Christ-force, preparatory to its perfect manifestation in the Sixth Great Race. In the fifth sub-race *manas*, or mind, reached a high state of development, for all during the Fifth Great Race thinking man was developing and perfecting that which had been begun and then perverted in the Fourth Race, especially in its fifth sub-race. Hence, as we are now just entering the cycle of the sixth sub-race of the Fifth, there will be a constantly growing tendency for mind to rise to greater heights and to correlate with the spiritual consciousness (*Buddhi-manas*) of the Divine Self. This will continue with increasing power all

---

[2] See *The Voice of Isis*, Curtiss, 186.

through the sixth and seventh sub-races and will become the dominant factor in shaping the evolution of the Sixth Great Race in the ages yet to come. Altho 6 is the number of the unrest of the Christ-force back of evolution, we must now out of the unrest begin to reap for the Race the spiritual fruit, or the Christ-man, with his mind illumined by the Christ-consciousness. This can be completed, however, only in the Sixth Great Race.

The Fifth and Sixth Angels mentioned in the ninth chapter of *Revelation* are the rulers of their respective sub-races, the Fifth coming to close the cycle of the fifth sub-race and the Sixth to prepare for the coming sixth sub-race. But "another Mighty Angel," mentioned in our text, refers to the great Divine Teacher whom all the world is now expecting after the Sixth Angel has sounded his trumpet. And it is comforting to those who follow the Christian teachings to find both how and when the Great One will appear clearly set forth in their own scriptures, namely, after the first and second woes are past, for the third woe will not be *completed* until the close of the sub-race, many ages hence.

While we are told that: "It is not for you to know the times or the seasons," still, according to our general calculations, the four phases of the second woe[3] should end approximately about 1940, for we know that we are now entering upon this second woe, and that each of its four phases must yield to mankind its great lesson. The fields of Earth must be purified, the chaff gathered together and burned; the minds of men must be plowed and harrowed by the bitter experiences of the woes through which humanity is passing that they may be prepared for the sowing of the new seed, ere the great One can come and gather his elect from the four winds.

Then there must be a period of overlapping while the seed takes root, springs up and begins to bear fruit. This

---

[3] See Chapter XIX herein.

will be a time of turmoil and testing, for the old is being swept away and the new has not yet manifested. Only those who, by their love and wisdom, their devotion and patience, prove their ability to receive from the Master the seed of the new ideals and sow it, even during the dark and discouraging conditions of this transitional period, will be proved worthy to be His chosen disciples when He comes; for in this age are the words especially true, "By their fruits ye shall know them. . . . . Not everyone that saith unto me, Lord, Lord, shall enter into the kingdom of heaven; but he that doeth the will of my Father which is in heaven."

While a definite understanding of the period in which the Great One shall appear may relieve the minds of some who have feared the end of the world was at hand, it may also tend to discourage others who are keyed up to great effort to be especially "good" for a time that they may be selected as His special followers within a short period. Yet, considering all the preparation necessary and the work to be accomplished in humanity, the time is all too short. For the first it will be a test of faith, for the second a test of endurance. "Blessed is the man that endureth temptation: for when he is tried, he shall receive the crown of life, which the Lord hath promised to them that love him." It is far easier to endure pain and harrowing experiences or patiently to plod through daily duties for a time when buoyed up by the hope of a quick reward, than it is to go on working, striving and conquering through an indefinite period. The latter is the greater test, for it can be continued only when patience and trust have been built into the character.

The "cloud" in which the Mighty Angel is clothed as he descends to Earth, refers not only to the cloud of radiant "glory of his Father with the holy angels," but also to the appearance of physical embodiment, which will seem so physical as to cloud or obscure His divinity, except to those whose intuition and love are so developed as to correlate with His consciousness, and thus penetrate the cloud and know Him as He is.

The manner of the manifestation is clearly set forth by the angel who spoke at the time of His ascension, namely, *"This same Jesus, which is taken up from you into heaven, shall so come in like manner* as you have seen him go into heaven." While they were talking with Him about His kingdom, suddenly He "disappeared from their sight," and *"in like manner"* shall He reappear. This plainly shows that an Avatar is not a mortal who enters the world through the gate of birth, but is a Celestial Being, who descends into manifestation only under certain conditions, as we have fully explained elsewhere.[4]

Because of the many misconceptions that have grown up around the story of Jesus' life, and the many cruel misunderstandings that have been fastened like millstones around the neck of humanity in His name, and because of the many crimes of inhumanity of man to man that have been excused through the literal interpretation and arbitrary enforcement of man-made creeds erected on medieval conceptions of natural laws, science and religion; because of all these misapplications of His teachings, that Great Teacher must come at the close of His cycle to straighten out all the crooked mental paths and to bring comfort to all His true followers who, in spite of all these drawbacks, have met Him in the inner sanctuary of the heart and who, therefore, know Him face to face and heart to heart.

Just as Jesus appeared to His disciples (and to His disciples and their followers only) thirteen times[5] after His resurrection, by lowering the vibratory rate of His spiritual body until it became visible to their physical senses, and just as He again raised its vibrations until it disappeared from the physical plane when His message was given, so

---

[4] *The Voice of Isis*, Curtiss, Chapter X.
[5] See *The Key of Destiny*, Curtiss, 140.

will He appear at His second coming, according to the promise, "So shall (He) come *in like manner.*"

"In like manner" also means that these phenomenal appearances will take place only in the presence of His disciples, those who have not been deceived and who are "gathered together into one place," and who are looking steadfastly toward heaven. In other words, He will appear only to those who can meet together in such love, harmony, purity and unselfishness as to make conditions in which He can manifest. Just as lightning strikes only at points where the Earth-forces draw it, so will the Spiritual Light manifest only where conditions on Earth are such as to attract it. But since the second coming is for the world, and not for any one order, society or sect, such groups of disciples will be formed all over the world in all countries, wherever the aspirations of human hearts have opened to His love and human consciousness has responded to His message, the message of the feminine aspect of the Godhead; the power to bring forth the Christ-consciousness and its fruit in the daily life.

It matters not under what name the various groups recognize Him, whether as "the Western Buddha" expected by the Thibetans and certain Buddhist sects of other countries or under the Western term of the Christ used in Christian countries. It will be the same Celestial Being we know as Jesus who will manifest to all, first to one group and then to another in all parts of the world until all mankind have had the message of the New Age proclaimed to them. To avoid the mistake of believing every cry of, "Lo, here is Christ, Lo there," we have only to determine whether or not the claimant be a mortal born of woman; if so, he is not the Avatar, for the Avatar is not a mortal.

The rainbow about His head symbolizes the light of His complete and perfect spiritualized aura in which, like a rainbow, all the seven colors or forces of the seven planetary Hierarchies are perfectly blended. His face is said to be like the Sun because of the white Light of Absolute Truth and the warmth of Divine Love which His presence radiates and which shall quicken the seeds of the teachings for the New Age. "His feet as pillars of fire" indicates that His contact with the Earth plane will illumine the understanding and also consume the false ideas of mankind as with fire.

As this Mighty Angel or Avatar draws closer to the Earth, the Light of Truth penetrates more and more clearly through the clouds of misconception and misunderstanding, and many, many minds awaken and determine to see and understand the Truth for themselves, for they can no longer accept as Truth that which another says they must believe. In other words, the little mind-seeds of advanced Cosmic Truth which have lain so long hidden in the darkness of ignorance and spiritual blindness and covered up with the demands of trade, the seductions of the senses and the allurements of selfish ease, all over the world are beginning to feel the stir of spiritual life at this new springtime of humanity.

Soon the hard shells of the seeds will burst asunder and the tiny sprouts of cosmic Truths for humanity's guidance and salvation will force themselves up into the Light. And these shoots are destined to grow, multiply and produce a mighty crop of advanced ideals which will demand new world conditions. For as the Light of Truth shines into the minds of men they begin to think for themselves, to see more clearly, to reason, compare and draw conclusions. Already they refuse any longer to be led like children or driven like cattle by those who lay claim to divine authority. Especially is this true after all the suffering that humanity has experienced during the first woe now past, during which mankind has been brought face to face with his own creations and their results.

The woes of the closing cycle are symbolized in all occult teachings by the glyph of the serpent swallowing or biting its tail, for it is the evil creations of man—the serpent in its lowest aspect—that have slimed the fair ideals of mankind, and until the serpent's power thus to degrade and debase is recognized by the race and is lifted up by a majority and made to swallow its tail or close the old cycle—a process preparatory to growing a new skin—it cannot be turned into the Rod of Power for the new sixth sub-race to take up and, like Aaron, make it swallow all the crawling vipers of the Egyptians. These woes are also symbolized by the scorpion stinging itself to death with its own tail. The same idea is suggested in the ninth chapter of *Revelation*, where we read of the forces which close the old cycle "For their power is in their mouth, and in their tails: for their tails were like unto serpents, and had heads (stings) and with them they do hurt."

How shall we know Him and He know us? To know others we must be able to enter into their thoughts, share their aspirations and ideals and work side by side with them. Just so shall we know Him and He know us. Those who are already dwelling in the Christ-consciousness are feeling His deep love and compassion for humanity. His impersonal desire is to help all who will listen, without recognition or praise for Himself. All such are even now being "caught up to meet Him in the air" or in thought. And all who are doing His works, helping to prepare the world for His coming, verily all such shall find Him very near, ready to give loving counsel and reach out His powerful hand and make His presence manifest when sorrow, discouragement and fear sweep over their Souls and they cry out like frightened children for light and comfort.

We will know Him in the only way that real knowing can ever manifest, by personal and intimate experience and realization. Merely to have a mental conception of such a Divine Teacher will avail us little, for we must know Him face to face and heart to heart, hence these years of preparation are given. He is now very close to earthly manifestation and can be both seen and felt and personally communed with by all who are truly His disciples. Let us pray that none of us shall hear the fateful words when He comes: "Depart from me . . . . . I never knew you."

Let us then gather together in one thought and remain looking steadfastly toward heaven or living in the consciousness of the higher life and endeavoring to do His works here on Earth "until He comes."

Chapter XXXIX

THE SOUL'S GUERDON

"Behold, the Lord hath proclaimed unto the end of the world. Say ye to the daughter of Zion, Behold, thy salvation cometh; behold, his reward is with him, and his work before him." *Isaiah*, LXII, 11.

"Now he that planteth and he that watereth are one; and every man shall receive his own reward according to his own labour." *I Corinthians*, III, 8.

A guerdon is defined as a reward, a recompense and a requital, but it is nevertheless much more than all these. It is a reward given, not by any power outside oneself, but a reward which comes as a result of one's own definite effort, struggle and attainment. It is something that rewards the Soul because the Soul has to a greater or lesser degree fulfilled a certain stage in the manifestation of its destiny. Hence, as each Soul has been sent to this Earth with a definite lesson to learn and a personal work to perform in each incarnation in the environment in which it is placed, each will receive the guerdon of its own efforts as a result of its own travail or birth pangs. And its work is found in just those opportunities for constructive expression which the Great Law brings to it, just as the Soul enters Earth-life in a body and in an environment which are the result or Karma of its own efforts in former lives.

While the Soul in the heaven world is perfect and pure and one with God, yet to complete its mission of individualization it must come down to Earth and learn to do God's will under Earth conditions, even as it does that will in heaven; for only by the help of the countless incarnate Souls can God's will—the work of perfecting every manifested thing—be carried to completion. Therefore, as Jesus told us, we come down from heaven, not to do our own will, even if that will be the perfection of ourselves, but to do the will of Him that sent us.[1] And His will is that we should be ambassadors of God, to unfold our credentials—our God-given powers—and manifest them in this new field of earthly manifestation.

We can definitely accomplish His will only as we are born into the consciousness of it, *i.e.*, into the realization that in the last analysis we and our Father are one, and His work is our work. The method of embodying this consciousness is analogous to that manifesting through the physical Sun. For instance, the Sun is in the heavens and we can see its glory, rejoice in its warmth and its vivifying powers, yet it is not the Sun itself that descends to bless us, but its countless emanated rays, which are sent to Earth each with its own particular work to accomplish toward the manifestation of the Divine Plan; light rays, heat rays, chemical rays, actinic rays, magnetic rays, etc. Also all the color rays have each their potency, power and part to play. Only as man advances in knowledge of Nature's laws does he learn to take advantage of more hidden rays or rates of vibration, such as X-rays, N-rays, ultra violet rays, etc., altho these were always present and did their work silently in Nature. But only as man advanced in understanding of Nature's finer forces could he utilize them for a definite end.

There are still more wonderful secrets which Nature holds for man, waiting until he is ready to use them wisely. Yet, if man does nothing to take advantage of these rays, does not prepare the soil, plant selected seed, water, cultivate, weed and protect it, the Sun, with all its magic potencies, cannot do more than bring forth the cruder and less evolved forms of vegetation or bake the Earth into desolate sterility or into stagnant morasses. Similarly, if man persistently lives in a cold, damp cave or cellar, and shuts out every ray

---

[1] *St. John*, VI, 38.

of sunlight, he will be benefited but little by the Sun's shining, altho the Sun will still be shedding its benign radiance upon the Earth as freely as ever. "Help Nature and work on with her, and Nature will regard thee as one of her creators and make obeisance. And she will open wide before thee the portals of her secret chambers, lay bare before thy gaze the treasures hidden in the very depths of her pure, virgin bosom."[2]

So it is with the rays of Spiritual light from the Sun of Righteousness. Each Soul comes to Earth as the outshining of God's graciousness; comes to unfold its latent possibilities according to the Grand Plan, to bless the Earth and to aid in bringing all things upon it to their perfect manifestation. In other words, we are individualized Rays of God, shining forth as the Light of His vast countenance. Therefore, let us not be swallowed up in the darkness of ignorance, lest we fail to accomplish that for which we were sent forth.

Each one holds within himself or herself the mighty powers and potencies of God, each with its own mission to perform in the personal life and in the world, yet only as all are combined, each giving its peculiar gift, to make the pure white Light, can the destined end be attained, either personally or for humanity or for the planet. The great Divine Law of God has, therefore, predestined every son of man, every movement that is put forth for the betterment of conditions for humanity; in fact, everything that takes place, to work toward and contribute its quota to the perfection of the whole. Nevertheless, this predestination is not fate; for the crowning gift of God to man is free-will.

While man is predestined ultimately to attain perfection of expression and then return to God whence he came, even as each ray of the Sun is destined to be released from its objective embodiment and be drawn into the Sun and to be sent forth again and again until it has accomplished its

---

[2] *The Voice of the Silence*, Blavatsky, Fragment I.

mission, so is the Soul sent forth. Yet man differs from a ray of the Sun in the important particular that he is given individual self-consciousness and free-will; freedom to do or not to do the Divine Will, or, to speak more correctly, to take his own time about it and to use his own methods, altho *ultimately* he must return to his Father, bringing his sheaves of accomplishment with him.

And he receives as his guerdon just that which he has chosen to accomplish. If he has chosen unwisely his guerdon will be a lesson to him, for ultimately he must learn to choose wisely. Ignorance of the law does not excuse one for its breaking, for guidance from within is freely given to teach the Soul, if the Soul will seek for and follow it; but it must choose. It may be like a boy who refuses to go to school: the school is there and his parents may urge him to go, but if he ignores it or refuses to attend, his guerdon in life must be ignorance and lack of mental training and all that results therefrom.

That which we call destiny is, therefore, the ultimate perfection of all things. Hence, *no one need worry about losing or saving his Soul. The Soul is immortal and cannot be lost*, hence needs no saving, except saving from the suffering that it will experience by making mistakes, setting up causes which are not in harmony with the Divine Law and which, therefore, must result in inharmony and suffering to the Soul. Each Soul—and by the Soul we mean the Higher Self, the three higher principles of man (the higher or spiritual mind, the Ray of pure Spirit and Buddhi or the spiritual body which unites man and Spirit)—takes its destiny into its own hands when it descends to Earth. And it is told: "Behold, your reward is with you, and your work is before you! Ultimate perfection is yours, and you must come back to your Father's home, bringing with you the sheaves of experience garnered in the lower worlds. But unto your own Soul will be the guerdon according as you travail, *i.e.*, as you bring to birth the will of the Father, the highest and best that is in you." In one sense the guerdon is the wisdom and love, the poise and power and other godlike qualities we have brought into expression. Hence, the guerdon is ours according as we live and bring forth and manifest our part in the Divine Plan. During our struggle, very often through the bitter experiences of want and misery, we are forced to take cognizance of many of the hidden blessings which are prepared for us against the time of our need, which we might never perceive if all went well with us continually. Many of the great discoveries have been the result of pressing necessity, therefore the saying, "Man's extremity is God's opportunity."

God Almighty is the power hidden within each Soul and within each manifestation in the universe; for there is no personal God in the orthodox sense of a great anthropomorphic Being, entirely separate from us. Personality is a part of the manifested creation, hence is not even immortal. Since God is not a created entity, He can have no personality; hence, there can be no such thing as a personal God in the orthodox sense, altho the individualized Ray of God which constitutes our Real Self is a personalized aspect of God ever present with us and ever conscious of our every thought. God created the manifested universe and all things contained therein, and as a personality is a product of creation, God could not be merely one small product of His own creation. The only personality of God is manifested in His works. Therefore, our personality should also be expressed in our works; our ability to manifest God in the flesh and to make the flesh the expression of the Real Self.

God is the mighty outbreathing of Divinity; the Great Urge, the Great Force, the Mighty Good, the Divine Love which is everywhere pushing forth into greater and greater expression. Each Soul grows more and more godlike as it unfolds the God-powers within it. Thus, man does not grow spiritually by worshiping in abject servility some Supreme Being. Nor is it some far-off God who bestows upon him perfection in response to many prayers and supplications, altho we can hasten our growth, and consequently our power to manifest, by correlating with and aspiring to oneness with the Divine through prayer. We grow spiritually by realizing that we are Rays of God, embodying all His powers and potencies, either active or latent, which are sent forth to accomplish His will on earth, and by striving to bring into manifestation those powers and potencies, just as man strives to put forth all his powers—his will, his thought, his patience, faith, judgment, etc.—when he wishes to accomplish any chosen work in physical affairs. Ultimately we grow so close in manifestation to our Father-ray which sent us forth, that we consciously need the hand of our Initiator or Spiritual Parent to help us take the final step from mortality to immortality.

Spiritual development is, therefore, the unfoldment from within, firstly, of the realization of all this and, secondly, a persistent effort to manifest it in our lives. For altho most of us have vague haunting memories of our Father's home of glory, and of the great and eager desire which led us to offer ourselves as volunteers to come into this world of spiritual darkness to uplift, conquer and subdue it and make it a fitting kingdom for "our Lord and his Christ," we fail to apply these memories to our daily lives.

We often awake from deep sleep feeling that we have had experiences of unspeakable glory, and for days we may feel something we cannot express hovering over and inspiring us, yet, unless we understand that this is the result of our momentary union with the Divine in heaven, and of our being filled with the glory of the Sun of Righteousness that we may radiate it in our lives, we will not be able to make the most of it. Such glimpses are given to all from time to time, whether fully recognized or not; else we could scarce endure our exile on this dark star. And always, as we return to Earth for a new incarnation, we bring this haunting memory of our spiritual home with us. It is said that at the moment of death a vision of this divine truth is revealed to us, and this explains why on many faces of the dead, even when they pass out in great suffering, there is a look of peace and joy. We can often see this same light in the eyes of babes, and the old adage, "A babe which smiles in its sleep is listening to the whispers of the angels," in reality contains more fact than poetic fancy.

To one who will seek for them within instead of without, there are many proofs that the seeds of Divine Love, almighty power, supreme consciousness and goodness (Godness) are to be found within each heart; that they are ours now to recognize, nourish and bring forth into manifestation; for we are here to manifest God in the flesh. Therefore, each Soul will receive its guerdon according to how it is able to bring to birth the forces and powers of the Godhead inherent within it; for within each there is the possibility of ultimate perfection.

Ultimate perfection means the perfect expression of the One in the many and the many in the One. Even as we see in Nature many manifestations of the One—mountains, plains, rivers, trees, flowers, vegetation, rocks, minerals, etc.—each evolving toward its own perfection according to the perfect pattern it is destined to express, yet all together making one perfect Earth—so do we see many manifestations of the One in the various races of mankind, yet all together making up humanity as a whole. So does it take the gifts of the Spirit, expressed in the hearts of each of God's children, all brought to their highest perfection, to manifest the one God. Hence, all should ask within for enlightenment and guidance, and strive to find out just what God intends them to manifest; what part in the Divine Plan they are to play, and then strive to unfold the godlike powers which are implanted within them to enable them to accomplish their mission.

We can never be successful or perfect if we seek to copy another or to do the work which is the task of some other

Soul; for to do so we must neglect to be ourselves and to perform our own task, and at best can become but an imperfect copy or a freak of nature, thus retarding the expression of our own Real Selves. Nevertheless, we have free-will and can try this method if we so desire; for God never forces us to do right, altho He could do so if He so desired. But in supreme wisdom He permits us to try all experiences if we so wish, waiting in powerful and undisturbed patience for us to awaken and turn our faces back to Him for guidance and for the power to carry out our mission as His representatives.

Therefore, let us try every day to realize our place and work in the world and our powers to manifest as a Child of God in that place in which we find ourselves. Let us say to ourselves daily and frequently: "I am not only a Child of God, but a very Ray of God himself, a part of God. And the part of me that is God is the power of God that I am able to bring into expression. All the rest of me must gradually become the servant of this God-part, to do its will, even as I do the will of Him that sent me. I am accomplishing little of my mission until I have recognized this and begun to use my God-given powers." The power of God is like a steady stream of electricity from a great dynamo. It is impotent or latent until the power is turned into some avenue of accomplishment. Once this is realized, it is as simple as turning a button to have either light or heat in our homes. But we must consciously turn the button. If we do not, we cannot blame the power-house for our lack of results.

Again, we are like wireless stations. We can communicate with all the worlds if we are properly attuned. And to become attuned we must reach out and touch God; not God outside of us, but the manifested power of God within us; our power to be true, to love, to accomplish, to radiate peace, harmony and purity; our power to be well and strong, to be magnetic, to be happy; our power to be a positive, vital factor for good in the world.

There is no way of attaining these powers except by expressing them from within. No amount of outer observances — ceremonies, dress, diet, posture, etc. — will suffice. "Believe thou not that sitting in dark forests, in proud seclusion and apart from men; believe thou not that life on roots and plants, that thirst assuaged with snow from the Great Range — believe thou not, O Devotee, that this will lead thee to the goal of final liberation."[3] The guerdon must be in all *the birth of a new consciousness*, a new understanding, new power, new love, new joy, new helpfulness. And it must be brought forth in spirit and in truth. When a child is brought forth it is a tangible thing, to be fed and nourished, cherished, taught, trained and given every help to promote its growth and perfect expression. So must be the power of God which we are destined to bring forth.

(To be concluded)

---

[3] *The Voice of the Silence*, Blavatsky, II.

CHAPTER XL

THE SOUL'S GUERDON
(Concluded)

"The first man is of the earth, earthy; the second man is the Lord from heaven.... And as we have borne the image of the earthy we shall also bear the image of the heavenly." *I Corinthians*, XV, 47,49.

"Be not deceived; God is not mocked: for whatsoever a man soweth, that shall he also reap." *Galatians*, VI, 7.

Many sincere students are wondering just what they may expect as a guerdon for the personal self. Must they supinely accept poverty, incompetency, illness and misery, and say, "It matters not what my personality is, for my Real Self is divine and is master of all worldly conditions"? As the result of such an attitude we see many earnest workers either neglecting to develop and perfect the personality, or even cultivating eccentricities which often make their personalities very unattractive.

On the other hand, some claim that the personality is everything, is all that the world can see, hence they feel that they must conform to the opinion of the world and use their power of will to suppress all that does not meet with the world's approval. They say: "If I would help humanity I must impress it by making great claims. I must strive to appear as Super-man or I cannot expect a following." Thus do many who are seeking to do the Father's will strive to build up a great personality that will attract the admiration of the world. They feel that the work they would do is truly the Father's work, yet since they have not learned to separate the eternal from the transitory, the Real Self from its outer vesture or instrument (personality), or the inmate

from the house in which it dwells, they truly believe that only as
their personality attracts can they become effective and useful
spiritual teachers of men. And many there be who follow after
such personalities, the greater the claims put forth the greater the
crowd, and the greater the adulation of the crowd the greater the
inflation of the personality.

But since every claim that is made must be faced and proved,
many who express either of the above extremes find their laudable
intentions either miscarry or they are taken out of incarnation long
before their work is accomplished, as the long list of failures,
premature deaths or sudden collapses of teachers and spiritual
movements only too sadly proves. And such failures often do
as much harm to the followers of their teachings, in the way of
disillusionment, discouragement and lack of faith in all similar
teachings, as the good those who put forth the teachings had
hoped to accomplish. And the Karma of everyone whose faith
has been thus destroyed must be connected with and borne by
or be the guerdon of the one whose misconception permitted the
personality to strive to do that which only the Real or Divine Self
could accomplish.

The fact that the more we try to perfect the personality for
its own sake and become Super-man, the more our personal
traits grow, the more egotism takes possession of us and the less
humble, loving and helpful we become, is evidence that we are
not following the Law; for God manifesting in us as God-likeness
is always impersonal. When we think more of others and take
more pleasure in helping them and trying to bring out the best in
them, the result is a sweetening and perfecting of our personality;
for we are thus dwelling in the Light of God and that Light must
shine through and illumine the mask of our personality. "Verily,
by their fruits shall ye know them."

All personal claims are of the Earth earthly. We dare not
expect the first or personal man, made from "the dust of the
earth," to do the work of "the Lord from heaven," the Inner

or Divine Man. God manifests His works silently yet persistently, forever overcoming the opposition of earthiness by the radio-activity of the inner spiritual life-force which is ever bringing forth perfection out of imperfection. So will every true child of God accomplish His will on Earth in proportion as he lets the inner Divine Self silently yet persistently manifest through him.

As in man, so in Nature. The tree, the flower, the grass, all have a personality or outer vehicle of expression, yet only as the universal Life-essence permeates them and the sap flows uninterruptedly through them do they become beautiful and perfect. Let this mystic Life-force be cut off by any mishap and the tree, the flower, the grass soon grows sear and yellow, soon fades and dies; becomes first unattractive and then but cumbersome trash which must be consumed or done away with.

We are told that God is Spirit, and that we must worship Him in spirit and in truth. This does not mean, as some suppose, that God is merely that personalized Ray of the Divine which is individualized in us and which can be worshiped only in the silence of our hearts, and therefore that we need no outward observances, no temples, no ceremonies, no prayers, no studies, etc. It means that the all-pervading Spiritual Essence, the same Spirit or Divine Life which is both Be-ness and Being and which manifests in us, also manifests in all God's manifested universe. In fact, just as all worlds and systems are brought into being through the outworking and manifesting of this Spirit of all Truth, so our personalities must become so perfected as to out-picture this same Spirit, the all-creative, living, spiritual radio-activity within, and correlate with that same Spirit of all Truth in its expressions without, thus developing and perfecting the personality as an instrument and servant, yet not worshiping or exalting it as of supreme importance. A good and faithful servant in the house will be much appreciated and admired by the guests, yet if that servant attempts to usurp the place of the master of the house he will be despised, pitied and avoided because he is out of place. All work is equally honorable and every personality is honored if in its own place it tries to accomplish its own work, and reflect the just honor due to the Real Self, who is "the Master whom thou hast not seen yet whom thou feelest."

To worship God in Spirit and in Truth we must recognize this two-fold relation and give this Spirit our understanding worship. We worship the thing which we dwell on continually in thought; for thought is a dynamic generator of power and that to which we turn our thought *lives in and has power over us*. If, therefore, we continually turn our thoughts from the concerns and ambitions and desires of the personality toward those of the Spirit, the former have less power over us and the Spirit lives to a greater degree in us and gains greater power over us. And it is this Spirit which will bring to each Soul as its guerdon the birth of the God-consciousness within.

In proportion as we turn the dynamic power of thought upon it, it will gradually manifest in our outer lives, even in the outward appearance of the personality. It will bring to birth new powers, new strength, new health, new beauty, new love, new joy of life, new ability to help our fellow men. This will be the guerdon of the personality; for the personal self, having been created as an instrument through which the Divine Self could manifest on Earth, must be perfected, yet its greatness must be built into it *from within* with Spiritual Essence drawn from the Spirit of all Truth as expressed by the Divine Self. It cannot be built up with physical atoms of the Earth, earthy, in an effort to exalt the personality; for all true development must come from within outward. And as all earthly things are transitory and shortly pass away, nothing built up of earthly atoms, thoughts and forces can endure. Only that which comes from the Divine, Immortal Self within can endure.

Therefore, we may confidently expect, as the guerdon of our personality, when made subservient to the Divine, such guidance from within as will illumine our minds and give us the understanding that every condition that confronts us comes to help perfect us. We will then see that adverse conditions came to us because we are not worshiping in the Spirit of Truth; that they are sent not to punish, but to lead us back to the true worship.

To remind ourselves of this God-consciousness within and to aid us in focusing the creative power of our thought upon it, we should avail ourselves of every aid to this end, such as ceremonies, prayers, mantra, set times for devotion and worship, the occurrence of sunrise, noon and sunset or any other factor that will help to keep before our mind's eye the ideal to be attained. Hence, the importance this Order places upon definite times of meditation, definite prayers for morning, noon and night, before meals, before sleeping, etc.

At the present period in human evolution we are facing the dawning of a New Day. Like eager children we are waiting for the curtain to roll up and a new act in the wonderful drama of man's unfoldment to begin. We know that this act is but the continuation of the Great Drama with which we are familiar, but we are ignorant as to the details of its further unfoldment. We know that it is destined to turn out well, yet we see the characters so harassed and the action so complicated and seemingly disastrous that we scarce dare hope for a pleasant ending, much less that it will result in some great good for the world.

We who have recognized ourselves as Children of the Household are called together by our Great Teacher in a very definite way. We are told to look back over the way we have come and to realize that the first act in the present-day presentation of the drama of this Order is finished. In this act we have seen the Order, through many and various scenes, grow from an obscure and insignificant beginning into a mighty Ocean of Spiritual Light, Love and Truth, which washes the shores of every land.

Yet we know that the drama has only begun, and as the curtain rolls up for the second act a thrill of expectation fills the air, and a mighty cry goes up, even as it did from the Children of Israel when they stood on the border of the Promised Land and viewed it from afar. The cry is: "O Lord, through Thy prophets and messengers Thou hast led us out of the land of Egypt (spiritual darkness and sense pleasures) and we will follow Thee and Thy law until we enter into the Land of Promise to possess it. We know that our pillar of cloud by day and our pillar of fire by night is none other than the mighty Law of God and that Thy messengers are its servants, even as Moses and Joshua were the servants of that Law. We know that when we grow faint and weary with the journey or when we thirst for the living waters, they will strike the rock of hard physical conditions and the water of Divine Love shall gush forth to refresh us. We know that when we are hungry for spiritual truth and ask for bread we will not be given a stone, but will be fed with the bread and fishes given by Thy Son and broken for the multitude by His disciples. We know that every day each Soul that asks shall be fed by the sustaining power of the heavenly manna falling for us even in the most dreary wilderness of our lives, and not only feeding us, but comforting, sustaining and healing us. We know that when we seem alone in the darkness a pillar of fire shall lead us on. And when in the day we grow forgetful or are distracted by the pressure of physical affairs a pillar of cloud shall appear that we may turn our thoughts to Thee." Let us then press on with cheerful courage, never fearing, never doubting, knowing full well that ultimately the waters of adversity and opposition will divide and that some day we shall find ourselves in the Promised Land.

This Order must, as a whole, bring forth its own guerdon. For this Order, as well as every other spiritual work or movement, has a Soul, and that Soul must bring to birth its guerdon. Every effort toward the enlightenment and uplift of humanity must come back home and lay its sheaves of accomplishment at the feet of the Lord God that they may be taken to the threshing floor and every golden grain be stored up to feed the hungry, while the chaff is winnowed and consumed in the Fire of the Lord.

This Order came into manifestation because of the world's great need; the need of a simple yet heart-satisfying presentation of the world-old principles and laws of Divine Life. To accomplish its work two "children in spiritual things" answered the call. They answered because they had dreamed the memory-dreams of their glorious heritage in the Father's home and their hearts' desire was that all might know of, realize and share in that heritage which is for all. They answered: "Here are we, Lord, use us. We are weak and poor and small in personality, yet we fear not and can obey, and with Thy help we will do the best we can." And the reply came from the great storehouse of all wisdom: "The Teachings must be all, and we will supply them. Only be true and faithful and persistent. Keep the personality in the background. Lean altogether upon the Truth and the Truth shall set you free." These children have made many mistakes, yet they have never faltered, and the Order has gone steadily on growing and ever growing. And it will ever continue to grow, because the Teachings are living spiritual truths which transcend and shall ultimately swallow up the personalities of their interpreters.

This Order also has its personality or expression "of the earth, earthy," and yet it is ruled by its "Lord from heaven." And since its personality is made up of all the atoms or personalities of all its students, only as its students strive to purify, control and perfect their personalities and allow the Spirit of Truth which pervades its Teachings to sink deep into their consciousness—thus touching in consciousness the hem of the Robe of the Christ with which it is clothed—will they feel its virtue go out to them and manifest in their lives. Then, be they sick or weak or ignorant or poor, the mighty river of Divine Love which is poured forth to sweep this Order onward throughout the world on its mission of Light, Love and Comfort, will manifest in their own hearts and lives.

And as we all together strive to let the "Lord from heaven" rule in our lives and in the Order, we will find that the Order's personality or outward expression will more and more out-picture its Soul, the Spirit of Truth, and it will more and more have added to it the power the more perfectly to accomplish its mission in the world, and thus receive its Soul's guerdon.

We speak of the Divinity within, but in our present state of evolution that Divinity is scarcely more than the radiance of the emanations which the Divine Indweller left enmeshed in us when we were forced to leave the Garden when the mind usurped the authority of the spiritual will. But even this radiance is a very real Flame of spiritual force and through it we can always "ascend into the hill of the Lord" and reach the Indweller. Therefore, we must dwell in the thought of its radiant shining until it grows more and more intense; for through the misuse of mind we have driven it out, and by the proper use of mind must we bring it back. Yet we have never been left comfortless. Always the power of the Holy Ghost has overshadowed us. And in our darkest hours the Flame of Divine Love has dwelt with us as a pillar of fire that has guided us through the wilderness of life, and the Lord God has spoken to us out of the fiery cloud.

Because of the very brilliancy of this shining man sees reflected on the darkness of his life his creations of sin and disobedience. Therefore, only as he seeks to embody and follow the guidance of the Divine Light which shines within can he learn how to re-enter his lost heritage.

Unless we often dwell in thought on the glorious possibilities which the Light unfolds we cannot prepare ourselves to manifest the Divine Indweller. To actually attain this higher consciousness, and not have merely an intellectual conception of it, we must open the door of our minds to the Divine Light, cleanse the sanctuary of our hearts, purify our bodies and invite our Lord of Life, the Divine Indweller, to enter in and take possession of that which is his own. There we must allow him to reign supreme as the Vice Regent of God and give willing and glad obedience to him, for only then can we say with Jesus: "I and my Father are one." Until then we can only listen to the voice which says: "Behold, I stand at the door and knock: if any man hear my voice, and open the door, I will come in to him, and will sup with him, and he with me."[1]

To apply this conception to the practical development of our spiritual consciousness let each sincere student repeat the following mantram night and morning and as often as possible during the day, meditating upon it and visualizing it and endeavoring to realize its significance until it becomes a reality in his life.

Invocation to the Divine Indweller

Come, O Lord of Life and Love and Beauty!
Thou who art myself and yet art God!
And dwell in this body of flesh,
Radiating all the beauty of holiness and perfection.
That the flesh may out-picture all that Thou art within!
Even so, come, O Lord. Amen.

---

[1] *Revelation*, III, 20.

PRAYERS

Prayers of *The Order of Christian Mystics*

———

PRAYER FOR LIGHT

O Christ! Light Thou within my heart
The Flame of Divine Love and Wisdom,
That I may dwell forever in the radiance of Thy countenance
And rest in the Light of Thy smile!

MORNING PRAYER

I have within me the power of the Christ!
I can conquer all that comes to me today!
I am strong enough to bear every trial
And accept every joy
And to say
Thy will be done!

HEALING PRAYER

O thou loving and helpful Master Jesus!
Thou who gavest to Thy disciples power to heal the sick!
We, recognizing Thee, and realizing Thy divine Presence with us,
Ask Thee to lay Thy hands (powers) upon us in healing Love.
Cleanse US from all OUR sins, and by the divine power of Omnipotent
    Life,
Drive out the atoms of inharmony and disease, and
Fill our bodies full to overflowing with Life and Love and Purity.

PRAYER OF PROTECTION

O Christ! Surround and fill me and Thy Order with the Flame of Divine
    Love and Wisdom,
That it may purify, illumine and guide us in all things.
May its Spiritual Fire form a rampart of Living Flame around me and
    Thy Order,
To protect us from all harm.
May it radiate to every heart, consuming all evil and intensifying
all good.
In the name of the Living Christ! Amen.

PRAYER OF DEMONSTRATION

I am a child of the Living God!
I have within me the all-creating power of the Christ!

It radiates from me and blesses all I contact.
It is my Health, my Strength, my Courage,
My Patience, my Peace, my Poise,
My Power, my Wisdom, my Understanding,
My Joy, my Inspiration, and my Abundant Supply.
Unto this great Power I entrust all my problems,
Knowing they will be solved in Love and Justice.
(Mention all problems connected with your worldly affairs, visualize
    each and conclude with the following words)
O Lord Christ! I have laid upon Thy altar all my wants and desires.
I know Thy Love, Thy Wisdom, Thy Power and Thy Graciousness.
In Thee I peacefully rest, knowing that all is well.
Not my will but Thine be done. Amen.

PRAYER TO THE DIVINE INDWELLER
Come, O Lord of Life and Love and Beauty!
Thou who art myself and yet art God!
And dwell in this body of flesh,
Radiating all the beauty of holiness and perfection,
That the flesh may out-picture all that Thou art within!
Even so, come, O Lord. Amen.

PRAYER TO THE DIVINE MOTHER
O Divine Mother!
Illumine me with Divine Wisdom,
Vivify me with Divine Life and
Purify me with Divine Love,
That in all I think and say and do
I may be more and more Thy child. Amen.

GRACE BEFORE MEALS
I am a creator.
By the power of my spiritualized Will
I consciously gather all the forces from this food,
And use them to create food, health, strength and harmony
In all my bodies (physical, astral and mental).
And we thank the Father for this manifestation of His bounteous supply.
May we use it to his glory.

PRAYER OF DEVOTION
We, Thy chosen servants, to whom Thou hast given the great privilege
    of becoming co-workers with the Masters of Wisdom, ask that we
    may have Wisdom and Power and Courage and Humility to carry us
    through the work of this day.

We open our hearts that the Divine Love of the Master may fill us; that all irritation, inharmony and slothfulness may be transmuted into Love that shall draw us closer in unity to all our fellow workers both seen and unseen; that we may grow absolutely one with the force of Wisdom and Compassion that is sent forth to accomplish the great work for humanity.

Give us all things necessary, that there may be no hampering conditions.

Lead us through this day, in the name of the Divine, Everliving Christ, that the will of the Father may be done in us and through us forevermore. Amen.

PRAYER FOR WORLD HARMONY

Glory and honor and worship be unto Thee, O Lord Christ,
Thou who art the Life and Light of all mankind.
Thou art the King of Glory to whom all the peoples of the Earth should give joyful allegiance and service.
Inspire mankind with a realization of true Brotherhood.
Teach us the wisdom of peace, harmony and co-operation.
Breathe into our hearts the understanding that only as we see ourselves as parts of the one body of humanity can peace, harmony, success and plenty descend upon us.
Help us to conquer all manifestations of inharmony and evil in ourselves and in the world.
May all persons and classes and nations cease their conflicts, and unselfishly strive for peace and goodwill that the days of tribulation may be shortened.
Bless us all with the radiance of Thy Divine Love and Wisdom that we may ever worship Thee in the beauty of holiness.
In the Name of the Living Christ we ask it. Amen.

PRAYER FOR THE CHRIST POWER

O Lord Christ! Thou who hast planted within me
The Immortal Power of Spiritual Love and Life,
Help me so to correlate with Thy divine overshadowing Presence,
That all hampering conditions shall be swallowed up
In the Light of the Living Christ Power. Amen.

EVENING PRAYER

As the physical Sun
Disappears from our sight
May the Spiritual Sun
Arise in our hearts,
Illumine our minds
And shed its radiant blessing
Upon all we contact.

INDEX

www.ingramcontent.com/pod-product-compliance
Lightning Source LLC
Chambersburg PA
CBHW062144080426
42734CB00010B/1559